V&R

Towards Mutual Security

Fifty Years of Munich Security Conference

Edited by
Stiftung Münchner Sicherheitskonferenz
Wolfgang Ischinger

Editorial Team
Tobias Bunde, Antje Lein-Struck, and Adrian Oroz

Vandenhoeck & Ruprecht

You can find additional material to this book on our website:

www.v-r.de/Munich-Security-Conference

Bibliographic information published by the Deutsche Nationalbibliothek

The Deutsche Nationalbibliothek lists this publication in
the Deutsche Nationalbibliografie; detailed bibliographic data
available online: http://dnb.d-nb.de.

ISBN 978-3-525-30054-1
ISBN 978-3-647-30054-2 (E-Book)

Copyediting by Rebecca van Dyck
Image editing by SchwabScantechnik, Göttingen
Layout and typesetting by textformart, Göttingen | www.text-form-art.de

Printed and bound in Germany by ⊕ Hubert & Co, Göttingen

Printed on non-aging paper.

Table of Contents

The Chairmen

Wehrkunde and the Cold War

New Challenges after the End of the Cold War

Euro-Atlantic Security in a Globalized World

Spotlights on the Conference

Mutual Security in the Twenty-First Century

Acknowledgments

We would like to thank all of the authors as well as their respective staff members for their personal commitment and enthusiasm. This project would not have been possible without their support and dedication.

We would also like to extend our thanks to the team of our publisher, Vandenhoeck & Ruprecht, for their advice, patience, and cooperation throughout the project. This applies especially to Dr. Wilhelm Ruprecht, Dr. Martina Kayser, Daniel Sander, Ulrike Bade, and Rebecca van Dyck.

Working on this book, we were grateful for the kind support of a number of archives and committed individuals regarding documents and photos. We particularly thank the Political Archive of the Federal Foreign Office, the Archives for Christian-Social Politics, and the *European Security & Defence Magazine* for granting printing rights and providing the necessary scans, as well as Karin Ehinger and Haide Hormann from the German Federal Foreign Office for the transcription of the conversation with Chancellor Helmut Schmidt.

For their legal consulting throughout the project, our gratitude goes to Ksenia Ilina, Matthias Lupp, and Hans Peter Wiesemann.

We are particularly grateful to Munich Re and the Federal Foreign Office, without whose generous contribution the compilation of this volume would not have been feasible.

We extend our thanks to Dr. Timo Noetzel for his valuable academic advice throughout this project. Our most cordial thanks go to Thomas Bauer for crucially reinforcing the editorial team. His work and dedication ensured thoroughly observed style guides, turning individual contributions into a homogeneous volume.

Last but not least, we would like to offer a special note of appreciation to Helmut Bialek, Björn Boening, Kathleen Damerius, Dr. Benedikt Franke, Tim Gürtler, Michael Heller, Mirjam Issing, Marcel Lewicki, Barbara Mittelhammer, Mirjana Richter, Oliver Rolofs, Jean-Pierre Schnaubelt, Florian Wiesböck, and Sara-Sumie Yang, the team members of the Munich Security Conference Foundation, and to Sabine Schulz-Plink and Gonca Treu. They spent endless hours supporting us by contributing ideas toward the volume's concept, arranging for photographs, identifying interesting documents, and providing the necessary administrative support for the project.

Finally, it should be noted that the opinions expressed in the contributions to this volume are the opinions of the respective authors alone and do not necessarily reflect the opinions of the Stiftung Münchner Sicherheitskonferenz gGmbH. The authors were last able to review the manuscripts in early fall and were thus unable to include any developments that may have occurred afterwards. All information in this book, including biographical information about the authors, was last updated on November 30, 2013.

Wolfgang Ischinger
Tobias Bunde
Antje Lein-Struck
Adrian Oroz

Anniversary Messages

Message from the Federal Chancellor to Mark the Fiftieth Anniversary of the Munich Security Conference

Angela Merkel

The Munich Security Conference, a unique forum for the debate on international security policy, is taking place for the fiftieth time in 2014. It brings together decision-makers and opinion leaders who shoulder a special responsibility in the constant struggle for peace, freedom, and stability. This conference enjoys a high standing, largely owing to dedicated individuals who devote their energies to promoting dialogue year after year. All of them deserve our thanks and recognition for the great success of the conference, which now has a long tradition.

The success story of the Munich Security Conference is and remains first and foremost linked to the name Ewald-Heinrich von Kleist. As a young lieutenant, he was one of those willing to risk their lives in the resistance to Hitler. After the end of World War II, the promotion of transatlantic relations was a matter very close to his heart. A key expression of this endeavor was the establishment of the International Wehrkunde Conference fifty years ago, later renamed the Munich Security Conference, which

▲
Chancellor Angela Merkel speaking at the 2011 MSC

Ewald-Heinrich von Kleist developed within a short space of time into a central forum for exchanging views on transatlantic security policy and which he chaired until 1998. This conference offered an excellent opportunity for Germany to actively take part in the dialogue on the global political situation.

Ewald-Heinrich von Kleist died in March 2013. We have honored his memory. His achievements as the long-standing chairman of the Munich Security Conference have received a particularly fitting tribute in the form of the award that bears his name. The Ewald von Kleist Award, first presented in 2009, is granted to individuals in recognition of their outstanding commitment to peace and conflict resolution.

Although the aim of the conference, to give substance to the dialogue on security policy, has not changed during the last half-century, the political environment has changed fundamentally. While the first conference years were marked by the Cold War, new challenges came to the fore once the East-West confrontation was overcome, initially in the Balkans and then in particular in the wake of the appalling terrorist attacks of September 11, 2001.

The Munich Security Conference has always addressed topical issues and further developed its areas of focus in the spirit of networked security. Inevitably, this has also resulted in the circle of participants being expanded—a real boon for the conference—to include representatives from other regions, from Central and Eastern European countries, from Russia, and from Asia.

However, the transatlantic dialogue—the cornerstone and fixture of the Munich Security Conference—has retained its outstanding importance, especially when it is put to the test, for example by data protection issues. The unique partnership between the United States and Europe remains the fundamental basis for our security and freedom.

We work closely together within NATO. In partnership with other allies, we stand shoulder to shoulder in carrying out missions such as the one in Afghanistan. We Europeans and Americans are cooperating to tackle key foreign policy challenges. This applies—to name just a few examples—to the situation in Syria and the changes sweeping the Arab world, the Middle East peace process, Iran's nuclear program, the promotion of democracy and stability in Mali, as well as to the fight against terrorism and piracy.

Ewald-Heinrich von Kleist called Europe—once a divided and today a united continent—a fortunate oasis. And he added: "However, it has to be looked after." This is the aim of the Munich Security Conference. It is always open to new participants and themes. It thus remains in step with the times as an international forum for fostering understanding and mutual appreciation. On that note, I would like to wish all participants a sure hand and continued success.

*Dr. **Angela Merkel** is chancellor of the Federal Republic of Germany.*

Congratulating the Munich Security Conference on Fifty Years of Contributions to Transatlantic Security[1]

Joseph R. Biden

For more than fifty years, American foreign and defense ministers, legislators, and academics—and even vice presidents—have regularly made the annual pilgrimage to Munich to share in an open dialogue with our closest friends and Allies on the most pressing issues affecting the transatlantic partnership and beyond.

I first went to the Munich Security Conference during the grip of the Cold War in 1980, when it was still known as *Wehrkunde*. Those were very different times, but even then there was not a question in my mind, or in the minds of those who had traveled to Munich with me, that our work was essential and that the opportunities before us were genuine and significant.

Since that time, much has changed. The Iron Curtain that once divided Europe was replaced by an open door. NATO grew from fifteen allies in 1980 to an ever strengthened and more inclusive alliance of twenty-eight countries. During the same period, the size of the European Community tripled.

US Vice President Biden addressing the 2013 MSC

New forces have begun shaping the twenty-first century. We have realized that neither the United States nor Europe can afford to look inward, that instead we must engage in the world around us. And we have.

Today's threats are as real and, at times, as daunting as those we faced during the Cold War. They transcend borders and nation states and impact global security and economic prosperity in profound ways. And so the work of the Munich Security Conference has become even more essential.

Preserving stability and peace for our children and grandchildren requires constant vigilance, dialogue, and cooperation. It requires that we strengthen our ability to prevent cyber attacks, to stop the spread of the world's most dangerous weapons, and to mitigate the consequences of a warming planet. And it requires continued work at home, from stimulating new growth to continuing the important work of building a Europe that is whole, free, and at peace.

And just as the transatlantic relationship has evolved, so too has the Munich Security Conference, in part thanks to the vision and leadership of my good friend Ambassador Wolfgang Ischinger.

Munich started out as a small gathering of Germans and Americans focused on defense and security in Europe. Over time, it added other Europeans, other disciplines, and other countries. And now instead of looking inward at the Euro-Atlantic space, today's Munich is focused on how Americans and Europeans engage in the world around us.

Today, Munich is the place to go to hear bold policies announced, new ideas and approaches tested, old partnerships reaffirmed, and new ones formed. Like no other global forum, today's Munich connects European leaders and thinkers with their peers from across the world to have an open and frank exchange of ideas on the most pressing issues we currently face— from the crisis in Syria to the global financial crisis and its impact on security, as well as cyber security. And while the formal discussions are important, it is the informal chats in the coffee bar and the *Stuben* that cement relationships, foster intellectual ferment, and bring people from disparate political stripes together, including many of my colleagues from Congress.

That's why I chose Munich as the place to outline the Obama administration's new approach toward foreign policy, including our desire to reset relations with Russia while maintaining our principled position rejecting spheres of influence.

It's why, in 2013, I returned to Munich to take stock of what America had accomplished with our friends and partners over the previous four years, including responsibly ending the war in Iraq and drawing down our forces in Afghanistan, to lay out a new agenda of cooperation for the next four years—challenges we face together, such as strengthening our global trading system and creating jobs on both sides of the Atlantic, and broadening our engagement in the Asia-Pacific.

All of us who have participated in the Munich Security Conference over the years know something simple and fundamental: important partnerships do not build themselves. They require hard work and constant conversation, and are best fostered at forums like the Munich Security Conference. I have every confidence that Munich's best days are yet to come. Congratulations on fifty years of essential work!

Joseph R. Biden is vice president of the United States.

Notes

1 This foreword is meant to commemorate the fiftieth anniversary of the Munich Security Conference and does not suggest approval or endorsement by the vice president or the White House of any particular views expressed in the anthology.

The 50th Munich Security Conference— Security Policy in the Era of Globalization

Wolfgang Reitzle

When, in the fall of 1963, the first *Internationale Wehrkunde-Begegnung* was held in Munich, nobody could guess how significant the conference would one day become. It was the time of the Cold War, the Cuban missile crisis, and the historic speech by President John F. Kennedy from the balcony of Berlin City Hall.

Today we know: that beginning, fifty years ago, marked the start of a success story. *Wehrkunde* was to become one of the most important international conferences on questions of foreign and security policy: the Munich Security Conference, which has been held under the leadership of Ambassador Wolfgang Ischinger since 2008.

Ewald von Kleist, the formative chairman of the conference for more than three decades, had conceived the conference as an independent private discussion forum, bringing together international personalities and experts from the worlds of transatlantic politics, military, and diplomacy. From the very start, the opportunity for an informal exchange untrammeled by protocol and for confidential discussions on the margin was an essential feature of the conference.

The conference hall during the 2013 Munich Security Conference

Against the background of the Cold War, the conference in those initial decades was characterized above all by questions of military cooperation and collaboration within NATO. After the end of the Cold War, it was continuously opened up and expanded to include new themes and regional priorities. This development was steadily pushed forward under the auspices of Kleist's successor as chairman, Horst Teltschik, and led to more intensive collaboration in particular with the states of Central and Eastern Europe. Furthermore, Horst Teltschik emphasized the significance of the rising powers.

Under the current chairman, Ambassador Ischinger, the Munich Security Conference has continued to explore new topics, building his concept of the conference on a more extended understanding of security.

Today, topics such as threats to global trade routes and data streams, economic espionage and cyber security, the secure procurement of raw materials, and environmental and climate risks complement the agenda of the conference—of course, without losing sight of more traditional areas of security policy.

This diversity is also apparent among the participants: alongside heads of state, ministers, and high-ranking military representatives, guests now also include Nobel Peace Prize laureates and representatives of organizations such as Greenpeace. In the future, the objective is to continue to make the conference a bit younger and less predominantly male.

In recent years, the Munich Security Conference has become even more relevant internationally under the leadership of Ambassador Ischinger. We in the MSC Advisory Council would like to express our very sincere thanks to him for his vision and his great personal commitment to modernizing the focus and organization of the conference.

The end of the Cold War was not—as many had hoped—"the end of history." Given the current conflicts and challenges, the Munich Security Conference remains an essential institution in the international debate on foreign and security policy. With that in mind, the Advisory Council wishes everyone a successful fiftieth conference—and hopes that you will find the diverse mix of essays in this book both entertaining and insightful.

*Prof. Dr. **Wolfgang Reitzle** is chief executive officer of Linde AG and chairman of the Advisory Council of the Munich Security Conference.*

Advisory Council of the Munich Security Conference

Chairman

Reitzle, Prof. Dr. Wolfgang
Chief Executive Officer, Linde AG

Members

Achleitner, Dr. Paul
Chairman of the Supervisory Board, Deutsche Bank AG

Al Saud, Prince Turki Al Faisal bin Abdulaziz
Chairman, King Faisal Center for Research and Islamic Studies

von Bomhard, Dr. Nikolaus
Chairman of the Board, Munich Re

Diekmann, Michael
Chairman of the Board of Management, Allianz SE

Gref, Herman O.
Chairman of the Board and Chief Executive Officer, Sberbank RF

Harman, Jane
Director, President, and Chief Executive Officer, Woodrow Wilson
International Center for Scholars

Haun, Frank
Chief Executive Officer, Krauss-Maffei Wegmann GmbH & Co. KG

Lauvergeon, Anne
Chairman and Chief Executive Officer of A.L.P. S.A.; Member of the Board
of Directors of EADS

Rudloff, Hans-Joerg
Chairman of the Investment Bank, Barclays

Solana, Dr. Javier
Former Secretary General of NATO; former High Representative of
the European Union for Foreign Affairs and Security Policy; Distinguished
Fellow, the Brookings Institution; President, ESADE Center for Global
Economy and Geopolitics

Stoiber, Dr. Dr. h.c. Edmund
Former Minister-President of the Free State of Bavaria

The Chairmen

Towards Mutual Security:
From *Wehrkunde* to the Munich Security Conference

Wolfgang Ischinger

Since its inception in the fall of 1963,[1] the conference we today call the Munich Security Conference has changed in many ways—not just in terms of its name. Yet in some ways, it has not changed at all. What was the main rationale behind the first conferences remains true today. Munich was, is, and will hopefully continue to be an important independent venue for policymakers and experts for open and constructive discussions about the most pressing security issues of the day—and of the future. These debates take place both on the podium and, crucially, behind the scenes, at the margins of the conference. Since its inaugural meeting under the name of *Internationale Wehrkunde-Begegnung,* the conference has built a unique reputation as a not-to-be-missed meeting for the strategic community, particularly for those from NATO member states. As Ivo Daalder, at the time US ambassador to NATO, remarked last year via Twitter, Munich is the "Oscars for security policy wonks."

The Munich Security Conference has attracted many of the West's leading practitioners and thinkers on security issues. In 2013, more than sixty

▲
Wolfgang Ischinger opening day three of the 2012 Munich Security Conference

foreign and defense ministers were in attendance, along with eleven heads of state and government. We have hosted United Nations secretary generals, heads of international organizations, the president of the European Council, vice presidents of the United States, and Nobel Peace Prize laureates such as Tawakkol Karman. Given the limited space at the Hotel Bayerischer Hof—the conference venue in the heart of Munich—and the few spots on the different panels, setting the agenda, inviting participants, and selecting the speakers is not always an enviable task. Yet it is a challenge we happily embrace.

Nonetheless, the participation of high-level speakers is not the only feature that makes the Munich Security Conference unique. Most importantly, there is a very special atmosphere that fills the corridors every year when decision-makers and experts from different fields of foreign and security policy invade the Hotel Bayerischer Hof. Where else do you find a couple of European ministers in a small corner of the rustic Palais Keller restaurant in the hotel's basement arguing—amicably, I should add—with Cathy Ashton over a beer, without protocol, without staff, without a preset agenda? Where else is the mix of high-ranking participants so diverse, and the physical space so limited, that you can hardly avoid running into officials whom you would rather not talk to? Where else can you see, just a few steps from the hotel, a head of government running into another leader right after one of them snuck out to buy a pair of *Lederhosen* and both having a good laugh about it? We may not spend much time during the MSC weekend celebrating *Fasching* anymore—as the attendees did in the early *Wehrkunde* years—but the event continues to be, despite so many official delegations, an informal event featuring Bavarian hospitality, and with the always welcome opportunity to sneak away for an hour or two into downtown Munich, right outside the door. Many of the foreign participants have also enjoyed coming to the conference for these very reasons.

In turn, the extraordinary commitment not only of the German government but of every single US administration and of key members of Congress has contributed enormously to the success and the reputation of the conference. For Germans, *Wehrkunde,* which literally translates as "military science," is a rather old-fashioned notion, but the fact that our US participants continue to refer to the conference as *Wehrkunde* underlines the powerful tradition of the institution. Over the years, the annual meeting has built lasting ties across the Atlantic, in many cases personal friendships. I am glad that the US commitment to the Munich Security Conference is as strong as ever. Last year, one full tenth of the US Senate attended the conference. Where else do you ever find ten senators—from both parties—in one room together outside the United States? I very much appreciate the continued dedication by the congressional delegation, especially by its long-time leaders William Cohen, John McCain, and Joe Lieberman, who have all contributed personal essays to this book.

Moreover, it is certainly no coincidence that, in 2009 and in 2013, Vice President Joe Biden came to Munich for the Obama administration's first major foreign policy addresses of both the first and second term, and that Munich was the place Secretary of State Hillary Clinton and Secretary of Defense Leon Panetta attended together in 2012 to try and dissipate European worries about the so-called rebalancing of the United States toward the Asia-Pacific. While the transatlantic security relationship will certainly change, US representatives have underscored in recent years that Europe remains America's most important partner in engaging with the world, which is why the conference will remain an important date in the calendar of our US allies. As Secretary of State John Kerry writes in his contribution to this volume, "President Obama's plan to rebalance our interests and investments in [the Asia-Pacific] region does not diminish in any way our close and continuing partnership with Europe."

Our participants come to Munich to talk—and to listen. The conference itself does not "produce" any direct "result," and this is actually a good thing. Since there is no need to agree on a final communiqué, participants are free to voice their views and explore their divergent opinions. This does not mean that the conference does not have an impact. On the contrary, contributions to this volume point out how some of the debates have had a major influence on a number of diplomatic initiatives. In contrast to many other diplomatic events controlled by protocol, the Munich Security Conference is a rather unregulated marketplace of ideas. Here, new or old proposals are floated—sometimes successfully, sometimes not. But if they are uttered here, they will be heard and not soon be forgotten by the community. One example among many: when NATO secretary general Anders Rasmussen proposed his Smart Defence initiative in 2011, he did so in Munich.

The annual meeting also often becomes a hub for diplomatic initiatives and the preparation for important decisions in response to crises. After all, it is hard to imagine a place where it is easier to get as many key players into a single room than here. In 2012, for example, informal UN Security Council deliberations essentially took place in Munich, as many key foreign ministers were present, arguing the merits of the proposed Syria resolution both on the podium and behind closed doors. And the essays contributed to this volume by Rudolf Scharping and Klaus Naumann, for instance, provide insight into the decisions relating to Kosovo during the 1999 conference.

In addition, the MSC offers protected space for informal meetings between representatives from governments who might not be on the best terms but who may wish to meet informally, behind the scenes. Where else do you have the chance to see so many of your colleagues in one spot? Some ministers have been known to hold up to two dozen bilateral meetings over the span of a conference weekend.

Sometimes, foreign and defense ministers even use their joint presence in Munich to agree on and sign important bilateral documents. One particularly noteworthy example could be witnessed during the 2011 conference, when Russian Foreign Minister Sergey Lavrov and US Secretary of State Hillary Clinton exchanged the instruments of ratification for the New START treaty in the Hotel Bayerischer Hof.

Increasingly, the conference also serves as a meeting place for a number of nongovernmental initiatives and events. For instance, important Track II initiatives such as the Euro-Atlantic Security Initiative or the Global Zero Commission have met in the context of the MSC and presented reports, providing independent food for thought for the decision-makers present in the audience or the wider public. And side events like the "women's breakfast" or a CEO lunch provide unique opportunities to bring key people together.

Today, the debate about security issues involves an ever-increasing number of people. For the first decades of the Munich Security Conference, the participants did not hail from as many countries as they do today—and that was entirely by design. Back then, the audience was relatively small, not exceeding a few dozen people. While *Wehrkunde* was an international conference from the very beginning, it was first of all a venue where German participants met their counterparts from their most important ally, the United States, but also from other NATO member states. Mutual security at that time meant, first of all, shared security among the transatlantic allies. Debates in Munich concentrated on Western policy within the overarching framework of the Cold War confrontation. Long-time participants such as Lothar Rühl, Karl Kaiser, Richard Burt, Sam Nunn, and others describe some of these debates in this volume. The basic idea of *Wehrkunde* was to bring together decision-makers and experts from NATO member states to discuss and develop a common strategy *vis-à-vis* the Soviet Union and the Warsaw Pact. Just like today, these intra-alliance debates were far from uncontroversial, at times even heated. Yet *Wehrkunde* was an important meeting place where differences could be voiced and mitigated, and where conceptual thinking beyond the urgent issues of the day had a place. As a result, the conference has often been dubbed the "transatlantic family meeting." It is a testament to the extraordinary work and personality of Ewald von

Kleist, who sadly passed away in March of 2013, that it developed and kept such a high reputation. The Munich Security Conference will always be his conference. We will continue to honor his name by each year dedicating the Ewald von Kleist Award to a leader who has contributed to global peace and security.

When the Cold War came to an end, both von Kleist and his successor as chairman from 1998 on, Horst Teltschik, built on the unique character of this transatlantic meeting, but they also decided to invite participants from countries that had not been part of the Western world before. They made room for participants from Central and Eastern European countries that had begun their transition processes from Soviet-dominated state economies to liberal democracies with a market-based economy. As these countries made clear that they wanted to become a part of the West, where they felt they belonged anyway, they also became regular participants of the Munich conferences. But even beyond those states that would soon become members of NATO and the European Union, Kleist and Teltschik reached out to the successor states of the Soviet Union, notably the Russian Federation. They understood that the conference—much like NATO—had to move beyond the confines of one "side" of the Cold War if it were to remain relevant.

In fact, it is this ability to transform itself that a number of contributors to this volume see as one of the key reasons that the MSC's relevance has managed to remain so remarkably high. As US Secretary of Defense Chuck Hagel writes in his essay, "[t]he Munich Security Conference has stayed relevant for fifty years because of its ability to adapt to a constantly changing world."

Over the years, as the number and variety of important players in international security has increased, the circle of conference participants has continued to grow wider. At the same time, the core of the conference will always be transatlantic. It is sometimes said of NATO that it is not a global alliance but an alliance in a global world. The same is true for the Munich Security Conference. It cannot and will not become a global conference, but it has to be a conference reflecting a globalized world.

Today, we welcome high-ranking participants from key rising powers, such as China, Brazil, and India. They will have an important role to play in any future international security architecture. Moreover, I am glad that, over the past decade, the MSC has evolved into a meeting that allows both NATO member states and prominent representatives from the Russian Federation to address their respective grievances and to attempt to find more common ground. As such, both Vladimir Putin's speech in 2007 (as well as the reactions to it) and Joe Biden's "reset" speech in 2009 reflect the role of Munich.

In this volume, Igor Ivanov, former foreign minister of the Russian Federation, and Frank-Walter Steinmeier reflect on the ups and downs of NATO-Russia relations.

In addition, in recent years, both the Arab uprisings and the debate about Iran's nuclear ambitions brought leaders from the Middle East to Munich, sparking both controversial arguments and the opportunity for further dialogue on and off the conference stage.

The audience today is not only more diverse in terms of geography, it also mirrors the broader understanding of security itself. Now, when the participants gather at the Hotel Bayerischer Hof, you still see military leaders—and rightly so. But you also see CEOs, human rights activists, environmentalists, and other leaders representing global civil society. Munich will not lose sight of its core themes belonging to traditional "hard security." We will continue to debate traditional topics such as regional crises, arms races, nuclear proliferation, the purpose and role of NATO, transatlantic burden sharing, or European military capabilities. However, current security policy is more than counting missiles and debating military doctrines. When the financial crisis hit our economies, I welcomed participants to the conference by saying that we would have to discuss "banks, not tanks" in the opening session. We have also invited specialists who inform our audience about issues such as cyber security, energy, or environmental challenges that affect our mutual security. Moreover, together with the Körber Foundation, we initiated the Munich Young Leaders program, bringing a group of younger experts and practitioners to Munich each year.

Another aspect in which today's Munich Security Conference clearly differs from *Wehrkunde* is the degree of transparency. The early meetings were held behind closed doors. Security policy, and NATO military doctrines in particular, were discussed by elites and often kept secret. Over time, the conference has become more transparent. For a number of years, the panel debates have been transmitted not only in parts by our broadcast partners, Bayerischer Rundfunk and Deutsche Welle, but also as a live stream on our website. Whereas space in the Hotel Bayerischer Hof itself is limited, this service offers the opportunity to everyone with access to the Internet to follow the debates in Munich. Increasingly, this will cease to be a one-way street. We have already welcomed input by our friends and followers on Facebook and Twitter and are confident that these new ways of interacting with the interested public can strengthen the social debate on security policy. In 2013, our hashtag #MSC2013 became trending on Twitter for the first time, with participants at the Hotel Bayerischer Hof commenting on the panel debates and interacting with people who followed the debates online.

Of course, the increasing level of transparency does have its drawbacks. High-level speakers who know that their words will be immediately spread across the globe are understandably more careful about what they say. As a consequence, speeches may be less controversial than they used to be. However, given the technological advances, the public interest, and the number of participants, keeping the entire proceedings off the record would today be futile and next to impossible. With that said, we are mindful of the importance of smaller formats, which is why we have begun to introduce breakout sessions during the main conference. Similarly, we have initiated a number of smaller conferences throughout the year: the MSC Core Group Meetings held in a number of capitals around the world, bringing together roughly fifty high-level participants, as well as day-long events such as the Cyber Security Summit in 2012 and 2013 or The Future of European Defence Summit in April 2013.

Thus, as it turns fifty, the Munich Security Conference is evolving, and it is as alive and well as it has ever been. Instead of asking you to take my admittedly biased word for it, I would simply point you to the table of contents of this book. I am proud that the conference enjoys such a reputation that not only is it a must for so many to find their way to Munich each year, but that so many also found the time to contribute to this volume. The authors provide unique perspectives on the first fifty conferences held in Munich and on key security challenges that the international community has faced and continues to face.

In many ways, this is a book much like the Munich Security Conference, and the essays are much like the debates and speeches. Some are short, others long. Some focus on one or two concrete arguments or events, others span decades. Some refer in particular to the debates in Munich, while others frame a certain issue more broadly. A number of essays mostly look ahead—on key issues such as European security policy, cyber security, the "rise" of the Asia-Pacific, or the future of transatlantic and Euro-Atlantic security.

Finally, it is important to note that this is not, and cannot be, a work of history. The conference itself does not have an official archive dating back to the first meetings. The book does, however, aim to illuminate some aspects of the conference's history. You will be able to read a number of very personal, heartfelt reflections about *Wehrkunde* and Ewald von Kleist. A number of authors shed light on specific conferences, including the one held in 1999 just before the Kosovo intervention, and, depending on where you stand, highly publicized highlights or lowlights of the conference, such as the transatlantic crisis over Iraq, epitomized by the proceedings in Munich in 2003. I am delighted that former German chancellor Helmut Schmidt, who came to the conference for the first time in the mid-sixties, found the time to reflect on a number of key debates of the *Wehrkunde* era.

When the *Internationale Wehrkunde-Begegnung* first took place, mutual assured destruction and zero-sum thinking were the ideas of the time. The term "mutual security" could only be applied within NATO. Today more than ever before, the quest for "mutual security" is a global proposition. National interests will not suddenly disappear, and neither will those instances when states understand them too narrowly. Munich is a place where we can and should define and search for our common interests, understood as enlightened self-interest that thinks in win-win categories. As Poland's foreign minister Radosław Sikorski puts it in his essay, in the future "what defines a superpower will not be its weapons of mass destruction that can never be used or the ability to conquer and destroy. It will be the ability to combine and build, the power of mass innovation and mass teamwork based on flexibility, tolerance, and inclusiveness."

The conflict that helped give birth to the conference no longer exists, but that does not mean that the Munich Security Conference's reason to exist has become any less relevant. Quite the contrary: it may well be even more important in an era in which global governance in general, and international security in particular, is certain to become messier and more difficult to manage, and in which the transatlantic partners will have to both stick together as well as reach out to new partners.

*Ambassador **Wolfgang Ischinger** took over from Professor Horst Teltschik as chairman of the Munich Security Conference in 2008. His career in the German foreign service included positions as director of policy planning, as political director, and as state secretary (deputy foreign minister), followed by appointments as German ambassador to the United States and the United Kingdom. He is currently global head of public policy and economic research at Allianz SE, Munich.*

Notes

1   A quick note on why the 2014 meeting is the conference's fiftieth edition, although a 1963 founding might suggest 2012 would have been: a few years after the meeting was founded, one year was skipped when the conference date moved from late fall to early February. Moreover, in 1997, when Ewald von Kleist had indicated his intention to retire as chairman, the conference did not take place. In 1991, the planned and prepared conference was canceled at the very last minute due to the start of the Gulf War, but was always counted.

The Munich Conference on Security Policy—Continuity and Change

Horst Teltschik

When I took over the chairmanship of the Munich Conference on Security Policy, now the Munich Security Conference, in 1999, it was a case of continuing a great tradition: a tradition that my predecessor, Ewald-Heinrich von Kleist, had established in 1963 and carefully fostered. The thirty-fifth conference was to be my first.

The conference was not new territory for me, since Ewald-Heinrich von Kleist had previously invited me to be a participant on numerous occasions. He had twice invited me to a private discussion to talk about his succession. We discussed various names but never mine, until one day a request came via the chairman of my supervisory board at the BMW Group, Mr. Eberhard von Kuenheim, asking for me to take over the conference. Our first joint response was negative. There followed calls from the German chancellor Helmut Kohl, the Bavarian minister president Edmund Stoiber, and even Egon Bahr from the Social Democratic Party urging me to chair the conference. The latter was particularly important for me, as his call showed the impartiality of the conference. With that, the decision was taken.

Horst Teltschik (left) with Secretary of Defense Robert Gates in 2007

In the run-up to my first conference in February 1999 I was frequently asked what I wanted to do differently than my predecessor. As a result, I said rather provocatively in my opening speech: "It is impossible for anyone trying to follow in the footsteps of their predecessor to overtake him." However, I added that anything that had proved its worth should not be changed, and I quoted the German chancellor, Gerhard Schröder, who was present, and who had said during the election campaign that he did not want to do everything differently than his predecessor but just do some things better.

I was absolutely determined to continue with Kleist's important decisions in principle and experience.

Although the Munich Conference on Security Policy was generously funded almost exclusively by the Federal Press Office of Germany's federal government, it nevertheless had to preserve its private character. The chairman of the conference has sole responsibility regarding the subjects to be discussed, the speakers, and the participants. That did not rule out recommendations or consultations with respect to content. They were, and remain, a natural element of the preparations. Only experts on foreign, security, and defense policy from politics, the military, academia, and the media were invited, together with a few representatives from commerce and industry. To keep costs down, volunteers handled the entire organization and running of the conference. The civilian staff and soldiers of the German Bundeswehr deserve special thanks for their diverse and selfless support.

The Munich Conference on Security Policy had to retain its nonpartisan character. The participation of the current German chancellor and that of the opposition leader had to be guaranteed.

The prevailing and future policy of the Atlantic alliance and the development of transatlantic relations had to remain a constant in the content of each conference, and so it was taken as a given that the secretary general of NATO would take part. For the same reason, the participation of a strong American delegation from the administration and Congress was inevitable. To some extent, the impressive number of senators and members of the House of Representatives from both parties as well as participants from the State Department, the Pentagon, and the White House, and other American experts taking part year after year formed the backbone of the Munich Conference on Security Policy. A high point was reached in 2000, when fifteen members of the US Congress came to Munich. For the first time, seven members of the House of Representatives took part, together with eight senators. The two US senators John McCain (R-AZ) and Joe Lieberman (D-CT) led the annual American delegation very successfully and vigorously.

It was essential to maintain the tradition of speaking openly at the Munich Conference on Security Policy, developing new ideas and options for action, and holding intense discussions while nevertheless keeping the conference public. Up to a peak of around seven hundred journalists from all over the world followed the live broadcast in adjoining rooms. Two German television stations broadcast the speeches and discussions simultaneously. To facilitate an intense and lively debate, it was traditional for the chairman himself to lead the conference.

However, what was supposed to change?

It was the American senators who immediately expressed a wish to return to the traditional venue, the Hotel Bayerischer Hof. After a firm promise by the new owner and manager of the hotel, Mrs. Innegrit Volkhardt, to host the conference at her hotel, subject to possible security requirements, there was no longer anything to prevent a return. Mrs. Volkhardt was to prove to be an extremely charming and obliging hostess for all the participants.

The nonpartisan nature of the conference was reinforced by the invitation—for the first time—to the Bündnis 90/Die Grünen party. Foreign Minister and Vice Chancellor Joschka Fischer, Antje Vollmer, and Jürgen Trittin, to name just a few, were not only regular participants but also active speakers and contributors to the discussions. In the following years, the first, proficient representatives of NGOs, such as Kenneth Roth of Human Rights Watch, were also to come along.

It was a particular concern of mine to increase the number of participating countries. In view of international developments toward a multipolar world, the emergence of new hotspots, particularly in Eastern and Southeastern Europe and the Middle East, and the growing significance of the Asia-Pacific area, it was absolutely essential to invite high-ranking politicians from these regions: first and foremost from the People's Republic of China, Japan, India, Singapore, but also from Pakistan, Egypt, Israel, Palestine, Jordan, and Iran. Finally, there were also representatives from Latin America who had expressed their own interest in attending. Since the number of participants was of course limited, observers were invited as well.

With the additional new participants, the range of subjects to be discussed was equally expanded. Naturally, attention focused on the latest crises such as the wars in Iraq and in Afghanistan and the necessary political decision-making processes in NATO, the European Union, or at a national level. However, the bloody terrorist attacks of September 11, 2001, in New York and Washington demonstrated new threats such as international terrorism. The so-called asymmetric threats came to the forefront and were to have a determining influence on the conference agenda.

The large number of personal meetings and talks on the fringes of the Munich Conference on Security Policy, particularly between parties to a conflict, proved to be the major and indispensable capital of the annual meeting. Year after year, completely confidential personal talks took place between conflicting parties in the side rooms and suites of the hotel, without any minutes, note takers, press, or public, and unnoticed by the other participants. These informal talks gave and still give cause for the hope that new approaches to conflict resolution are being sought and, hopefully, found, and they underline the value of the conference.

The latest crises, such as the two Iraq wars and the military intervention in Afghanistan, were also to change the environment of the conference. It had regularly been accompanied by protest demonstrations since 2001. On one occasion, during the First Iraq War, Ewald-Heinrich von Kleist even had to cancel the conference. Thanks to the precautions of the Bavarian state government and the Munich police and their discreet courses of action, the safety of participants and of the city of Munich was never jeopardized. In order to emphatically underscore the peacemaking character of the conference, I organized it under the overarching slogan "Peace through Dialogue." This was backed up by selected invitations to conflicting parties to take part in public discussions, be they representatives of Iran, Israel and Palestine, India and Pakistan, or others. A "peace prize" in the form of a "Peace through Dialogue" medal has been awarded since 2005. The first recipient of the prize was United Nations Secretary General Kofi Annan, followed in 2006 by Senator McCain, who had pushed a law on a general ban on torture through Congress. In 2007 NATO Secretary General Javier Solana was honored, and in 2008 soldiers of the Canadian armed forces who had been wounded during an international peace mission in Afghanistan.

Less helpful in these public disputes with the demonstrators was the leadership of the City of Munich, who certainly stressed the importance of the Munich Conference on Security Policy for the worldwide reputation of the Bavarian capital in personal discussions and through their role as host, but who nevertheless failed to adequately address the public.

The ten years of the Munich Conference on Security Policy under my leadership produced a wealth of high points that were particularly characteristic of the conference. I shall recall just a few here.

The opening speaker at the first conference I hosted was Chancellor Gerhard Schröder, who continued the fine tradition of his predecessor, Helmut Kohl. It is self-evident that the speeches by the German chancellors from Helmut Kohl and Gerhard Schröder right up to Angela Merkel were always among the high points of the conference. International participants see them as defining the position of German foreign and security policy in general and on the latest crises in particular. Gerhard Schröder was eagerly awaited in 1999. Only in office since October 1998, he announced a "joint foreign and security policy" for Europe and the "development of a European security and defense identity" at my first conference. His message was: "A new Europe for a new NATO, and the new NATO for a new Europe!"

These two topics were to substantially define all of the conferences in the light of the Kosovo War of 1999, 9/11, and the American intervention in Afghanistan in 2001 and in Iraq in 2003.

The lessons of the Kosovo War for NATO and for the European Union were drawn jointly at the 2000 conference. Not least, it was the first "out-of-area" deployment of the German Bundeswehr in the context of NATO, which was, moreover, undertaken without a United Nations mandate.

On the other hand, it was striking that Munich Conference on Security Policy participants initially paid only little attention to the high-ranking representatives from the rising world powers in Asia, China, India, and Japan, with their analyses of regional and global security. The potential for conflict between India and Pakistan, China and Taiwan, and the arming of North Korea with ballistic missiles still seemed to be a long way off for European participants at that time.

US Secretary of Defense Donald Rumsfeld had only been in office for thirteen days when he came to Munich in 2001. In subsequent conferences he was to become an influential and quite invigorating factor for the Munich Conference on Security Policy on a series of controversial themes. It started with the announcement that the United States intended to set up a missile defense system. The high point was reached in 2003 with the almost proverbial exchange of blows with Foreign Minister Joschka Fischer, when the latter, reacting to the American plans for intervention in Iraq, fired back at Rumsfeld by saying: "Sorry, I am not convinced!"

From 2001 onwards, the politics of Russia and its position in a European security architecture have increasingly been placed on the agenda. Year after year, Defense Minister Sergei Ivanov vigorously represented Russian interests, particularly against American participants. However, the speech by President Vladimir Putin in 2007 was to meet with a worldwide response. Candidly and directly, he addressed the entire catalogue of Russian interests and the existing differences of opinion with the West. Unfortunately, the answers largely failed to materialize. It almost seemed as if the conference participants had been paralyzed.

After the terrible terrorist attack of 9/11, international terrorism dominated the Munich Conference on Security Policy agenda in 2002. NATO had for the first time invoked the assistance clause of Article 5 of the North Atlantic Treaty. American intervention in Afghanistan took place in October. A military confrontation with Iraq was looming on the horizon.

The question of military intervention in Iraq was to dominate the 2003 conference. The political atmosphere had intensified. The US saw the end of diplomatic efforts for a peaceful solution to the Iraq conflict approaching. Three days before the conference convened, Secretary of State Colin Powell presented alleged proof of Iraq producing weapons of mass destruction to the UN Security Council. On the other hand, Chancellor Schröder, speaking at a market square in Goslar during the Lower Saxony election campaign, announced that Germany would not advocate intervention in Iraq, even if the United Nations voted for it. There were rumors of an independent Franco-German initiative. CDU party leader Angela Merkel spoke cautiously in favor of supporting the US. In the run-up, Donald Rumsfeld had ridiculed the "old" and the "new" Europe. The general mood was that the Iraq conflict divided NATO.

The fact that a high-ranking representative from the Islamic Republic of Iran spoke at that conference for the first time was virtually drowned out.

At the next Munich Conference on Security Policy, in 2004, it was absolutely necessary, in view of the "disaster" caused by the dispute regarding the Iraq conflict in the Atlantic alliance and in view of the war in Afghanistan, to focus on the future of the transatlantic relationship and the future of NATO. Jaap de Hoop Scheffer appeared for the first time as successor to NATO Secretary General George Robertson. At the same time, the conference directed its attention to the overarching crisis in the Middle East. King Abdullah II of Jordan gave introductory talks on this, as did high-ranking representatives from Israel and Palestine. Foreign Minister Fischer and Defense Minister Peter Struck proposed new transatlantic initiatives.

This discussion on the future of the Middle East was continued at the 2005 conference with the Egyptian foreign minister, among others, and once again a top representative from Iran. However, the high points were speeches by German President Horst Köhler and UN Secretary General Kofi Annan. They were concerned with discussing the subject of security policy in detail—beyond the latest military conflicts and the terrorist threat. It was the task of President Köhler to open the discussion on the interaction between economic underdevelopment and security. Kofi Annan dealt with the future role of the United Nations, on which US Senator Hillary Clinton also made a notable speech.

However, as it did every year, the Munich Security Conference also dealt with the future tasks of NATO. The speech by Gerhard Schröder also caused a stir. As he fell ill at short notice, it was read out by Peter Struck. Schröder regretted that NATO was "no longer the primary venue where transatlantic partners discuss and coordinate strategies." The same applied for "the dialogue between the European Union and the United States … ." Consequently, he proposed "a high-ranking panel of independent figures from both sides of the Atlantic to help us find a solution." This proposal led to fierce controversy regarding the future of NATO.

In the following year, 2006, Angela Merkel, who had since become the German chancellor, set out her foreign and security policy program for the first time. Right at the start, she triggered a lively exchange with the Iranian deputy foreign minister with her unequivocal criticism of Iran's nuclear policy and President Mahmoud Ahmadinejad's statements on the Holocaust. Frank-Walter Steinmeier, the new foreign minister, emphasized the significance of close cooperation with Russia in European and global security matters. The discussion on the future of NATO continued. Central to this was the question of whether and how the Alliance should take on global responsibility. The importance of this discussion was underlined by the speeches by leading politicians from China, India, and Japan on their foreign and security policy interests.

A sensational inquiry loomed in the run-up to the 2007 Munich Conference on Security Policy. Mahmoud Ahmadinejad wanted to take part. However, that would have jeopardized the conference as a whole. The speech by Vladimir Putin was sensational enough. Russia's policy remained an essential component of the conference agenda. In her speech, Angela Merkel had gone so far as to propose further development of NATO-Russia relations. Israeli Foreign Minister Tzipi Livni had given conference participants an introduction to the crisis situation in the Middle East. Leading political representatives from Pakistan, Afghanistan, and Iran went into the subject in more depth. The first appearance of US Secretary of Defense Robert Gates, who stated, after six years of NATO intervention in Afghanistan, that there was still no joint comprehensive strategy and that the available civilian and military resources were insufficient, caused general disillusionment. The despaired cry by NATO Secretary General George Robertson—who had already declared at the 2002 conference that what was needed were "capabilities, capabilities, capabilities"—was unforgettable.

This discussion on burden sharing by NATO in Afghanistan continued at the last Munich Conference on Security Policy that I chaired. The high point, however, were the speech by Turkish Prime Minister Recep Erdoğan on Turkish foreign and security policy and the speech by Serbian President Boris Tadić, who had been elected only a week before. For the first time there was a discussion panel on issues of pan-European development that included three presidents from Eastern and Southeastern Europe.

In the ten years of the Munich Conference on Security Policy, its international importance increased dramatically. This is reflected by the number of high-ranking participants, which has risen year after year—from presidents and heads of government, fifty foreign and defense ministers, to American senators and large numbers of parliamentarians from more than fifty countries, who often had registered of their own accord during the year. It became more and more difficult to limit the number of participants to a maximum of five hundred. The rapidly growing number of journalists from throughout the world demonstrated the great public interest in the conference.

In the end it was possible to say: the Munich Conference on Security Policy has become a guaranteed success. For me, that was the right time to pass the chair of the conference on to someone new.

*Professor **Horst Teltschik** was chairman of the Munich Conference on Security Policy from 1999 to 2008. Prior to his chairmanship of the BMW Foundation Herbert Quandt from 1993 to 2003 and his membership in the Board of Management of the BMW Group, he served as national security advisor to Chancellor Dr. Helmut Kohl.*

Remembering Ewald von Kleist

John McCain

The Munich Security Conference, for me, will always be synonymous with Ewald von Kleist. It was Ewald who created the annual *Wehrkunde* conference fifty years ago. It was Ewald who turned it into the world's premier gathering for policymakers, military officials, civil society leaders, and journalists to debate the world's most pressing security challenges and strive to overcome them. And despite his passing last year at the age of ninety, it is Ewald who will always be *Wehrkunde's* deepest inspiration, just as he was my inspiration for over thirty years as well as a personal hero and friend to me.

I have known quite a few brave and inspiring people in my life, but never anyone quite as brave as Ewald von Kleist, who twice prepared to sacrifice his life to rid the world of one of the cruelest, most depraved, and dangerous tyrants in history. It is never easy to answer fully the demands of conscience and always to have the courage of your convictions. There is always some price to be paid to live that nobly.

However, the kind of choice that Ewald made—to choose honor and duty over every personal consideration, to choose the world over his place in it, to choose history over his own future—that is a price that only people who possess the most sublime sense of honor and humility are willing to pay. To

John McCain surrounded by reporters during the 2003 conference be that brave and selfless, that morally irreproachable, at the age of twenty-one, in the springtime of life; to confront with courage a regime built on fear; to die rather than submit to tyranny; to leave the world rather than allow its continued destruction is an inspiration that should endure far beyond the lives of the generations who witnessed it.

That Ewald's mission did not succeed, and that his sacrifice was not required, does not diminish the nobility of his attempt or the power of its inspiration. For Ewald, his father, and the others who took part in the effort to assassinate Adolf Hitler belonged, as Winston Churchill described it, to one of "the noblest and greatest of resistance movements that have ever arisen in the history of all people."

It is the heroism of Ewald and people like him, who, in the face of unspeakable horrors, kindled the world's moral imagination to see the sufferings of millions without illusions and inspired others to act to save good from evil. His story reminds us that history is made not by abstract, inexorable forces but by human beings who have the courage to make the hardest decisions and the selflessness to pay whatever price necessary to ensure history is the record of humanity's progress and not just a series of tragedies wrought by iniquity.

After World War II, Ewald could have lived the rest of his life in leisure and comfort, having done his duty, and more, to save the world from darkness. No one would have begrudged him that. But that is not who Ewald was. He devoted himself not just to the defeat of the Third Reich but to building something decent in its place—to the defense of Western democracies and the advance of our values against new threats. From the ruins of a cataclysmic war, Ewald helped build and preserve an alliance that would make the world safer and freer. We cannot celebrate his legacy without paying tribute to his great contributions to the transatlantic alliance, the cause to which he devoted the rest of his long and accomplished life.

Ewald was my friend for three decades. I was blessed to have enjoyed the distinct pleasure of his company and blessed to have learned so many important things from his wise and generous counsel. And I have been influenced greatly by the many years I have attended the Munich Security Conference, which was among Ewald's greatest creations.

I was even more influenced by Ewald's personal example of statesmanship, leadership, courage, and civility, although my debating style at *Wehrkunde* might have caused a few observers to speculate that Ewald's possession of that last quality failed to make an adequate impression on me. I assure you, it did, although I have to admit that I have little hope of ever possessing as great a measure of any of Ewald's many virtues as I would like to. He set too high a bar for courage and civility than most of us can match. But it is worth aspiring to Ewald's high standards, even if it is in vain, even if only to keep us humble.

Since I first attended *Wehrkunde* at the height of the Cold War, the world has transformed in unimaginable ways: from the collapse of the Iron Curtain to the rise of the European Union, from the attacks of September 11, 2001, to the dawn of the Arab Awakening. Hundreds of millions of people have been lifted out of poverty from China to India and elsewhere. Technological advances have transformed the way we live. I am reminded when I return to Munich each February that none of these developments happened by accident. They were made possible by the principled leadership of the transatlantic alliance and the international system we forged together with diplomacy and defended with military power.

It is easy to forget just how audacious an idea the transatlantic alliance was six decades ago. America had a long tradition of avoiding entangling alliances, and the nations of Western Europe had a long history of going to war with one another. But we had learned the lessons of World War II that we had failed to learn after the Great War. The founders of our alliance believed we could transcend our differences, allies, and former enemies together, with a diplomatic and security architecture designed around not only our shared security interests but also our shared values. This was a new promise made—a promise not just of security but of a better, freer way of life. In fact, it promised security because of our shared values.

What I came to understand about the Munich Security Conference and Ewald von Kleist's vision in creating it is that, at its core, this conference embodies the same idea that animates our broader transatlantic community. It is the idea that Euro-Atlantic democracies, the stewards of freedom, human rights, and the rule of law should not confront our challenges in isolation. It is the idea that we are stronger, safer, freer together. We broke with history and created our world anew—a community of independent nations with different languages, characteristics, and customs and occasional disagreements that had the wisdom to recognize an essential common identity as free and just civilizations and a common purpose to remain so.

Whether in the face of Soviet aggression in 1963 or the threat of terrorism in 2014, the transatlantic idea is the idea that our individual struggles are a shared endeavor that transcends time and place. In this way, one of the enduring values of the Munich Security Conference is the solidarity it creates and recreates each year through dynamic debate and in pursuit of common solutions to new problems and challenges.

The security challenges we discussed at *Wehrkunde* when I attended my first conference three decades ago were different than those we discussed last February. And the challenges that will be at the center of conversations at *Wehrkunde* three decades from now will undoubtedly be different than the ones we are grappling with today. But I am confident that the central idea that unites the transatlantic alliance and defines Ewald's legacy will endure: solidarity with each other and with the universal longings of the human heart for security, for basic rights and equality, for liberty under the law, for tolerance and opportunity.

At a time when America and Europe face many challenges at home and abroad, and when it has unfortunately become all too fashionable to suggest that our best days are behind us, Ewald von Kleist's legacy—his moral conviction, his optimism, his abiding faith in our shared interests and values—should lift our spirits and inspire us to carry on with confidence.

Though we have said goodbye to our friend last year and celebrated his extraordinary life, his memory must inspire us all to live as he did—for the right reasons and causes, cherishing the example of courage and humility this brave man gave us, and the laughter and loyalty that were his personal gifts to us. It was an extraordinary privilege to know Ewald, to help shape history with him, and to be considered his friend. We must endeavor always to be worthy of that privilege.

John McCain has represented Arizona in the United States Senate since 1986. He is a member of the Senate Committee on Armed Services, the Senate Committee on Homeland Security and Governmental Affairs, and the Senate Committee on Foreign Relations. For many years, he has led the congressional delegation to the Munich conference.

Ewald-Heinrich von Kleist:
The Man behind *Wehrkunde*

Peter C. Hughes and Theresa M. Sandwith

The worldwide tributes paid to Ewald-Heinrich von Kleist following his death on March 8, 2013, at the age of ninety-one were effusive in their respect and admiration for the man who had passed away. It was perhaps inevitable that much of the commentary would focus on Kleist as the last surviving member of the July 20, 1944 plot and his role in the Stauffenberg-led assassination attempt against Hitler. Kleist would have accepted the tributes paid to him for his role in this important event in German history with demure resignation. However, the recognition that he received for his role as the founder of the *Internationale Wehrkunde-Begegnung,* his *Wehrkunde* conference, and the acknowledgement of it and its role in NATO history, meant much more to him than his heroic participation in the German Resistance. *Wehrkunde* was Kleist's life work, a work he pursued with enormous skill and great passion. It grew out of his experience during World War II, the lessons of which he carried with him throughout his entire life. This essay addresses his story. It offers a personal and private perspective on this remarkable man within the greater public history of *Wehrkunde* and NATO. Moreover, it discusses what Kleist set out to accomplish and what, in fact, he

▲
Ewald-Heinrich von Kleist (center)
with Vice President Dan Quayle (left) and Peter Hughes[1]

did accomplish, and it pays respect to him and the friends who helped him on his journey.

Ewald-Heinrich von Kleist frequently observed that his father, Baron Ewald von Kleist-Schmenzin, was the man who had the most import-ant and most profound influence on his life. Indeed, it was his father, his family, and the history the von Kleist family name carried with it, that shaped Kleist's life-long values and principles and gave him his unerring moral compass, which could not be compromised. Kleist's father became an early and active opponent of Hitler who regularly wrote and published in opposition to the Nazis. His writings culminated in his 1932 publication *Der Nationalsozialismus—Eine Gefahr* (National Socialism—A Threat), in which he urged all Germans "who believe in democracy, Christianity, free-dom, humanity, and the rule of law, [to] join together in opposition to Hit-ler and the Nazis."[2] Kleist-Schmenzin's active opposition made him a target for murder by the National Socialists during the Night of the Long Knives on June 30, 1934.[3] Warned by friends, he escaped and stayed in hiding until the threat passed. Nevertheless, Kleist-Schmenzin remained actively involved with the Nazi opposition.[4] When the Stauffenberg plot failed, he was ar-rested and taken to Gestapo headquarters, where circumstance allowed him to see his son, who had also been arrested for his participation in the plot and was being processed at the same time.[5] When discussing this experience, Kleist frequently told the story of how his prison guard would sit and talk to him, incongruously offering him huge slices of his black bread slavered thick with liverwurst, amid the evil and inhumanity that surrounded them. This was a memory that left Kleist shaking his head. However, for reasons one can suspect but which Kleist could never fully explain, this same guard allowed Kleist to meet with his father in private for a few minutes, which allowed them to say their final farewells. Kleist-Schmenzin was executed in Plötzensee on April 9, 1945, two weeks before the Soviets occupied Berlin.[6]

Standing in the shadow of this "great man," as he referred to his father, Ewald-Heinrich von Kleist readily embraced his father's principles and val-ues as well as the responsibilities they brought with them.[7] In 1940, at the age of eighteen, Kleist became a *Wehrmacht* officer, joining the 9th Infantry Regiment in Potsdam. From the outset, Kleist intended to use his position in the military to actively oppose Hitler.[8] His first opportunity to make a meaningful contribution to the resistance came in early 1944, when he was asked by Stauffenberg to blow himself up with Hitler during a display of new military uniforms. The entreaty led Kleist to ask Stauffenberg to give him twenty-four hours to consider the request. As Kleist frequently told the story, he used the twenty-four hours to visit his father and explain what was being asked of him, emphasizing that he was also being asked to kill himself. Although Kleist claims that he was holding out the hope his father might discourage him from undertaking the mission, knowing his father as he did, there are more layers to this story than he lets on. The more compelling explanation is that Kleist wanted his father's blessing and also the opportunity to say his farewell. He said that after he talked to his father about Stauffenberg's request, the latter stood up and walked over to the window. Looking out of the window, he responded: "Ja, das musst Du tun. Wer in einem solchen Moment versagt, wird nie wieder froh in seinem Leben" (Yes, you must do it. He who fails in such a moment will never again find happiness in his life). Reflecting upon their conversation years later, Kleist summed up: "Fathers love their sons and mine certainly [loved me]. But as always, I had underestimated him. He was a great personality [probably] the most important [and for me the most influential] man I ever met."[9]

The plot could never be executed, and several other assassination attempts against Hitler also failed. However, Kleist was now part of Stauffenberg's inner circle and so found himself at his side in the Bendlerblock on July 20, 1944. Kleist described the chaos in Berlin and the desertion of those who had planned to take part in overthrowing the government once it became apparent that Hitler had survived the attack. Although pandemonium surrounded them, Kleist said Stauffenberg was "magnificent, acting absolutely heroically and with an utter calm to the very end; it was like watching history in slow motion while standing on the edge of a bending knife." Even as the conspiracy collapsed, Kleist, who had been sent out on a reconnaissance mission, chose to return to the Bendlerblock to be with Stauffenberg and his fellow conspirators for their inevitable capture.[10]

Ewald-Heinrich von Kleist was arrested and became what he termed the "frequent guest of the Gestapo" before finally being sent to the Ravensbrück concentration camp.[11] He was subsequently released under a ploy: his captors hoped he would lead them to a fellow conspirator from the Stauffenberg plot.[12] However, warned of this and also told that he would be quickly re-arrested, Kleist went to Italy under false military orders. He stayed on permanent travel to evade capture until the war ended, after which he surrendered to the Americans.[13] Although he declined an offer to collaborate with them in the immediate post-war period, he was nevertheless given a so-called *Persilschein,* a clean slate freeing him from any association with the Nazis or war crimes. Kleist came out of the war bearing lessons he called *prägende Erfahrungen* (defining experiences). He loathed the Nazi regime, which he called "a corrupt and criminal totalitarian dictatorship, an incarnation of evil that had violated and destroyed the *Rechtsstaat* and had not even maintained the pretense of recognizing any basic human rights." Thus, this man, who had been prepared to give up his life during the war for his country, both intuitively and consciously, sought a path that would allow him to serve Germany in the postwar era. He was committed to the West German democracy, a civil society governed by the rule of law; this was a cornerstone of the *prägende Erfahrungen* he carried with him throughout his personal life and public career. The other and equally important cornerstone he carried with him was his horror of war and the value he placed on individual life, which he called a nation's "greatest treasure."[14] Moreover, like his father, Kleist was above all a German *Patriot* in the classical nineteenth-century tradition. He was a man who placed loyalty and love of country above party politics or a particular government.

The post-World-War-II geopolitical reality was not only that Germany lay at the center of the East-West divide, itself divided by the two opposing power blocs, but that the world lived under the threat of nuclear weapons, *ein Wahnsinn,* as Kleist termed the condition on which world peace rested. However, he also believed that the "right kind of atomic weapons" contributed to the maintenance of peace through deterrence, a better alternative than war itself.[15] Kleist viewed the geopolitical circumstances as both an opportunity and a challenge for West Germany, which he believed needed to establish itself as a stable democracy and demonstrate that it could become a responsible and reliable member of the West. The opportunity came with the establishment of the Federal Republic of Germany in 1949 and the 1955 dissolution of the Occupation Statute governing the status of Germany, accompanied by the decision for Germany to re-arm and join NATO; this decision was controversial in Germany as well as abroad. Kleist's commitment to become part of this debate and contribute to the development of policy, particularly security policy, in the fledgling West German democracy, became the foundation of his life's work.[16]

Following the study of law and economics, Kleist founded what became a well-known and successful publishing house, the Ewald von Kleist Verlag, which published books on law and jurisprudence. He did this on the basis of his belief in and support for the new German democracy. He also believed he had found a niche with his books in the field of law (which proved to be correct) that would make his publishing house a successful commercial enterprise.[17] Kleist viewed the domestic and international opposition to German rearmament and Germany joining NATO with concern; he believed it was essential for Germany to become a member of the transatlantic security partnership. Together with friends he became a founding member of the *Gesellschaft für Wehrkunde* in 1952, a nonpartisan group established to promote Germany's creation of a military founded on the concept of the citizen soldier and integrated into NATO as a responsible member of the transatlantic alliance.[18] The organization also began publishing a newsletter and topical pamphlets. These were the forerunner of his later publication, begun in 1954, the *Wehrkunde-Zeitschrift,* later the *Europäische Wehrkunde,* which became the foremost international security journal in the German language, a journal that continues to be published to this day.[19]

Concerned about nuclear weapons and the strategy and policy deliberations taking place at NATO over which Germans and Germany, in his view, had limited understanding and even more limited say, Kleist saw an "urgent" need to overcome the "lack of German experts on politico-strategic (meaning nuclear) matters." He believed that there was a need to make the country's political leaders, pundits, and opinion makers aware of the "ideas, knowledge, and theories behind the American projects (policies) and decisions" before they became NATO policy.[20] For Kleist this need came to the forefront in the early sixties. After the election of President John F. Kennedy in 1961, US strategic nuclear defense policy shifted from what was popularly called a policy of "massive retaliation" to one of "flexible response." This shift in US policy precipitated a controversy within NATO, where NATO's defense policy at the time was governed by a Military Committee Document known as MC 14/2. Agreed to in 1957, NATO's defenses relied heavily on the first and early use of theater and strategic nuclear weapons to deter conflict, or if deterrence failed, they would be used to defend Europe. NATO's reliance on this policy of "massive retaliation" was intended to offset the shortfalls in NATO's conventional defense capabilities.[21] Thus began a persistent debate within NATO and at *Wehrkunde* during the Cold War concerning NATO nuclear strategy and capabilities, and the (in)adequacy of NATO's defense expenditures and conventional defense forces.

Ewald-Heinrich von Kleist viewed this entire nuclear debate with aghast; the notion of defending Germany and Europe with ("the wrong kinds of") nuclear weapons, effectively destroying the people(s) and the countries NATO was supposed to be defending, while absurd to him, was a reality nonetheless, and one in which he believed Germans and Germany needed to take an active role. Kleist closely followed the developing conventional-nuclear defense theories, including concepts such as *Brandmauern* (firewalls) and *Eskalationstheorien* (escalation control theories), and he sought greater German participation in the evolution and formulation of policy. As he watched the debates over doctrine and policy within NATO, much of which he saw emanating from a US community of influential academic and think-tank experts, he saw the need for German counterparts to also become engaged in the dialogue. This objective became the near-term catalyst for initiating his first gathering of political leaders, security experts, and pundits, which convened at the Regina Hotel in Munich, from November 30 to December 2, 1963, under the name *I. Internationale Wehrkunde-Begegnung.* This would remain the title for his meetings throughout the Cold War.[22]

In planning for his gathering, he said he wanted a "roundtable encounter of politicians, experts, political writers, and publicists, [which would be] the first of this kind in Germany ... not a desk and auditorium conference in which speech after speech was delivered, endless speeches by politicians who enjoy speaking ("also nicht Reden zum Fenster raus, was Politiker ja gerne machen"). He sought "a discussion between equal and active participants ... [with] the debate field [ranging] from matters of general policy to that of strategy. ... The task and aim is a) taking up contact and favoring personal relationships between American, French, British, and German experts in matters of the political strategy, and b) an exchange of opinions between experts from abroad and the German politicians and publicists working in the field of political strategy and policy of defense." Kleist's plan was to start the conference with attendees coming from NATO's core countries, in which Germany and the United States were to play a major role, "Germany as the host country and the United States as the most important NATO partner."[23] However, guests were to come from across the political spectrum and reflect divergent views.[24] He wanted to create a pleasant but also a familial atmosphere; this latter goal explains why to the end Kleist did not invite participants from outside of what he called "the NATO family." Although this atmosphere and this format, his roundtable, would expose divergent opinions, Kleist hoped they would also lead to the participants better understanding each other as well as to an overall better understanding of the issues at hand, thereby creating a broader basis for finding common ground.[25] For the early gatherings (1963–67), he turned over most of the actual work of implementing his plans, especially in dealing with the US, to Alfons Dalma, who was the editor for Kleist's *Wehrkunde-Zeitschrift* (and who also served as an editor for the *Münchner Merkur*). He also allowed Dalma to serve as host and moderator. At these early meetings Kleist achieved his objective of bringing America's leading security experts to the conference, of which as early as 1963 Henry Kissinger represented a notable example.[27] Kleist's focus on questions of nuclear strategy became evident with the very first paper presented at his first conference, Henry Kissinger's "Nukleare Strategie des Westens und Aufteilung von Potential und Verantwortung" (The Nuclear Strategy of the West and the Sharing of Resources

and Responsibility). The other papers that followed similarly dealt with nuclear weapons and nuclear strategy.[28]

Between 1963 and 1967, and later in 1968 when Kleist took over as
host and moderator, *Wehrkunde* reflected the security debates of the era.
These included the debates over the role of nuclear weapons in NATO's defense posture, who would control them, the composition and capabilities of
NATO's conventional forces, and the contentious views of France regarding the US role in Europe as well as Europe's role in the transatlantic security partnership. These issues confronted NATO and *Wehrkunde* throughout the Cold War. Another of NATO's perennial themes also emerged at the
first *Wehrkunde,* that of "NATO in crisis." Richard Jaeger, a member of the
German Bundestag, would write in his article following the first *Wehrkunde*
that it was clear that NATO found itself in a real crisis, "Es lag vor. Die NATO
befindet sich in einer Krise." Then Bundestag member Friedrich Zimmermann defined the problem as the three negative Ds: "Dis-Integration, De-
Nuklearisierung, and [US] Dis-Engagement."[29]

During these debates at the early *Wehrkunde* encounters, Helmut Schmidt
was in attendance. In fact, he participated in the very first *Wehrkunde* and
was joined by Ewald-Heinrich von Kleist's friend, Karl-Theodor Freiherr
von und zu Guttenberg, at the second conference. Both men became core
members of the early meetings and not only contributed papers and participated as speakers, but also worked with Kleist on the planning and execution
of the conferences. Like Schmidt, Guttenberg would rise to political prominence.[30] The immediate issue confronting them, *Wehrkunde,* and NATO
was the question of who should control NATO's nuclear weapons. Should
NATO have a multilaterally controlled nuclear force (MLF), a position advocated by France, that included vocal support from several prominent German political figures? The French position was that "the countries of Europe
needed to be part of the controlling authority over the atomic weapons, because [NATO] could not at all times count on the reliability of the American
alliance partner."[31] German Chancellor Konrad Adenauer had endorsed an
MLF, and US President Johnson had agreed to provide a draft agreement for
NATO to review. Advocacy within NATO for an agreement to have an MLF,
which was driven by France, eventually collapsed after France's withdrawal
from NATO in 1966.

Other topics covered at these early conferences also involved questions of
nuclear strategy. This included debates over US plans to develop an anti-ballistic missile (ABM) system and what this would mean for European security and strategic nuclear deterrence, a debate eventually settled with the
ABM treaty of 1972. The second *Wehrkunde* also reflected the significant

debate concerning a nuclear non-proliferation treaty (NPT), which France objected to on principle, because it meant the sanctioning of the geopolitical status quo under US and Soviet dominance. Many of Germany's political leaders also expressed reservations over an NPT, not so much for the restriction that would prevent Germany from acquiring such weapons (though some argued that a future united Europe should have that option), but instead that it placed a Soviet imprimatur on the division of Germany. The debate over the NPT would continue into the 1968 *Wehrkunde* and thereafter until the Treaty on the Non-Proliferation of Nuclear Weapons entered into force in 1970. The debate over the NPT, however, demonstrated that *Wehrkunde* was not just a forum for reflecting the security debates taking place within NATO, but that it was also impacting and influencing the policies being debated.[32]

Between 1963 and 1967 Kleist successfully institutionalized *Wehrkunde*. The German and international media publicized the debates from the conference, and Kleist succeeded in bringing the leading American security experts and leading figures from NATO's core countries to Munich to engage in and inform Germany's politicians, security experts, and pundits of the great debates pending and coming to NATO and its *Gremien*. Evidently still not entirely satisfied with his meetings, in 1968 he took over complete control at the *V. Internationale Wehrkunde-Begegnung,* which again took place at the Regina Hotel from February 9 to 11. Kleist for the first time also served as host and moderator, a position he would retain until his retirement in 1998. Opening the gathering and welcoming his guests, he announced that "one should not leave all the work that needed to be done for the common security in NATO's *Gremien*" and that this forum "should prove useful and helpful for NATO's deliberations." In closing his remarks he left his guests with a central theme to which he would always return: 1) No matter how those at the table today might disagree with each other, "we must discuss our different opinions with candor and respect for each other;" and 2) "Our common foundation ... our shared community [the transatlantic community] of interests, is the most important condition for our future; if we treat this too lightly, we will have to pay the consequences."[33]

The geopolitical developments within NATO leading Kleist to take over at *Wehrkunde* had been dramatic. France's withdrawal from NATO's integrated military command structure in 1966 had paved the way for NATO's adoption of MC 14/3 in 1968, the new "Overall Strategic Concept for the Defense of the North Atlantic Treaty Organization Area;" the companion document, MC 48/3, "Measures to Implement the Strategic Concept for the Defense of the NATO Area," was approved in 1969. With approval of these documents, NATO had effectively adopted the strategy of "flexible response," and this adoption would fuel the debates at *Wehrkunde* and at NATO about the proper role and capabilities of nuclear forces and the role and capabilities of conventional forces. In parallel to these developments, NATO's foreign ministers had developed and approved the so-called Harmel Report, the 1967 "Report of the Council on the Future Tasks of the Alliance." With approval of this policy, NATO established a dual-track approach in which NATO's "military defense deterrent would be balanced alongside political détente," an effort to "seek a relaxation of tensions" with the Soviet Union.[34]

As these developments took place, Kleist forged some personal bonds through *Wehrkunde* in 1968 that proved decisive for its role and evolution, and ultimately gave it much of the character with which it became identified. One of these bonds was the personal friendship with Sir Arthur Hockaday, a senior British civil servant who attended his first *Wehrkunde* in 1968 as NATO's assistant secretary general for defense planning and policy (1967–69). Hockaday had gone to NATO having served as private secretary to various British ministers of defense and returned to the UK Ministry of Defence rising to the most senior level of the British civil service. Kleist's friendship with Hockaday ensured a high-level continuing presence of British politicians and defense officials at *Wehrkunde,* including the attendance of the first defense minister, Dennis Healey, in 1969. Beyond their common commitment to the importance of *Wehrkunde* as a forum for NATO deliberations, Hockaday and Kleist shared another bond. Hockaday was a devout Christian, who despite his positions in the UK Ministry of Defence and at NATO, "struggled with the [moral] dilemmas of war" throughout his career and private life. This struggle was a continuing topic in the personal relationship between Kleist and Hockaday, as they discussed what was needed for a moral defense and for a moral deterrence in the nuclear age, and the important role they believed *Wehrkunde* could play in this debate.[35]

Ewald-Heinrich von Kleist was not, as some commentators have observed, a pacifist. He saw the pre-World-War-II policy of "appeasement" as an important underlying cause of the war. However, he also did not view war as a tool of diplomacy, certainly not in the nuclear age. He did believe in nuclear deterrence, saying "we want deterrence not war," and he saw the United States and the Soviet Union similarly constrained in the Cold War, because they shared a common view of life and death. The loss of this consensus view about the value of life and death, and especially this problem in the context of the contemporary proliferation threat of weapons of mass destruction, is probably the security problem that concerned Kleist most about today's world. Confronting the prospects of wars today he believed that war was always to be the last resort, only to be considered when no other alternative was available and only when "vital national interests" were at stake. "Vital interests," he conceded, needed to be decided case by case by a nation (its people) and its allies. Through his conferences he sought to make a contribution to deliberations about such matters. In fact, he would often say that there was no more compelling purpose for his conferences than dealing with the moral quandary of war.[37]

Central to the relationship the US would adopt towards *Wehrkunde* was the attendance in 1968 of Senator John Tower. Tower became a committed friend of Kleist's and a faithful friend of *Wehrkunde*, attending uninterrupted for twenty-three years (V–XXVII). Tower's attendance encouraged not only strong US government participation at *Wehrkunde*, but he also worked on bringing future political leaders to the conference. With his retirement Tower turned over the leadership of the US congressional delegation (CoDel) to long-time participant and Kleist friend, US Senator (and later) Secretary of Defense William Cohen (R-ME). Another of Tower's young wards took over from Cohen to lead the US congressional delegation to *Wehrkunde*, Senator John McCain (R-AZ). McCain continues today in this position, a remarkable lineage that began with Tower's first attendance at *Wehrkunde* in 1968.[38] Yet another of Kleist's "young friends" was then Congressman and (later) US Vice President Dan Quayle (R-IN), a member of Tower's Senate delegations to *Wehrkunde* who would come as the first US vice president to address *Wehrkunde*.

For Ewald-Heinrich von Kleist, another important friendship developed in 1970 with the attendance at *Wehrkunde* of Congressman Sam Stratton (D-NY), an important subcommittee chairman of the House Armed Services Committee. It was Stratton who introduced Kleist to a young member of the committee who would become its chairman and an enduring Kleist friend, later US Secretary of Defense Les Aspin (in the Clinton administration).[39]

Kleist's goal of bringing senior US political leaders and pundits to *Wehrkunde* was growing rapidly, as was his goal of bringing senior NATO and German-European government officials; he was also successfully encouraging a new generation of German security experts and pundits.[40] As part of his outreach he was also focused on Germany's future political leaders, and in this outreach he was always non-partisan or *überparteilich*, which was consistent with his belief that Germany's security policy needed to carry a broad spectrum of political support. Such an "outreach" came one evening in 1968 "over Cognac" with Helmut Kohl, after which Kleist wrote Kohl and encouraged him to attend *Wehrkunde* as a *Landesvater*, an often-used expression to refer to the *Ministerpräsident* of a *Bundesland*. Kohl did not attend, but he and Kleist formed a life-long friendship. Another of Kleist's most enduring friendships was established with (German) Defense Minister Manfred Wörner, who attended *Wehrkunde* in the early seventies and served as defense minister in the critical years of the eighties from 1982 to 1988. He ended his career as Germany's first and only NATO secretary general, also at a critical juncture in NATO history, serving there from 1988 to 1994. Both Kleist and Wörner shared a common belief and commitment to German-American relations and the transatlantic security relationship. Indeed, it was Wörner whom Kleist asked to become his successor and lead *Wehrkunde* after his retirement. The succession plan failed because of Wörner's untimely death in office due to cancer in 1994.

For much of the seventies, US focus and involvement remained with Vietnam. America, not unlike today, had become war weary. This era nonetheless became one of the most tense periods in US-Soviet and NATO-Warsaw Pact relations, popularly referred to as the era of the US-Soviet nuclear arms race. It was also shaped by both superpowers using proxies to confront each other around the world, increasingly in a surrogate conflict throughout Latin America. During this era *Wehrkunde* reflected the widely divergent views over how the US and NATO should confront the Soviet Union. Moreover, US relations with NATO were becoming increasingly strained as NATO, critics argued, remained in its "permanent state of crisis." In the US, Senator Mike Mansfield (D-MT) led a general US frustration about the inadequacy of Europe's burden sharing and began recommending that America start a drawdown of its forces stationed in Europe. This again raised questions in Europe and NATO about the reliability of the US commitment to Europe, and it became one of *Wehrkunde's* perennial themes. The threat of a US troop withdrawal from NATO was finally averted when in 1978 NATO reached agreement on various proposals to improve its conventional defenses anchored in an agreement to increase defense spending by 3 percent annually in real terms. However, when NATO failed to meet its obligations under this agreement, Senate Armed Services Committee Chairman Sam Nunn (D-GA) renewed US proposals to reduce US personnel in Europe unless Europe raised its defense expenditures and did more to improve its conventional defense capabilities. It should be noted that Nunn was always a strong proponent of NATO, and that his efforts were intended to strengthen, not weaken, the Alliance.

It was during the late seventies that Kleist's friend, US Under Secretary of Defense for Policy Bob Komer (in the Carter administration), and his deputy, Walt Slocombe, Under Secretary of Defense for Policy (in the Clinton administration), became regular participants at *Wehrkunde*. US Under Secretary of Defense for Research and Engineering William J. Perry also attended *Wehrkunde* for the first time during this period, beginning in 1978. Komer, Perry, and Nunn became creative forces in promoting transatlantic defense cooperation with a series of proposals designed to improve US and NATO's conventional forces. US Secretary of Defense Perry returned to *Wehrkunde* as a member of the Clinton administration.

The decade of the seventies ended with the Soviet invasion of Afghanistan. It also represented a nadir in German-American relations, which was the result of a poor personal relationship between German Chancellor Helmut Schmidt and US President Jimmy Carter. This relationship deteriorated further over what became known as the "neutron bomb debacle." The contentious debate within Germany and between the US, NATO, and Germany over the neutron bomb, also known as the enhanced radiation weapon (ERW), became the basis for equally contentious debates at *Wehrkunde*. The debate produced a rebellion for Chancellor Schmidt within his own party, with one leading Social Democrat defense expert not atypically referring to ERWs as a "perversion of human thought."[41] The decision ultimately not to deploy the ERW left bitterness between the US and German governments as well as within Germany itself. Also at NATO there was a sense that the Alliance had mishandled an issue that went to the core of its *raison d'être*, its military security.[42] The experience became an important subcurrent for NATO's debates in the eighties over the so-called intermediate nuclear forces (INF) "dual track decision," which came to dominate NATO and *Wehrkunde* deliberations for much of that decade.

Ewald-Heinrich von Kleist frequently said that the period of the eighties produced some of the most serious and intense discussions at *Wehrkunde*, requiring him perhaps more than at any other time to remind, even admonish, his guests that *Wehrkunde* had always been characterized by great frankness and candor without personal recriminations or *ad hominem* attacks, and on this he continued to place the utmost importance and the greatest priority. This is also the period, however, that many participants consider to be the great heyday of *Wehrkunde*, the era of the eighties, with which many of its greatest moments and episodes in NATO history are associated.[43]

The election of President Ronald Reagan in 1980 brought about fundamental changes in US defense and security policy and in its dealings with the Soviet Union. Chancellor Helmut Kohl's election in 1982 (and his selection of Manfred Wörner as defense minister) and the election of Prime Minister Margaret Thatcher in 1979 also brought together a unique international political constellation in the West that would prove defining for the developments in the Cold War that followed. This constellation was also decisively influenced by Mikhail Gorbachev coming to power as Soviet leader from 1985 to 1991. He dramatically transformed the conduct of Soviet relations with the West and the conduct of Soviet relations with its alliance partners in the East Bloc. For *Wehrkunde*, these changes in political leadership were also of great significance, because these new leaders in the West, and many of the officials who flowed into government, especially in the United States and Britain, had long associations with Kleist and his conference. The United States, in particular, increasingly used *Wehrkunde* as part of its outreach to shape the political and public security and arms control debates in Europe, and it regularly sent over its most senior officials to speak and engage at the conference.[44] The active participation of US government officials was also intended to shore up political support within European NATO countries generally, and within Germany in particular, where sharp divisions between the Kohl government and its political opposition were increasingly apparent. The defining security and arms control initiative that came to symbolize the divisions that existed was NATO's INF dual-track decision and the contentious debates that accompanied it. The disagreement within Europe over this NATO decision soon went to the heart of the debate that had confronted NATO from the outset of its creation, that is, a debate over the role, purpose, and composition of nuclear weapons, the issue of the possible decoupling of the United States from Europe, and the possible "Finlandization" of Germany; these became dominant *Wehrkunde* and transatlantic themes. At the core of this debate was the conflict between East and West, yet again, as it was throughout the Cold War, over the future of Germany and who would control it. During this period, *Wehrkunde* demonstrated that it had become a critical forum for and a requisite part of NATO's deliberations.[45] For Kleist it also represented the closing of the circle that he had begun with his first *Wehrkunde* in 1963, that is, Germany's political leaders, security experts, and pundits had become a critical part of NATO's deliberations over nuclear policy, and the German public had participated in a debate directly affecting German security. Lawrence Freedman, a leading British academic, would later write that the debate that began with Helmut Schmidt's 1977 speech at the International Institute for Strategic Studies and the deliberations that followed reflected Germany's "coming of age" by its participation in NATO deliberations regarding nuclear weapons policy, doctrine, and deterrence strategy. It was a development Freedman described as Germany coming out of "The Wilderness Years." Kleist and *Wehrkunde* had played a pivotal role in this development.[46]

The INF agreement and the developments that followed proved critical to the events leading to the end of the Cold War. Improvements in US-Soviet relations following the INF agreement and the changes in Soviet policy reflected in Gorbachev's policies of *Glasnost* and *Perestroika* brought rapid and uncertain changes to the countries of Eastern Europe under Soviet dominance. These changes were felt in East Germany, the German Democratic Republic (GDR), where through a series of events and unusual circumstances, which are now historically well documented, the government mistakenly opened the Berlin Wall the night of November 9/10, 1989.[47] Therewith began a rapid and dynamic process that led to German unification with the GDR acceding to the Federal Republic of Germany on October 3, 1990. Despite the rapidity of these developments, there had again been a serious challenge over the future of Germany between it and its alliance partners, between it and the Soviet Union, and even within Germany's own domestic politics. These fissures were prominently on display at *Wehrkunde*. Once the decision for German unification was settled, the subsequent debate at *Wehrkunde* paralleled the ongoing discourse between the US and Germany. This debate was also occurring between the US and Germany and the Soviet Union, as well as within German politics. It centered on the terms and conditions under which German unification might take place. Again, from the left to right in German politics there were calls for the abandonment of the NATO alliance and, if not that, then some of Germany's political leaders advocated that Germany should be excluded from remaining a NATO member. When these ideas faltered, some of Germany's political leaders proposed that a unified Germany should not allow nuclear weapons to be stationed on its soil. These and other proposals provoked heated discussions within German politics that were exposed at *Wehrkunde*, and they became part of *Wehrkunde's* discussions between Germany and its NATO partners. They were also central themes in Kleist's meetings and discussions with US and British government officials during his visits to those countries. Determined US support for German unification and Kohl's strong leadership in Germany ultimately proved to be the essential determinants that allowed German unification to move forward.[49] However, it was a critical period of history, often taken for granted now but far from preordained at the time. For Kleist the debate went to the core of his post-World-War-II vision for, and his belief in, a Germany anchored in the continuing security relationship with NATO, the Atlantic community, and the transatlantic partnership.

With German unification and the end of the Cold War, Kleist believed that the time had finally come to change the name of his conference. He renamed it the Munich Conference on Security Policy, which reflected his belief that the time of (the Cold War) confrontation had passed and that there was a need to move from "confrontation to cooperation" for dealing with contemporary security problems. He would never waiver from this position, and it became the underlying theme of all of his subsequent conferences through to his retirement in 1998. He also retained this heading for all subsequent roundtable discussions the authors organized with him.[50] The dramatic developments taking place in Central and Eastern Europe became NATO's and *Wehrkunde's* focal point, as the countries of that region declared their independence from the Soviet Union and began the process towards forming national democratic states. The Union of Soviet Socialist Republics also began to unravel, and its dissolution was finalized by agreement between the twelve republics in December 1991. For NATO and participants at *Wehrkunde* the question became what kind of relationships should be established with the new Russian Federation and the new states of Eastern and Central Europe. The political instability that followed in Russia and what this might mean for the West also became part of *Wehrkunde's* annual debates. Similarly, NATO policy towards the countries of the East and, in particular, if and which countries should be allowed to join NATO, and should, in fact, NATO expand its membership, also became part of NATO and *Wehrkunde* discussions. Kleist feared that NATO expansion would weaken the alliance by making NATO consensus and decision-making more difficult to achieve, that NATO would not be able to make timely decisions, would become *entscheidungsunfähig,* as he termed it, and that NATO would eventually just become a "coalition of the willing" long before that term was popularized. Such developments, he feared, would undermine transatlantic security relations and make NATO (and Europe) increasingly less relevant in global security affairs.[51]

The peaceful transformation of Europe in the late eighties and into the nineties seemed to presage hope for a new and more peaceful world, but any hope for that came to an early end with the Iraq invasion of Kuwait in August 1990 and the US-led multi-national coalition military response to free Kuwait. Kleist invariably derived his views concerning war from the premise that it was always to be a last resort and should only come after all other options and alternatives had been exhausted. In the case of the First Iraq War, which came to be known as Desert Storm, he respected President George H. W. Bush, General and Chairman of the Joint Chiefs of Staff Colin Powell, and National Security Advisor Brent Scowcroft for their conception, plan, and prosecution of the war: it came in response to military aggression as a rejoinder by the international community, it followed a clearly defined mission based on internationally agreed upon objectives, and it stayed with a clearly defined exit plan. This war became a topic of discussion, particularly in the context of later US interventions, between Kleist and his friend Brent Scowcroft, a key architect of the war. Despite any private concerns Kleist harbored over the later Afghanistan war and the second Iraq conflict, he was not hesitant to privately express dismay over the manner in which German Chancellor Gerhard Schröder chose to denounce the 2003 US invasion of Iraq in a joint public declaration with France's Jacques Chirac and Russia's Vladimir Putin.[52]

It was, therefore, with a sense of satisfaction that Kleist attending the forty-second Munich conference in 2006, now as a "guest," heard Angela Merkel, the new German chancellor, announce an unequivocal endorsement of the transatlantic partnership and NATO as the cornerstone on which German security would be based. She unambiguously dismissed any notion of a "Paris-Berlin-Moscow" axis. Kleist held Merkel in high personal regard; he greatly respected her political skills, and he welcomed her clear and unequivocal endorsement of and commitment to NATO. The Merkel government's commitment to NATO as the cornerstone of German security policy was reaffirmed in 2013 by German Defense Minister Thomas de Maizière at the Munich Security Conference, by which time Kleist was already too ill to attend. Kleist, however, to the end remained a committed Atlanticist who believed in the transatlantic security partnership for Germany-Europe and the United States.[53]

Kleist had announced that he would be retiring from leading the conference following the completion of the 1998 gathering. He turned over the leadership of his conference to his selected successor, Dr. Horst Teltschik, Kohl's long-time security advisor, who had also personally been involved in so many of the historical events leading to German unification and the end of the Cold War. This transfer took place on the eve of what became the Kosovo War. That conflict posed a decade of serious political and military challenges for NATO, but it also demonstrated that NATO still functioned as a viable political and military alliance. Despite this conflict, Kleist could look back on his tenure of *Wehrkunde* from 1963 to 1998 with a great sense of accomplishment. Who could have envisioned that during this era Europe would emerge from the depths of the Cold War and achieve a peaceful end to that conflict, that the "hair trigger" on nuclear war would be removed, and that perhaps what had been the twentieth century's greatest international political challenge, the political resolution of Germany's status through unification, would also be achieved peacefully? The dissolution of the USSR, the collapse of Soviet dominance over Central and Eastern Europe, and the attainment of the political freedom for the peoples of Central and Eastern Europe were the final events to signify the end of the Cold War. *Wehrkunde* and Kleist, as US and European NATO officials have continually observed, made important contributions to this process and to this history.[54]

Ewald-Heinrich von Kleist would demur, but it was his vision and skill that enabled *Wehrkunde* to take on the character it had during this era, which had allowed it to become the forum it was and empowered it to play the important role it played in NATO history. *Wehrkunde* under Kleist became an extra-transatlantic NATO forum, arguably an indispensable forum, which enabled a larger participation by a broader community within NATO's member states to confront the challenges and their differences but also to find common ground. Perhaps best capturing what Kleist set out to achieve, and what he did achieve, was expressed by Javier Solana, when as NATO secretary general (later the EU's first foreign minister) he delivered his farewell tribute to Kleist in 1998 at the thirty-fourth Munich Conference on Security Policy. Calling his speech "The End of the Post Cold War Era," Solana acknowledged and paid tribute to the unique role Kleist and his conference had played in this process. Kleist, Solana observed, had "made [*Wehrkunde*] into what it is … a unique forum on transatlantic security relations. … *Wehrkunde* meetings have always been more than ritualistic meetings. They are occasions which offer—no, which demand—that we use them to refresh our thinking about security issues. In masterminding [*Wehrkunde*] Kleist has created more than a widely acclaimed international conference; he has created a transatlantic family, held together not only by shared interests but by personal friendships. This achievement cannot be overestimated."[55]

On June 10, 2013, The American Academy in Berlin gathered a distinguished group of US, German, and transatlantic leaders. They came together to honor Kleist posthumously with the award of the 2013 Henry A. Kissinger Prize. Of the many honors Kleist has received, arguably none is more fitting in terms of the history it symbolized. Kissinger, attending the American Academy event, had been a keynote speaker at Kleist's first *Wehrkunde* in 1963, well before he became one of the twentieth century's most important and most influential statesmen. These two great historical figures, Kissinger and Kleist, who had much respect and admiration for one another, had for many years been respectfully shy and reserved in their dealings with each other, and it was only in later life that they had been able to overcome their respective reticence and be at ease in each other's company.

While Kleist's clear preference would have been to accept the Kissinger Prize in person, it fell to his youngest daughter, Vera, to accept the award on his behalf. She displayed the same sense of modesty, demureness, and dignity that her father would have exemplified. Her presence also reminded those attending the event of the private Kleist that so few knew. He was indeed a devoted family man, whose love for his children and grandchildren underlay his life-long work and aspiration to create a better and more peaceful world. His daughter's presence also served as a reminder of the great and untold love story that Kleist shared with his wife of more than fifty years. This love story provides proof of the adage that behind every great man there stands a great woman, and Kleist was always the first to offer obeisance to his wife, who was the great love and epicenter of his life.[56]

Joining the American Academy's awards ceremony for Kleist was his old friend, Senator John McCain. Paying recognition to his friend, McCain spoke for all when he said of Kleist that "There is no worthier recipient of [this] prize," and he observed that he had known many "brave men and inspiring people" in his life, "but never quite someone as brave as Ewald." This was a gracious statement by McCain, who like Kleist was a great war hero, and who like Kleist always prefers to talk about the heroism of others. However, even more important for Kleist than the heartfelt personal tribute paid to him by McCain would have been the senator's concluding assessment:

"I'm confident the central idea that unites the transatlantic alliance and defines Ewald's legacy will endure: solidarity—solidarity with each other and with the universal longings of the human heart for security, for basic rights and equality, for liberty under the law, for tolerance, and opportunity."[57]

This, without doubt, is a legacy Kleist would welcome. However, there is another tribute that was paid to Kleist by his old friend John Tower some years earlier. When Kleist was informed of what Tower had said, it brought a smile to his face.[58]

The story goes back to Kleist announcing that he had changed the name of his conference from *Wehrkunde* to the Munich Conference on Security Policy. One evening, as the American delegation convened its annual US-only delegation meeting at the first Munich Conference on Security Policy, Senator Tower announced: "My good friend, the Baron, has asked me to inform the American delegates attending this conference that the new name for *Wehrkunde* is the Munich Conference on Security Policy. The Baron has asked me to request of you that we start using this new name." Then pausing for emphasis, Tower slowly took a cigarette out of his cigarette case, tapped the cigarette gently against the case, while still pausing for dramatic effect as the delegates waited in suspense to hear what was coming. "Gentlemen," said Tower, looking up and speaking slowly and deliberately, "Gentlemen,

I am here to inform you now that the American delegates to this conference will continue to call this conference *Wehrkunde*. Anyone who does not use the name *Wehrkunde*, let me assure you, will not be a member of an American delegation that attends *Wehrkunde*." And so, for Americans, the name *Wehrkunde* remains. For Americans the name is not the Munich Conference on Security Policy; the name is not the Munich Security Conference. The name was and remains simply *Wehrkunde*. It is a name evermore interwoven with the name of Ewald-Heinrich von Kleist. It is also a living legacy and an endearing tribute of affection and respect paid by his American friends to Kleist the man and all he embodied, while also reflecting respect for the conference he created and the consequential role it played in NATO history from 1963 to 1998 under his guardianship.

Peter C. Hughes, a Kleist friend, has attended Wehrkunde *continually since the seventies and served as assistant to Kleist since the eighties, including organizing his US visits. Appreciation for the work in support of Kleist also goes to his colleagues Dr. Joseph D. Halgus, Dr. Manfred von Nordheim, and Dr. Theresa Sandwith.*

Theresa Sandwith, whose godfather was Manfred Wörner, was a Kleist family friend. She worked closely over the years with Kleist, Freya von Moltke, and Hava Kohav Beller and now frequently works at Wehrkunde *with Alexander Kluge conducting TV interviews, including Kleist's 2010 TV Kluge interview,* Der Letzte Zeuge. *She received her PhD from Cambridge University in 2012 for her dissertation* Excavating German History: Memory, Mourning, and Myth in the Films of Alexander Kluge, 1966–1986.

The authors had numerous conversations and conducted several formally taped interviews with Herr von Kleist over several years; these have not been published. Therefore in footnoting the authors have provided public sources, where possible, for documentation purposes, which reflect the views Kleist expressed to the authors.

There are several film interviews with Kleist. Of special note are: Hava Kohav Beller's 1991 documentary film, *The Restless Conscience*, which was nominated for an Academy Award for best documentary feature. Also of special interest would be what is possibly Kleist's last television interview, *Der Letzte Zeuge—Ewald-Heinrich von Kleist,* which was conducted in 2010 together with Alexander Kluge and offers a very special exchange between Kleist and Kluge. In January 2009, the public broadcasting service ZDF also presented an in-depth documentary on Stauffenberg—*Die Wahre Geschichte*—which includes extensive interviews with Kleist.

There are two very special speeches that were made by Kleist in which he very deliberatively lays out his own World-War-II experiences and the lessons he learned from these. These are his lecture on July 19, 1998, in the Henning-von-Tresckow-Kaserne, Potsdam, "Eine Frage des Gewissens und der Moral," and his July 20, 2010 speech "Rede von Ewald-Heinrich von Kleist beim Feierlichen Gelöbnis vor dem Reichstag in Berlin am 20 Juli 2010."

One of the last print interviews given by Kleist, which provides some wonderful insights, appears in Antje Vollmer and Lars-Broder Keil, *Stauffenbergs Gefährten: Das Schicksal der unbekannten Verschwörer* (Munich: Carl Hanser Verlag, 2013), 221–236.

Kleist was frequently asked if the Stauffenberg plot was too little too late. In explaining the circumstances, which made challenging Hitler so difficult, he would nonetheless point out that had the plot succeeded many lives would have been saved. For example, Germany alone—quite apart from the extraordinary losses by the allies—lost 2.8 million lives between September 1, 1939, and the July 20, 1944 plot. After the plot and until the war's end in May 1945, 4.8 million German lives were lost. Moreover, as Joachim Fest points out in his book, the Stauffenberg plot was not the first attempt to overthrow Hitler; it was the last attempt with many failures in between.

For an excellent historical account of the military resistance to Hitler, see Joachim Fest's *Plotting Hitler's Death* (New York: Henry Holt Company, 1994).

Notes

1   This photo shows Kleist (center) and Dr. Hughes (right) in a meeting with Vice President Quayle (left) in 1991. During the visit, Quayle awarded Kleist (on behalf of the Bush Administration) the first of the three US Government Department of Defense Distinguished Public Service Medals that Kleist would receive. The photograph was always one of Kleist's favorites because of the inscription. Referring to Kleist, Quayle in his inscription wrote : "Peter herein lies the key to US/German relations."

2   See Peter Hoffman, *The History of the German Resistance* (Cambridge, MA: MIT Press, 1977), 20.

3   In mid-January 1933, Kleist-Schmenzin had gone to meet with Hindenburg and thought he had agreement not to allow Hitler to become chancellor following the 1932 election, instead perhaps allowing him to become *Postminister*. Two weeks later, Hitler was made chancellor. See Bodo Scheurig, *Ewald von Kleist-Schmenzin: Ein Konservativer gegen Hitler* (Oldenburg: Gerhard Stalling Verlag, 1968), 264. In 1938, Kleist-Schmenzin was one of the emissaries sent to England by German Army Chief of Staff Ludwig Beck to see if he could get the British to announce that they would resist a German invasion of Czechoslovakia, which Beck believed would enable him to mount a military coup to overthrow Hitler. The initiative failed. It was rejected by Prime Minister Neville Chamberlain, who believed that he could control Hitler, avoid war, and achieve "peace in our time" through his policy of "appeasement." See Ernest L. Woodward et al., eds., *Documents on British Foreign Policy 1919–1939* (London: His Majesty's Stationary Office, 1949), 684–685.

4   "Das Ausland fragt immer wieder: Habt ihr Deutsche denn eigentlich niemanden, der von Anfang an gegen Hitler war? Ewald von Kleist[-Schmenzin] können wir Deutsche vorweisen." Fabian von Schlabrendorff, "Dem Untergang geweiht," *Der Spiegel* (January 27, 1969).

5   Writing to his wife, Kleist-Schmenzin wrote, "mich quälte der Gedanke an Ewald-Heinrich, von dem ich wusste, das der auch im Gefängnis saß, da wir beide zufällig im selben Augenblick eingeliefert wurden und uns dabei gesehen haben." See Helmut Gollwitze et al., eds., *Du hast mich heimgesucht bei Nacht: Abschiedsbriefe und Aufzeichnungen des Widerstandes 1933–1945* (Munich: Chr. Kaiser Verlag, 1954), 44.

6   Kleist-Schmenzin was tried along with several other conspirators before the notorious Nazi judge, Roland Freisler, in a series of brutal sham show trials and sentenced to death. Several commentators have noted Kleist-Schmenzin's courageous and heroic appearance before Freisler. Asked if he had committed treason, Kleist-Schmenzin responded: "Yes, I have pursued high treason since January 30, 1933, always and with every means. I made no secret of my struggles against Hitler and National Socialism. I regard this struggle as a commandment from God. God alone will be my judge." See Michael Burleigh, *The Third Reich: A New History* (New York: Hill and Wang, 2000), 715. Fabian von Schlabrendorff was a conspirator who only escaped his death sentence because Freisler was killed in an Allied bombing attack before sentencing him. Schlabrendorff later became a judge for the Federal German Republic's Constitutional Court (Bundesverfassungsgericht) and wrote of Kleist: "Wer Kleist in diesem Augenblick erlebt hat, stolz und ungebrochen vor den Menschen, aber demütig vor Gott, dem drängte sich unwillkürlich der Wunsch auf, gleich ihm in solcher Haltung sterben zu können." See Fabian von Schlabrendorff, *Offiziere gegen Hitler* (Zurich: Europa Verlag, 1946), 177.

7   Kleist would explain: "I was very much influenced by my father who hated National Socialism. He loathed Hitler and his ideology. … I had a very good relationship with my father … a father loves his son and a son his father, [but much more] I liked and admired him, very much. … He was a great influence for me. I also had many friends who hated Hitler. … Also for me there were no illusions after the Night of the Long Knives. What Hitler and his thugs did was a premeditated cold-blooded mass murder perpetrated by the German state. … I am still shocked by the events of that night … in a civilized state even criminals have the right to legal protection and a trial by jury. Here was the German Reich head of state behaving like Al Capone … like a mafia don … outrageous … . The German Army should never have allowed this to happen … the Army High Command did not so much as whisper a protest." See Hava Kohav Beller's film *The Restless Conscience* (1991).

8   Kleist's father objected to his son joining the army and swearing the oath of allegiance to Hitler. As Kleist tells the story: "My father asked me: 'Do you think Hitler is a criminal? If so, how can you swear [the oath of personal allegiance to Hitler]?'" Kleist responded that it would be neither good nor wise "not to swear the oath … I would be shot." His father countered, "That is very dangerous thinking, because if enough people refuse to take the oath, then nobody would be shot but if everyone obeys Hitler's orders then, of course, he gets away with it." Kleist tried to assuage his father by telling him of his private oath "to break the oath of allegiance and oppose Hitler in any way that I can." See Beller, *The Restless Conscience*, op. cit. The Potsdam 9th Infantry Regiment is famous in history for serving as the First Guard for the Kings of Prussia. It distinguished itself during World War II for having so many of its officers executed by the Nazis because of their active opposition to Hitler.

9   See Beller, *The Restless Conscience*, op. cit.

10 See Antje Vollmer and Lars-Broder Keil, *Stauffenbergs Gefährten: Das Schicksal der un-bekannten Verschwörer* (Munich: Carl Hanser Verlag, 2013), 228. Kleist, never able to speak of any personal heroism on his part, explains that he returned to the Bendler-block to be arrested with his fellow conspirators because, having just advised a young colleague not to abandon his friends, he felt compelled to heed his own advice.

11 Following German unification, Kleist and the authors were in Berlin together. We met him at his hotel on the Gendarmenmarkt to go to lunch; he had made reservations at a well-known restaurant, Borchardt, on the Französische Straße. However, as we arrived he was most interested in the adjacent building. We walked up to it and he looked at the floor where the *Süddeutsche Zeitung* had its offices. He gestured towards it and said this is one of the locations where I was "the frequent guest of the Gestapo." He did not want to ring the bell and go up to the office.

12 See Vollmer and Keil 2013, op. cit., 234–235. Kleist was frequently asked if he knew why he had not been summarily executed along with Stauffenberg. He would say he did not know. One possible explanation came from an article written by Jim Woolsey in 2003 (director of the CIA 1993–95). In the article, Woolsey mistakenly identified Kleist's father as the German World-War-II Field Marshal Paul Ludwig Ewald von Kleist. When pointing out the error to Woolsey, he said this information came from his old organiza-tion's historical files and it was understood that believing the field marshal was Kleist's father the Gestapo chose not to summarily execute Kleist, which gave him the oppor-tunity to survive that first night. See Jim Woolsey, "Not All Bad," *Wall Street Journal*, February 20, 2003.

13 See Vollmer and Keil 2013, op. cit., 234–235.

14 Ibid., 236. Asked by the authors why he started his conference, Kleist bluntly stated: "Es geht mir um das Verhältnis zum Krieg." In his *Spiegel* interview Kleist was equally clear: "[D]ie Aufgabe der Sicherheitspolitiker ist es, Blut und Leben der ihnen An-vertrauten zu schützen. Nichts ist teurer als das Blut der Menschen, für die man Ver-antwortung trägt. Das muss man den Leuten klar machen. … Deswegen interessiert mich Sicherheitspolitik. Und deswegen macht es mir Sorgen, dass wir zum Teil sehr leichtfertig mit solchen Dingen umgehen." Ralf Neukirch and Martin Doerry, "Angst halte ich für sehr vernünftig," Spiegel-Gespräch [with Kleist], *Der Spiegel* (February 28, 2011), 42.

15 The reality of nuclear weapons and deterrence in the Cold War, in Kleist's view, re-sided not in the *Wahnsinn* (insanity) of nuclear war fighting theories but rather in the ability of the US and the Soviet Union to hold each other hostage. As he told *Der Spie-gel*: "Wir sitzen hier und unterhalten uns, weil in der Vergangenheit die großen Atom-mächte, nämlich Amerika und Russland, die gleiche Einstellung zu Tod und Leben hatten. Beide sagten: Leben ist gut, Tod muss verhindert werden." Then he expressed his concern about today's world: "Das sehen nicht mehr alle so. … Bin Laden hat vor einiger Zeit gesagt: Der Unterschied zwischen uns und euch ist: Ihr liebt das Leben, wir lieben den Tod. Ich fürchte, er hat recht. … Irgendwann gibt es wieder einen Hitler. … Man (muss) die Proliferation von Atomwaffen unterbinden. Es dürfen nicht noch mehr Länder in den Besitz dieser schrecklichen Waffen kommen." Ibid., 43.

16 "Ja, warum? Ich hatte große Sorgen, und zwar wegen der allgemeinen Akzeptanz einer Verteidigungsbereitschaft. Denn die war ja damals ja noch wirklich nicht stark gegeben. Man darf nicht vergessen, dass bis 1945 ungefähr 95 Prozent der Men-schen geglaubt haben, Soldat sein sei etwas Notwendiges und Wichtiges. Dann ha-ben die Alliierten in einem Ratschluss von ungewöhnlicher Weisheit ein Gesetz erfun-den, die 'Befreiung vom Nationalsozialismus und Militarismus,' und es wurde also dem Deutschen Volk in der *re-education* mitgeteilt, dass Soldat das Schlimmste und

Schrecklichste war, was man überhaupt tun könnte. Dieses glaubte auch nach einiger Zeit der Manipulation wieder ein großer Teil der Deutschen. … Die Wiederbewaffnung gab es dann erst seit 1955. Wo also, die allgemeine Meinung wieder um 180 Grad sich verändert hat. Das ist ein sehr interessanter Vorgang. In neun Jahren ist dreimal um 180 Grad die offizielle Meinung manupuliert worden, umgedreht worden, etwas was es sonst vergleichbar, nach meiner Ansicht nach, selten gibt. Dies war ganz offensichtlich natürlich fehlerhaft, denn eine Verteidigungsbereitschaft kann nur funktionieren, wenn sie von einer möglichst breiten Basis getragen wird." Conversation with Kleist.

17 "Wie ich … Jura studiert habe, habe ich bemerkt, dass es eigentlich nur drei Dinge gibt, Lehrbücher, Kommentare, und Gesetzestexte, und für den jungen Juristen, den Studenten, fehlt etwas, nämlich die Erklärung und die Verweisung auf die Zusammenhänge innerhalb der einzelnen Paragraphen. Da habe ich mir gedacht, da ist ein Bedarf dafür, und da habe ich versucht zu publizieren und das gelang dann auch … war auch sehr erfolgreich." Conversation with Kleist.

18 "Wenn ich mich richtig erinnere, habe ich mit verschiedenen Bekannten die Gesellschaft für Wehrkunde 1952 gegründet. Und der Grund dafür war, dass die Meinung in Amerika, Deutschland und der westlichen Welt war, dass Deutschland nie wieder Soldaten haben würde. Das war offensichtlich töricht und naiv, denn es war vorauszusehen, dass die Besetzung mit Russland eine Wiederbewaffnung Deutschlands notwendig machen würde." Conversation with Kleist. Kleist expained further: "In der Annahme, dass Deutschland in absehbarer Zeit aufgefordert werden würde, einen eigenen militärischen Beitrag zu leisten, wollten die Gründungsväter der GfW aktiv daran mitwirken, Fehlentwicklungen der Vergangenheit zu vermeiden und die Neugestaltung der Streitkräfte den Erfordernissen des neuen demokratischen Systems in Deutschland anzupassen." Kleist's Gesellschaft für Wehrkunde files.

19 The magazine *Wehrkunde* had its origins in the *Gesellschaft für Wehrkunde's* newsletters: "Daraus entstand dann ein kleines hektographiertes Blatt, haben wir herausgegeben, zwei Seiten, und das war der Anfang der späteren Zeitschrift Wehrkunde. Dann habe ich im Jahre 1954 den Verlag Europäische Wehrkunde gegründet, und dann wurde die Zeitschrift auch regelrecht als Zeitschrift herausgegeben, auch ganz erfolgreich." Conversation with Kleist.

20 Kleist's 1963 Wehrkunde Conference Files.

21 Gregory W. Pedlow, ed., *NATO Strategy Documents 1949–1969* (Brussels: NATO Information Service, 1997).

22 1963 Wehrkunde Conference Files. When the Regina Hotel closed, Kleist moved the conference to the Bayerischer Hof. During that time, and until he moved the conference to the Hilton Hotel am Tucher Park in 1992, the hotel was open to the public and home to many *Fasching* balls. Wehrkunde, especially for Americans, therewith became associated with *Fasching*, a not unpleasant association. In fact, Horst Teltschik was encouraged by several senior US government officials to return the conference to the Bayerischer Hof, which he did when he took it over in 1999. By then, however, security requirements had closed off the hotel to the general public and *Fasching* festivals could no longer take place at the hotel during the conference, thus leaving only memories and associations of a pleasant past for Americans who remembered the history.

23 "[A]lso wie ich den Kreis zusammengestzt habe…ich wollte eine Familie schaffen … die NATO war Mittelpunkt, denn eine nationale Verteidigung gibt es nicht, gab es zu diesem Zeitpunkt schon nicht mehr … und es war wichtig, dass man in einer Allianz die Verteidigungssicherheit herstellen konnte. Deswegen waren die NATO-Mitglieder, also sagen wir mal der Kern der ursprünglichen Gruppe. … NATOs Kern, ja (Deutschland, USA, Großbritannien und Frankreich) … wobei natürlich die Amerikaner und

die Deutschen eine große Rolle spielten, die Deutschen nicht weil sie besonders viel zu bieten hatten ... aber sie waren immerhin Gastgeber, und die Amerikaner weil sie die wichtigsten Partner der NATO waren." Conversation with Kleist.

24 "Wie ich schon sagte, eine Verteidigungsbereitschaft kann nur funktionieren, wenn sie von einer möglichst breiten Basis getragen wird, und es reicht nicht, dass die regierende Partei im Augenblick hierzu bereit ist, sondern man muss auch sehen, dass große Teile der Opposition den notwendigen Maßnahmen zustimmen und sie mittragen ... man muss alle, das Spektrum, vor allem was für Sicherheitspolitik von Bedeutung ist (in jedem Land) berücksichtigen. ... Es gibt nicht Prioritäten nur von einer Partei, die gerade regiert ... der Zusammenhalt und das Ringen um die Probleme der gemeinsamen Zukunft ... das war für mich das Wesentliche, die gemeinsamen Ziele für die gemeinsame Zukunft zu bearbeiten und zu fördern, das war für mich das Entscheidende." Conversation with Kleist.

25 Kleist would explain in his various interviews that he wanted the conference to bring political leaders together from across the political spectrum in Germany and abroad. In one of his last published interviews and looking back, he described one of the principal motivating factors for his conference: "Ich habe gesehen, dass die Politiker kaum Zeit für solche (Sicherheits-)Debatten haben, dass sie eingezwängt sind, auch in parteipolitische Vorgaben. Aber wenn man mit den Leuten einzeln sprach, merkte man schon, dass es Brücken zwischen den Lagern gab. Das wollte ich ausnutzen mit der Konferenz. Es ist dumm zu sagen, in einer Demokratie kann man nichts machen, außer alle paar Jahre zur Wahl gehen. Man kann sehr wohl etwas machen. Den Politikern eine Hilfestellung geben. Mit der Erkenntnis, etwas präventiv machen zu können, und eine Gesprächsebene zwischen Menschen zu schaffen, die sonst nicht so leicht zueinander gefunden hätten. Die Konferenz war somit ein mächtiges informelles Gremium während des Kalten Krieges." See Vollmer and Keil 2013, op. cit., 236.

26 Kleist was also frequently asked if his conference should broaden its participation to include non-NATO members to which he would politely demur, "I am not sure about it ... our priority should be to first find out in our own family where we want to go. ... So I would prefer, I guess, that we do this first among ourselves (and once) we have found our way, and know what we are going to do ... then I think it would be useful to invite responsible people from the 'former' other side." See House Committee on Armed Services, *The New Europe: Security and Political Arrangements for the Post-Cold-War World*, 101st Cong., 2nd sess., 1990.

27 The second conference included Zbigniew Brzezinski, and among the many other leading US security experts and nuclear strategists who would come over the years there were Robert Bowie, Ashton Carter, Donald Cotter, Alain Enthoven, Fritz Ermarth, Richard Garwin, William Griffith, Samuel Huntington, Phil Karber, Morton Kaplan, Albert Latter, Edward Luttwak, Andy Marshall, Hans J. Morgenthau, Robert Osgood, Richard Pipes, Stefan Possony, Henry S. Rowen, Thomas C. Schelling, William Schneider, Robert Strauss-Hupe, Edward Teller, Paul Warnke, and Albert Wohlstetter.

28 Other papers included Robert Bowie, "Nuclear Strategy and the US-European Partnership in Politics and Defense; Pierre Gallois, "Alliance and Partnership Under the Sign of Nuclear Weapons"; and Helmut Schmidt on "The Foundations of German Security," with Richard Jäger, member of the German Bundestag, addressing "Balancing the Security Interests within the Alliance."

29 1963 Wehrkunde Conference Files: The great debates at *Wehrkunde* in the early years were not just the "nuclear debates." Until France withdrew from NATO in 1966, the "crisis" in the alliance was invariably precipitated by France and its views on the US role in NATO and the transatlantic partnership. The French criticisms of the US found

some support among German politicians, which Friedrich Zimmermann, member of the German Bundestag, defined as the "three negative Ds" referenced in the essay.

30 Schmidt became defense minister and chancellor. Guttenberg became parliamentary foreign policy spokesman for the CDU/CSU and later parliamentary secretary of state in Chancellor Kurt Kiesinger's office from 1967 until 1969, during which time he played a formative role in German foreign policy. He was a friend of Kleist's, and his uncle, Karl Ludwig Freiherr von und zu Guttenberg, was part of the Nazi resistance in the German army who was executed after the failed Stauffenberg July 20,1944 plot. His grandson, Karl-Theodor zu Guttenberg, would later represent his grandfather's seat in the Bundestag and served as minister for economics and minister of defense in Chancellor Angela Merkel's cabinet. Like his grandfather, he became a good and "dear young" friend of Kleist's, and they stayed close to the end.

31 Pierre Gallois, 1963 Wehrkunde Conference Files.

32 The 1968 *Wehrkunde* conference was the first one to be attended by US Senator John Tower. He was so impressed by his discussions with European officials over their concerns with the NPT that he would later offer an amendment in the US Senate deliberations of the treaty. He addressed these concerns, which included a press release, John Tower Press Release, February 17/18, 1968.

33 Kleist's opening remarks, 1968 Wehrkunde Conference Files.

34 For a comprehensive review of this NATO history, see: Richard L. Kugler, "The Great Strategy Debate: NATO's Evolution in the 1960s," *A Rand Note N-3252-FF/RC* (Santa Monica: Rand, 1991).

35 For a discussion on Hockaday's views see "Sir Arthur Hockaday, A Christian Civil Servant Struggling with the Dilemmas of War," *The Guardian*, September 17, 2004. Kleist personally believed in the defense and security provided by atomic weapons during the Cold War, by which he meant intercontinental missiles through which the US and the Soviets held each other hostage. Regarding other nuclear weapons he would say that "The short range [nuclear] missiles … are the most successful method by which to kill ourselves. That, of course, is not extremely pleasant." See House Committee on Armed Services 1990, op. cit., 7–8.

36 Although it is apparently not well known, during part of his internment Kleist shared a prison cell with Helmut James von Moltke, a co-founder of the Kreisau Circle who was also executed following sentencing by Freisler. Kleist said they had many heart-wrenching discussions about the morality of war and whether assassination could ever be morally justified. During their time together, Kleist said he came to greatly respect and admire Moltke. Kleist also became a source of solace for Moltke's wife, Freya, because he was one of the few men who survived the war who had also shared time with her husband during his final days. Both Freya von Moltke and Kleist gave the authors a much more nuanced interpretation of Moltke's final views concerning the efforts to assassinate Hitler than generally appears in the literature on the subject.

37 In his interview with *Der Spiegel* in response to the question, "Wofür lohnt es sich zu sterben?" Kleist responded: "Es ist nur dann gerechtfertigt, das Leben deutscher Soldaten zu riskieren, wenn vitale Interessen gefährdet sind. Was vitale Interessen sind, muss man im Einzelfall entscheiden. Dann muss man prüfen, ob man die Mittel hat, seine Ziele zu erreichen. Und schließlich muss ich mich fragen: Wie komme ich wieder raus? Erst wenn man eine überzeugende Antwort auf diese Fragen hat, ist ein militärischer Einsatz gerechtfertigt." Neukirch and Doerry 2011, op. cit., 43.

38 McCain had actually already attended *Wehrkunde* in the late seventies as the military escort officer supporting the Tower CoDel. He had a particularly distinguished military service record during the Vietnam War, where he served as a US Navy pilot who

was shot down over Hanoi. His treatment as a prisoner of war was particularly brutal because his father, a Navy admiral, was the Commander-in-Chief Pacific Command (CINCPAC) responsible for US forces in Vietnam. McCain also distinguished himself by refusing to be released out of order before other prisoners who were ahead of him were first released. His refusal led to further extreme torture by his captors. He returned to the US after the war a hero but physically savaged. Like Kleist, McCain was always modest, preferred not to talk about his own role, and instead would always speak of the heroism of his fellow prisoners. However, as a result of their shared experiences they had a special affinity for each other that few could share. In 1980, McCain brought another military escort officer to accompany the delegation, USMC Colonel Jim Jones, later to attend *Wehrkunde* as USMC commandant, SACEUR, and national security advisor to President Barack Obama.

39 In 1990, the chairman of the House Armed Services Committee, Les Aspin, convened a hearing of the committee to honor Kleist and give recognition to his work and *Wehrkunde*. See House Committee on Armed Services 1990, op. cit.

40 One of Kleist's goals was to promote German security expertise not only in government but also in academia, think tanks, and the media. Similar to the US model, he encouraged individuals who might move in between these worlds and who could engage with their US and NATO counterparts, build up influence and relationships, and contribute to the shaping of NATO security policy. Among the earliest of such attendees were Lothar Rühl and Theo Sommer, whose attendance began in 1964. They subsequently pursued distinguished careers in government and journalism. Uwe Nerlich joined *Wehrkunde* in 1966 and pursued a growing role in NATO's nuclear debates through his position at Ebenhausen. Walter Stützle attended in the early seventies and assumed increasingly important roles in the German Ministry of Defense and German security policy, as did Hans Rühle, Manfred Wörner's long-time aide and confidante. Rühle played a central role in US-German relations during the eighties. Michael Stürmer and Karl Kaiser came to *Wehrkunde* in the eighties and also played increasingly influential roles in the transatlantic security debate. Josef Joffe also came to *Wehrkunde* in the eighties and became a leading arms control expert and commentator with strong ties on both side of the Atlantic during NATO's great debates of that era.

41 The "neutron bomb debate" was precipitated by a 1977 Walter Pincus article in the *Washington Post* entitled "Neutron Killer Warhead Buried in ERDA Budget" (*The Washington Post*, June 6, 1977, A1). After this article appeared, a contentious public debate erupted. Raymond Garthoff would later write, "In important respects the neutron weapon was unfairly characterized: it was not a capitalist weapon to 'kill people but not property'; it was not a 'bomb' ... the radiation effects would not be appreciably greater than the munitions it would replace, while the blast damage would be less." See Raymond Garthoff, *Détente and Confrontation: American-Soviet Relations from Nixon to Reagan* (Washington, DC: Brookings Institution, 1964), 851. Although it was Egon Bahr who used that term, Herbert Wehner and other SPD party leaders, as well as rank and file members, challenged Schmidt over the issue. See Jeffrey Boutwell, The German Nuclear Dilemma (London: Brassey's, 1990), 66.

42 For a discussion of the inner German debate, see ibid.

43 Conversation with Kleist.

44 Among these were Secretary of Defense Weinberger, Under Secretary of Defense for Policy (and long-time Kleist friend) Fred Ikle, and Secretary of the Navy (and Reagan administration insider) John F. Lehman (also a Tower and Kleist friend). The US ambassadors and the chief negotiators for the ongoing arms control negotiations also

became regular participants. These included Ed Rowney for START, Max Kampelmann for CSCE, and Paul Nitze for INF.

45 The meetings would not have been complete without the attendance of Assistant Secretary of Defense Richard Perle, and his counterpart at the State Department, Assistant Secretary of State for Europe and Canada Rick Burt. Both men were highly respected security experts and influential members of the Reagan administration. Members of the media as well as many of *Wehrkunde's* European participants focused much of their attention on them because of their reported policy differences, which received widespread attention in the press. Perle was the architect of what critics called the "non-negotiable zero-zero option," a ploy that they argued was designed to prevent an arms control agreement so that NATO could deploy its Pershing and GLCM missiles. With the signing of the INF agreement, Perle would later claim with some satisfaction that his critics had been proved wrong. Both Perle and Burt called *Wehrkunde* an indispensable part of their diplomatic forays during this period.

46 See Lawrence Freedman, "The Wilderness Years," in Jeffrey D. Boutwell et al., eds., *The Nuclear Confrontation in Europe* (Dover, MA: Auburn House, 1985), 44–67.

47 On the morning of November 9, 1989, Kleist had a meeting in Washington at the Department of Defense with Under Secretary of Defense for Policy (USDP) Paul Wolfowitz, Assistant Secretary of Defense Steve Hadley, the USDP's director for Germany, Dr. Joseph D. Halgus, and several other senior US defense officials and German experts. The purpose of this meeting was to discuss the program for the upcoming *Wehrkunde* conference, the state of affairs in Germany, and what could be expected over the near term. Regrettably, Kleist later conceded, no one in our meeting that morning anticipated the events that were about to unfold later that evening. During our busy day of meetings the first we learned of what was happening in Berlin came over lunch at Maison Blanche, a restaurant adjacent to the White House, where the first of Kleist's afternoon meetings was scheduled. Halgus, who had become a friend and was accompanying us, suddenly received a call requiring him to return immediately to his office for meetings because of "something big going on in Berlin."

48 Kleist would later comment that (US Ambassador) Vernon Walter was the only person he knew who had kept predicting the imminent fall of the Berlin Wall. Walter's departure as US Ambassador to Germany was greatly eased for Kleist by the arrival of Robert M. Kimmitt, his wife Holly, and their family. Kleist considered Kimmitt to be one of the US's great ambassadors to Germany and a great friend as he continued his distinguished service in successive US administrations. Kleist also held the last US ambassador to Germany he would know, Phil Murphy, his wife Tammy and their family in high regard for what he considered their love of Germany and their very personal commitment as a family to US-German relations.

49 Horst Teltschik's book *329 Tage* (Berlin: Siedler Verlag, 1991) is the definitive work in German on Kohl's leadership and the events leading to German unification. In English, Condoleeza Rice and Philip Zelikow's book *Germany Unified and Europe Transformed: A Study in Statecraft* (Cambridge, MA: Harvard University Press, 1995) remains the definitive work. Moreover, it carefully details the shoring up of French and British support for German unification, which they had opposed, and the steps entailed in dealing with the opposition of the Soviet Union, as well as the inner-German political debate within the German government and the German political opposition.

50 See Vollmer and Keil 2013, op. cit., 236, in which Kleist says: "Nach dem Zusammenbruch des Ostblocks habe ich sofort das Motto ausgerufen: Kooperation statt Konfrontation und Siegerposen." In 1990 he had planned to convene the conference under the umbrella question "From Confrontation to Cooperation?" However, he soon dropped

the question mark because of "the conviction that cooperation is a must in the future." See House Committee on Armed Services 1990, op. cit., 17–18. Thereafter and until his death, whenever the authors asked him for the title for our round tables he would invariably say, "let's call it 'From Confrontation to Cooperation' and examine our topics within that framework."

51 Kleist always provided an unambiguous response to the question of whether he thought we will need NATO in the future. He would say, "Without NATO ... we would not be here. My answer is a clear yes. NATO is indispensable ... NATO is [the] close and successful link between the United States and the states in Europe. This link is also a necessity in the future, maybe even more so than in the past time." Ibid., 5–6.

52 Kleist was frequently asked, "Why don't you seed the *Wehrkunde* discussions with more of your own views or questions?" to which he invariably responded: "If you add your personal thoughts about what is right or wrong and start to put weight on one view or another, it would ruin everyone's trust. And trust, in the meeting, is the biggest capital I have." See Benjamin F. Schemmer, "Exclusive AFJ interview with: Ewald Heinrich von Kleist, Editor-in-Chief, Europaische Wehrkunde—On the 25th Anniversary of the Wehrkunde Encounter," *Armed Forces Journal* 125 (February 1988), 40–41. In private meetings with government officials Kleist was not so hesitant. In fact, during a visit to Washington, Kleist was meeting with his old friend, Brent Scowcroft, who had been declared a persona non grata by the Bush 43 White House because of his views on the Second Iraq War. Scowcroft asked Kleist whom he would be next visiting. When Kleist told him he was meeting with National Security Advisor Condoleeza Rice and Deputy National Security Advisor Steve Hadley, both of whom were Scowcroft protégés of a previous era, Scowcroft told Kleist they would no longer meet with him. His parting words to Kleist were: "Now, Ewald, I trust you will give them hell as you always did with me." The two old friends smiled at each other as they parted. But the conversation reflected a truth: Kleist could meet with any US official and offer his personal views even if they were not consistent with the prevailing orthodoxy, because officials knew that their conversations with him always remained private.

53 Merkel defined German security and alliance policy noting that NATO "muss der Ort sein, an dem politische Konsultationen über neue Konfliktherde, die auf der Welt entstehen, geführt werden, und sie sollte nach meiner Auffassung der Ort sein, an dem politische und militärische Aktionen koordiniert werden" (2006 Wehrkunde Conference Files). Kleist was concerned that France rejoining NATO in 2009 would lead to a repeat of NATO's earlier history and a weakening of NATO itself. As with most Germans of his generation, he was a strong proponent of the Franco-German reconciliation and saw it as a cornerstone of a successful economic and political European Union. However, he held no illusions about France's designs for the transatlantic security partnership, and he was dismayed by the obsequiousness of many of Germany's politicians to France on this issue.

54 One clear illustration of this respect is seen in the fact that Kleist is the recipient not only of his country's *Großes Bundesverdienstkreuz mit Stern und Schulterband*, but also of Great Britain's Knight Commander of the Order of the British Empire and of France's Legion of Honor. As noted, he is also a three-time recipient of the US Government's Department of Defense Distinguished Public Service Medal, receiving it in 1991, 1997, and 2004. Awarding it in 1997, Secretary of Defense Cohen noted, "Kleist established *Wehrkunde* [and used it] to promote US-European cooperation ... his personal leadership and exceptional dedication to the defense of Europe ... have made invaluable contributions to the security of NATO." In honoring Kleist with a hearing of the House Armed Services Committee devoted to Kleist, Chairman Aspin observed:

"I believe the fact that NATO pulled together long enough to emerge victorious in the Cold War against communism is in very significant part due to the efforts of Baron von Kleist."

55 Javier Solana, "The End of the Post Cold War," Speech by the Secretary General, Thirty-fourth Munich Conference on Security Policy, February 7/8, 1998.

56 Speaking at the American Academy event in memory of Kleist, his not so "young friend" Tom Enders recalled a belated birthday celebration we spent with Herr and Frau von Kleist in the fall of 2012. Enders noted that he saw a man that evening with "a never before seen melancholy (not when his wife was by his side) … he was a man as intellectually sharp and forward looking as ever, but one who knew his body was failing him. … Here sat a man who had done so much for his country, the cause of peace, and the transatlantic partnership and friendship with the US … he still had so much to offer but so little time left to give … that is how I will remember Herr von Kleist," sitting with his wife by his side, which is when he was always at his happiest.

57 Laudation from Senator John McCain of Arizona on behalf of Ewald-Heinrich von Kleist at the American Academy in Berlin for the award of the 2013 Henry A. Kissinger Prize, June 10, 2013.

58 The co-author, Dr. Hughes, sat with Kleist and Tower as Kleist requested Tower to inform the American delegation of the conference's new name, the Munich Conference on Security Policy. Following the US-only delegation meeting, Kleist asked Hughes whether Tower had announced his request that the new name be used from now on. When Hughes told Kleist the story and how Tower had informed the US delegation of the request, but had nevertheless made it clear that Americans were to continue calling the conference *Wehrkunde*, he smiled and nodded wryly, understanding Tower's gesture.

Wehrkunde and the Cold War

Theo Sommer in Conversation with Helmut Schmidt[1]

Theo Sommer: In the ten years preceding the first *Wehrkunde-Begegnung,* as the Munich Security Conference was known then, in 1963, you had matured into one of the most knowledgeable and forthright defense politicians in the Federal Republic. You had joined the *Realpolitik* wing of the Social Democratic Party of Germany [SPD] at an early date; for you, it was soon no longer a question of a fundamental "yes" to rearmament but primarily a matter of "how?" You had written your book *Verteidigung oder Vergeltung* in 1961. At the second security conference in December 1964 you were interior minister in the Free and Hanseatic City of Hamburg, and you were introduced on that occasion as the SPD candidate for defense minister. In your contributions you called on the European NATO partners and the United States to work toward an integrated, rationally designed military strategy and an equally rationally designed arms control policy. The commonality of interests between the allies appeared to you at the time—and I quote— "obscure and even questionable." "How much unity do we need?" you asked. "How much pluralism can we allow ourselves in the Alliance?"

What were the contentious issues at that time, in 1964? Was it the MLF, the Multilateral Missile Force? Was it the Americans' failure to consult its partners? What preoccupied and concerned you at that time?

▲
Helmut Schmidt and Henry Kissinger at Hotel Bayerischer Hof, 1974

Helmut Schmidt: By 1964 we had been through the Cuban missile crisis, which was the climax of the Cold War. We had put it behind us, but we were still in the midst of the East-West conflict. Germany was still divided. The Federal German Armed Forces were being built up, but that process was by no means complete. And it was embedded in a military alliance whose official strategy was, in my view, absurd, but which I was nevertheless bound to pursue.

TS: The official strategy at the time was "massive retaliation."

HS: Because, in terms of numbers, the West was no match at all for either the Soviet army or the Soviet air force. It had developed the harebrained idea of making up for the conventional deficit by deploying nuclear weapons, that is to say, first use of nuclear weapons by NATO. I thought to myself that this retaliatory strike against a conventional attack would naturally itself attract retaliation in the form of a second strike by the Soviets. Both strikes would be focused on targets on German soil, perhaps to some extent on Dutch soil and northern France, but essentially on German soil. That meant that millions of Germans would be killed. For that reason I considered such a strategy to be wrong and—as a minor senator from Hamburg—attempted to counteract it by writing a book. The English translation of that book, *Defense or Retaliation,* had a real impact in Great Britain and the US in 1962.

TS: At the time, there was an ongoing debate over whether the Alliance partners should have a say in the nuclear strategy. You argued that the Germans should give up any nuclear co-ownership, that is, involvement in the MLF, but not give up joint planning or a regional veto. Your idea of a regional veto was to be able to say "no" as soon as nuclear weapons were fired from German soil or against targets on German soil. That was important to you. Were you granted enough of a say, or even a right of veto, in the talks and consultations being conducted at the time?

HS: At the time, I was a senator in Hamburg, which was not particularly important in foreign policy terms. I later became defense minister. By then, the allies had set up the Nuclear Planning Group. Yet I nonetheless stuck to my demand. However, it did not receive a positive response.

TS: In 1967, as well as in 1970 and 1971, you were again among the participants at the *Wehrkunde-Begegnung.* By that time you had already become the federal minister of defense, and in that position, too, you were concernedabove all with nuclear strategy, especially the American idea of burying atomic munitions on German soil in holes along the GDR border that would automatically detonate in the event of a Soviet attack. Did you speak about this at the security conference?

HS: I don't remember. But I do recall that I didn't know in advance of the existence of those plans for ADMs—that's what they were called, atomic demolition means, nuclear weapons buried in the soil. The holes had already been drilled, and the warheads for them were stored in nearby bunkers. I became aware of these facts a couple of days after I took office as defense minister in 1969. The project had been kept secret; not even the German cabinet knew anything about it, nor did the Bundestag. Only the chancellor and the defense minister of the day were aware of it. I was horrified, because the deployment of these weapons would certainly have resulted in huge numbers of German casualties. I opposed it then, but not with loud talk. Rather, I went to see my American colleague, Melvin Laird. A wonderful guy, a veteran who understood immediately that Germans had to oppose this, and who fundamentally shared my concerns. And then Laird and I came to an agreement: that we would put an end to this nonsense. Altogether, it took us over three years to get there. In fact, these systems were not dismantled and removed until 1973.

TS: It wasn't discussed at the security conference?

HS: Barely.

TS: In 1970, when you participated for the first time as defense minister, you set out six principles of your defense policy. First: the Atlantic alliance is indispensable; second: a strong American military presence is also indispensable; third: we must attempt reconciliation with our East European neighbors; fourth: we must not give up the relationship with the West, because it was possible that détente would fail; fifth: you called for concerted efforts to achieve greater economic and political unity in Western Europe; and sixth: European unity might one day include defense. These were your public statements. Do you remember the discussion?

HS: I remember the speech, but I don't recall the ensuing discussion.

TS: At the time, the Mansfield resolution was still in the air. Mike Mansfield was an American senator who demanded that US troops in Germany be reduced by at least fifty thousand.

HS: It was at the same time that the debate about maintaining and abolishing compulsory service in the United States began, and I remember that public debate. Myself, I was reserved when speaking in public. I didn't want to unsettle our French neighbors unnecessarily. Of course, my ideas were quite different from those of the French.

TS: As defense minister, but also as finance minister, you were continually confronted with American demands that the Germans should pay higher "stationing costs" for US troops deployed in the Federal Republic, and in general should increase the defense budget.

HS: The finance minister was under pressure to cut the budget. We were more or less successful in muddling ourselves through those discussions.

TS: But you also said that the Americans, who of course were themselves trying to reduce their defense spending, should be careful—their cuts might have a contagious effect in Europe. You were also concerned that the Americans might be withdrawing too many of their troops.

HS: Yes. In reality, the Americans were the backbone of NATO. If they detached themselves physically from Europe, the risk was that their influence would be gravely diminished. I could see that coming, and so I opposed it.

TS: What were the most important issues discussed at the security conferences you attended?

HS: The role of nuclear weapons as well as financing the build-up of our armed forces was very important. You have to remember: all of this was going on in the landscape of a divided Europe—characterized by Germany and the capital Berlin divided in two and by an unpleasant regime in what was then the GDR, a regime in Poland that was impenetrable to us in the West, and to some extent an aggressive Soviet rearmament, which became visible for the first time toward the end of the seventies.

When I was chancellor, it came to light that the Russians had a new missile, the SS-20. Its range was basically limited to Europe. It was essentially aimed at German cities. Initially there were a dozen, a year later two dozen SS-20s. This relatively rapid build-up happened at the same time America was absorbed by the Watergate affair. Richard Nixon was replaced by Gerald Ford, a wonderful guy. But by 1976 Ford had already been replaced by Jimmy Carter, who was not quite so admirable in my view. He was highly intelligent, a very hard worker, but as far as grand strategy, military strategy, and disarmament strategy were concerned, he was for all practical purposes an amateur. Moreover, when he considered the issues he sometimes arrived at different conclusions at different times. That made everything even more complicated. But by that time I was no longer attending the Munich Security Conference.

TS: Did Carter's indecision and the to-ing and fro-ing in his policy perhaps also have to do with his national security advisor, Zbigniew Brzezinski, whom you met several times in Munich?

HS: I had known Brzezinski since the fifties. At the time he was a member of the American defense community. I got to know him along with Henry Kissinger, Tom Schelling, Bob Bowie, Arnold Wolfers, and people like them. During the late seventies and early eighties, Brzezinski was national security adviser to Jimmy Carter. Presumably it was really he who armed Jimmy

Carter with arguments in response to my constant pressure for balancing the SS-20s.

TS: You expressed your concern over the Russian SS-20 build-up for the first time in the early fall of 1977, during a speech at the London Institute for Strategic Studies.

HS: Really not so much in the speech itself but afterwards at a small private dinner. There I pulled no punches. That shocked the Americans. They talked about it in Washington. The result was that Jimmy Carter invited the three Europeans whom he thought mattered to a joint meeting in Washington: the British prime minister Jim Callaghan, Valéry Giscard d'Estaing, the French president, and myself. Giscard's view was that we must not be summoned by President Carter. Instead, he invited us to Guadeloupe, a French island in the Caribbean.

TS: The man who had passed on your concerns to the White House after hearing you at the dinner after your speech in London was Helmut (Hal) Sonnenfeldt, a frequent participant at the security conference and Henry Kissinger's right-hand man. You held your speech in 1977; the double-track decision—either the Russians scrap the SS-20s or the West will build up its medium-range arsenal—was reached in 1979 at a NATO special meeting. Five years after that famous London speech, you left office as federal chancellor. Ten years later, for the first time ever an entire category of nuclear weapons was totally eliminated.

HS: There's a story behind that. After 1979, I expressed my views very clearly and unambiguously on the subject of the SS-20 and the NATO double-track decision, both in the West and in the East. I remember, for example, that I spoke about it in Catherine Hall in the Kremlin. The Soviet participants—actually the entire politburo—had my text, translated into Russian, in front of them on the table. So they were able to follow everything in detail, their fingers moving down line by line. At some point, Mikhail Suslov, who was the senior Soviet ideologue at the time, banged his paper down on the table, completely outraged, and stood up. I thought he was going to fly off his handle. But opposite me sat the old man, Leonid Brezhnev, and he just calmly continued reading. Suslov had to sit down again. At the time, I had come to know Brezhnev quite well. I knew that he would not start a war. But I did not know his successor—he might later on blackmail West Germany, against whose cities his SS-20s were mainly targeted. And I was not sure of the American answer. With Carter I reasoned just as candidly.

TS: As the Russians wouldn't disarm even after four years of negotiations, NATO said, we'd also deploy new weapons.

HS: In 1986 there was a summit meeting, held in Reykjavik in Iceland, between Mikhail Gorbachev—who was the third successor after Brezhnev had died in October 1982—and Ronald Reagan. Gorbachev very openly and quite convincingly put forward my position and made it his own. The two men got along very well, but ultimately no agreement was reached in Reykjavik. When it came right down to it, Reagan didn't want to abandon his Star Wars ideology. But George Shultz was there, then secretary of state. I knew him well, and I still consider him a friend, a very trustworthy friend. Shultz must have, after a few months, persuaded his president to agree to the double-track decision. The first real disarmament treaty between the East and the West came into force in 1987. Two years later, the Berlin Wall came down.

TS: For many years, another issue played a significant role in Munich: the Non-Proliferation Treaty. We now know that the German Defense Minister, Franz-Josef Strauss, was eager to develop, together with the French and the Italians, a European nuclear weapon. For a long time, the Bonn government was therefore officially opposed to the treaty.

HS: It was Chancellor Willy Brandt who finally signed it in 1969 or 1970. The CDU [Christian Democratic Union] opposed it under Chancellor Kurt Kiesinger, but once it entered into force, they finally came to accept it.

TS: Who were the people at the conference in Munich who made the biggest impression on you and also influenced your thinking? You've mentioned a few already, but you didn't mention the American general Maxwell Taylor, or the French generals Pierre Gallois and André Beaufre.

HS: I already knew Gallois, Beaufre, and Taylor before Munich. After retiring, Taylor wrote a book entitled *The Uncertain Trumpet*—a biblical metaphor describing the questionable effectiveness of nuclear deterrence. I saw Taylor as an undeclared ally against the threat of massive retaliation.

TS: You also had your doubts—and expressed them forcefully in Munich—about the strategy that replaced the strategy of massive retaliation: flexible response.

HS: In reality there was no flexibility.

TS: You said in Munich that you thought defense by employing tactical nuclear weapons made little sense militarily, because defenders also had to concentrate their forces, not just attackers. Moreover, you were certain that after a few days it would escalate to the employment of the big strategic weapons.

HS: I can't remember that part of the speech, but it sounds very familiar.

TS: And what impression did Beaufre or Gallois make on you? In Munich you frequently demonstrated your vehement support of Franco-German cooperation.

HS: I certainly did, although I really didn't agree with Charles de Gaulle's nuclear strategy. On the other hand, I was sufficiently conscious of history to know that any German foreign and security policy had to make cooperation with France a top priority. When I became defense minister, I found in my French colleague a man who was indeed a protagonist of the Grande Nation, Michel Debré, a Gaullist. Nevertheless, he became a true friend of mine.

TS: Who was important among the British? Alastair Buchan, the first director of the London Institute for Strategic Studies?

HS: Alastair Buchan died young, and I can't remember the details of our acquaintance very well. Two British ministers were particularly significant for me. One was Denis Healey—now Lord Healey from the Labour Party, who took part in Munich for the first time in 1969. Then there was Peter Carrington, Lord Carrington. He was foreign secretary under Maggie Thatcher, a conservative who later became NATO's secretary general. Actually, the four of us—Gerry Ford, Giscard d'Estaing, Carrington, and I—managed to heave him into office. When we met in the mountains of Colorado we were all "has-beens." Carrington had had an argument, a difference of opinion with his prime minister, Maggie Thatcher. He lost his job as defense secretary, and we thought that was a waste of talent. We knew Peter Carrington and thought he should become NATO secretary general. Indeed, NATO did us the favor of accepting our proposal and appointed him to that very post.

TS: In the early days, Air Marshall John Slessor or Admiral Anthony Buzzard also took part in the conferences that you attended. They were among the cofounders of the International Institute for Strategic Studies. Were they important for the development of your thoughts?

HS: They were part of the international defense community in the fifties and sixties, and were probably my senior by ten or more years. Someone else who should be mentioned in that context is Basil Henry Liddell Hart, who was still alive at the time. I visited him before I wrote my book and had lengthy conversations with him.

TS: What were your impressions of the atmosphere prevailing during the talks in Munich?

HS: It was quite normal, which was usually the case at such international conferences.

TS: How important are such conferences for politicians in office?

HS: Some politicians rely on their instinct, the best examples in my opinion being Winston Churchill, Charles de Gaulle, and in his own way Konrad Adenauer too. None of them needed such meetings. Others need places like Munich to make contacts—to test out their ideas, find their ideas confirmed or rejected, and adjust or change them.

TS: Actually, politicians, as long as they are in office, have many types of official bilateral contacts. Inside NATO as well, discussions and negotiations take place all the time. What is the specific value of the Munich Security Conference in comparison with those official contacts?

HS: The so-called official contacts are those between the military and diplomats, and occasionally ministers. They all have their professional qualifications, they have grown into their professions over their lifetime, they have a horizon, and they can make judgments. However, they do not have contact with outsiders. It's possible to enter the defense community laterally, as did, for example, Franz-Josef Strauss—in German we call them "Quereinsteiger," career changers. Diplomats and military people rarely have such contacts. The Munich Security Conference brings them all together.

TS: In the early years of the conference, a fifth to a quarter of the participants were editors-in-chief, because there was clearly a desire to introduce journalists to the subject of security policy. When one reads through the records of those conferences and the numerous newspaper articles about the meetings, one is struck by how many anxieties were expressed then and later over the future of the Atlantic alliance. *"Die NATO fällt der Schwindsucht anheim"*—"NATO is falling victim to consumption"—read a headline in 1964. Friedrich Zimmermann, then chairman of the Defense Committee in the Bundestag, was afraid of "disintegration, disengagement, and denuclearization"—the three Ds. The newspapers wrote: *"Es knistert im Gebälk der NATO"*—"The NATO woodwork is creaking." You yourself lamented the signs that NATO was breaking up. The Vietnam War had already triggered a great deal of anxiety that the US was pivoting toward Asia.

HS: I don't think those anxieties could have gone very deep.

TS: At the time there was also a protracted discussion about the order of sequence and priority: "security before détente" or "security through détente"? And there was a discussion then, just as forty years later in the time of Dmitry Medvedev, about the Kremlin's proposals for a European security system. Americans and Europeans were at odds about it. How do those ancient discussions differ from those today?

HS: The debates then and now take place in two different worlds. The world then was characterized by the Cold War between the Soviet-dominated part of the world and the West. That Cold War has ended. As always, there is no friendship between the US and Russia, but cooperation has grown closer between Russia and China. I can still remember how frightened Brezhnev was of a war with China in 1975, 1976, and 1977. And I also know that at the same time Mao Zedong was very much aware of the Russian military deployment north of the Soviet-Chinese border. Mao thought the Russians were far superior to the Chinese. He could list the cities; he could list the missile targets. And he told me: "We must let them in, but in the end they will drown in the enormous masses of Chinese."

TS: Did he say that to you when you met him in 1975?

HS: Literally, yes. I can remember his exact words. The Cold War was still on, but the hostility between Moscow and Beijing was quite marked.

TS: Is it not still latent in Moscow today?

HS: Subcutaneously, perhaps, but it is not as ostentatious. If you ask a Russian how many Chinese there are now in Siberia, he will perhaps hesitate and say, "About ten million, I would think." And if you ask a Chinese person the same question, he will say, "One million, and they are traders who will go home again." The truth probably lies somewhere in the middle. In fact there are 140 million Russians, of whom at least 20 million are Muslims. And there is this gigantic Russian territory. How are they ever going to fill this gigantic territory, given the ever-increasing population of the mainly Muslim countries in the south? The Russians still have lots of unexplored mineral resources, without even mentioning those being exploited already—but there are not enough people.

At the same time, in China and India and all over the world there is a trend toward urbanization. Humanity has increased fivefold since 1900. There were 1.5 billion in the world then, now we number almost 7.5 billion. By the middle of the twenty-first century there will be around nine billion. And while in the past the 1,500 to 1,600 million people in huts lived side by side in villages, these days they live on top of one another in urban high-rise apartment complexes. Chongqing now has a population of thirty million, Shanghai more than twenty million, Beijing more than twenty million, and Kuandong twenty million. I still remember Shenzhen as a small village in the hills north of Hong Kong—now it has a population of twelve million. The same is true for Cairo, Mexico City, São Paulo—in fact for the whole world. Such cities can be hard to govern.

TS: Does this create security problems as well?

HS: Initially, problems of internal security. But it can also lead to external security problems, because many people in these cities are poor. They might want to move to Europe. This poses problems of external security. What is going on in Lampedusa is only a prelude.

TS: Looking at the global picture, we see the rise of China and Vladimir Putin pivoting toward Asia like Barack Obama. We see the decline of

America's capacity to shape the world and the Europeans' inability to agree on a common, effective European security policy. What would you advise the Munich Security Conference to do today, given this fundamentally changing geopolitical and geostrategic situation?

HS: The MSC must acknowledge this change and deal with it, and take note that the question is not just one of security in the traditional sense but of a grand strategy, of global strategic ideas, of geopolitical, geo-economic, and geodemographic problems. One concrete geo-economic example is that the United States will probably become self-sufficient in terms of energy within this decade. Currently it is one of the largest importers of energy/oil, but the picture will probably be very different by 2020.

TS: Does that mean that the Americans will lose interest in the Middle East when they no longer need its oil?

HS: I don't think so. Rather, I think that the effect of demographic change on domestic politics will result in the American public losing some of their interest in dominating the world. By 2050, the Afro-Americans and their children and grandchildren, and Mexicans and Latinos and their children and grandchildren will together form the majority of US voters. In social terms, they are mostly members of the lower classes. They will be interested in decent social security, pensions, healthcare, unemployment benefits, possibly even care insurance in the long term. In any case, they are interested in ensuring that their clever children can go to Harvard rather than to a run-down state university. Those things will be much more important to them than getting involved in disputes about some islands in the South China Sea.

TS: Do you expect a new American isolationism?

HS: It wouldn't be quite so novel. American isolationism goes back two hundred years. It is called the Monroe Doctrine. There has always been a tendency toward isolationism in the United States, at other times toward imperialism and improving the world.

TS: There have always been phases of internationalism as well.

HS: That is true. From Wilson to the Marshall Plan.

TS: A final question. One principle has always marked your entire thinking about global strategy: "balance of power." How should this concept shape Western policy today and in the decades to come?

HS: In the course of the twentieth century we saw the gradual emergence of a new factor in world politics, something that did not exist in the nineteenth century: the spread of Islam. When you ask for balance, the point is not a balance only between China and America but one between Asians, Muslims, and the West. It is a different world. We have at least about as many

Muslims in the world as there are Catholics. The world has not taken it in yet, but this is a fact. And we can't exclude the possibility of the Muslims uniting, though perhaps not just now. At present, it seems they're divided into various sects: Sunnis, Shias, Salafis, Alawis ...

TS: ... jihadists.

HS: Jihadists, yes, all of them. They may form alliances.

TS: And what sort of structures should emerge from this new dispensation? How should the balance of power principle be applied in the world of the future?

HS: I'm too old to trust myself to answer that one.

Helmut Schmidt *was chancellor of the Federal Republic of Germany from 1974 to 1982 and minister of defense from 1969 to 1972.*

Dr. **Theo Sommer** *is editor-at-large of the weekly newspaper DIE ZEIT. He was its editor-in-chief from 1973 to 1992, and subsequently, until April 2000, one of its publishers (with Marion Gräfin Dönhoff and Helmut Schmidt). In 1969–70 he was head of the planning staff at the West German Ministry of Defense and served as a member of the German Defense Structure Commissions in 1970–72 and 1999–2001.*

Notes

1   This is the transcript of a conversation that took place on October 18, 2013, in Hamburg.

The Discussions in the Critical Period of the East-West Conflict from the Mid-Sixties to the Early Nineties

Lothar Rühl

Following the split between Moscow and Beijing, which caused the Sino-Soviet bloc to collapse and changed the global geopolitical scene, the *Internationale Wehrkunde-Begegnung,* which was initiated in 1963, focused on the following related group of seven major strategic policy challenges for North Atlantic security:

1. The nuclear arms limitation policy introduced in 1963 by the treaty between the United States, the Union of Soviet Socialist Republics, and Great Britain banning nuclear weapon tests in the atmosphere leading to a switch from nuclear deterrence to the strategic protection of Europe by America.

The Nuclear Non-Proliferation Treaty (NPT) of 1968/69 and, from 1972 onwards, the Strategic Arms Limitation Talks (SALT) on US-Soviet nuclear arms limitation agreements (later the Strategic Arms Reduction Treaty [START]), on which preliminary talks had been in progress since 1968,

Lothar Rühl (left) and Paul Nitze at the 1984 *Wehrkunde*

dominated East-West relations, strategic negotiations, and security policy as a whole under the banner of arms control. Initially, there were more than fifteen years of confrontation with profound disagreements as to the definition of "forward based systems" in strategic nuclear forces, the criteria of numerical or qualitative symmetry, the equivalence of the operational strategy options on both sides, and the numbers of nuclear weapons to be classified as strategic. The tension eased somewhat from 1986 onwards, and new agreements could be reached. The point at issue was always the interests of the European allies, in particular Great Britain and France, and their link with the US *vis-à-vis* the USSR and ultimately, in 1972, China as well.

This was the background of the negotiations over an independent European nuclear deterrent. The subject took up much time at the Munich conference in the late sixties and gave rise to extremely heated debates. The exchange of correspondence between US Secretary of State Dean Rusk and European governments on the recognition of the right of a European authority, to which nation states were subordinate, to exercise independent control of European nuclear forces and on cooperation with US forces took center stage in this discussion, for the time being ending the disputes over the NPT.

The equally controversial plan for a European multilateral deterrent force, the Multilateral Force (MLF), which had been accepted by NATO, with American nuclear-armed missiles mounted on ships manned by European crews was debated vigorously and in depth in Munich but later abandoned by President Lyndon B. Johnson, so that the matter went off the agenda. (France had not taken part in the MLF program.)

However, the much wider strategic question as to the application of the "flexible response" to an attack by Western nuclear weapons stationed in Europe remained unanswered, as did the question of the wider deterrent held by the US in relation to the bilateral American-Soviet negotiations on strategic nuclear weapon delivery and antiballistic missile defense systems under the Moscow SALT I Treaty of 1972.

2. In this context, the crisis in the relationship between France and NATO and the conflict with both Anglo-American allies over the French national nuclear deterrent and France's position in the Alliance, in particular President Charles de Gaulle's demand, rejected by both Washington and London, for a board of three powers to control the Alliance based on sovereign nuclear weapons and the powers of veto in the UN.

These disputes began in 1965/66; they affected the European NATO partners in particular, who were also armed with American nuclear weapons under dual control, but also all the European allies, because de Gaulle was calling for political privileges for France and Great Britain. This was incompatible with the formal sovereign equality of all allies, the existing NATO structures, and the Washington Treaty of 1949.

3. Moscow's offense initiatives for a pan-European security conference designed to distinguish between the security of Europe as a whole and that of North America, to deactivate if not to dissolve NATO, and to push the US out of Europe.

Between 1968 and 1973 the West responded to the talks in Carlsbad, requested by the Warsaw Pact in 1966, with counterproposals for the parallel dual process of the Mutual and Balanced Force Reductions (MBFR) talks in Europe and the Conference on Security and Cooperation in Europe (CSCE).

Both sets of negotiations continued beyond the Helsinki CSCE Final Acts in 1975 until 1990/91 and ended in the Paris Agreement of 1991, before the break-up of the USSR but after the dissolution of the Warsaw Pact.

4. The emergence of the so-called Eurostrategic threat from Soviet "assault weapons," in the words of German Chancellor Helmut Schmidt, and the new ground-based SS-20 medium- or intermediate-range missiles.

Launched from the USSR, these would be effective almost 5,500 kilometers across Western Europe but unable to reach North America and therefore impacted the nuclear weapons deployment strategy quite differently in the territories of Europe and America. This made a nuclear war limited to Europe conceivable, particularly given the enhanced precision of the targeting capability of these missiles, reducing the terminal miss distance of the weapons and accordingly limiting the radius of collateral damage in the area surrounding the target. This facilitated limited nuclear strikes on selected targets, and a nuclear attack on Europe became a strategic option for Moscow. Heated discussions on this policy took place in Munich.

The West responded controversially by counter-arming in the nuclear medium range with the NATO double-track decision in 1979 on the deployment of American medium-range missile systems in five Western European countries. This included an offer to Moscow for both sides to dispense with such ground-based weapons worldwide—including East Asia, which was similarly threatened. A crucial factor here was the modernization of Soviet potential through the new SS-20 missile, with three multiple independently targetable reentry vehicle (MIRV) nuclear warheads and reloading capability, including in the case of mobile ground launch systems, which in any event meant a tripling of targeted attack capability.

5. President Ronald Reagan's 1983 decision to move from the strategic doctrine of mutual assured destruction to assured missile defense in inner space between the US and the USSR.

This ushered in a new strategy epoch, yet after a quarter of a century it is still not generally accepted or technically complete. The supporters of Reagan's Strategic Defense Initiative (SDI) saw it as total and definitive security against missile attacks, that is, full deterrence but without the threatened use of nuclear offensive weapons. Other voices in the debate saw it as partial coverage of selected targets on the ground, hence as strategic coverage of priority targets for second-strike capability and strategic leadership by the US. This view would see the system as only a partial deterrent, essentially along the lines of earlier doctrines on nuclear missiles, such as "sufficiency," namely adequate weapons (Robert McNamara 1963/65).

One of these voices was the US secretary of defense in the Carter administration of the seventies, Harold Brown. He considered medium-range weapons unnecessary for NATO in Europe but accepted them for the sake of peace of mind for Europeans. These American nuclear weapons in Europe, on sites from which they could reach targets in Soviet Russia, were therefore "political weapons," or, more precisely, instruments of the European-Atlantic alliance policy designed to stabilize NATO.

6. In 1964/65, the US involvement in the Vietnam War, which had broken out again in 1963 and which was to last until 1973/75.

This brought in Laos and Cambodia, escalated the crisis in the Alliance with the withdrawal of France from the military integration structure in 1966/67, and cut the US military commitment in Europe by means of troop reductions. This led to increasing the need, and strengthening US calls, for a greater European effort by building up stronger defense capabilities, thus relieving the burden on the US—a topic that was to increasingly define discussions between Europe and America.

7. The conflict between Greece and Turkey over Cyprus from late 1963.

This disrupted NATO's southeast military flank in Europe over a long period, practically dissolved the integrated military structure in Southeastern

Europe. The conflict between the two allies over the demarcation and use of each other's territorial waters in the area of the Aegean Archipelago grew. Repeated military confrontations, and later, after Turkey occupied the whole of northern Cyprus in 1974, brought the sides to the brink of war.

Such were the issues that occupied the Munich Security Conference over the years. Then in 1968 the Soviet army occupied socialist Czechoslovakia along with several allies in the Warsaw Pact, triggering a general state of military alarm in Central Europe. The USSR intervened in the Afghan Civil War from 1979 until early 1989, and in 1980/81 there was the threat of Soviet intervention in Poland against the freedom movement set in motion by the Solidarność trade union. This was supported in different ways in Western Europe and therefore became a topic of controversy among NATO partners, particularly in terms of German policy during the crisis.

The two wars in the Middle East in 1967 and 1973, with the closures of the Suez Canal, the Arab League oil embargo against Western European NATO countries in 1973, and finally the Israeli intervention in Lebanon in 1982 against the Palestine Liberation Army and its political umbrella, the Palestine Liberation Organization, brought the Middle East conflict back onto the international political center stage. In 1973, the US put its combat forces, including its strategic forces, on the highest alert in order to deter a Soviet intervention.

It was inevitable that the Munich talks would be shaped and determined by the reality of the link between developments and events in the major areas for discussion, which in any case related to international security and power politics. It was also inevitable that three strands would always be interlinked—dialogue between America and Europe, dialogue within Europe, and dialogue within Germany—as well as, now and then, debate within America.

The Talks between the United States and Europe 1964–94

Leaving aside those topics that surface only occasionally and those that are marginal, we can clearly discern a common thread running throughout the three decades of discussions in Munich: Europe's need for protection under the umbrella of the American deterrent, which is sometimes wide open and sometimes slightly closed, together with the American call for burden-sharing for joint security, hence for a greater European effort to defend Western Europe. All the other topics fit comfortably around this central core.

To set a timetable of priorities, we have to look at the direct connection between nuclear deterrence and conventional defense in relation to the negotiations with the USSR and the Warsaw Pact, and between nuclear and conventional arms control and the goals of disarmament. Equally important for an understanding of both the security policy processes and the strategic problems and approaches to solutions up to the 1989/90 treaty is how the Western threat is perceived on the Eastern horizon. There was some argument at the Munich debates: firstly, because the facts could never be precisely verified and were often contradictory, and secondly because interpretations diverged. At the time of the East-West conflict, no one from Soviet Russia or other Eastern European countries attended the Munich Security Conference. Moreover, the governments of the Warsaw Pact states themselves opted out of the then ongoing MBFR discussions on conventional weapons in Europe and for a long time even from the bilateral SALT talks with the US on the controversial areas of the detailed discussions on practical questions. Not until nearly the end of those talks, when Mikhail Gorbachev was in power in Moscow from fall 1986 onwards, could Soviet Russian negotiators and participants in other international forums get involved in real discussions on facts. These were then introduced into the Munich Security Conference and once again were the subject of heated argument, primarily among representatives of the German government and the opposition, where the latter often inclined to give more credit to information from Moscow than to information from Washington and Brussels. Finally, official USSR figures for nuclear systems and conventional weapons in 1989/90 showed that Western assumptions, far from being exaggerated, were actually below the real figures for Soviet armaments and armed forces in Europe.

The outcome in Munich reflected the results of the official exchange of information in Vienna and Geneva: the threat as perceived by the West was less than it actually had been for a quarter of a century. With few exceptions, neither those involved in political debate nor the media or the academic community addressed this topic in its aftermath. After German reunification it was forced from the political center stage, but in Munich it was taken very seriously and evaluated. However, the question remained as to the consequences of these findings for the future.

During the entire era from 1964 to 1994, the period during which Russian troops were withdrawn from Germany, the Western doctrine on security policy strategy was that equivalence in essentials and an effective extended deterrence, the substance of which was discussed over the next two and half decades in Munich, did not require absolute numerical parity with the East, whatever the geographical boundaries. The main point was always equivalence of operational options, the goal being to effectively and reliably deter a major attack on the territory of the Alliance—in other words, demonstrating to the enemy that even a major planned offensive against Western Europe or in the Middle East could not succeed and that the risk of survival could not be defined, even for the attacker, because the operations would not continue to be either conventional or confined to Europe or to Turkey. This was the meaning of the theory of putting a potential attacker at risk from the start, using the strategy of flexible response. This was the background to the German and European insistence on counter-arming in the nuclear medium-range area to offer a credible threat to the USSR in Western Russia and Ukraine as a counter-threat for an attack on the West. On strategy grounds, the US military in Europe as well as in Washington supported these arguments and political targets, supported primarily by German Chancellor Helmut Schmidt but also, at the critical moment, by French President François Mitterrand, although France was not involved in the program. In Munich, not only were the contours of the problem sharpened and the fronts clearly drawn, but a great deal was achieved for the solidarity of the Alliance and the commitment of the US, which could at times waver.

The American participants, who always met as a delegation on the evening before the conference so that, as far as possible, they spoke with one voice, clarified Washington's nuances and reservations: the United States Congress would approve resources for new nuclear weapon systems only if deployment in Europe ensured that the USSR was within range. On the other hand, it was more inclined towards modernizing the nuclear short-range weapons in order to strengthen US forces in Europe and the Mediterranean/ Middle East (known as Lance II or Follow on to Lance, a missile with nuclear capability and a range of up to approximately 650 kilometers compared with Lance's 350). However, this implied tooling up for a nuclear battle in Europe and triggered protest on the part of Europe, especially Germany (the Turks in any case refused to take any part in the deployment of new or additional nuclear systems on their territory).

Since numerical parity with Soviet weaponry seemed neither necessary nor achievable in the talks, but rather that an "adequate" deterrent would suffice, the discussions in Munich, like Western arms control diplomacy, were flexible—until the "zero solution" proposed later, following the NATO double-track decision in 1979 on deployment of a particular number of medium-range systems and talks on a parity ceiling, namely worldwide abandonment of this category of armaments between the US and the USSR.

It is true that the talks in Munich on this complex topic were usually controversial, but they were well targeted overall in the sense that they prepared the ground conceptually for the synthesis found later with Moscow, namely the "double-zero solution" for ground-based missiles with ranges between 500 and 5,500 kilometers worldwide. This was only possible thanks to the active participation of the most important American negotiators, such as Paul Nitze and Richard Burt. The conversations in small groups on the margins of the conference made a significant contribution, as, of course, did the regular consultations between allied governments and NATO Council meetings in Brussels.

Through three decades from beginning to end, these discussions were relevant to the total SALT/START negotiation process on strategic nuclear disarmament, which in SALT only provided for limiting the growth in armaments in numerical terms rather than disarmament as such, and did not until later cover the qualities of the weapons, such as MIRVs. Moreover, for Europe, eliminating the continental invasion capability of the Soviet forces and their allies, in other words reducing conventional weaponry, was of prime importance. Yet because the East bore a disproportionately greater burden this could only be done asymmetrically to the detriment of the Warsaw Pact, and in particular the Soviet army, if the goal in the sense of true equivalence and strategic and operational parity of options were to be reached. Over the years, the subject and underlying arguments were worked over in Munich until MBFR ended and, with the subsequent negotiations on conventional forces in Europe, the necessary conventional weapons control and disarmament complement for 1991 to the Intermediate-Range Nuclear Forces Treaty of 1989 could be agreed. Afterwards, the Munich Security Conference could also be opened to Eastern Europe and turn its attention much more widely to the Middle East—although outside Europe, it is strategically relevant to Europe's security—and beyond to the East as a whole. However, the southern arc of crisis from the Indian Ocean and Southwest Asia to the Near East and North Africa as far as Gibraltar was an area that had always appeared clearly on the radar horizon in Munich.

In Europe, the policy of consolidating security that was introduced in 1993 following the demise of the USSR and the pulling-back of Russia's western borders (to those of Moscovy at the end of the sixteenth century after the defeats of Ivan the Terrible against Poland-Lithuania, Sweden, and the Crimean Tartars) was to be continued and end in agreement. The loss of the forward territory in Central Europe and the old West Russian land with Belarus and Ukraine, together with Crimea, in other words all of the conquests of Peter the Great and Catherine the Great in the eighteenth century as well as Central Asia, was more than simply the "loss of empire," a phrase frequently quoted even in Munich. The problem of pan-European security and territorial stability discussed in depth and with some heat at the Munich Security Conference from 1991 onwards concentrated on Russia and Ukraine, but also focused on the newly independent South Caucasus, while the Baltic states were already preparing to join NATO and the EU. Participants from Eastern Europe, particularly from Poland and the Baltic states, prioritized the subject of their security against Russia, while the Russians concentrated on the security and territorial integrity of Russia and the "Russian Federation," together with the "Commonwealth of Independent States," and the concept of a "Slavic Union" in Europe, facing NATO with the US as its backbone.

The United States as a "European power," as President George Bush senior proclaimed in Mainz in May 1989, became a discussion topic central to all sides at the Munich Security Conference, together with the START nuclear strategy questions, the first real reduction of strategic nuclear weapon delivery systems and nuclear warheads, missile defense, and the new American SDI program.

The reduction in conventional forces, particularly in the southeast, in the Russian North Caucasus, created an associated problem, given the Russian need to strengthen forces in the event of a crisis. This delayed the implementation of the full CFE Treaty, although its core terms were implemented in Central and Eastern Europe as far as the Ural Mountains and Russian superiority was eliminated. Despite this, East-West confrontation remained in people's minds even in 1993 and into the second half of the nineties. Critically, this was to be demonstrated later in the Georgian conflict and in the excessive, almost automatic NATO expansion to Russia's western border, which had moved back by 600 to 1,000 kilometers. In 1993 this involved only the eastern part of Central Europe with Poland, then Czechoslovakia, which still existed at the start of the process, and Hungary. Later, the three Baltic states and, in the southeast, Romania and Bulgaria were added, which also gave the West a border on the Black Sea. These milestones in 1991–93/94 describe a development that had made NATO the foundation for European security far beyond the NATO area and had thereby reinforced a continuing geopolitical conflict with Russia—still going on two decades later. This development was reflected in the Munich Security Conference, particularly in a spectacular intervention by Russian President Putin and in the lasting dispute over the American forward-deployed strategic missile defense in Europe and the Mediterranean.

The next subject was the planning for deployment of US interceptor missiles in Romania and the movement of fighter aircraft and ground-based air defense to Poland and Romania. On both sides, this development could be called, as indeed it was called in Munich, a "continuation of the Cold War by other means," particularly as regards the 2008 plan in Bucharest to open up preliminary negotiations with Ukraine and Georgia regarding membership in NATO. This question did indeed receive a positive response, but, since the decision by President Barack Obama not to take the plan forward for the time being, it has remained pending for political reasons, regularly occupying the Munich Security Conference from the point of view of European security, relations with Russia after the tensions of the Balkan Wars of 1994–99, and the problems of the Middle East in the Levant. Thus, the interlinked group of topics involving strategic and geopolitical challenges on both sides leaves questions of policy and strategy unanswered, and even since 1993 the relationship has still not become a Vancouver-to-Vladivostok solution for transatlantic joint security between America and Europe as intended by foreign ministers James Baker and Hans-Dietrich Genscher. The relationship has remained confrontational but cooperative, and hence politically ambivalent, as has been repeatedly affirmed in the Munich conferences.

*Professor Dr. **Lothar Rühl** was state secretary in the German Ministry of Defense (1982–1989) and deputy spokesperson of the federal government (1981–82). For many years, he has taught international relations and political science at the University of Cologne. He served on the boards of numerous institutes, such as German Institute for International and Security Affairs (Stiftung Wissenschaft und Politik).*

Wehrkunde and the Transatlantic Nuclear Discourse

Uwe Nerlich

Tracing back a chain of fifty annual events like the *Wehrkunde* and its sequels leads back into a period of fateful history, or, for witnesses of the times, it means observing the vanishing of what was felt as a unique presence. The annual conferences had a special aura from the start—meetings of American and European minds in search of common formulas, if not political solutions, for what needed to become explainable to political audiences that had just lived through the second Berlin crisis and the Cuban missile crisis.[1]

The *Internationale Wehrkunde-Begegnung* and its successor, the Munich Security Conference, have prevailed as a seemingly indispensable platform for exchange in the political universe of discourse. When it was initiated in the early sixties, defense policy was a top priority within domestic politics. Yet at the same time issue formation became more complex along with the increasingly direct involvement of European allies, and the Federal Republic of Germany found itself in the middle of the intense debates that ensued after the second Berlin crisis and the Cuban missile crisis. It took creative private initiatives, and it needed the informal, competent involvement of politicians and key experts from allied countries, above all the United States,

▲

Fred Ikle, Ewald-Heinrich von Kleist, and
Franz-Josef Strauss (from left to right) at the 1986 conference

Great Britain, and France—inspired by the longstanding British and American culture of public discourse. The first *Wehrkunde* conferences were thus a sort of cultural pioneering.

Public discourse on war and peace is dependent on cultural conditions. The World War I experience had led to the foundation of the Council on Foreign Relations in the United States and Chatham House in Great Britain. In both countries, postwar reflections cumulated in great political and strategic literature, and institutionalized public discourse through new academic endeavors fertilized the political culture in both countries and beyond. There were also beginnings in Germany before they were exiled, only to enrich the US discourse on war and peace.

The world after World War II was very different. Destruction and fatigue in Europe combined with a United States that was inclined to both retreat again and to shape global structures toward "a world environment in which the American system could survive and flourish."[2] The challenges facing the US and, in different ways, Europe presented an unprecedented combination of systemic global competition, a global reconstruction of trade and financial relations, the European and German divide with the peer countries opposed and at the time deeply entangled, and the advent of nuclear weapons in search of strategic and political concepts. Prudent advice and public discourse were badly needed.

It required above all farsighted former military leaders assembling the experience from World War II and new technology, yet it was not until the late fifties and early sixties that the new thinking on strategic competition under uncertainty met the public, which adapted only slowly to the new political currencies. While deterrence was primarily about reassuring allies, the public and domestic politics were divided over tactical orientations toward the East-West competition.

In Europe, only Great Britain had close links to US decision-making, although recovering continental nations felt affected. NATO was virtually run by US bureaucracies. Transatlantic exchanges had little more than restricted and largely one-sided official channels. Informal dialogues across the Atlantic remained scarce, although since the Suez Canal crisis political consultation had been acknowledged as imperative.

It was the achievement of a few individuals that led to the foundation of the Institute for Strategic Studies (ISS) in London in 1958—inspired by the Anglican Church and realized above all by Alastair Buchan and supported by Michael Howard and other evolving "nuclear strategists"—in the spirit of Edward Burke. "In the intercourse between two nations ... the secret, unseen, but irrefragable bond of habitual intercourse holds them together even when their perverse and litigious nature sets them to equivocate, scuffle, and fight about the terms of their written obligations."[3]

The debate spread to continental Europe inspired by Raymond Aron in France and Wilhelm Cornides in Germany. And it initiated a dialogue with counterparts in the United States, where an increasing number of new foreign and defense policy institutes was beginning to immerse into public discourse after having achieved preliminary conceptual and institutional foundations. A new platform evolved in Western Europe, where officials in uniform and without from both sides of the Atlantic could enter debates and exchanges on common approaches without prohibitive prior commitments.

Germany was then in the middle of all central controversies—systemic competition, European and German division, and nuclear deterrence in search of minimal European participation. With the emergence of arms control approaches in 1960, a new political language developed that was more inviting for Europeans than nuclear strategy and which allowed a conceptual approach to the mix of structural political and nuclear strategic matters.

In Germany, Wilhelm Cornides had founded the Deutsche Gesellschaft für Auswärtige Politik (German Council on Foreign Relations) and a top-level study group with the participation of politicians from all major parties, the relevant governmental segments, and from research and the media. Fritz Erler was the pace-setting chairman, followed by Helmut Schmidt. For several years, this group served as a main driver in German policymaking on matters relating to East-West, transatlantic, and European matters. It led to the foundation of the Stiftung Wissenschaft und Politik (German Institute for International Security Affairs, SWP), which increasingly became one of the major integrating mechanisms in the West. In 1963, Ewald von Kleist founded a forum for having policymakers, analysts, and media representatives from both sides of the Atlantic meet annually to review priorities, choices, and visions ahead: the *Internationale Wehrkunde-Begegnung* thus widened public interest and debate in and about Germany.

Throughout the five decades since this forum has developed, its attendees have changed, and its agendas have of course been driven by events. But there has been something special about *Wehrkunde* that differs from any other public discourse. A strategic community developed around Ewald von Kleist—a charismatic figure, known for having been ready to sacrifice his life to end the Hitler regime. The *genius loci* of Munich worked. It fostered lively and public exchanges between fragmented, segmented, and dispersed actors—particularly important for Germany, which was lacking the tradition of public discourse and in fact the culture of public debate of major capitals like London. Moreover, *Wehrkunde* sought to be up-to-date without itself engaging in problem solving. It brought together opinion leaders and leading problem solvers to provide opportunities for explaining and winning arguments with political impact. Typically, participants positioned themselves in view of evolving major political debates or indeed opportunities to shape political agendas for the months, if not years, to come.

This would not have been possible in the fifties. In the early sixties—that is, after the second Berlin crisis, the Cuban missile crisis, the beginnings of strategic dialogue between the United States and the Union of Soviet Socialist Republics and, oddly, the building of the Berlin Wall—a somewhat precarious normalization had developed. As Walter Lippman observed at the time: "The Europeans believe that the East-West political stalemate which results from the nuclear deadlock is not soon going to be broken, and that therefore while there will be no nuclear war, and no small conventional wars about Berlin and Germany, nothing constructive and large can be negotiated either."[4]

Global affairs had thus reached a certain level of stability and dependability of the status quo, resulting from a combination of an increasingly controllable stalemate in peer relations and regional conflicts that had largely been suppressed by the strategic conditions of peer competition. Domestic politics in Europe and to a degree in the US was thus evolving along fairly stable dividing lines between support for deterrence versus détente and for Atlanticism versus European primacy. The formation of movements was driven by controversies over mostly abstract and hypostasized notions about relations with the USSR and/or relations within the Alliance. Given these domestic dimensions of the debates, issues of strategic policy could nevertheless become headline topics and at times forge domestic outcomes. Compared with the current public ranking, defense policy remained a top priority, not least importantly mirrored in budgetary decisions.

Informal exchanges thus became critically important, providing decision-makers with a new platform for public diplomacy. *Wehrkunde* played a rather unique role almost from the outset in that it involved key decision-makers from both sides of the Atlantic with confidentiality and yet with intended publicity. It took Ewald von Kleist to create an unmistakable aura, early on supported by an American "co-organizer," usually from the US Senate.

There are various ways to look back at those fifty years to evaluate the role of this impressive sequence of meetings of minds, to highlight meetings at critical watersheds, to retrieve episodes of the Cold War in the light of *Wehrkunde* debates, to give credit and praise to the founder and his charisma and unimpeachable credibility, or to discuss the importance of this conference tradition as an essential part of the public discourse on nuclear policy that had spanned a major part of the Cold War.

This essay seeks to review how the public discourse on nuclear policy became a pivotal driver. The annual event in Munich has time and again generated political impulses, political bridge-building, and embryonic solutions to contested issues in this vein. *Wehrkunde* became a kind of transatlantic *agora*.

In hindsight, it is an unprecedented cultural phenomenon how the world public avoided thinking about nuclear weapons. During the formative years of the Cold War, neither political theory, international law, philosophical ethics, nor theology provided a framework for judging the political role of the new means for strategic action that had been demonstrated over Hiroshima. It had ended the horrors of the war in the Pacific, and the public response was captured by what Tom Schelling some twenty-five years later called "the tradition of non-use," one that in McGeorge Bundy's words "has strengthened with each decade."[5]

Nuclear weapons became a unique background factor amidst the tectonic changes following World War II—reassuring for some and downplayed by others. The amazing fact was that the huge political shadow of nuclear weapons notwithstanding, it was precisely their constraining effect—over time becoming the basic concept of deterrence—that allowed a degree of normalcy in the political conduct of the new dominant powers amid a global systemic competition, an evolving military confrontation without precedent, and a regional division in Europe that was bound to harden by the way the USSR and the US were entangled and tied to that regional context. The problem was, in the words of an authority on nuclear fears, "that thinking remained stuck in old patterns, and would continue there except when overwhelming new facts forced it into new paths."[6]

This normalcy, however, implied that nuclear weapons were in the hands of political authorities, desperately in need of control and yet bound to proliferate, albeit at a much slower pace and with lessening impact than expected in the early days. Yet the nuclear competition between the US and the USSR introduced the challenge of comparative risk-taking into the dynamics of the great power competition—first within the European context and eventually in direct bilateral strategic relations.[7]

Wars by proxy involving the two peer countries added a degree of reality to nuclear deterrence, exacerbated by the direct and precariously asymmetric military confrontation in Central Europe. Political choices became unavoidable. European countries depended on US protection and were prone to become victims should competition between the US and the USSR get out of control and escalate. They were thus seeking some sharing of responsibility for the control and use of nuclear capabilities.

Unlike the fifties, the more erratic phase of the Cold War, exacerbated apprehensions about nuclear risks were to be reconciled with an increasing expectation of political normalcy. In retrospect, the dual crisis over Berlin and missiles on Cuba did in fact represent the watershed in the drama of the US-Soviet competition over Europe. Yet given the complexities on both sides and the need for establishing confidence and dependable institutions, it took another thirty years before it could be seen to have been the change in the course of events of the Cold War.

While the fifties involved competition over positioning in what was perceived as a secular competition of public discourse on nuclear policy, during the following three decades it became ever more important and eventually offered key boards for influencing the public on the "other side." Within the "troubled alliance," controversies over how to reconcile détente with deterrence, extended deterrence with stability, European strategic freedom to act with alliance cohesion, et cetera, increasingly entered the agendas of domestic politics. A universe of nuclear discourse evolved, and a sort of meta-level of nuclear policy moved into the center of political controversy.

Nuclear deterrence thus developed into both a political currency and a political language for coping with what was prohibiting the kind of unequivocal commitments and decision-making that would seem to be imperative in view of the monumental risks involved. While strategic analysis required complex theoretical systems that allow evaluating choices and dealing with uncertainties, it was bound to enter the political discourse, and indeed it did. Throughout the Cold War, three types of hypothetical reasoning became part of the political discourse: (1) All things, including conventional armament and warfare, would continue as if nuclear weapons did not make a difference, in other words the very capabilities that made "normal" conduct possible in the first place; (2) if deterrence failed, nuclear warfare would still serve overriding political objectives, even though mutual deterrence was based on the expectation of ultimate mutual annihilation; and (3) extending nuclear protection to third countries would maintain sufficient credibility and thus provide reassurance, although if credible it exposes the protector to existential risks.

No political calculus was able to avoid the consequences of these three hypothetical approaches that dominated in large measure the Cold War years and led at best to what Henry Kissinger called "constructive ambiguity." At a few junctures it could indeed have gone in very different directions.[8]

The year 1983 is a case in point. NATO conducted its Able Archer exercise, and the United States was conducting the even more ambitious Proud Prophet exercise—both involving Pershing II missiles deployed in Germany.

The Soviet side tended toward nervous responses. Yet on the political plane, the eventual deployment of Pershing II missiles in Germany and the subsequent federal election won by Helmut Kohl over this very issue was seen by Mikhail Gorbachev as the last and lost option to influence the European public by coercive nuclear diplomacy—backed by the preceding SS-20 deployment that was designed to hold Europe hostage as a step toward disconnecting Western Europe from US protection.

Few, if any, decision-makers had the full picture at the time. Nor would the prevailing political jargon have allowed reconciling political and operational considerations in the pursuit of political strategy. Never has military jargon played a bigger public role than throughout the nuclear era. It served consensus building and thus public support and sustainability. It was conducive to pursuing the processes that have produced Europe's recovery.

On domestic levels it allowed degrees of bipartisanship, although differences over deterrence and how to deal with the Soviet Union defined political positioning. Within the Atlantic alliance it provided the glue between partners who were exposed to very different roles, risks, and opportunities. It eventually provided enough of a common language between the declared antagonists, although for both sides it related to the most existential risks. And finally, like in other areas of novel challenges, nuclear learning produced high levels of expertise that required its own language, and the more joint expertise developed, the more the intrinsic confrontational nature vanished to be superseded by concepts of stability and parity.

Expertise on nuclear strategy was followed by moral reflection. Shared reflections by officials and experts, spreading to media and politics, generated a universe of discourse that gave nuclear deterrence and the management of nuclear stability its role in how political structures and processes evolved under conditions of extreme uncertainty.

A seeming paradox is that nuclear learning had reached its level of maturity when the Cold War was ending. At this stage nuclear policy had less to do with the physical weapons than with the images they aroused, that is with old, autonomous features of our society, our cultures, and our psychology. To become politically consequential, big "public splashes" such as the one made by President Reagan's Strategic Defense Initiative (SDI) speech became instrumental. Yet as soon as the Cold War was over, they had and have little or no value, except when new players threaten to jeopardize this state of nuclear tranquility by assertive efforts to gain recognition of their status as a nuclear weapons state. Past experience would suggest, however, that the proliferation phase rather than the actual possession of nuclear weapons offers political leverage. In effect, the maturity of coping with nuclear risks and options together with asymmetric developments of economic and social conditions in the Soviet orbit, within the Atlantic alliance, and between the two thus turned out to be a decisive factor in how the Cold War ended.

Could the Cold War competition and its nuclear dimensions have been avoided by some political short-circuiting, echoing Kant's dictum that good will should have done, but did not, what sheer helplessness finally has achieved? But controlling nuclear weapons under conditions of political competitiveness that did not originate from the existence of nuclear weapons means sustained work: to ensure control and technical reliability, build military and political structures for their handling, cope with proliferation to more independent potential users, and pursue silent competition with the opponent over denying versus achieving degrees of flexibility and freedom of strategic actions under conditions of mutual deterrence.

This competitive process focused on comparative risk-taking and actually drove both horizontal and vertical nuclear proliferation. In fact, in various critical states of imbalance political payoffs were slim or nonexistent, such as during the first Berlin crisis, when the city was surrounded by Soviet forces with only symbolic US forces left in Germany and US nuclear capabilities almost nonoperable. However, at times armament moves were intended to drive the opponent into self-deterrence: the SS-20 deployment is a case in point to impress on Western publics its indefensibility and trigger public movements to prevent responses. So was the US SDI that led Soviet leaders to conclude that the military-technology race cannot be won under worsening economic conditions.

In other words, while it was not a strictly interactive process, denial or response options or the creation of flexibility in response had critical importance for the political competition. The arms competition and its central nuclear dimension represented a key element in the ongoing political competition. In Hannah Arendt's words, it was a kind of "hypothetical warfare," that is, a sequence of virtual wars. This was not helplessness but persistent work on many levels.

Nuclear weapons thus do serve political purposes. Both sides were increasingly committed to develop some sort of stability that would favor their own political objectives, the USSR even more clearly than the US. But in the end, the USSR and its European empire collapsed; Russian forces were withdrawn without a shot fired.

Eventually, nuclear arms control became the currency and the language that served both ends—political normalcy and process management. The actual outcome of the Cold War, however, still needs a different interpretation, and it should be reconstructed before the Cold War has vanished into history. Future strategic behavior will be difficult to be guided and shaped unless the "relevance of the past" is understood in terms of its origins, its dynamics, and its outcomes. Today, the public ranking of defense and nuclear deterrence is minimal. So is the intensity of the public discourse, except in cases of political ostracism through "investigative journalism." By the same token, the nature of the Munich Security Conference has changed. It has become a political calendar event, routinized, with wide participation, providing stages for politicians and addressing "what the world offers up." And it no doubt provides a unique network and diplomatic niches that are hard to overestimate. However, in the years to come, the conference could in fact once again play a pivotal role if it were—as it has begun to do with its Core Group Meetings—to engage in agenda-building and political strategy development.

The *Wehrkunde* meetings and their successors have changed profoundly along with the changing strategic circumstances.

- During the sixties, key decision-makers from core member states within the Alliance met head on to judge projects like the NATO multilateral force or the Non-Proliferation Treaty (NPT) with "external" experts.
- During the seventies, the in-house capacities of governments had significantly increased, thus changing the chemistry of the meetings along with increasing US-European tensions.
- During the eighties, apprehension across the Atlantic grew, and *Wehrkunde* became part of the political process, driven by the deep controversies over nuclear deployment.
- During the nineties, outreach to Eastern Europe and the search for a new rationale for the Alliance dominated and led to the widening population of the meetings.
- During the first decade of the twenty-first century, the various consequences of 9/11 shaped the agendas, and, in the absence of common projects and with the growing size of the meetings, positioning became the name of the game with staged performers rather than heated interaction.

The potential for a productive future role is there. And so is the need for it. To mention just three key issues that are likely to shape future Munich Security Conference agendas:

- European defense in a future global strategic environment;
- the strategic US-Chinese relationship in an increasingly competitive global context; and
- coping with non-declared nuclear weapons states: prospects for constraints and deterrence.

Positioning, like on interventionism, will not suffice. The key lesson from the Cold War is that avoiding war between major and competing powers is the overriding common interest, but below rules of stability military power is pivotal in view of an increasingly competitive global strategic environment. With new players involved, the conditions for reconciling requirements of stability, and the challenges of complex competitiveness need to be reinvented under changing circumstances. New kinds of political solutions will become essential. And an increase in public attention and strategic outlooks will be needed. It will ensure rich agendas at the Munich Security Conference in the years to come, as it has time and again over the last fifty years.

Uwe Nerlich is a Wehrkunde loyalist, attending the conference more than forty times. He is director of the Centre for European Security Strategies (CESS) in Munich. He was a member of the board of the German Institute for International and Security Affairs (Stiftung Wissenschaft und Politik) and senior vice president of IABG.

Notes

1   A comprehensive history of the Cold War is still missing, in particular in view of large numbers of recently declassified documents from the Department of Defense, the Central Intelligence Agency, NATO, and so on. For a brilliant account of how the various levels of the competition were interrelated throughout the Cold War, see Gordon S. Barrass, *The Great Cold War: A Journey through the Hall of Mirrors* (Stanford: Stanford University Press, 2009).

2   United States Department of State, Planning Staff, National Security Council Paper NSC-68, *United States Objectives and Programs for National Security,* April 7, 1950.

3   Edward Burke, *Letters on a Regicide Peace,* cited in Alastair Buchan, *Power and Equilibrium in the 1970s* (New York: Praeger, 1973), 53.

4   Walter Lippman, *Western Unity and the Common Market* (Boston and Toronto: Atlantic Little Brown, 1962), 6.

5   McGeorge Bundy, *Danger and Survival: Choices about the Bomb in the First Fifty Years* (New York: Random House, 1988), 587.

6   Spencer R. Weart, *Nuclear Fear: A History of Images* (Cambridge: Harvard University Press, 1988), 422.

7   See Uwe Nerlich, "Theatre Nuclear Forces in Europe: Is NATO Running Out of Options?" in Kenneth A. Myers, ed., *NATO, the Next Thirty Years: The Changing Political, Economic, and Military Setting* (Boulder: Westview Press, 1981), 63–93.

8   See the thoughtful comments by Hannah Arendt in the introduction to her book *On Revolution* (New York: Viking Press, 1963).

"The Shorter the Range, the Deader the Germans"

Egon Bahr

The German word *Wehrkunde* sounds old-fashioned. In Plato's *The Republic,* Martin Luther came across the tripartite division of social classes into the appetitive, the logical, and the spirited, the last of which is known in German as *Wehrstand.* Even before that, this Middle High German word took on the meaning "to defend oneself" via the medieval tournaments of the time. I do not know who coined the term *Internationale Wehrkunde-Begegnung,* the name by which the Munich Security Conference was first known. For me it was synonymous with Ewald von Kleist, and not because of his historic family name. Rather, I saw in him the young officer who was prepared to blow himself up with Hitler and who, very fortunately, escaped the fury directed against the survivors of the July 20, 1944 plot. Here was a man who represented the other, better Germany to the outside world, without arrogance but inviolable in the firmness of his stance, from which he observed the power and interests of allies and adversaries; a man who was always glad to be German and who did not lose sight of the smaller part of that divided country.

He once said the following in an interview: "There are a number of people who are great idealists but simply do not have both feet on the ground. Then,

▲
Ewald von Kleist (center) and Manfred Wörner (fourth from right) at the 1986 meeting

quite the opposite, there are the cool calculators. A mixture of the two is almost unheard of. Graf Stauffenberg was one of those rare examples. An ardent idealist with incredible charm but quite matter of fact, as we would now say; quite clear and precise. This mixture of hot and cold, as it were, exerted an enormously attractive influence on me, the like of which I rarely experienced again in my life. A quite unique person."

That was a self-portrait. I came to know Ewald von Kleist after he had founded the *Internationale Wehrkunde-Begegnung* in 1963, and I remain deeply indebted to him for the discussions that we had outside the conference. His analyses were valuable and provided orientation for a self-confident way of thinking.

The Berlin Wall was built in 1961, and the four victors demonstrated at the time that the Germans, on both sides, were the objects of their power and inalienable rights. Then, two years later, came the modest, tentative beginnings, when we in West Germany started to participate knowledgeably in defense matters, although we did not have sovereignty over Germany and Berlin. At any rate, it was a sign of naturally growing self-confidence that from those beginnings emerged a security conference that is now emblematic of an exchange of views on foreign and security policy and has grown annually, even beyond Europe.

Looking back over the past five decades, what stands out are the enormous changes. The Soviet Union no longer exists, there is no more Warsaw Pact. The division of Germany has ended. China has grown to be a major nuclear power and holds the largest dollar reserves. It will probably overtake the United States in economic terms. India and Pakistan have nuclear weapons, and North Korea is handled with kid gloves now that it has demonstrated its nuclear capability, however limited. In 1963, the names Barack Obama and Vladimir Putin were still unknown, even to the population of their respective countries. Both of those countries are now weaker and have to turn to Asia, a continent with a growing population, growing economic power, growing performance, and a growing hunger for raw materials, a continent with unresolved territorial claims and without the stability that Europe's policy of détente created for the Old Continent.

Above all, it seems to have been forgotten that the two presidents, George Bush senior and Mikhail Gorbachev, were the only leaders to get rid of the nuclear medium- and short-range missiles they had previously brought to Europe. Moreover, they both had the power to reach agreement on the biggest conventional arms reduction treaty in history and to establish the security structure for a united Germany, without asking François Mitterrand, Margaret Thatcher, Helmut Kohl, or Erich Honecker. However, once they had completed this Herculean task, they lacked the power to foresee that, just a year later, the Soviet Union would no longer exist. The Munich Security Conference need not feel any shame that it had no idea what the future would bring in 1989.

What surprises me is how many well-known figures from the past have survived into the new era. The perennial worries about an existential NATO crisis are now gone. There were internal discussions in the West following the American change of strategy from massive retaliation to flexible response and France's sudden decision to withdraw from military integration in the Alliance. I admit my error, namely thinking that a pan-European security structure would be conceivable without the Warsaw Pact but also without NATO. Today, NATO is not called into question, either in the West or in the East. The stabilizing guarantee provided by the United States through its presence in Europe also ensures that a politically and economically strong Germany can develop neither military nor territorial ambitions, however improbable that may be.

In the meantime, NATO has decided on a new strategy. It has thereby become, more than ever, an American instrument with multilateral appendages. Militarily, it has become weaker since Washington decided to seek differing coalitions of the willing for different actions, even if they are not members of the Alliance. The political problems of expansion have largely been overcome, as indeed has the need for unanimity, which appeared indispensable during the East-West conflict.

In Munich, I expressed the positions held by the Social Democratic Party of Germany (SPD) in three speeches between 1985 and 1989. If Ronald Reagan and Mikhail Gorbachev reached agreement on the demand for the wholesale abolition of nuclear weapons, why should the SPD demand any less?

New threats have almost allowed those debates to fall silent. US attempts to put the Maginot Line into space in order to become invincible once more were abandoned in favor of new medium-range weapons, against which Soviet short-range weapons were stationed in the German Democratic Republic (GDR). The two major powers had created the opportunity for themselves to protect their sanctuaries and, if necessary, restrict the nuclear fireworks to the two German states before stopping, terrified. Whether they would succeed in this, we would never find out. At the 1985 Munich conference, Alfred Dregger of the Christian Democratic Union and I, to the great amazement of the foreign participants, came to the same conclusion: "The shorter the range, the deader the Germans." It may not have been proper German, or proper English, but it was catchy and, what is more, it was right.

We had learned from former US Secretary of State Cyrus Vance that there were chemical weapons, that is to say American chemical weapons, only in the Federal Republic and there were no such Soviet weapons in the GDR, and that a nuclear-weapon-free corridor with a total width of three hundred kilometers, as proposed by the Palme Commission, would be in line with US interests.

No nuclear weapons on the soil of states that have none—that was a logical but at that time unrealistic conclusion. Yet as early as in 1985 it could be said from experience, and not foresight: "The technological and scientific development was moving toward weapons systems that are increasingly beyond control. The history of arms control negotiations shows that it is easier to develop new weapons systems than to have political control of them. Scientific and technical development is faster than the ability of politicians to conclude limiting or stabilizing agreements. Science and technology are always ahead of politics. At some point, the moment must come when politics creates for itself the time and space not to be overtaken once again."

Politics is on the point of becoming hostage to military technical development. That was true in the past with respect to the lack of coherent negotiations on space weapons, on strategic missiles, and on tactical missiles with conventional weapons. It is still true today with respect to the issue that the two major powers forgot in 1989. There are still twenty nuclear bombs in Germany that are to be flown by an out-of-date squadron (and for what purpose?). In addition, there is the nuclear missile defense project in Poland with radar support in the Czech Republic. Both topics should have been settled between Obama and Putin in St. Petersburg, after Edward Snowden had revealed new US abilities of global control and data collection, and thus new military and economic dimensions. Obama's reaction was, first, to cancel the meeting, and then, the willingness to speak about a more cooperative approach towards Syria for twenty minutes.

It was not so much the civil war in Syria as the use of toxic gas, which had been prohibited for ninety years, that attracted the keen interest of world politics and diverted it from Europe. In that context, the relationship between Washington and Moscow is among the longest and most successful in the history of the postwar era. Since John F. Kennedy and Nikita Khrushchev reached the unwritten agreement that no war should break out between their countries on account of the Berlin Wall or a divided Germany and divided Europe, the two sides have conducted themselves responsibly. The agreement between Obama and Putin on the margins of the G20 summit in St. Petersburg has reinforced these unique foundations and has apparently averted the risk of the unilateral use of external military force in Syria. It was true in the Cold War and it is true today, although no end is in sight. The nuclear shield across the Atlantic has changed from mutual deterrence to an instrument of common interest, notwithstanding all other divergent views.

It is in this situation that Europe wishes to define itself. I was shocked by how little had changed in over twenty-five years since my speech in Munich in 1987, when I said that "European self-assertion is a demand but not a reality. A world power like the US with its global interests and responsibilities is unlikely to act differently in future, specifically on the basis of the experience it has had with Europe in recent decades. The United States' strategic shield cannot be replaced by any European shield. To that extent it is impossible to see a time when the strategic powerlessness or the dependence of Europe on the US might change. Without the political willingness to take on the appropriate conventional responsibility for its security, we should stop talking about European self-assertion or an expanding European role within the Alliance."

Nuclear weapons make the issue more complex. Charles de Gaulle's insight into the character of nuclear weapons is probably accurate. No nuclear power will be prepared to share with another state the decision on the use of those weapons, which touches on the very existence of its own nation. It is impossible to eliminate the imbalance that resides in the fact that nuclear states decide on the fate of nonnuclear states; the opposite is never true. This can even be taken further: nonnuclear states will not even be given a right of veto against the use of nuclear weapons. Nonnuclear states will never be in a position to push the button, but why can't they be at the table where negotiations take place on field weapons and short-range missiles that affect them?

There will be no Europeanization of Franco-British nuclear weapons. There will be no European nuclear weapon and no European decision on the matter. In practice this means that the European pillar of the Alliance can be thought of only in conventional terms. Europe's self-assertion can only be organized if the independent sovereign decision on French and British nuclear weapons is not called into question. It is still true today that if Europe follows up on its decisions and wishes to achieve a certain capacity for action on foreign and security policy, it has to establish a conventional European army.

Egon Bahr served in numerous capacities in the German Federal Foreign Office, the Federal Chancellery, and as federal minister during the sixties and seventies. He was a key advisor to Willy Brandt.

NATO's Double-Track Decision, the Peace Movement, and Arms Control

Karl Kaiser

NATO's double-track decision of December 1979 to station cruise missiles and Pershing II missiles in Western Europe and simultaneously offer negotiations to the Soviet Union to reduce or eliminate long-range theater nuclear weapons stands out as one of the most controversial events in the history of the Alliance. To be sure, other controversies, such as the ill-fated neutron weapon and the notoriously difficult relationship between President Jimmy Carter and Chancellor Helmut Schmidt, had an impact on the events surrounding the double-track decision, as did the dramatic international developments of that time, notably the taking of American hostages in Teheran and the Soviet invasion of Afghanistan. Moreover, never before in the history of the Alliance did a protest movement of such magnitude oppose a decision by the governments, notably in Germany.

But the double-track decision was also one of the great moments in the history of *Wehrkunde,* today's Munich Security Conference. It provided the venue where under the wise chairmanship of Ewald-Heinrich von Kleist the protagonists of opposing opinions on these issues reasoned together in a civil manner sitting around a table (as was the custom then), united by

Karl Kaiser, Josef Joffe, and Jackson Janes (from left to right) at the 2013 Core Group Meeting in Washington the belief that whatever the differences between them, they shared the goal of preserving peace in a nuclear environment and of maintaining a strong US-European relationship as the foundation of the Alliance.

The Context

The double-track decision, though involving NATO as a whole, was primarily shaped by the United States as NATO's leader and West Germany as both a pivotal actor and the central theater of the East-West conflict. In Washington, epic bureaucratic battles were fought to determine American policy on these issues, notably under the Reagan administration. In Germany, Helmut Schmidt, himself a renowned expert on strategic affairs in his own right, had to reconcile the exigencies of national interest with maintaining a coalition government, all the while dealing with a divided Social Democratic Party (SPD) and domestic public. In fact, growing opposition from his coalition partner, the Free Democrats, and his own party on these issues was to eventually cost him the chancellorship.

There had been some disagreements between the American and German governments after Schmidt took over from Willy Brandt, but they had been manageable. In fact, Schmidt's relationships with President Gerald Ford and Secretary of State Henry Kissinger were close and characterized by friendship. However, this changed after Jimmy Carter took over the presidency in January 1977. Their relationship was tense from the beginning, since Schmidt had openly supported Ford in the election campaign, and substantive policy disagreements soon began to plague their relations. These ranged from American opposition to German sales of sensitive nuclear technology to Brazil and Argentina, American pressure on Bonn to stimulate the economy (the famed "locomotive theory"), to the neutron bomb, a project Schmidt had reluctantly supported against energetic protest from within his party and the public, only to learn that Carter had dropped the idea like a hot potato. The neutron bomb incident not only established the perception of Carter in Germany and Europe as being unsteady and unreliable; it jump-started the antinuclear peace movement in Germany that was supported by parts of the SPD. The party's general secretary, Egon Bahr, described it as "perversion of thinking."

When Carter, in this respect no doubt also encouraged by his national security advisor, Zbigniew Brzezinski, made an offensive policy on human rights a priority of his policy toward Moscow, basic differences on how to deal with the Soviet Union began to emerge. Schmidt and numerous

German Social Democrats considered some of these approaches to be devoid of realism, naïve, and even a potential threat to détente and a continuation of *Ostpolitik*. More than anything else, this difference in approach rendered dealings between the American and German government difficult throughout the controversies over the double-track decision.

The Road toward the Double-Track Decision

After some prodding by the German and other NATO governments, the Carter administration engaged the Soviet Union in negotiations on strategic nuclear weapons, culminating in SALT II with an agreement in principle as early as September 1977. Yet when the German chancellor heard the terms, he immediately raised objections to the administration's agreement not to deploy cruise missiles with a range of more than six hundred kilometers without getting any restriction in return on the new mobile Soviet SS-20 missile that was already being deployed in Europe and had a range of five thousand kilometers and three warheads. Though cruise missiles were not to become available for three years, Schmidt feared that this concession might prejudice the future and block development of a Western alternative to the growing threat of the SS-20. At the time, NATO did not possess any long-range theater nuclear forces (LRTNF) except nuclear-armed planes, which were vulnerable to Soviet air defense.

In Schmidt's opinion, the absence of viable Western LRTNF would "decouple" Europe from the strategic level of deterrence, thus raising the possibility of a war, including nuclear war, confined to Europe and, because limited, thereby more probable. He expressed his critique in a speech at the International Institute for Strategic Studies in October 1977, arguing that the parity between the US and the Soviet Union negotiated in SALT II would neutralize the strategic deterrent of the US and that consequently, the growing imbalance at the nonstrategic level would represent a threat to European security. Since the speech indirectly criticized Washington's negotiation approach and questioned the credibility of America's commitment to use its strategic arsenal for the defense of Europe, it greatly annoyed the administration. As an official put it to the author in Washington a few days after the speech: "Does he [Schmidt] realize how traitorous this is?"

The imbalance in the nonstrategic weapons area became an issue of intense diplomacy at the bilateral and NATO level. At the same time, developments around the neutron bomb and disagreements on economic policy were also plaguing relations between Washington and Bonn, but the administration eventually changed course and proposed including the SS-20 in negotiations with Moscow while expecting the European allies, notably Germany, to be willing to station LRTNF if necessary.

A "high-level group" in NATO agreed that Western LRTNF should be modernized, not to match the Soviet system in every respect but to provide a credible counterweight to the Russian systems by requiring a range to reach Soviet territory. The force was to consist of cruise missiles and a modernized version of the Pershing I that had been stationed in Germany with a range of 1,800 kilometers. At the same time, negotiations were to be offered to the Soviet Union that proposed including the SS-20 in a future SALT III agreement. A summit of the United States, Great Britain, France, and Germany in Guadeloupe in January 1979 agreed on this package in principle, although the Europeans were somewhat reluctant—France actually declined—to make firm commitments on stationing in case of a failure of the negotiations.

During the run-up to the NATO decision in December 1979, cooperation between the American and German governments was significant. Carter needed European support to overcome opposition by conservative senators against the ratification of the SALT II Treaty. Germany provided that support by declaring a package deal: no NATO decision without ratification of SALT II, which Carter used extensively in dealing with the Senate. Schmidt needed a clear commitment to negotiations, since he was facing rising opposition in his party and needed the SPD to support the decision at a forthcoming party conference. For the first time in the history of arms control, the NATO decision combined the threat of a new weapons system with an offer to negotiate, thus responding to those Germans and Europeans who were afraid that the issue could undermine détente and who wanted a continuation of an active *Ostpolitik*.

Implementing the Double-Track Decision and the Rise of the Peace Movement

Not surprisingly, the Soviet Union tried to prevent NATO's modernization plans. President Leonid Brezhnev traveled to East Berlin in October 1979 and delivered a speech in which he sharply criticized the Alliance's intention to introduce new weapons in Europe. He offered a reduction of medium-range Soviet systems if NATO abandoned its project as well as negotiations on reductions of LRTNF based on the principle of "equal security." His speech was obviously aimed at the deeply divided SPD, which was preparing a resolution for its forthcoming party congress, but failed to have the desired impact. The SPD endorsed the double-track decision but added the "zero solution" (of LRTNF on both sides) as a goal of the negotiations. (This had been considered unrealistic in earlier internal NATO deliberations, since it was assumed that Moscow would not totally abandon its LRTNF.) On December 12, the foreign and defense ministers of NATO finally approved the project.

But the international situation, already aggravated by the taking of American hostages in Tehran in November 1979, sharply deteriorated when in December the Soviet Union invaded Afghanistan in a major, carefully prepared military operation, the first outside the socialist camp since the end of World War II. It had a profound impact on internal Western and East-West diplomacy as well as on the increasingly volatile domestic politics around the double-track decision. It is in this context that the peace movement really took off. Amid strong American reactions to the Soviet invasion, calls for sanctions, and a boycott of the Moscow Olympics, European governments, the German government in particular, began to wonder whether the interaction between the superpowers might endanger the achievements and the future of East-West détente.

An atmosphere of pending catastrophe and doom increasingly gripped the public, particularly in Germany, and provided the driving philosophy of the peace movement. Analogies to the situation of 1914 were popular, and Chancellor Schmidt himself further stimulated spreading alarmism by issuing a warning of a third world war. The rhetoric of presidential candidate Ronald Reagan during the election campaign further strengthened European anxieties, notably his assertion of returning to a "policy of strength," planning to open negotiations with the Soviet Union only after America had overcome its shortcomings in tactical nuclear weapons. His election in November 1980 interrupted East-West negotiations, since the new administration first wanted to conduct a fundamental reassessment of arms control policy before approaching the Soviet Union, and to do so from a position of strength. Germany itself experienced a highly divisive election campaign in 1980 in which Franz-Josef Strauss, the candidate of the opposition, vigorously questioned the promises of détente.

The peace movement constantly grew in strength and turned from a formerly ecological movement to an antinuclear mass movement organizing a multitude of rallies all over the country. It was joined by numerous splinter parties of the left, including the communists, the Greens, and church groups. An appeal ("Krefelder Appell") organized by these groups to the German government to withdraw from the double-track decision and refuse any stationing attracted four million signatories by 1984 (the East German *Staatssicherheitsdienst* files later revealed that it had financed the appeal). Many SPD politicians sympathized with the peace movement or joined it. When in October 1981 it organized its largest mass rally with 300,000 participants in Bonn, to the great embarrassment of the Schmidt government, Willy Brandt, the chairman of the SPD, took part.

One of the leaders quite representative of the views of the movement was Oskar Lafontaine, chair of the SPD in Saarland (with whom the author exchanged several public controversies on these issues). His critique went beyond the double-track decision, accusing the United States of being the only force driving the nuclear arms race, citing as (highly disputable) evidence the assertion that the US had always been the first to introduce each new nuclear system, while the Soviet Union only reacted. Central to his critique and of the entire movement was the argument that nuclear deterrence is inherently dangerous, unstable, und could lead to a war of which Germany would be the first victim. In this respect, his argument found resonance in German society, which like other Western societies had difficulty understanding and accepting nuclear deterrence as a means to preserve peace. Of course, he and the movement also criticized elements of the double-track decision itself, for example an allegedly unacceptable shortening of the warning time for Moscow of the Pershing II, which, in fact, was not very different from the warning time for nuclear attacks on Washington from Soviet submarine-launched missiles.

At the core of the controversies around the double-track decision was not so much the question of whether or not the Soviet Union would be able to wage a nuclear war, which in view of the risks was improbable anyhow, but the future of the West European political system. If, as a result of these controversies, the established cooperation between the US and Europe had been undermined or destroyed, new dependencies on Moscow would have emerged in which Soviet nuclear weapons superiority would have become a means of political influence and pressure over Western Europe. The peace movement simply ignored this political question and exclusively focused on nuclear weapons, as did those parts of the SPD that joined it.

The Reagan administration was deeply divided over future policy on LRTNF, and its rhetoric no doubt fired up the peace movement. Inside the bureaucracy, powerful voices argued that modernization should have priority before negotiations were to begin. The European allies, however, demanded a resumption of negotiations on the double-track decision, and the administration finally came to an agreement with Moscow to restart negotiations in the fall of 1982. But they made no progress. Reacting to growing opposition to the double-track decision within the SPD and also to some of its economic policy positions, the FDP had left the coalition and switched sides. And on October 1, 1982, in its vote of "constructive no-confidence" the German parliament replaced Helmut Schmidt with Helmut Kohl as chancellor.

The new government basically implemented the policy for which Schmidt had paid such a high price. Moscow had hoped that internal resistance to the double-track decision in Germany would prevail. As Yuli Kvitsinsky, the Soviet negotiator on LRTNF, once laughingly told the author: "You're never going to make it!" In November 1983, the German parliament voted in favor of a stationing and negotiations, but it took until March 1985 for negotiations on LRTNF, now called intermediate-range nuclear forces (INF), to be resumed. The immensely intricate negotiations did not produce a result. In the end it required two game changers to do that: Ronald Reagan, who was basically skeptical of nuclear weapons, and a courageous Mikhail Gorbachev. In December 1987 they signed the INF Treaty, which eliminated all nuclear weapons with a range of between five hundred and five thousand kilometers. It was the first genuine disarmament measure between East and West. Helmut Schmidt's perseverance was rewarded, albeit belatedly. It was Gorbachev who once remarked that for Moscow, the initial double-track decision was the beginning of the end of a Soviet policy that conceived of security exclusively in the context of a costly arms race.

The Role of *Wehrkunde*

When Ewald-Heinrich von Kleist created the *Wehrkunde* conference in the early sixties, he undoubtedly wanted to create a better understanding for problems of peace and security among the elites of Germany, which was not only growing in economic and political importance but was a country on whose soil East and West confronted each other and thus had a very special interest in security and the prevention of war. The conference indeed went on to provide the forum where the transatlantic community could constructively and repeatedly discuss three major problems throughout the Cold War.

First, President John F. Kennedy had initiated a new approach to the Soviet Union that aimed at seeking common ground between East and West for the sake of preserving stability under nuclear conditions. It eventually led in 1967 to NATO's adoption of the recommendation of the Harmel Report to add détente to the Alliance's goal of deterrence and defense. And since then, the difficulties of reconciling the politics of détente with the requirements of deterrence and defense had to be constantly reviewed and debated at *Wehrkunde*. Second, the changing circumstances of the arms process continually required discussion of how to adapt and relegitimize nuclear deterrence. Third, the conference had to deal with policy differences and problems within the transatlantic community, beginning with the Vietnam War in the sixties, which affected and potentially threatened the cooperative base of the US-European relationship.

The double-track decision reflected all three themes: it activated concerns and even fears that it could destroy détente, it raised complex questions of reconciling regional and strategic nuclear deterrence, and it created a wave of public criticism of the United States, indeed of anti-Americanism, which was considered a threat to the European-American relationship. As a result, the various aspects of the double-track decision dominated the deliberations of *Wehrkunde* for years. Unlike its globalized composition during the post-Cold War period, the participants then came only from NATO or Western countries. Moreover, the limited number of participants allowed for a relatively intimate style of discussion. Participants sat around tables, not only able to face each other but, more importantly, allowing immediate responses in give-and-take discussions.

The participants' positions on the issues of the double-track decision were often diametrically opposed and usually clashed with passion and vehemence in the public discourse outside the conference, but not so in the halls of the Hotel Bayerischer Hof. Kleist always radiated civility, politeness, and fairness in chairing the discussion. The model of this truly great personality with his natural authority made the participants adopt his style of discussion, so that the pros and cons of complex and divisive issues were debated in a rational and civil manner.

The conference therefore played a major role not only in clarifying these complicated issues among relevant elites but helped to maintain links across the inevitable divides, particularly with regard to maintaining a functioning and strong American-European and American-German relationship while facing a common adversary in an existential conflict. The composition of the conference, which consisted of ministers, officials, parliamentarians, think-tank experts, and journalists, had the dual effect of bringing a multitude of relevant aspects into the debate, thus guaranteeing a maximum of feedback into government activity, expert work, and public discourse. Finally, *Wehrkunde* made a major contribution to creating and strengthening a network of individuals—politicians, officials, experts, journalists—

who knew and respected each other independent of their possibly differing positions and who were therefore better empowered to maintain a strong transatlantic relationship as the basis of their common security.

Karl Kaiser was director of the Research Institute of the German Council on Foreign Relations, Bonn/Berlin, from 1973 to 2003. Since then he is adjunct professor of public policy at the John F. Kennedy School of Government and director of the Program on Transatlantic Relations of the Weatherhead Center for International Affairs, Harvard University.

Wehrkunde and the End of the Cold War

Richard Burt

Given the global character (and stature) of the Munich Security Conference, it is hard to remember that twenty-five years ago it occupied a very different niche. *Wehrkunde*, as it was universally called by its participants, was still, at its core, a German-American dialogue: while other attendees—mainly from NATO states—could be found prowling the corridors of the Hotel Bayerischer Hof, it was the West German and American defense establishments that dominated the dialogue. And that dialogue focused almost exclusively on the Soviet political-military threat. Issues like international terrorism, security and change in the Middle East, nuclear proliferation, and the rise of China and India would wait until a later day.

In the mid-eighties, the participants in Munich had a very different set of concerns. In late 1983, the United States had begun the deployment of Pershing II warheads in Germany and air-launched cruise missiles in Britain. The missiles were a counter to the earlier Soviet deployment of the SS-20, but more importantly, their deployment represented a significant political victory by NATO over a determined Soviet effort to divide the Alliance and what many analysts at the *Wehrkunde* meetings saw as Moscow's effort to achieve "escalation dominance" over the West. In this era at *Wehrkunde*, simple

▲
Richard Burt (right) and Paul Nitze (center) at the 1986 *Wehrkunde*

fifties-style "massive retaliation" was not sufficient; as NATO commander Bernie Rogers told *Wehrkunde* in 1983, NATO needed to not only modernize its nuclear deterrent, but President Ronald Reagan's "zero option" for intermediate nuclear forces meant that Western governments also needed to increase spending on conventional forces by 4 percent (in real terms) annually.

Indeed, American pressure for increased European defense spending became a permanent feature at the conference in the late eighties, with perhaps the strongest statements coming from members of the US congressional delegation, including Senator Bill Cohen and Representative Dan Quayle (both of whom apparently used the conference to prepare for higher-ranking political jobs in the nineties).

By 1985, the American drive for stronger conventional forces was complemented by another, far more controversial US policy initiative, the Strategic Defense Initiative (SDI), or "Star Wars." There was perhaps no more eloquent spokesman for the concept in Munich than Dr. Edward Teller, the self-described father of the H-bomb, who enthusiastically endorsed the idea of space-based systems capable of protecting the West from nuclear attack. Interestingly, unlike the goals of conventional force improvement or strengthened nuclear deterrence, "Star Wars" enjoyed few European adherents at *Wehrkunde.* Not surprisingly, the French defense minister, Charles Hernu, saw the concept as threatening France's deterrent, while Geoffrey Pattie, the British defense minister, questioned the cost of SDI. Senator Gary Hart was also a critic, as was SPD theorist Egon Bahr, a *Wehrkunde* regular, who propounded a concept of "shared security" with the Soviet Union rather than strategic defense.

As lively as this debate was, it was only a prelude to the debates at the meeting over the implications for the Alliance of Mikhail Gorbachev's arrival in the Kremlin. One of Gorbachev's first Western interlocutors, Canadian Prime Minister Brian Mulroney, told Ronald Reagan in 1986 that the new Soviet leader resembled "Brezhnev in a $1,000 suit." However, that certainly was not the view of Margaret Thatcher, who said that "we can do business" with this man. Gradually, as the press accounts of the 1987 and 1988 conferences indicate, there was a growing but grudging acceptance that Gorbachev offered the Alliance an opportunity for seeking cooperative solutions to European security problems. At the same time, the *Wehrkunde* debates during this period underscored the conceptual and political difficulties of transitioning from one security paradigm to another. The debates that took place on three separate—but related—issues also highlighted the difficulties of migrating away from the eighties consensus in the West on defense policy and posture.

The Reykjavik Summit of October 1986 came as a shock to security and defense analysts on both sides of the Atlantic. The willingness of the American and Soviet leadership to think big thoughts about arms control and security was something new. This "new thinking" was exhilarating to publics, especially in Western Europe, who were tiring of both the stress and the rhetoric of the Cold War. Thus, there was a keen sense of disappointment felt by many (including Secretary of State George Shultz) that in the end, Reykjavik did not produce an agreement. This sense of disappointment, however, was not in display at the Munich meeting in early 1987, when German Defense Minister Manfred Wörner warned of an "appeasement psychosis" in the West, and Assistant Secretary of State Richard Perle said that it was "absurd" to think that European security could be achieved without the threat of using nuclear weapons.

Second, the 1987 Intermediate-Range Nuclear Forces (INF) Treaty stimulated a lively discussion in Munich, when a variety of Europeans (who always seemed to support arms control in general) voiced misgivings that the treaty could weaken deterrence in Europe because it would ban the deployment of US INF missiles. Having fought so hard to get the Pershing IIs and cruise missiles in, the *Wehrkunde* "hard core" clearly had trouble with the idea of taking them out. American spokesmen (including myself) tried to settle these nerves by pointing out that the SS-20 was being removed and that a US nuclear presence would remain in Europe. During the course of this Munich debate it became clear to me that the Reagan-Gorbachev achievement highlighted another Cold War principle: while the Europeans did not like it when US-Soviet relations got too tense, they also got uncomfortable when the two superpowers seemed to get along too well.

Third, and finally, there was the rather absurd (at least from today's perspective) debate over short-range nuclear modernization at Munich in 1988. In the aftermath of the INF Treaty, German participants, such as Wörner, expressed concern over the "singularization" issue, the idea that with longer-range missiles removed from Europe, Germany faced a unique threat from Soviet shorter-range, forward-deployed missiles. The US response, as expressed by Secretary of Defense Frank Carlucci at Munich, was appreciative of the German concern. But the American solution to "singularization" was also unsettling to Chancellor Helmut Kohl and his foreign minister, Hans-Dietrich Genscher: Carlucci wanted to deploy a new, modernized Lance missile on German soil. After the agony of the INF debate in Germany some eight to ten years earlier, only a very conservative CDU constituency supported further nuclear modernization. Despite this, American representatives, such as Senator Bill Cohen, lectured their German counterparts: "Reject existentialism and Genscherism," he pleaded.

By the 1989 meeting, less than a year before the fall of the Berlin Wall, the US-European debate over deterrence, nuclear modernization, and, yes, "existentialism" was beginning to wind down. Interestingly, even before the collapse of the Soviet Union (two years away), American officials were focusing on threats beyond the Cold War. Secretary of Defense designate John Tower called on the allies to provide security assistance to pro-Western Middle Eastern countries, such as Egypt and Tunisia. Senator McCain, meanwhile, expressed concern over Libya's chemical weapons efforts and criticized West German technology exports to Iran. A new US-European security agenda was beginning to emerge.

The end of the Cold War, of course, did not mean the end of the German-American security debate. But it did force thoughtful people on both sides of the Atlantic to reexamine prevailing doctrines and continue the dialogue on new policy terrain. In the fall of 1996, Ewald-Heinrich von Kleist indicated that he would not be able to continue as chairman of the conference. Fearing that the meeting might not reconvene, I sent Chancellor Kohl a letter expressing concern that the absence of *Wehrkunde* would create an important hole in the European-American security dialogue and I convinced John McCain to also weigh in. Thankfully, the conference continued to play its unique role, addressing security issues from an increasingly global perspective. As it took on a broader and more complex agenda in the nineties and, under Horst Teltschik's leadership, into the twenty-first century, it would continue to perform its most important function: forcing security elites to question their assumptions. In this important sense, Ewald-Heinrich von Kleist's remarkable vision would continue to live on.

*Ambassador **Richard Burt** is managing director at McLarty Associates and US chair of the "Global Zero" initiative. He was the US chief negotiator in the Strategic Arms Reduction Talks with the former Soviet Union, US ambassador to the Federal Republic of Germany (1985–89), and assistant secretary of state for European and Canadian affairs (1983–85).*

Countering Nuclear Threats:
From Cold War *Wehrkunde* to Today's
Munich Security Conference

Sam Nunn

The *Internationale Wehrkunde-Begegnung*—the global security forum now known as the Munich Security Conference—has both influenced and paralleled my five decades of interest and involvement in the security field. At the helm at its founding in 1963, Ewald von Kleist was an inspirational figure and a hero—a man who through his leadership of this forum helped inspire, support, shape, and maintain NATO's firm and sustained response to the threat from the Soviet Union and the Warsaw Pact. He was also one of the first to recognize, in the early nineties, that the post-Cold War era presented both new challenges and new opportunities and that we must think anew. This remarkable forum has played an enormous role on numerous fronts during its five decades of influence. Let me relate just a few examples of its impact on security developments where I was directly involved.

One year before *Wehrkunde* initiated its rapid climb to become the world's leading forum for the exchange of ideas among policymakers, elected officials, and security experts, I made my first trip to Europe. The year was

Sam Nunn addressing the 2012 MSC

1962, and I was a twenty-four-year-old staff lawyer working for the House Armed Services Committee in the United States Congress. I happened to be on an Air Force trip to NATO bases during the Cuban missile crisis, perhaps the single most dangerous period of confrontation between the US and the Soviet Union during the four decades of the Cold War. President John F. Kennedy responded to the Soviet threat by imposing a naval quarantine around Cuba, and to the world's great relief, Soviet Premier Nikita Khrushchev ordered all Soviet missiles removed from the island, albeit reluctantly.

At one of the tensest moments in the confrontation, I was at Wiesbaden Air Force Base in Germany, the headquarters of US Air Forces Europe. There, I first was brought face to face with nuclear reality when the commanding general told me that if ordered to strike, he would have only a couple of minutes to get his forward-based aircraft launched with their nuclear payload. Because those planes were likely to deliver the first US weapons to their Soviet targets, the commander knew that they, in turn, would be the first to be targeted by the Soviets. It was during this period of maximum danger that I decided that if I could ever play a role in reducing nuclear dangers, I would make the effort.

Fast-forward to 1974: *Wehrkunde* had become the world's premier security forum, and I had become a US Senator from Georgia. It was more than ten years after the Cuban missile crisis, and I was on my first European-NATO trip since my election in 1972. By this time, I was well aware of *Wehrkunde* and von Kleist's leadership in strengthening the NATO Alliance in the post-Vietnam period. It was a time of considerable concern about the future of the Alliance. The concept and practice of nuclear deterrence by the United States and NATO—including the deployment of thousands of shorter-range American non-strategic (or "tactical") nuclear weapons in Europe—played a crucial role in NATO's strategy and defense posture. Several important points became evident to me during that trip:

NATO's conventional weaknesses combined with the enormous Soviet forward-based tank and artillery forces arrayed against NATO made front-line US and NATO commanders not only reliant on the first use of tactical nuclear weapons but, more dangerously, on their *early* first use. This was a very high-risk and dangerous policy for NATO, for all of Europe, and indeed for the Soviet Union and the Warsaw Pact. Because of the short range of these tactical nuclear weapons, it left the NATO Alliance reliant on a strategy of destroying the territory we were sworn to defend if a conflict occurred. The lack of conventional warning and decision time caused by the Soviet-Warsaw Pact forward-deployed heavy forces and NATO's early first-use strategy response made war—indeed nuclear war—more likely, whether by intent or accident.

Policy discussions at *Wehrkunde* around that time helped me formulate a report that I made to the US Senate Committee on Armed Services, in which I noted that that the NATO Alliance was in a "watershed period." Europe's conventional force capabilities at the time were sorely lacking, leading to frustration within the Alliance, particularly in post-Vietnam America. It was clear to me that the European allies would have to step up their efforts to improve their conventional defense capabilities and develop a long-term commitment to a strong European conventional defense, with the full support of the United States.

Based on my findings and considerable discussions with defense experts, I proposed two policy changes as amendments to the Senate Defense Bill. One amendment, which became law, would allow formation of a new US Army brigade in Europe, funded by reducing excessive support forces in Europe. My other proposal threatened partial withdrawal of US forces from NATO unless the European allies strengthened their own financial and security contributions. David Abshire, then US ambassador to NATO, was a strong proponent of the additional brigade, which he called the "good Nunn Amendment." He disagreed with the threat of partial withdrawal of US forces from Europe and labeled it the "bad Nunn Amendment." It did not become law. All of this was the subject of more than a few debates and discussions among friends and allies at the *Wehrkunde* during the mid-seventies. During this period, I considered each meeting to be crucial—both because of the ongoing Soviet-Warsaw Pact threat as well as the growing demands in the United States following the Vietnam War to bring the troops home unless our allies increased their own defense budgets. As I wrote in the 1974 Senate report:

The nuclear threshold in Europe is quite low. There is a considerable danger that tactical nuclear weapons would be used at the very outset of a war, leading to possible or even probable, escalation to strategic nuclear war. Our plan to use tactical nuclear weapons "as soon as necessary" is heavily emphasized—but as "late as possible" does not get enough emphasis. I believe that much more emphasis should be given to the latter.

The nuclear threshold is low because of the short time that NATO military commanders feel that they could fight conventionally, and because of the psychological reliance by Allied military and political leaders on a rapid American nuclear response. In a Warsaw Pact attack, the initial shock of conventional fighting, probably with some initial military setbacks, combined with the desire to assure a US nuclear commitment, could result in enormous and possible irresistible pressure to use nuclear weapons at the outset.[1]

Wehrkunde provided a crucial outlet for policy discussion and development among those of us who felt we must firm up the NATO alliance, firm up US-Europe cooperation, firm up our economic cooperation, and stand firm on a containment policy *vis-à-vis* the Soviet Union until, we hoped, the situation there one day would change. That day came much sooner than expected in the late eighties and early nineties with the reunification of Germany, the breakup of the Soviet Union, and the expansion of NATO and the European Union. *Wehrkunde* also made enormous changes, with Russia and former members of the Warsaw Pact becoming important participants in a much broader Euro-Atlantic dialogue.

In my mind, the key challenge in the wake of the breakup of the Soviet Union in the early nineties was how to safely secure and dismantle weapons of mass destruction and the infrastructure around them in Russia and other former Soviet states. During the Cold War, the world faced the high risk of nuclear confrontation—but also a high level of security around the weapons held by the two superpowers. Much of the security inherent in communist control disappeared with the end of the Cold War. We entered a new period of lower risk of all-out war but also low stability and a much higher risk of nuclear terrorism as ethnic, religious, and class conflicts took the place of global superpower rivalry.

During the course of these radical changes, Senator Richard Lugar and I, as well as many others, concluded that cooperation between Russia and the United States had to replace confrontation. We had to begin to act as partners in keeping the world and ourselves safe from the arsenals we had built.

To help secure those arsenals, Senator Lugar and I proposed offering funding and expertise to former Soviet states to help them decommission nuclear, biological, and chemical stockpiles, which could be targets for terrorists looking to steal weapons or the materials needed to make them. *Wehrkunde* was the essential forum where we could present our ideas and hopefully gain broad support from our European friends and allies. In 1992, the US Congress approved legislation for the program, and President George H. W. Bush signed the bill into law. The Cooperative Threat Reduction Program, known as Nunn-Lugar, is so far responsible for contributing to the deactivation and destruction of 7,601 nuclear warheads, 792 intercontinental ballistic missiles (ICBMs), 498 ICBM silos, 182 ICBM launchers, 33 nuclear-weapons-carrying submarines, and much more. The program continues to this day and must become a global program in the years ahead.

Under the dynamic and capable leadership of Wolfgang Ischinger, the Munich Security Conference continues to make important contributions toward avoiding, addressing, and mitigating urgent threats around the globe. One such effort came to fruition in 2012 with the release at the conference of the report of the Euro-Atlantic Security Initiative (EASI), a project sponsored by the Carnegie Endowment for International Peace under the leadership of Jessica Mathews. As the co-chairs of the commission that produced the report, Wolfgang, former Russian Foreign Minister Igor Ivanov, and I worked with senior officials from government, the private sector, and nongovernmental organizations to address the future security needs of the Euro-Atlantic region. This comprehensive report addressed military security, human security, economic security, and historical animosities and urged the leaders of the United States, Russia, and Europe to take specific, practical steps to build a more secure future. As the report states:

[W]e concluded that the only means to assure the long-term security of our peoples lies in building an inclusive, undivided, functioning Euro-Atlantic Security Community—a community without barriers, in which all would expect resolution of disputes exclusively by diplomatic, legal or other nonviolent means, without recourse to military force or the threat of its use. Governments within this community would share a common strategy and understanding in the face of common threats and a commitment to the proposition that the best and most efficient way to tackle threats, both internal and external, is through cooperation.[2]

Building on the foundation of the EASI report, Wolfgang, Igor, and I, joined by former UK Defense Minister Des Browne, formed a new group of more than thirty senior military, political, and security experts from the Euro-Atlantic region to develop a new and sustained approach to improving security in the region. Thanks to Wolfgang Ischinger's leadership, we were able to preview our report to the influential audience gathered at the conference in 2013 before releasing it six weeks later.

Our report, *Building Mutual Security in the Euro-Atlantic Region*, was released in April 2013.[3] We warn that twenty years after the end of the Cold War, there is still no security strategy for the Euro-Atlantic region. Filling the void is a corrosive lack of trust that is blocking progress on a range of security issues. This leads to increased risks and costs at a time of unprecedented austerity and fiscal demands across the region. Our report recommends a fresh approach that begins with a politically mandated dialogue among senior civilian and military leaders to engage in a set of practical, concrete steps on core security issues, including nuclear forces, missile defenses, prompt-strike forces, conventional forces, cyber security, and space. Together, the steps—to be taken over a period of years—could increase transparency, mutual understanding, decision time for political leaders in extreme situations, and mutual defense capabilities.

Today, the Munich Security Conference provides a platform for broad discussions on a new vision of Euro-Atlantic security, including how to address the ongoing security problems posed by proliferation, terrorist threats, vulnerable nuclear materials, missile defense disagreements, and regional conflicts, not to mention persistent mistrust, entrenched Cold War mindsets, and a lack of transparency and economic insecurity. Participants now include leaders from Eastern Europe, Turkey, the Baltic states, and Russia, among others, reflecting today's range of global security concerns as well as the promise of a more secure future.

The call for regional and global cooperation on security threats—and the development of concrete ways to get there—has been at the core of the Munich Security Conference's philosophy and its work since its inception. In Ischinger's highly productive tenure as chairman, he also has greatly broadened the scope of the issues addressed by the conference to include the impact of global economic forces, conflict in the Middle East and South Asia, emerging China, and the evolving nature of global threats. This is a crucial leap forward for the conference and ensures that it is well positioned to address the pressing security challenges that lie ahead.

Global cooperation and the kind of strong, bold leadership stimulated by the Munich Security Conference will be required to meet twenty-first-century threats and, ultimately, to fulfill Charles de Gaulle's vision of a Europe that stretches from the Atlantic to the Ural Mountains—a political and geographic space that includes Europe, Russia, and North America.

I am honored to have worked closely with the conference's esteemed leaders over the years, and I congratulate the Munich Security Conference on the occasion of its fiftieth anniversary.

Sam Nunn served in the United States Senate for twenty-four years and is a former chairman of the Senate Armed Services Committee. He is currently co-chairman and chief executive officer of the Nuclear Threat Initiative.

Notes

1 Senate Committee on Armed Services, *Policy, Troops and the NATO Alliance: Report of Senator Sam Nunn,* 93d Cong., 2d sess., 1974, 3.

2 *Toward a Euro-Atlantic Security Community, EASI Final Report* (Washington, D.C.: Carnegie Endowment for International Peace), February 3, 2012, carnegieendowment.org/2012/02/03/toward-euro-atlantic-security-community/9d3j, 7.

3 *Building Mutual Security in the Euro-Atlantic Region: Report Prepared for Presidents, Prime Ministers, Parliamentarians, and Publics* (Washington, D.C.: Nuclear Threat Initiative), April 2013, www.buildingmutualsecurity.org/

New Challenges after
the End of the Cold War

Why Didn't We Stop the Bosnia War Earlier? Thoughts and Lessons

Carl Bildt

Otto von Bismarck is often quoted as has having said that the issues of the Balkans are not worth the life of a single Pomeranian soldier. And as chancellor he certainly took a somewhat detached view of the region even as he hosted the crucially important Congress of Berlin in 1878.

When the *Wehrkunde* series of conferences started in the early sixties, I doubt that anyone paid much attention to the issues of the Balkans. These were the decades of the Cold War, and although Tito's Yugoslavia had been expelled from the Soviet bloc in 1948, attention was clearly focused on other issues. The Balkans were yesterday's news.

But this was to change dramatically as the Cold War faded away, the Soviet Union and its empire collapsed, and we suddenly had to search for a new order of peace and stability in Europe. The Balkans went from yesterday's to today's news with breathtaking speed. The last decade of the twentieth century turned into one of war in the Balkans in much the same way as the first decade of that century had been, and our policies struggled to understand new realities and handle challenges very different from the well-known ones of the Cold War years.

Carl Bildt, Stefan Kornelius, and
Manouchehr Mottaki (from left to right) at the 2010 MSC

The Balkans in general and Bosnia in particular became a defining experience for the new phase in international affairs that we were entering. The post-Cold War order in Europe was to a large extent to be shaped by the experiences of that decade.

The controversies over the decade of wars in the Balkans are still too raw to allow a detached analysis of the extraordinarily complex series of events that came to define the period. We will probably have to wait years before historians start to give us their more analytical perspectives on that period.

As *Wehrkunde* gave way to the Munich Security Conference, thus broadening its approach from defense to security, the issues of the Balkans were very much in the focus of the discussions. In modern mythology it is often claimed that "the hour of Europe" failed, and that it was only possible to end the wars of the region when a more robust—kinetic would be the word today—approach by the United States asserted itself.

If we look at the most protracted and most difficult of the conflicts—the war in Bosnia that raged from April 1992 to October 1995—there is little doubt that the advent of a more determined US diplomatic and military push from the summer of 1995 onwards made it possible to end the fighting and put the country on the path to peace.

Richard Holbrooke, who was certainly instrumental, gave an account of the drama of these months in his book *To End a War,* and I gave a slightly less dramatic account from a European perspective, also encompassing the difficult first years of peace implementation, in *Peace Journey—The Search for Peace in Bosnia.* But even more important than discussing, and trying to draw lessons from, the end of the war in Bosnia is to look at the failure to prevent it from breaking out in the first place—and to bring it to an end far faster than turned out to the case. Every war sooner or later comes to an end, but not all conflicts and challenges should turn into open war. The necessity of conflict prevention is the real lesson we need to learn from the decade of wars in the Balkans.

The recent publication of a large number of formerly classified US documents on the Bosnia conflict, primarily from the intelligence community but also from the high-level deliberations on the issues—*Bosnia, Intelligence, and the Clinton Presidency*—provides the debate with new material. Noticeable in these documents is how distant the US was from the issues when the storm clouds started to gather over Yugoslavia. The intelligence community wrote its papers, but high-level attention was obviously elsewhere, and there is hardly a trace of any effort to put together a true policy of conflict prevention in the regions.

The efforts by what was then the European Economic Community were, for obvious reasons, more energetic, initially under the Dutch presidency in the second half of 1991 with Peter Carrington as the lead personality, then under the succeeding Portuguese presidency and, from the London conference in the summer of 1992, with David Owen as the European Union representative working in tandem with Cyrus Vance representing the United Nations.

It remains a highly controversial issue to this day whether the EU decision to recognize the independence of Croatia and Slovenia in January 1992 fuelled the conflict or made it easier to rein it in. It was a decision to a large extent driven by Germany, with both the United Kingdom and France being hesitant, the UN secretary general openly critical, and the US in essence on the UN line. The controversy was hardly over the aim—that both Croatia and Slovenia were heading toward independence was hardly disputed anywhere, including Belgrade—but over whether a negotiated and comprehensive approach would have been possible and better.

In his detailed memoirs from this period, *Balkan Odyssey,* David Owen certainly talks of this recognition decision as "dangerous," but he believes that the biggest mistake was the failure in late 1991 to rule out any revision of the borders of what were then the six republics that made up Yugoslavia. Negotiated border adjustments could, he argues, have paved the way for a more peaceful breakup of the region.

But resistance to border adjustment was solid, and the reason for this was to some degree to be found in the parallel breakup of the Soviet Union. The Belavezha Accord of December 1991 had opened up the prospect of independence for all Soviet republics, but also made clear that it had to be within the then established boundaries, although the irrationality of some of them were obvious. There is little doubt, in retrospect, that this was a wise approach to the breakup of the Soviet Union. It did not prevent fierce fighting resulting in conflicts that remain unresolved to this day in the Transnistrian part of Moldova, in the Abchazia and South Ossetia regions of Georgia, as well as in Nagorno-Karabach in Azerbaijan, but it prevented the opening up of even more difficult issues, most notable of which is that of the Crimea.

The Badinter Arbitration Commission set up by the EEC took the same approach in Yugoslavia, and the door that David Owen would have liked to open up in order to resolve some of the most difficult issues was then definitely closed. Whether an approach that had paved the way for an agreement on boundary revisions would have made possible a comprehensive approach that would have prevented the open conflicts remains uncertain. I fail to see that the key issues of the Bosnian conflict would have been easier to solve, although the approach might have been productive in some other cases. The key failure in terms of conflict prevention, or early conflict termination, was clearly Bosnia.

In retrospect it is obvious that there was insufficient understanding of the complexity of the Bosnian situation in the key capitals, and one cannot avoid the impression that this contributed to them all stumbling into the Bosnian war.

The Bosnian Muslim leader Alija Izetbegović was among those opposing a premature recognition of the independence of Croatia, and he worked energetically to preserve some form of "light framework" that could prevent the confrontation between Croatia and Serbia, which he feared would otherwise threaten Bosnia. In his autobiographical notes *Inescapable Questions,* Izetbegović would later note that "the fate of Yugoslavia, and its dissolution, was not an inevitability; and dissolution itself, when it came about, could have developed quite differently."

When the issue of recognition of Croatia and Slovenia was off the table of EU leaders, and UN forces started to deploy in the "protected areas" in Croatia, attention turned to trying to see if Bosnia could be guided to a stable future under circumstances that President Izetbegović saw as increasingly dangerous. Tension had already been building up in the country, with Serbs setting up their autonomous areas and Croats claiming that Muslims upstream of the Drina River were in reality just Croats of another faith.

It came to the then Portuguese presidency of the EU in the first half of 1992 to take responsibility for a last-minute effort to prevent open conflict in Bosnia. The negotiations between the Bosnian parties undertaken by the EU, with José Cutileiro in the lead, in Lisbon and Brussels during the early months of 1992 were the last attempt to prevent the mounting tensions in the region from igniting all the volatile material of Bosnia. Its eventual failure made war inevitable. In March, however, the three key ethnic leaders of Bosnia signed to a plan that envisaged an independent and sovereign country organized in three essentially ethnic "cantons." But soon thereafter, the consensus around this plan collapsed.

The reasons for the failure remain controversial to this day. Fingers of accusation are pointed in different directions both within Bosnia and in the international community. However, it seems clear that different perceptions by the different actors in Bosnia of the attitudes of the key players in the international community played an important part in causing the collapse. And there is little doubt that different perceptions by the different actors involved in the policies of the different parts of the international community played a role in causing the collapse of Cutileiro's peace plan.

Overall, it is unfortunately obvious that the international community was insufficiently aware of the dangers, insufficiently united in its approach, and insufficiently determined in its efforts. By April 1992 the war in Bosnia was a fact, and it would last until the fall of 1995 and cost approximately 100,000 people their lives, drive millions from their homes, and cause massive destruction to a society that has yet to recover.

When the end came with the signing of the Dayton Agreement in December 1995, its essence was not dissimilar from what had been on the table in the Cutileiro peace plan nearly four years earlier—essentially, the three "cantons" had been replaced by the two "entities." But the suffering in the intervening years had been of a magnitude Europe had not seen since 1945—and has not seen since.

With war in Bosnia a fact, a new mechanism for achieving peace was set up in the form of the International Conference for Former Yugoslavia taking a more comprehensive approach to conflict resolution under joint EU and UN auspices with David Owen and Cyrus Vance in the lead.

The year 1992 was one of horror in Bosnia, with major fighting and massive ethnic cleansing. It established the broad lines of division that were to hold more or less until the end of the war.

That the war lasted until the fall of 1995 must be attributed to the failure of the succession of peace efforts and plans during this long period. There were a number of them: the Cutileiro peace plan of March 1992, the Vance-Owen peace plan of May 1993, the EU action plan in December 1993, the Contact Group plan in July 1994 and its plan B in the spring of 1995, and the endgame that finally brought everyone to Dayton in November that year.

It is easy in retrospect, as it was in those days, to be critical of different details of all these plans and efforts. They all had their faults. But no one can claim that what was eventually agreed to in Dayton was free from faults, and at the end of the day it was not in their perceived faults that the reason for the failure of these lie.

In his book, David Owen squarely places the blame on vacillating US policies during these years, claiming that "if President Bush had won reelection in November 1992 there would have been a settlement in Bosnia-Herzegovina in February 1993." Furthermore, "from the spring of 1993 to the summer of 1995, in my judgment, the effect of US policy, despite it being called 'containment,' was to prolong the war of the Bosnian Serbs in Bosnia-Herzegovina."

The recently disclosed US documents mentioned above lend a certain credence to the David Owen thesis. They show how the incoming Clinton administration wanted to question everything in the Balkan policy of the outgoing administration, thus naturally calling into question US support for the ongoing efforts by David Owen and Cyrus Vance. And Bill Clinton now makes it clear that he was determined to stop the Vance-Owen plan. Everyone who has been involved in peace efforts of this kind knows how sensitive parties of a conflict are to signs of international cohesion wavering.

That there were tensions across the Atlantic over Bosnia policy is hardly new, but instead of trying to discuss who might have been right and who might have been wrong, we should unite around the conclusion that the tensions in themselves undermined the efforts to achieve peace in Bosnia during 1992, 1993, 1994, and large parts of 1995. Whether the one or the other approach, had it had full international backing, would have succeeded must remain an open question. But going over the material available now it is clear that while the US focused primarily on the shorter-perspective military issues and the territorial issues associated with them, the Europeans tended to give more weight to the political and constitutional solutions necessary.

In my opinion, the most spectacular of the failures was the Contact Group plan of July 1994. It was certainly positive that it was possible to get the five countries of the Contact Group—the US, the UK, France, Germany, and Russia—to agree on a proposed territorial division of Bosnia, but since divisions prevented this to be associated with a political or institutional structure it was a peace plan in name only. It might have produced a temporary peace within the Contact Group, but it had the effect of prolonging the war in Bosnia.

The summer of 1995 saw a distinct escalation of fighting as all the parties expected this to be the last season of war, and it was thus important to capture ground before a deal was made. We saw an ultimately unsuccessful Bosnian Muslim effort to break the siege of Sarajevo, the Bosnian Serb capture of Srebrenica and the genocide that followed, as well as the Croat Operation Storm offensive that produced the single largest exodus and ethnic cleansing of the entire war.

With the UN Protection Force efforts on the ground failing, and with peace efforts stalled due to disagreements in the international community, we were approaching a situation where NATO troops, under the agreed Operational Plan 40-104, would have to enter Bosnia in order to get the UN forces out, then to leave the parties to the conflict to fight it out with new weapons supplies until further notice. We were about to descend from one circle of hell into a much deeper one. The political consequences, also within the various Western countries, would have been very considerable.

It was in this situation that Richard Holbrooke, working closely with Robert Frasure until he so tragically died on Mount Igman in July 1994, was able to persuade Washington to a push for peace that combined a more European political approach to peace in Bosnia with an amount of US kinetic thunder.

And now it worked. A meeting of the foreign ministers of all the parties to the conflict in Geneva in early September led to an agreement on all the key parameters of a solution. The three weeks at Wright-Paterson Air Force Base in Dayton were then spent on hammering out the details of the territorial delimitation, the international peace implementation efforts, and—although more time should have been spent on this—the constitutional structures. It could have faltered on the one detail or the other, but with the key issues already sorted out, it was primarily a question of time.

Modern mythology often claims that it was NATO air strikes that finally brought about peace. A previous CIA publication, *Balkan Battlegrounds,* dryly noted that "militarily speaking, the practical effect of the NATO air strikes was approximately zero," but that does not mean that they were not of political importance. Ironically enough, they were probably instrumental in getting President Izetbegović to accept a Republika Srpska within the future Bosnia.

However, the absolute key to success was the fact that the international community, after years of debate and division, came together in a strong, united and credible approach. US leadership was necessary, also because divisions in Washington were one of the key problems that had hampered previous efforts; yet it should not be forgotten that there was also the constructive cooperation and support of Russia. We were still in the Russia of President Yeltsin, and First Deputy Foreign Minister Igor Ivanov was among those who spent three weeks at the US Air Force base in Ohio.

What, then, are the lessons to be learned from the failure to first prevent the war in Bosnia and then from the failure to bring peace during such a long and painful period of time?

The number one lesson is that the international community—however it is defined—will never succeed in bringing peace to a divided country or region as long as it is divided—or even seen to be divided—itself. Even signs of division easily make the parties in the conflict see themselves as fighters in a proxy war with even more support from the perceived outside backer just around the corner. The conflict is intensified and prolonged.

To avoid this is, of course, far easier said than done. Confronted with new situations and challenges, there is legitimate divisiveness on what might be the best road ahead. Different national interests as well as different national strategic cultures easily come into play.

There are numerous aspects to the failure of the international community to prevent the full-scale war that broke out in Bosnia in April 1992.

Obviously, there was an insufficient understanding of the nature and magnitude of the challenge. Reading history books might have been a more useful guide to what could happen than diplomatic dispatches from Belgrade. But then maneuvering between the different approaches taken by the different diplomatic machineries of Europe and the US came into play, and the resulting discord seriously undermined the efforts undertaken to prevent the conflict. These were certainly not perfect, but had they been given more united, stronger, and more determined support it is not altogether excluded that they might have succeeded.

Carl Bildt has been Sweden's minister for foreign affairs since 2006. He was a member of parliament from 1979 to 2001, chairman of the Moderate Party from 1986 to 1999, and served as prime minister between 1991 and 1994. He also served in several functions in the Balkans, including as EU special representative to Former Yugoslavia in 1995 and as special envoy of the UN secretary general (1999–2001).

From the Fall of the Berlin Wall to the Admission of New Members to NATO

Ulrich Weisser[1]

The Berlin Wall fell on November 9, 1989; at the same time, the way was opened for German unity. Prevailing opinion was that the foreign policy key to German unity would lie in Moscow, as Mikhail Gorbachev had made the fundamental concession that it ought to be for the Germans in the East and the West to decide which direction they wanted to take. They had the right to aspire to unity and to find their proper place in a new pan-European security structure.

Of the Western powers with continuing responsibility for the German question, the governments of France and Great Britain were not greatly taken with the prospect of the unification of the German Democratic Republic and the Federal Republic of Germany. They feared dominance by a united Germany and disruption of the European balance of power; the British prime minister played a particularly destructive role.

A different, decisive position was adopted by the US administration under President George H. W. Bush, favoring German unity at an early stage and attaching the condition that a reunified Germany should be a member of the NATO alliance. In late February 1990, Bush reached agreement on this route

Wolfgang Ischinger (left) and Ulrich Weisser
at the 2010 MSC Core Group Meeting in Moscow

with Chancellor Helmut Kohl, with Bush being aware of a change of stance by Prime Minister Margaret Thatcher. The British government did not want to risk its close ties with the US because of its reservations concerning Germany unity.

Thus the American president proved to be the true "guiding spirit" of the European process that was triggered by German reunification. However, his thoughts extended beyond the "German unity" project, as Bush also had his eye on the fate of the Central European states—an approach that Bush expressed in the words: "Europe whole and free."

In 1990, the unification of the two German states brought to the agenda the final recognition in international law of the Oder-Neisse line as Poland's western border, as the issue of the border in the East had not been conclusively settled in the absence of a peace treaty. There was no meaningful alternative to this, as it had been required at an early stage by all of the Federal Republic's negotiating partners—President Bush had made his consent to reunification directly dependent on it.

George Bush doggedly pursued the primary US objectives for Europe—although distracted by lower-level operational measures. An expression of his geopolitical thinking, extending far beyond Germany, however, was his decision to commission the National Security Council to present a study that was to deal with America's long-term commitment in and for Europe.

Just a little later, the study was commissioned from the renowned RAND Corporation in Santa Monica. RAND had the reputation of answering controversial questions as objectively as possible, even within the US government, so that the results could be immediately incorporated into the political work of the administration.

James Thomson, the president of RAND, was delighted to take on the commission from Washington, as he understood which problems of global significance required a practical approach, and he immediately put together a small working group whose members—Ronald Asmus, Stephen Larrabee, and James Kugler—he regarded as being particularly suitable for getting to grips with the difficult terms of reference. At a meeting in Washington, then-German Defense Minister Gerhard Stoltenberg discussed the subject of the study with Thomson and suggested including a German officer in the working group—a request that was met by RAND, as a result of which the minister sent me to Santa Monica for six months in 1991. Our work quite quickly reached the conclusion that we saw the future of our neighbors in the East as members of NATO. But how could this objective be achieved immediately after the end of the Cold War? In practical terms it was a question of how Europe's nation states could be reorganized from the point of view of security—and how a special solution would be needed to overcome Russia's expected opposition to this. Russia openly conveyed its opposition to a policy that would be responsible for pushing NATO's eastern frontiers more than one thousand kilometers to the east. The study concluded that our neighbors would find protection and security only in the Atlantic alliance, which would not simply abandon the dividing line between stability and instability together with Germany's eastern frontiers. Any willingness by NATO to open its doors to the accession of Central and Eastern European states required a twofold approach: the integration of future European Union candidates was to be safeguarded with accession to NATO by means of a stability framework. The necessary counterpart to this process was a strategic partnership with Russia.

On returning to Germany, I was able to continue the long-standing strategic dialogue with Volker Rühe, the secretary general of the CDU at that time. When he became defense minister and asked me which major tasks I envisaged for him, my answer was: complete the *Armee der Einheit,* prepare the Bundeswehr for new tasks, and open up NATO to new members. I advised him to link his name inextricably with a major European and historical project—the opening-up of NATO. Rühe welcomed this proposal, because he knew from close contacts with Solidarność in the eighties that Poland preferred to have a democratic reunified Germany as a neighbor rather than the unnatural hybrid of the FRG/GDR.

With strategic and political far-sightedness, he had pointed out the strong binding effect of the Warsaw Pact in the border question at a time when his party was still a long way from this point of view. Thus, it was a question of harmonizing the broad lines of Volker Rühe's foreign policy with carefully conceived ideas on means and objective—the opening-up of NATO. The opportunity for this occurred on March 23, 1993. Rühe was invited to give the "Alastair Buchan Memorial Lecture" in London—an annual event at which Chancellor Helmut Schmidt had given his pioneering speech on the missile crisis in the late seventies. After Rühe's speech there was an icy silence, apart from the Eastern European ambassadors present, who applauded enthusiastically.

The mentality and professional career of Major General Klaus Wiesmann, assistant chief of staff for military policy at the Armed Forces High Command, who was a member of our small delegation, was shaped entirely by NATO. On the return flight to Bonn he expressed the view that it would take years before our country would recover from the Rühe speech. It became clear from all these signals what the project of opening up NATO would have to adapt to.

At the same time, the moment had arrived for Volker Rühe's (brilliant) foreign policy talent to be developed, to seek out and find support in the Alliance, and at the same time to eliminate any opposition within the organization. The minister and I agreed that we were faced with the opportunity, but also the need, to set the correct course for pan-European security and stability in the emerging complex process. We were convinced that we required competent advice for this demanding operation. I therefore recommended to the minister that RAND be consulted. The president of RAND responded positively to our request but pointed out that RAND had never previously dealt with security policy issues for a country outside the US. I therefore asked the competent official in the Pentagon for approval—pointing out that we could share and jointly utilize the results of the RAND work, while the German government would bear the financial cost of this initiative. The approval of the US Department of Defense arrived immediately.

Rühe was clear as to which German interests were to be pursued. It was evident that Germany was seen in the states of Eastern Europe as the decisive factor in the political and economic new beginning and reconstruction. Furthermore, these states were confident that Germany would further their integration into European structures. For Germany, such integration would mean moving from an unfavorable peripheral location to a highly advantageous central position, surrounded only by allies and partners.

This gave rise to the obligation and the opportunity for German policy to exercise a creative influence on the European process and, at the same time, to do something to stabilize the post-communist states in Eastern Europe. To ensure the transfer of stability eastwards, the two elements of integration and cooperation had become essential factors in the further development of European and transatlantic institutions. It was crucial here to take into account the interaction between integration and cooperation. Integration of the Central Eastern European states into Western structures was more likely to be regarded as a danger to stability and disruptive if such integration was not simultaneously linked with closer cooperation with Russia, which was given the name "strategic partnership."

Volker Rühe visited Moscow and almost all the NATO capitals in quick succession, examined the specific conditions of each host country, and at the same time "sold" his concept for a two-pronged approach of opening-up and balance. The allied governments without exception proved to be very amenable to discussions with the German defense minister. Politicians such as Czech President Havel, Polish President Kwasniewski, and even US President Clinton had recognized what a major European project it was to open up NATO to new members and a genuine strategic partnership with Moscow.

Nevertheless, our partners in the Alliance proved to be slightly irritated by the fact that the German chancellor failed to back Rühe with his full authority for reasons that were impossible to understand. This created the impression that it was a project of an individual minister—and, off the record, questions were asked in Washington and elsewhere as to what view should be taken of this situation and how it should be handled operationally. Finally, at the Munich Security Conference in February 1994, Helmut Kohl spoke in favor of the accession of new members to NATO and a strategic partnership with Russia—though in somewhat restrained terms.

It quickly turned out that Volker Rühe had to be prepared for varying degrees of support as well as powerful opposition. The governments in Copenhagen and The Hague proved to be steadfast friends. Incidentally, Denmark played a considerable role in reassuring the Baltic states, which, in their fear of Russia, responded more than skeptically to the initiative of the German defense minister. Our allies in the south made it clear to Rühe that, while Germany should look to the East and seek greater changes there, it should nevertheless recognize clearly the growing strategic importance of Spain, Italy, and Greece as well as the whole of the Mediterranean for Germany—with Rühe always saying that Italy was "our aircraft carrier." The American attitude proved to be difficult. Rühe did not know what position his American counterpart would finally adopt at the informal meeting of NATO defense ministers in Travemünde, which was to be held October 19–21, 1993. The minister therefore sent me to Washington to find out what stage he could and should expect American opinion to have reached. At the conference with his NATO colleagues, Volker Rühe wanted everyone to establish by common consent that, at the next summit of the Alliance, the states of Central and Eastern Europe should be given a clear sign of the prospect for accession to NATO, and that this should be in response to the question of "when" and "how" rather than "whether."

However, US Secretary of Defense Les Aspin did not deal with the issue of opening up NATO to new members at all; instead, he put forward his concept of a Partnership for Peace as an alternative. NATO Secretary General Manfred Wörner counterbalanced this serious difference of opinion with the formula that the concept was suitable as preparation for future accession to NATO.

The period from 1995 to 1996 was characterized essentially by the detailed diplomatic work for the approaching decision by the Alliance to determine at a summit in July 1997 which states could be and should be the first to become members of NATO. However, it also became clear that the work on the strategic partnership with Russia had fallen behind. At a meeting of the political directors from the foreign and defense ministries in fall 1996 there was an opportunity to discuss integration and cooperation as a whole and to compare the results achieved in the talks with the Russian government. We presented a paper, specifically the "NATO-Russia Charter," with due regard for the others' ideas but based mainly on the intensive preliminary conceptual work within the German government from fall 1995 to fall 1996. Our draft charter was intended to define and establish the principles of a partnership, to provide a mechanism for consultation, which would include Russia in processes of joint relevance, without allowing Moscow to be involved in internal NATO affairs, and finally to determine the areas for cooperation according to the principle of reciprocity. The primary objective laid down was to establish the closest possible cooperation between Russia and NATO in European crisis management and efforts to achieve regional stabilization. Our colleagues were rather astonished at how concrete the German ideas were. However, our proposal on the form of the desired charter was unanimously approved. In the meantime, Strobe Talbott, President Clinton's envoy to Russia, said that he was surprised that we Germans were so astute as to present drafts that had virtually reached treaty stage. He did not believe that it would be possible to achieve success in Moscow with this. He therefore advised us: "Go to Russia and take the Russians' pulse" before the NATO secretary general was given a mandate to negotiate by the North Atlantic Council in December 1996.

On November 11, 1996, we flew to confidential consultations with the Russian government, armed with the approval of the main alliance partners for the German ideas for a NATO-Russia Charter. In retrospect, these consultations must be rated as a significant factor in setting the course, opening up the way to results-oriented negotiations.

It became clear that Moscow's view was shaped by traditional ideas, and the fundamental change in the Alliance was not yet understood or had not been sufficiently considered. Nevertheless, the Russian side raised a crucial question that required an honest answer, namely whether, in principle, NATO intended to continue to regard Russia openly or implicitly as a threat or in future as a partner with equal rights. A NATO policy that spoke of partnership but which was at the same time geared to defense requirements against Russia—possibly with expansion of defense capability to new members—might inevitably be seen in Russia as contradictory. Therefore, for Russia the key to the success of the overall approach was for a charter between NATO and Russia to be characterized by a spirit of genuine and equal partnership that also had to allow for acceptable forms of Russian involvement in certain NATO decisions.

The German side produced three political and strategic key arguments on the deep-seated Russian skepticism about being treated as a latent threat and not as an equal partner:

1. NATO was pursuing a strategy that was basically determined by just two elements: cooperation and protection. NATO was prepared to go a very long way in cooperation. The more Russia responded to it, the more the element of "protection" against the vicissitudes of history could recede into the background.

2. Concerning the desired strategic cooperation, it was necessary, from a German perspective, to apply a logical rationale that could be approved by other members: Europe's security was indivisible; Western and Eastern Europe were equally interested in peace, stability, and security for the whole of Europe; in the future, it would be a case of jointly analyzing what factors for instability and what challenges might face Europe as a whole; if such an analysis came to the conclusion that it was necessary to act jointly, then appropriate action could be arrived at jointly in a NATO-Russia council.

3. From a German point of view, a cooperative security partnership organized in this way between a fundamentally reformed alliance and a Russia undergoing revolutionary changes would have to be combined with an appropriate arms control regime in Europe that, in the case of conventional forces, had to be geared to two core elements: flexibility and restrictions. Crucially, what mattered was to preserve or achieve the necessary flexibility for joint crisis management in and for Europe with corresponding availability of suitable armed forces for this, while at the same time other capabilities of the armed forces of both sides took a back seat as a result of reciprocal restrictions on movement and mobilization.

In the further discussions with the Russian government representatives, a broad fundamental acceptance of the German ideas began to emerge—fluctuating between enthusiastic approval and sober realization that the pattern of the negotiations should not be determined by rhetoric and polemic but rather by the joint desire to reach joint solutions. On November 23 and 24, 1996, the defense ministers of France, Germany, Great Britain, and the United States met at the Trianon Palace Hotel in Versailles to discuss the issues arising on the subject of NATO and Russia but also on further action regarding the opening-up of NATO. Defense Minister Volker Rühe was in the comfortable position that we could not only present the German proposals for the content of the charter but also report on the most important results of the consultations in Moscow. Rühe's counterparts proved to be impressed and agreed to the German approach without reservation. American

Secretary of Defense William Perry linked this approval to the proposal to give a far-reaching signal on the issue of stationing nuclear weapons in the territory of the new member states, even before the start of actual negotiations with Russia. He believed that the Alliance could say that there was no need to change NATO's nuclear strategy following the widening of the Alliance to include new members; therefore the NATO states had no plan, no intention, and also no reason to station nuclear weapons on the soil of the states that wanted to join the Alliance.

The question of how many states should form the first group to accede was still unsettled. Views fluctuated between three and five. This topic also dominated the Franco-German Defense Council, which met in Bourne in France in June 1997. German Foreign Minister Klaus Kinkel canvassed among his French counterparts for the accession of Poland, Hungary, and the Czech Republic, and also Romania and Slovenia. In the plenary session, French President Chirac proved to be annoyed about the different signals from the German delegation and gained the impression that the German government had not reached a united conclusion in this matter. In fact, Chancellor Kohl and President Clinton had already agreed on three over a meal of spaghetti at the Filomena Ristorante in Washington. In 1999, Poland, the Czech Republic, and Hungary joined NATO.

All of this originated from the fact that a single German politician concluded on the basis of a strategic and political judgment, but also out of responsibility for Germany and Europe, that NATO had to be opened up to new members. Against initially almost insurmountable opposition from NATO, this initiative quickly became a high-priority project of the Alliance, which was in principle aimed at nothing less than making the vision of President Bush of a "Europe whole and free" a reality. Volker Rühe joined his name to this historic project, which he justified in 1994 with his book *Deutschlands Verantwortung.*[2] It is only natural that at the end of the process many others allowed themselves to be celebrated as the originator of the success.

At no point did anyone question the approach that the opening-up of NATO to new members should be safeguarded and balanced out through a strategic partnership with Russia. However, the potential of such an approach with respect to Moscow has so far been underutilized. Now is the time, following the realignment of Europe in terms of security policy, for Europe, the United States, and Russia to reach an understanding on dealing with the joint challenges together. At the same time, it is about making a new strategic effort to overcome traditional ideas and meaningless structures.

Vice Admiral (ret.) **Ulrich Weisser** *was head of the policy and planning staff in the German Ministry of Defense from 1992 to 1998.*

Notes

1 Ulrich Weisser completed this draft a few weeks before his death in spring 2013. The article has been edited slightly.
2 Volker Rühe, *Deutschlands Verantwortung. Perspektiven für das neue Europa* (Frankfurt am Main: Ullstein, 1994).

XXXV.
Münchner Konferenz
für Sicherheitspolitik
5. – 7. Februar 1999

35th
Munich Conference
on Security Policy
February 5 – 7, 1999

The 1999 Munich Conference on Security Policy—Paving the Way for the Kosovo Air Campaign Operation Allied Force

Klaus Naumann

The 35th Munich Conference on Security Policy, which is how the Munich Security Conference was referred to until 2008, took place on the eve of the Rambouillet Conference near Paris, which was the last attempt to achieve a peaceful solution to the Kosovo crisis. It was the first MSC chaired by Horst Teltschik, who had succeeded Ewald von Kleist. It was also the first conference at which the new German chancellor, Gerhard Schröder, and two of his cabinet ministers, Foreign Minister Joschka Fischer and Defense Minister Rudolf Scharping, presented their views on foreign and security policy issues. Moreover, it was the last conference attended by sixteen members of NATO—and the first by many of the former Warsaw Pact countries and numerous Asian nations.

To some extent, it came as a surprise that the situation in Kosovo did not dominate the conference, although the Račak massacre in January 1999 had further deteriorated the tense standoff in Kosovo and the conference took place literally at the doorstep of the international conference at

▲
Javier Solana, William Cohen, Horst Teltschik,
and Rudolf Scharping (from left to right)

Rambouillet, which was widely seen as the last hope for solving the crisis in Kosovo.

The situation in the province, which the Serbs, the ethnic majority, saw as the cradle of their nation, had haunted NATO since the NATO Foreign Ministers Meeting in Luxembourg in spring 1998. The Alliance had issued statement after statement, and the tone had become increasingly threatening, yet the hostilities continued, and the Serbs deployed substantial numbers of police and troops to Kosovo. As all NATO members agreed that diplomacy sometimes works only when backed up by the threat of using force, in summer 1998 NATO drafted a set of operational concepts for a Kosovo peace enforcement operation ranging from air operations to a full-scale ground forces operation. For political reasons, and despite serious military doubts, the North Atlantic Council decided that any use of force by NATO should be limited to air strikes. Based on a Council-approved operation plan, NATO issued an activation order for an air campaign, Operation Allied Force, aimed at ending all hostilities and the subsequent withdrawal of Serbian military from Kosovo as the most convincing tool for the endgame in Ambassador Richard Holbrooke's negotiations. When he failed, NATO took over in another diplomatic effort, culminating in an ultimatum to launch air operations within forty-eight hours should the Serbs not cease hostilities. The Council tasked me as chairman of the NATO Military Committee and General Wesley Clark, Supreme Allied Commander Europe, to inform President Slobodan Milošević of the NATO ultimatum and to persuade him to agree to a cease-fire. As a result of a tense negotiation marathon lasting some twenty-six hours that we held in Belgrade at the end of October 1998, Milošević agreed to end hostilities and to withdraw all excess police and military forces within forty-eight hours. He honored his commitment, although he had clearly stated during our talks in Belgrade that he would seek, as he put it, a "final solution for Kosovo in spring 1999." However, as NATO's options of reining in the Kosovar side were extremely limited, new hostilities began as early as in November 1998, some of them undoubtedly provoked by the Ushtria Çlirimtare e Kosovës (UÇK), the Kosovo Liberation Army. The spiral of hostilities culminated in the Račak massacre in January 1999, when more than a dozen Kosovars were found dead, allegedly executed. As a consequence of Serbia's refusal to permit an international investigation, a new diplomatic effort to resolve the crisis was launched and the so-called Contact Group, consisting of the United States, France, Italy, Germany, and the United Kingdom, was established. It agreed with Russia to conduct negotiations and invited Serbia and a Kosovar delegation to come to Rambouillet on February 6, 1999. NATO was not part of this effort, but it was obvious that NATO would have to act should Rambouillet fail. Although this issue was not discussed in depth at the MSC, no one left the conference with the slightest doubt about what would happen if the negotiations in Rambouillet were unsuccessful. The fact that Chancellor Schröder, Foreign Minister Fischer, and Defense Minister Scharping had made it painstakingly clear that Germany would honor its obligation as a NATO member without any reservation was key to that. Scharping stated at the conference: "The credible threat of NATO air strikes to support international, diplomatic efforts ultimately resulted in Milošević agreeing last October to the verification missions of the Organization for Security and Co-operation in Europe and NATO and thus in the avoidance of a humanitarian catastrophe. Belgrade's continuous attempts to see how far it could go with a policy of massive oppression and violation of the human rights of the Kosovo Albanians made it essential for us to keep up the pressure. … At the moment we must keep all our options open until we know that a political solution has been achieved."

Nevertheless, the Alliance was deeply divided on the question concerning who should authorize such an operation conducted outside the NATO treaty area and definitely not entirely defensive in nature. The majority of the then sixteen members of NATO were convinced that a United Nations Security Council resolution (UNSCR) authorizing the use of force under Chapter VII of the UN Charta was mandatory, although the United States had indicated that there might be other options. Interestingly, the German chancellor had hinted at options that needed to be considered in case of atrocities and crimes against humanity, since the absence of a UN mandate does not necessarily mean inactivity on the part of the international community, and his defense minister had by no means insisted on a UNSCR as a compulsory prerequisite. Moreover, neither NATO Secretary General Javier Solana nor US Secretary of Defense William Cohen had mentioned UN authorization in their talks. The reason that the issue of authorizing operations beyond collective defense in accordance with Article 5 of the Washington Treaty was so controversial was that NATO also was in process of preparing for its fiftieth anniversary to be celebrated in Washington in April, where the new Strategic Concept was to be agreed. During the preparatory discussions in Brussels, some got the impression that the United States aimed at including wording in the concept that would open the door for a global alliance prepared to intervene elsewhere and, taking into account the failures of the international community in Rwanda and in Srebrenica, not necessarily based on a UN mandate. Some suspected that Washington wished to transform NATO into a global alliance.

In drafting the new Strategic Concept, this question remained open, as did the question of the future role of nuclear weapons when the some two hundred participants convened at Munich in February 1999. Chancellor Schröder, who stated unambiguously that he saw no need to debate the proposal of Foreign Minister Fischer to eliminate the first-use option, quickly defused the latter issue. The Americans in turn indicated that they would not object to emphasizing the need for a stronger European role, provided the Europeans would be willing to eventually invest more in defense. The European response to the unequivocal demands put forward by Secretary of Defense Cohen was lukewarm at best. Nevertheless, it was this issue that dominated the headlines in the media reports on the Munich conference.

The truly unresolved issues became NATO-Russia relations and the intervention question that some, notably the French, saw hidden behind the Kosovo case. French Defense Minister Alain Richard had explicitly stated in Munich: "For any 'non-article 5' operation implying the use of force we will never abandon the legitimacy which comes from the authority of the UN Security Council, which alone possesses an indisputable legal basis for any recourse to the use of armed forces." The assumption was that the US would use the precedent of intervention in Kosovo not mandated by the UN as the back door to getting a general intervention clause included in the Strategic Concept. The discussions at Munich, notably those at the margins and during bilateral meetings, did not produce a unanimous result, yet they helped tremendously for two reasons: first, they assured the Russians that a UN-mandated solution, which would include a NATO-led implementation force, was the common aim for the Rambouillet talks, and, second, they helped mitigate the worries of the UNSCR faction, thus laying the foundation for the decision that eventually had to be made on March 24, when Operation Allied Force began.

Munich thus sent a clear signal of resolve, unfortunately in vain, to the negotiators at Rambouillet. The debates at Munich regrettably did not eliminate restricting the Kosovo campaign to the use of air power, which turned out to be one of the reasons for the unexpectedly long duration of the operation, and, more importantly, they did not persuade the Russians to remove the protective hand they were holding over Milošević. Thus, one could get the impression that the price tag for intervention in Kosovo without a UNSCR would most likely include a setback and a pause of several years in NATO-Russia relations. On the other hand, it became obvious that Kosovo would serve as a trigger only. The main reason was Russia's uneasiness with the imminent NATO enlargement. The Russian side stated at the conference that they saw the future membership of Poland, the Czech Republic, and

Hungary as an attempt at widening NATO's sphere of influence to the detriment of Russia. One of the deputy foreign ministers of the Russian Federation stated that any inclusion of any of the republics of the former USSR would mean the West crossing a "red line," a statement that prompted me to remind him of the wording agreed to by the Russian Federation at the 1994 Commission on Security and Cooperation Conference, which assured that every state in Europe was free to make its own choice with respect to membership in an international organization.

In retrospect, the debates at the 35th Munich Security Conference sent a clear signal to all parties participating in the Rambouillet Conference: NATO supports the political process by exerting military pressure through ongoing preparations for air strikes as agreed in the operations concepts for the limited and phased air operations, and NATO hopes at the same time that it will not be necessary to execute those plans. Should the negotiations fail, however, NATO will act. This was the Munich message, which thus paved the way for the decision to be taken on March 14, 1999, to launch NATO's first comprehensive air operation.

But Munich 1999 paved the way for two other major developments as well. The debates had made it clear that a new step in shaping European military capabilities based on a European security strategy was urgently needed. Based on these deliberations and confronted with the inability of the European NATO nations to contribute substantially to the Kosovo air campaign in April/May 1999, the European leaders drew the proper conclusions at the Cologne EU Summit later that year. One could thus call the 35th Munich Security Conference the father of what was to be referred to as the Helsinki process, whose objective was to strengthen European military capabilities. The other major development was the beginning of a debate on how the international community should react in cases of crimes against humanity, mass killings, and other atrocities in the absence of an agreement at the United Nations Security Council. It remained inconclusive at Munich, but the notion that the international community cannot afford to be a passive bystander gained ground. Operation Allied Force of 1999, which was seen by most as being legitimate despite some legal flaws, may thus well have been the trigger that led to the Canadian initiative of establishing the International Commission on Intervention and State Sovereignty in 2000. The commission coined the phrase "Responsibility to Protect (R2P)," and its report paved the way for the adoption of the R2P concept by the UN General Assembly in 2005.

In conclusion, one could say that the Munich format of open debates in the plenary sessions, of confidential discussions at the margins, and of animated bilateral exchange once again proved its value in February 1999, when NATO prepared for its first armed intervention, which ultimately saved thousands of Kosovar lives, established a precedent in international law, and paved the way for the idea that much later would be called Responsibility to Protect.

General (ret.) **Klaus Naumann** *was chief of staff of the German Armed Forces and served as chairman of the North Atlantic Military Committee from 1996 to 1999. He was a member of the International Commission on Intervention and State Sovereignty and more recently of the International Commission on Nuclear Non-Proliferation and Disarmament.*

Key Meetings at the Margins— Kosovo and the Munich Conference

Rudolf Scharping

In the fall of 1998, the incoming German government had been confronted with a situation unlike any German government before. This was not so much because, for the first time, a government jointly formed by the Social Democrats and the Green party had just come to power—even before they formally entered office, the future chancellor Gerhard Schröder and his foreign minister, Joschka Fischer, had been confronted in Washington with the possibility of war, and the expulsion policy of the Slobodan Milošević regime in Kosovo was a particularly serious infringement on human rights. So serious in fact that in April 1999, in Geneva, UN Secretary General Kofi Annan spoke of it as the "dark cloud of genocide." Many people, and not only in Germany, could see that thousands had lost their lives and hundreds of thousands their homeland in the Balkan wars, particularly in Srebrenica, as a result of this failure—a view confirmed by the fact that it was interpreted by the Milošević regime as the inability of Europe and the international community to effectively intervene.

So it was that the intense negotiations in late fall in Paris and in 1999 in Rambouillet, conducted with great tenacity but with an increasing

▲
Rudolf Scharping (right) and Javier Solana
at the margins of the 2001 conference

sense of hopelessness, drew to a close in March 1999 without achieving anything.

Meanwhile, for the member states of the Organization for Security and Co-operation in Europe (OSCE), and in particular for NATO and the European Union, the OSCE mission that had been launched was an attempt to reduce, perhaps even to put an end to, the persecution in and expulsion from Kosovo by means of an international presence. Anyone who not only read reports but also had direct personal conversations with members of the mission came to the conclusion that the cynical refusal of the government in Belgrade to allow a rescue helicopter in Kosovo corresponded to the reality on the ground: continual obstruction, indeed a constant attempt at intimidation were the order of the day—despite all the negotiations and all the protestations in the international arena.

In any case, we had to decide whether OSCE observers could be sent into this crisis zone without effective protection. As it was essential to consider the danger to life and limb faced by the police and members of the OSCE mission from the start, an extraction force had to be, and actually was, stationed in Macedonia to demonstrate the willingness and ability to provide and, if necessary, to guarantee effective protection.

That was the subject of the confidential meeting of defense ministers from NATO and the countries of the Assembly of the Western European Union (WEU) on the margin of the Munich Security Conference in 1999.

There was much to consider; for example, how does one solve the logistical problem of transport from the port of Thessaloníki through Greece, where the population (and politicians) felt a special affinity with the Balkans (and Serbia)? Given the dangers ahead, how does one explain to the citizens of democratic countries that a civilian mission would require immediate and massive protection in a hazardous environment so as not to jeopardize the credibility of such OSCE missions as a pan-European organization, crossing the frontiers of old alliances and systems? Who can contribute which forces and resources, and how would negotiations with the Milošević regime influence a military presence on the ground and directly adjacent to Kosovo?

This round was something new, even for the Munich Security Conference, which has always been a place for representing, exchanging, and communicating one's own views and interests with others; gaining credibility with the "public;" at best, being able to communicate different viewpoints transparently and even to draw closer to them; yet at the least, recognizing and sounding out the scope for different ideas. In 1999 something new was added: the precise exchange of assessments of an acutely concrete situation with the aim of agreeing on joint action.

It was clear to the ministers that their will to protect the international police forces of the OSCE would have to be "translated" into military capabilities, and that such capabilities could be seen as effective and sustainable only if they could be brought into action in the Kosovo arena, should the need arise.

It was also clear that the Milošević regime would necessarily interpret this stationing of troops as a preparation for a ground war—not simply or primarily because of the effect on the public, citizens, the media, and above all parliamentarians in democratic countries, but in real terms (we are talking about heavily equipped NATO troops). The idea that the government in Belgrade (and indeed several others) would also view the situation similarly turned out to be wrong—but was able to serve as further pressure in the contact group negotiations with Belgrade.

I vividly recall the almost desperate efforts to achieve a political solution through negotiation and diplomacy, also thanks to Foreign Minister Fischer's vivid accounts. Milošević derailed everything. The course of subsequent events does not need to be described here, with one exception.

As soon as the defense ministers met, they were quite clear (as indeed were all the governments) that, even if military action were taken, there was no real question of a ground war. On the contrary: everything had to be undertaken to again seek political and diplomatic solutions as soon as possible. The meeting in Munich was an essential part of that basis of trust on which the respective efforts could be built. Here are two examples:

In May 1999, once again in the WEU format, the defense ministers met at the Hardthöhe in Bonn. Outside the weighty topics on the official agenda—such as the future of a EU Common Foreign and Security Policy coordinating it with NATO policy, targets, and capabilities, and the longer-term future of the WEU—striving for a fast return to a political solution to the Kosovo conflict was the main theme of every discussion. It was clear that this should take place on the basis of a UN Security Council resolution. It was also clear that there was an urgent need for careful and necessarily confidential consultations with the government in Moscow. As a result, Lieutenant General Harald Kujat was sent in a civilian capacity to Moscow, which was closely coordinated within the German federal government and with my colleagues Bill Cohen, Alain Richard, and George Robertson, whom I also count as close personal friends (which made things easier).

This contribution is not intended to, and indeed cannot, cover in detail what is better done by professional researchers in the fields of political science and history or described in more detail in books. Basically, Germany was not well prepared, either politically or militarily, for the situation that unfolded between the summer of 1998 and the end of the Kosovo war in June 1999. However, one can at least say that the close and trusted cooperation in the German government, principally between the chancellor, the foreign minister, and the defense minister; the close and trusted cooperation in Europe and within NATO; the collaboration on specific points with Russia (achieved after setbacks); and, last but not least, the involvement of the United Nations in keeping the peace and observing international law met the challenges of the time. After a decade of mass murder, expulsion, and devastation left by war, a new path to reconciliation and into the European democracies lay open to the countries of southeastern Europe.

Rudolf Scharping was minister of defense of the Federal Republic of Germany from 1998 to 2002. From 1994 to 2005, he was a member of the German Bundestag, and, from 1995 to 2001, chairman of the Social Democratic Party of Europe.

The Margins at Munich:
The Conference from Kosovo to Iraq

George Robertson

The timing of the Munich Security Conference seems fortuitously fated to occur just as a crisis needs an assembly of interested stakeholders. That was my experience as British defense secretary and then as the tenth secretary general of NATO. Its timing has regularly proved to be crucial.

However, Munich has in addition always provided a platform for the ideas and developments that swirl around the world of security policy. It has, over the years, proved to be an incubus of thinking that has provided key policy-makers with aids to navigation in an increasingly complex world. A venue for gossip, networking, challenging, debating, and socializing in the defense and security village—these have been the hallmarks of that winter weekend in the Bavarian capital. The "margins" of the conference, always where the most business was done, had to be very wide indeed.

But my memories of Munich are sharp and striking. In particular four conferences are still in my mind. At the 1998 conference, the new Labour government coming to power the summer before was, of course, a source of curiosity to European and American participants. In 1999, the agenda was dominated by the aftermath of Bosnia and the looming confrontation with

Slobodan Milošević over Kosovo. The Munich Security Conference of 2001 was the first at which the George W. Bush administration was on display, and the 2003 conference was on the eve of the invasion of Iraq and amid the crisis over the defense of Turkey.

Labour had come to power in 1997, and I was the first Labour defense secretary for eighteen years. Not only that, we had by Munich embarked on one of the most extensive strategic reviews of our defenses seen in a generation. Every capability was to be examined, modernization was the watchword, and a promised six-month timescale had been rapidly abandoned in order that we got it right. Fundamental change was necessary to convert static Cold War legacy structures, thinking, and equipment into what was necessary for the future threats we might face.

All this was a matter of considerable interest to Americans and Europeans alike. The two biggest military nations in Europe (the French Socialist Party had surprisingly won their election too) had been taken over by forces of the left, and it was not only the Americans who were wary about what might happen. The Munich conference was the ideal venue to lay out our plans. The key reassurance came in the pledge given by Prime Minister Tony Blair that his review was to be foreign-policy, and not finance, led. Many, both at home and abroad, were very skeptical on this promise, but it held the prospect of being a model if it was fulfilled. The promise was kept, and the results of the review lasted more than a decade.

I recall meeting up with Richard Perle at one of the functions. The "Prince of Darkness" was never likely to be a Labour government supporter, but he knew me and my team. His welcome was genuine, but I knew he still had his doubts. He presented me with a copy of his memoir disguised as a novel, *Hard Line,* and the clue to his approach was in the title.

The other preoccupation on stage and in the corridors was the aftermath of the Bosnian conflict. NATO had had to act "out of area" and not in "collective defense." The intervention after several years of dithering had been cathartic in the European countries, and there was much to reflect on after the use of the Cold War structures of NATO to deal with a very different, very local, yet very deadly enemy. A rethink about what NATO stood for and would have to stand for permeated the speeches and the corridor talk. A new United States secretary of defense, William Cohen—a former Republican senator and Munich veteran—had brought a breath of fresh air to the Pentagon, and Europe's hand-wringing needed his intelligent and calming influence.

My next conference of moment was the following year. It had its dramas too. It was only a matter of weeks after the signing of the St. Malo Declaration by the British and French governments. This was a truly momentous change of direction and one of the direct consequences of the post-Bosnia rethink. Here were the two principal European defense powers saying, for the first time and together, that Europe had to take more responsibility for its own defense and security. For a continent used to the long-time British reluctance to have a European defense capacity and to France being the awkward customer in relations with the United States, this was a bolt of lightning.

On the other side of the Atlantic, where there was some real surprise, it seemed initially that this was a bid to rival and ultimately replace NATO. Even though America had been yet again dragged into a local European conflict in Bosnia and had had to provide most of the sophisticated firepower and resented it, there was still suspicion. Alain Richard, the French defense minister, and I had to use the unique surroundings of the Bayerischer Hof to get over the message that St. Malo was designed to build European capabilities that would be as useful to NATO as to the European Union. It was to be a compliment to NATO and not a replacement. It was to require a lot of effort, but the conference was the ideal forum for persuasion.

But that persuasive effort—to both the Europeans and the Americans—was thrown into sharp relief by the next looming Balkan conflict, the murderous activities of Milošević in Kosovo. With all the main security players in one hotel in Munich, some deeply concerning intelligence was being shared and worried over. We were becoming aware of what the Serbs called "Operation Horseshoe," Milošević's plan to drive, with vicious violence and killing, the Albanian majority south and out of this sensitive province.

It has to be said that after Bosnia, and despite success there, there was still a reluctance to intervene again, and because intelligence was still hidden there was no great public appetite for military action. And yet pictures on television from Kosovo of displaced people in the winter forests, the burning houses, and the reports of rape camps and mass killings were all leading to inexorable pressure to act. The defense ministers of the big powers were all pretty new to this kind of dilemma, but we knew something had to be done, and there were fraught conversations between William Cohen, Alain Richard, Rudolf Scharping, Joschka Fischer, and myself along with General Wesley Clark, the Supreme Allied Commander Europe. By the end of the weekend, a consensus was almost there: that Milošević would have to be stopped, and that if diplomacy would not do it then force would be necessary.

The conference in 2001 was dominated by the incoming personalities of the Bush (43) administration, in particular an old Munich hand, Donald Rumsfeld. Newly appointed as President Bush's secretary of defense he was, but new he certainly was not: a former US ambassador to NATO, former secretary of defense, former White House chief of staff, former top industrialist, and not so former inter-agency guerilla warrior. He was back, like the Terminator, and he was in the mood for sorting out the Europeans. Despite the manifest success of the Kosovo air campaign, he misguidedly saw it as war by committee, and it was at Munich that he coined his memorable pronouncement "the mission determines the coalition, the coalition does not determine the mission." It was a deliberate provocation to the NATO allies, and I was at my first Munich conference as NATO secretary general.

Don Rumsfeld is a curious and complex character, as is now well documented, but newly back in office and with most of his support staff still not in place he was restive about conceding any ground to the Europeans. Faced with me, twenty years his junior and a Labour politician to boot, he was going to be difficult to impress. But I am not easily put off, and the politics of the west of Scotland can be as rough in their own way as those inside the Beltway. In the end, by fair means and foul, and through bitter experience he came to realize that a permanent coalition of the willing and the able, as NATO was, was infinitely preferable to some loose ad-hoc, US-led coalition. As his own cyclostyled work, *Rumsfeld's Brilliant Pebbles*, says, "Washington DC is 110 square miles, surrounded by reality."

Fast forward then to 2003, missing out for reasons of space the traumas of 9/11 and its aftermath and the "don't call us, we'll call you" approach from the Pentagon to allies' offers of help in defeating the Taliban. That was to do so much to sour allied unity in the lead-up to the Iraq invasion. The 2002 conference was still in shock over the attacks in the United States but also overwhelmed with solidarity and sympathy. By the following year, that solidarity was under severe pressure as Iraq had become the preoccupation, and as we assembled in Munich NATO was in its worst existential crisis of its sixty-year history.

The issue of Iraq had, by early 2003, consumed the foreign policy community. Afghanistan, now in the hands of the permanent NATO coalition, was subordinated to events in the Middle East. Even those, like myself, who believed that Saddam Hussein represented a real threat to his neighbors and the wider world and had to be dealt with, were nervous about diverting so much attention from the acquired burden of sorting Afghanistan. But after Iraqi defiance over producing evidence to the United Nations in December 2002, the tension was ramping up.

As the UN deliberated amid some acrimony, Turkey was increasingly fearful that Saddam might make a preemptive assault on them to divert attention northwards from the rising tension on the Kuwait border. It requested through NATO channels support from allies and specifically Patriot missiles for their border areas. Four countries—France, Germany, Belgium, and Luxembourg—refused to say yes but also did not say no. They claimed that this was too intimately connected to the fractious debate in New York, and they wanted a delay in answering the request.

NATO has a procedure for taking decisions in an organization requiring unanimity in everything it does. A Decision Sheet (in essence a draft resolution) is issued under a "silence procedure," and if silence is not broken it becomes policy. Because the four dissenters warned they would "break" silence, I played for time by refusing to issue the Decision Sheet. Knowledge of Turkey's request became publicly known, and our reticence to say anything started to become a newsworthy issue. This crisis was then escalated by an increasingly angry and apprehensive Turkey, who then chose to invoke Article 4 of the North Atlantic Treaty. Much less known than Article 5, Article 4 is invoked when a state believes it may be attacked and wants allied support. It had never once been invoked before.

NATO was therefore on the edge of a cliff as Munich approached. To have ultimately rejected Turkey's appeal would quite simply have broken the Alliance, but that was what we were heading for as we arrived in Munich. All the major parties were at the conference—all aware of the heightening sense of crisis and some with a determination to use the opportunity to get a deal and escape the arguments ongoing in the Security Council. The platform speeches were being made to the outside world, but below in the corridors and side rooms desperate attempts were being made to find a solution.

Michelle Alliot-Marie, the formidable French defense minister, and Joschka Fischer, Germany's former street-fighting foreign minister, became key allies in my search for a way round the tangle. Much as I would like to say for this book that Munich was the site of the eventual solution, sadly we left for capitals with no breakthrough. And yet the atmosphere and natural conviviality of the conference made the ultimate solution easier to find. The weekend and assurances given there did lead to me issuing the famous Decision Sheet. French President Jacques Chirac took my move as highly provocative (a view not shared by his defense and foreign ministers), but the move did stimulate the final act, and at the eleventh hour alliance solidarity returned. Turkey got the Patriots and NATO was saved. It was a very close-run thing, and the relief in other capitals, especially Washington, DC, was deep and genuine.

These examples serve to show that the Munich Security Conference is not simply a public platform for presentations of the obvious but a venue of significance where the security village sits together and tries to make sense of the challenges the world faces. An annual reunion of old warriors it is not—it has a vitality and relevance that makes it a must-go for those involved in the fraught issues facing democratic countries today.

The crucial point I make in conclusion is this: the Munich Security Conference, like so many organizations built to deal with the Cold War, indeed like NATO itself, has to modernize and refresh and update. There is a generation coming to power today with no memories of the Cold War or even the Balkans. They need to be, indeed have to be, stakeholders in tomorrow's security debate and conclusions. The conference, much bigger than ever and without some of the precious intimacy that made it so memorable, has despite that maintained in different ways its relevance and interest and will continue to do so. Its need is even greater than it has been in the past.

*Lord **George Robertson** of Port Ellen KT GCMG HonFRSE PC was secretary of state for defence of the United Kingdom (1997–99), and secretary general of NATO and chairman of the North Atlantic Council (1999–2003).*

Ewald von Kleist, US Defense Secretary Frank Carlucci, and, standing, German Defense Minister Manfred Wörner and US Senator Sam Nunn at the 25th *Wehrkunde* in February 1988 in Munich (from left to right).

Top: A look into the conference venue at the Hotel Regina during the second
Wehrkundebegegnung in 1964. Pictured are, among others, Zbigniew Brezinski (far left)
as well as Ewald von Kleist and Franz-Josef Strauss (center).

Bottom: Inside the conference hall at the Hotel Regina during the mid-sixties.

Top: US Defense Secretary William Perry, German Chancellor Helmut Kohl, Ewald von Kleist, and NATO Secretary General Javier Solana at the 1996 conference (from left).

Bottom: Chancellor Helmut Kohl (left) talking to Ewald von Kleist during the 1996 conference.

Top: Taking stock of the mission in Bosnia: NATO Secretary General Javier Solana and George Joulwan, Supreme Allied Commander Europe, at the 1996 conference.

Bottom: German Chancellor Gerhard Schröder (left) with conference chairman Horst Teltschik at the 2001 conference.

Top: German President Horst Köhler addressing the 2005 meeting,
then called the Munich Conference on Security Policy.

Bottom: UN Secretary General Kofi Annan speaking at the 2005 conference.

Top: Russian President Vladimir Putin addresses the 2007 conference.
Among those listening are, in the first row, Russian Defense Minister Sergey Ivanov (left),
NATO Secretary General Jaap de Hoop Scheffer (fourth from left), German Chancellor Angela Merkel
(center), and US Defense Secretary Robert Gates (across the aisle to Merkel's left).

Bottom: Russian President Vladimir Putin and German Chancellor Angela Merkel at the margins
of the 2007 conference.

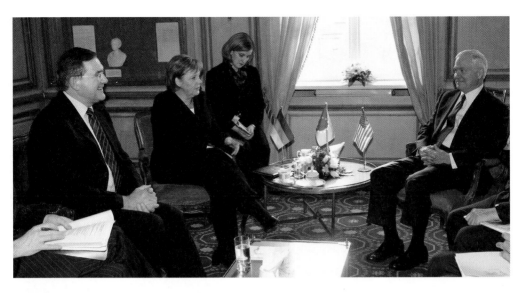

Top: German Defense Minister Franz-Josef Jung, Chancellor Angela Merkel, and US Defense Secretary Robert Gates at a bilateral meeting during the 2007 conference.

Bottom: A view of the conference hall during the 2008 conference: Chairman Horst Teltschik (left) and Turkish Prime Minister Recep Tayyip Erdoğan.

The passing of the torch: At the end of the 2008 conference, the outgoing chairman
Horst Teltschik (right) and the new chairman Wolfgang Ischinger shake hands.

Top: Polish Prime Minister Donald Tusk, German Chancellor Angela Merkel, French President Nicholas Sarkozy, and chairman Wolfgang Ischinger (from right) debate during the 2009 conference.

Bottom: The US congressional delegation, led by Senators John McCain (left) and Joe Lieberman (right), answering media questions at the 2011 conference.

UN Secretary General Ban Ki-Moon addresses the 2011 Munich Security Conference.

Russian Foreign Minister Sergey Lavrov and US Secretary of State Hillary Clinton shake hands after exchanging the instruments of ratification for the New START Treaty at the Hotel Bayerischer Hof on Saturday, February 5, 2011, at the margins of the 47th Munich Security Conference.

▲

Top: Russian President Dmitry Medvedev addresses the participants of the 2010 MSC Core Group Meeting in Moscow.

Bottom: The chairman of the European Union Military Committee, General Patrick de Rousiers, speaks at the Hotel Adlon, Berlin, during the MSC's The Future of European Defence Summit in April of 2013 (organized in cooperation with McKinsey & Company).

Top: A view of the conference hall during the Energy Security Forum, co-organized with the *Frankfurter Allgemeine Zeitung*, at the Gesellschaftshaus Palmengarten in Frankfurt in 2013.

Bottom: The conference venue in Bonn during the MSC's Cyber Security Summit, co-organized with Deutsche Telekom, in November of 2013.

Top: Kumi Naidoo, the International Executive Director of Greenpeace, on the big screen in the conference hall during the 48th conference.

Bottom: Nobel Peace Prize laureate Tawakkol Karman of Yemen speaks to the participants of the 48th conference in 2012 about the Arab uprising and the crisis in Syria.

Top: Ewald von Kleist (left) with former US Secretary of State Henry Kissinger at the 2012 Munich Security Conference. It would be the last conference von Kleist was able to attend.

Bottom: US Vice President Biden greets former NATO Secretary General Javier Solana at the 2013 Munich Security Conference.

A view of the atrium of the Hotel Bayerischer Hof during the 2011 conference,
as US Secretary of State Hillary Clinton and Russian Foreign Minister Sergey Lavrov
get ready to exchange the instruments of ratification for the New START Treaty.

The Munich Security Conference in the Post-9/11 Era

James L. Jones

There is no overestimating the importance of the role that the Munich Security Conference has played on the world stage over the past half-century. It remains the preeminent international forum for dialogue on global security. By bringing together the world's top security thinkers, leaders, and policy decision-makers, the MSC has enabled the international community to forge far greater levels of mutual understanding, cooperation, and partnership. Most importantly, it has fostered close personal relationships among influentials—vital connections that have contributed monumentally to international security and stability since the conference's inception in 1963.

My personal experience with the MSC is long and treasured. I first attended the forum in 1980 as a major in the United States Marine Corps serving as liaison to the United States Senate. This was when the conference was still led by its founder, the late Baron Ewald von Kleist. I marveled at the magnitude of the gathering, the discipline of the proceedings, and the sweeping dialogue on matters of enormous importance to humankind's progress. The atmosphere was electric, as heads of state, ministers, and a broad spectrum of leaders from around the globe conferred and caucused,

James L. Jones (center) with Sergey Lavrov (speaking), Catherine Ashton, and Guido Westerwelle at the 2010 conference talked and listened, argued and agreed, while building all-important bridges of communication and consensus on shared interests and values.

For fifty years, these links have helped the family of free nations identify and tackle common challenges. While the conference rarely achieves universal agreement on the issues of the day, it has never failed to provide for the useful exchange of viewpoints, perspectives, and positions—dialogue that is indispensable for coping in a multipolar and complex world where nations of goodwill are far stronger in concert than they are apart.

The conference's signature events, of course, have always been the official statements, panel discussions, and breakout sessions. They set the agenda and the tone for the proceedings, and provide a critical forum for the sharing of subject matter expertise and the presentation of national, regional, and institutional perspectives. Focusing on the preeminent topics of the day and on the emerging security challenges ahead, the official addresses prime the pump for the more interactive conference engagements.

My first invitation as a delegate was not until 1991, just after Saddam Hussein created a humanitarian crisis by stampeding the Kurds into the mountains of southern Turkey under the threat of attack by weapons of mass destruction (WMD). The animated debate that year focused on the growing problem posed by Iraq under Hussein's dictatorship. Indeed, the MSC had become an important forum for discussing the rising challenges in the broader Middle East.

I learned quickly that as important as the MSC's keynote speeches and the official run of show may be, the most fruitful activity would always be the sidebar conversations and informal meetings that provide attendees the opportunity to confer in small groups or one-on-one. These candid exchanges of views in such a discrete, personal, and enjoyable setting are indispensable to the broader process of gaining common understanding and consensus building. They also often allow the participants to enjoy the sights and delicacies of lovely Munich.

The history of the conference, like the history of global security itself, is marked by major crises and pivotal events. Among the most consequential of these transition points, of course, were the terrorist attacks on the United States that occurred on September 11, 2001, and the ensuing military response against al Qaeda and the Taliban. The atrocity in New York City, Washington, DC, and Pennsylvania claimed the lives of citizens from over ninety countries.

On 9/11 I was serving as Commandant of the United States Marine Corps and was in my office watching in horror at the events taking place in New York City that day, when I felt the impact of the jetliner hitting the Pentagon with such force that the pressure caused by the impact rapidly traveled the building's corridors. The events of that day, of course, shook the entire world. The plot hatched half way across the globe by a small group of conspirators spotlighted the threat posed by international terrorist organizations and radical Islam, and their future-defining challenge to human advancement.

The attacks demonstrated to the world that the nature of international security was changing and marked the true advent of the post-Cold War era. No longer was the security environment characterized predominantly by state threats and military-against-military conflict but by nonstate actors and asymmetric adversaries. Security in this new world would require new thinking, new doctrine, new partnerships, and new approaches by existing alliances—in particular NATO—based on the recognition of a common vulnerability and matched by cooperative action to solve it.

The 38th Munich Security Conference was the perfect forum to discuss how the United States, its transatlantic allies, and new global partners could address these challenges together. Held in February 2002, the conference took place in the shadow of the 9/11 attacks and amid the response by the United States and its partners to dislodge and dismantle the Taliban and al Qaeda from their lair in Afghanistan. As one might expect, the prominent topics at the conference were the goals, scope, and ramifications of Operation Enduring Freedom; the threat posed by al Qaeda and radical nonstate organizations; and how the international community should address state sponsors of terror.

The conference took place soon after President Bush's January 2002 State of the Union address. His speech had gained much attention because of its forceful declaration of US interests and prerogatives and, of course, the spotlight he placed on Iran, Iraq, and North Korea as state sponsors of terror and seekers of WMD. The passionate exposition by US leaders about the approaches necessary to confront the use of terrorism by nonstate actors and their state sponsors sparked an energetic, if not always harmonious, international debate.

As the attendees congregated in Munich in February 2002, the expressions of moral solidarity with the United States against terrorism were unquestionable, yet significant differences of opinion existed about what should be done and how. The dialogue on the multitude of issues arising in the post-9/11 security environment was lively, and the perspectives were manifold. The discussions did not yield uniform answers, but they helped frame key questions. What were al Qaeda's scope, organization, and capabilities? What were its true aims, objectives, and targets? What nations were at risk from this threat and why? What states were complicit in international terrorism or in fanning the flames of radical passion? Were terrorist attacks acts of war or criminal acts? What was our most effective toolkit for response?

Strategic questions included: What are the unilateral prerogatives of a state in responding to terrorist attack? What should be the response and strategic aims of the wider global security community in confronting an international menace that manifests itself in an attack upon the homeland of another country? What are the strategic pros and cons of various responses, of action and inaction—in particular the use of force in dislodging the Taliban from Afghanistan but also to addressing the broader collection of state sponsors of terrorism?

Among the central issues before the MSC was the question of NATO's proper role in this new threat environment. I remember very well Secretary General Lord Robertson's speech on this pivotal question. Acknowledging the perennial argument that in the post-Cold War context NATO's relevance was waning, his remarks to the conference argued the opposite. Indeed, thanks to his skillful leadership, the NATO Alliance had demonstrated its enduring relevance to the United States just months before the conference by unanimously invoking Article 5 of the NATO treaty on September 12, 2001.

Lord Robertson observed that NATO was about collective defense against common threats, regardless of their nature. The Alliance's relevance and endurance, he stressed, should not be dictated by the extent to which modern contingencies fit NATO's traditional constructs but rather how well NATO's constructs evolved to face emerging threats—as it had done in the Cold War, in responding to crisis in the Balkans and to Iraq's invasion of Kuwait, and eventually as it would have to do against international terror, including in Afghanistan through the International Security Assistance Force (ISAF). As Lord Robertson spoke, little did I realize that just two years later I would be serving as Supreme Allied Commander Europe briefing the North Atlantic Council just one day before the 2004 MSC on a proposed operational plan for NATO's engagement in Afghanistan.

In the concluding passages of his address in 2002, Lord Robertson stated, "These are two pillars of ordered freedom in this new age: the overthrow or forced conversion of rogue regimes that harbor terrorists and develop weapons of mass destruction, and the consolidation of a continent of secure peace unified in freedom's defense."

His speech sparked vigorous discussion at the conference. While it did not forge consensus on the best means of countering terrorism or exactly how to deal with its state sponsors, his address and others inspired healthy and productive dialogue about the extent to which the terrorist threat was a shared problem and the need for international solidarity in condemning and responding to it. In that regard the conference was transformational.

Robertson's speech set the stage for the historic NATO summit in Prague that same year; the Alliance undertook a significant transformation that left it better equipped to handle the challenge of international terrorism. His remarks laid the predicate for NATO's involvement in Afghanistan to eliminate al Qaeda from its base and remove the Taliban who vouchsafed the organization refuge and support. The Munich Security Conference discussions helped leaders gain a common appreciation for the scope, magnitude, and security ramifications of transnational terror in the era of WMD. They helped lay the groundwork for extensive cooperation across a broad range of international counterterrorism actions and initiatives to include defining the phenomenon, sharing intelligence and information on transnational terrorist groups, tracking terrorist financing, setting travel and transportation security standards, and undertaking joint operations to disrupt and dismantle terrorist cells.

The discussion at the 2002 MSC made clear that the global security community's aperture was widening. For almost four decades the focus had been on the protection of state borders, national militaries, weapons systems, NATO's strategic concept, and the level of security spending by allied nations. The weighty issues associated with the strategy and operations in Afghanistan were front and center, but from the addresses, discussion groups, and sidebars a more nuanced and complex security construct was emerging.

The dialogue was broadening to address less traditional issues of homeland security—ways and means of protecting critical international infrastructure, increasing social and economic resilience against asymmetric threats, and protecting civilian populations targeted by radical groups, big and small, capable of mass atrocity. The forum included richer debate on issues related to economics, social structures, religion, the roots of extremism, and the fundamental causes of insecurity and instability and how to address them.

Fortunately, the Munich Security Conference itself has adapted to take into account the historic changes in the international security landscape and the need to bring new partners and perspectives into the security debate. The conference has expanded its scope and membership vastly, moving far beyond the quiet German-American dialogue into the Cold War to incorporate global perspectives.

Under the magnificent chairmanship of Ambassador Wolfgang Ischinger, the MSC has helped inform the security dialogue not just in Munich but also in the capitals of over seventy countries. Even when there was no agreement, the debate yielded greater understanding of perspectives—a fundamental for building trust and cooperation necessary in the highly complex and quickly evolving security environment in the post-9/11 era.

Some would point to the disagreements, frank and sometimes even heated, that ensued a year later at the MSC in the lead-up to actions by the US-led coalition in Operation Iraqi Freedom as another landmark. The 39th MSC was historic given the differences of opinion among allies about the justification and wisdom of going to war in Iraq, particularly amid ongoing operations in Afghanistan.

Much of the debate and discussion focused on the question of proof regarding Iraq's possession of WMD, its level of support of al Qaeda, and the potential complicity in the 9/11 attacks. The difference of opinion on these matters is well chronicled, and history will render its judgments more objectively than can any of us. Critics will debate the implications of roads taken and not, but what is clear is the indispensable role of the MSC in providing a forum for the sharing of views and airing of differences on issues affecting the family of nations.

As the Munich Security Conference embarks on its next fifty years, what is clear is that the opportunity for global leaders and security policymakers to meet and talk candidly in an independent setting remains crucial, perhaps even decisive. We live in an increasingly borderless world, characterized by a highly integrated trade-based global economy. Nations are more interdependent than ever. Sustaining human progress and the global stability and security on which it depends will require greater levels of dialogue. This is necessary to affirm shared values, identify common threats and opportunities, and act collaboratively on the international security, development, and economic issues that affect us all. The importance of doing so will only intensify in a constantly evolving security environment.

This is not a century, so far, in which we are faced with the probability of major conventional war between major near-peer competitors. The asymmetric threats: the proliferation of chemical, biological, radiological, and nuclear weaponry; food, water, and energy insecurity; the trafficking of humans, weapons, and narcotics; and the collaboration of organized crime and terror pose the most significant perils to global security and must be combated. These are international threats and they must be dealt with on an international platform.

Security policy strategists and decision-makers must adjust to the reality that in the twenty-first century military might and state diplomacy alone are insufficient. Armed forces and security alliances will remain a central pillar of the international security portfolio, to be sure, but they must be part of a more sophisticated toolkit—one capable of synergizing security, economic development, and rule of law to achieve the broad human progress on which global stability is based.

Global stability is no longer defined solely by the ability of nations to deploy and defeat but rather by our capacity to engage and endow, to meet human needs, sustain economic growth, and turn promise and opportunity into jobs and a higher quality of life. In forging such a future it is clear to me as a former NATO commander that in the twenty-first century, no country, not even the United States, can go it alone and succeed. If we are to defeat radicalism, terrorism, nuclear proliferation, and the roll call of dangers facing the world, we must join forces to turn the tables on a set of more fundamental common threats: joblessness, hopelessness, want, corruption, and poor governance. In the long run, a proactive campaign on this challenge to global security will lead to the lasting defeat of radical fundamentalism and the triumph of the ideals that bring the MSC conferees together—a better future for us all.

What we have learned from Afghanistan, however, is that while greater international cooperation and engagement can solve many problems, it cannot solve all of them. Between the time Operation Enduring Freedom began in 2001 and the conclusion of the ISAF in 2014, we will have made significant progress in the security environment of Afghanistan, particularly in the troubled areas in the east and the south. We have tried our best to catapult economic programs into action, we have discovered potential vast resources of copper and other minerals that could prove to be very helpful for the Afghan economy, and we have pressed the government of President Hamid Karzai on governance, the rule of law, and corruption.

The challenge for NATO members and key partners is to forge a new relationship with the Afghan government, support credible and peaceful Afghan elections later in 2014, and assist an independent and sovereign Afghan state both economically and in the development of security forces. Yet the international community will merely take on a supporting role for the efforts of the Afghan people themselves.

As NATO forces depart Afghanistan in 2014 and wind down the ISAF mission, they will not face the luxury of being able to return to a static role of awaiting an unlikely land invasion from the East. Instead, NATO heads of state and government must once again define the future mission and role of NATO and how it remains relevant to our publics. The 2014 Munich Security Conference will be an ideal forum for that debate to continue among NATO allies and partner states.

In 1999, the MSC opened its doors for the first time to non-NATO countries. As we look to the next fifty years one can envision that the door will widen further to encompass an even greater circle of countries that accounts for the rise of the developing world. With it will come the opportunity to build greater understanding, consensus, and success on the security, economic, social, and diplomatic issues that will determine the quality of our collective future.

General James L. Jones, USMC (ret.), is founder and president of Jones Group International. He served as national security advisor to President Barack Obama, Supreme Allied Commander Europe (SACEUR) and commander, United States European Command (USEUCOM).

The Iraq War and the Transatlantic Rift

Kerstin Müller

On taking office, the SPD-Green federal government, which was responsible for German foreign policy from 1998, was immediately confronted with challenges in the field of security policy that no previous federal government had ever faced. Scarcely had we completed our participation in a painful but necessary military operation to put a stop to the killing in Kosovo when our political vision of a better world was put to the test as never before by the terrorist attacks of September 11, 2001. The United States, which had emerged from the Cold War as the only remaining superpower, was struck at its very heart and left traumatized.

Transatlantic Crisis and the Emancipation of Europe

President George Bush senior had handled the transition from Cold War to a new world order competently during his term of office and had earned a great deal of sympathy in our country, in particular through his role in the reunification of Germany. When Bill Clinton succeeded him, dreams of a new untroubled century began to germinate. In the Middle East, the

Donald Rumsfeld (left) and Joschka Fischer at the 2003 conference breakthrough to peace was within reach, the United Nations finally seemed to be acquiring political relevance in the quest for global peace, and the "dot-com industry" promised unbounded growth. The United States of America was popular and indispensable.

For us Greens in the governing coalition, there could be no tampering with the basic tenets of German foreign policy that had given us half a century of peace. Besides European integration and a special relationship with Israel, these basic tenets also include an irrevocably close relationship with the United States, despite an element of ambivalence that has repeatedly surfaced in postwar relations with the United States from a German point of view, and particularly from a Green perspective.

After 9/11, we initially took the logical step of proclaiming solidarity with the United States and participating in the pacification of Afghanistan, which included military intervention. That was right and proper, for the United States had every reason to defend itself against the terrorists that were operating from their safe haven in Afghanistan, and we also regarded their attacks as attacks on ourselves. Having thus taken on responsibility in the field of security policy, Germany under the SPD-Green government entered a new era by establishing itself as a reliable multilaterally focused player in the global political arena.

Within a short time, fresh developments were to put Germany's status as a responsible and emancipated player to the test. After 9/11, the Bush administration hastened unswervingly and utterly blindly toward war with Iraq. When George Bush and the neo-conservatives signaled their intention to take that step, the only possible response we could make was to say "Not with us!" One aspect of emancipation, after all, is the capacity to say no. The first steps had thus been taken on the road to a crisis in transatlantic relations. Driven by the determination with which the neo-conservatives were pursuing their mission, George Bush had overplayed his hand.

While German foreign policy underwent considerable development in the course of those years and ultimately acquired a new identity, Europe regrettably failed to come up with a common response. As a matter of fact, the crisis split our continent instead of uniting the European Union. Since the outbreak of that transatlantic crisis, it has been clear—or has become even clearer—how much the EU needs a common foreign and security policy that is worthy of the name for the twenty-first century. Europe's security cannot be guaranteed by the United States for all time to come.

The transatlantic crisis that the Bush administration triggered through the war in Iraq was an episode that ended with the election of Barack Obama. He is the president that the Germans themselves would have chosen, and so we laid a particularly heavy burden of hopes and expectations on his shoulders and were doomed to disappointment, even before the revelation of the National Security Agency scandal. It is important that Europe and Germany act with self-assurance, shaping transatlantic relations as a social and political partnership of equals. That is the best basis for both sides to maintain and cultivate their indissoluble ties.

The "Unfinished Business" and America's Break with the World

Not only Germany, no, the entire world showed solidarity with the United States following the September 11 attacks. Yet as closely as the Alliance was initially bound together in the war on international terrorism, as thoroughly did the United States isolate itself through the campaign in Iraq. Accordingly, the question of a crisis in transatlantic relations looks entirely different now, with the benefit of hindsight, than it did in the years from 2002 to 2005. Although we were already convinced, even then, that the neo-conservatives in Washington were on an ideological mission designed not only to complete the "unfinished business" of 1991, namely the overthrow of Saddam Hussein, but also to forcibly "democratize" the whole of the broader Middle East, the straightforward and initially successful military mission in Afghanistan had evidently conjured up some delusions of invincibility.

Our instinct had told us that the British dossier on the Iraqi weapons of mass destruction was merely being used as a pretext to justify a decision to invade that had long since been taken by the US administration and its allies. There was no sign of the "smoking gun" that, from the US perspective, would have warranted an attack under the prevailing American security strategy of preemption. Neither was there political evidence or intelligence to suggest the presence of weapons of mass destruction in Iraq. The body of evidence that was supposed to prove their existence was more than flawed. Moreover, it was never possible to give an affirmative answer to the frequently asked question of whether Saddam Hussein supported Islamist terrorism and might possibly even supply al Qaeda with such weapons.

Only after the event did we know for sure that our instinct had not erred and that CIA information on weapons of mass destruction in Iraq had been supplied to order for political reasons. Even our worst fears in those days have subsequently been realized. The US troops have been withdrawn, and Iraq has effectively disintegrated. For years, civil war between Shiites and Sunnis has raged with varying degrees of intensity by the Euphrates and the Tigris, while the Kurds in the north have made themselves virtually independent. The death toll has far exceeded 120,000 in the ten years since Operation Iraqi Freedom, and there is not the slightest prospect of early stabilization. At the same time, Iran has become the powerhouse of the region and is keeping the world on tenterhooks by pursuing a dangerous nuclear program and by fuelling conflicts in the surrounding area.

Not least by waging that futile war in Iraq, the United States has sapped its own strength. The war was costly, and losses were high, with 4,800 US troops killed and more than 31,000 injured; cost estimates range from 800 billion to 3 trillion dollars. The campaign also resulted in a reversal of the prevailing momentum in Afghanistan, where the situation was still far from under control, and its impact is still being felt in the current war in Syria. Since then, jihadists throughout the world have been able to pose as liberators. As a result of the war in Iraq, the United States and the West in general abruptly squandered the support they had received for the fight against terrorism and undermined its legitimacy. They set themselves up as targets in the jihadists' "global battlefield." In this way the United States unnecessarily forfeited its moral, political, and material claim to global leadership.

Accordingly, it is more appropriate—especially in light of the tragedy in Iraq—to speak of a crisis of US foreign policy and indeed of a blunder of historic proportions rather than a transatlantic crisis. With its policy on Iraq, the United States set itself against the rest of the world, regardless of the fact that the latter included its closest allies. The negotiating efforts of the United Nations and the objections to the use of force in Iraq, notably on the part of the respected UN weapons inspector Hans Blix, were simply swept under the carpet. In fact, it was actually France that, by announcing that it would exercise its veto, thwarted a Security Council resolution designed to legitimize the war. Even though the so-called coalition of the willing included countries such as Great Britain, Italy, and Poland, we should not forget that the governments of those countries had 90 percent of their populations lined up against them, with millions demonstrating against their government's policy on Iraq. In the years around the time of the war in Iraq, I never met a single interlocutor from outside the United States who seriously considered the American approach comprehensible, let alone supported it.

The SPD and Green government in Berlin was pilloried by the CDU/CSU and FDP opposition for its outright rejection of the war in Iraq. Although it was evident to us, and to the many thousands who took to the streets to protest against the war, that the United States was on the wrong track, there were still enough zealots accusing us of a lack of transatlantic solidarity. How far would we have had to bend to embrace the neo-conservatives' ideologically loaded perception of good and evil in the world and thus be able to justify the campaign against Iraq? Back in 1998, a group associated with Donald Rumsfeld was calling for military action against Iraq, asserting that diplomacy had failed. Had Angela Merkel and Edmund Stoiber been at the helm, Germany would surely have gone to war in Iraq as part of the coalition of the willing. A CDU/CSU and FDP government would certainly have signed the letter written by a number of European governments to express their solidarity with the United States and hence their support for the war in Iraq. There were even some dyed-in-the-wool transatlanticists in the ranks of the SPD-Green coalition who advocated a common front with the United States in that situation. A similar mood prevailed at the Munich Security Conference in February 2003, where a clear majority favored war against Iraq in the face of clear opposition from the German foreign minister of the time, Joseph (Joschka) Fischer of the Green Party, whose historic comment, "Sorry, I am not convinced," was a clear "red card" for Donald Rumsfeld and the US administration. Nevertheless, many of the German participants adhered to the majority view, chiefly because of an instinctive misinterpretation of transatlanticism, which, for many of them, evidently meant blind obedience and not the "partnership in leadership" that George Bush senior had once offered to the reunited Germany.

While relations between Berlin and Washington at the top governmental level were in deep freeze, the stability of transatlantic relations was in evidence in dealings between government departments and public authorities, whose working relations remained rooted in mutual trust. In exchanges between parliamentarians and even in talks with senior American military officers, it became evident during the crisis that relations between Germany and the United States were more than a matter of political expediency. Everyone truly suffered from the rift at the top. In hindsight, however, the predominant impression is that the relationship was strong enough to survive even a hefty clash over foreign policy. Friendship between Americans and Germans is deeply embedded within society. This is illustrated not least by the historic speech delivered in front of the Victory Column in Berlin by Barack Obama in 2008, when he was running for election as president of the United States, a speech that captivated a live audience of more than 200,000 as well as millions of television viewers.

As far as relations between the two countries are concerned, the dark clouds have long since cleared. The era of the neo-conservatives has come to an end, and in Barack Obama the United States has a president who is one of the few political figures in the country to have openly and publicly acknowledged that the war in Iraq was a mistake. That realization has not only been made in the United States but also by most of its erstwhile advocates in this country.

This makes it all the less comprehensible that Germany should display such weakness today in disputes over matters such as the NSA scandal. We can surely expect not to be treated as a third-class partner, particularly by a US president who commands a great deal of respect in Germany. If "partnership in leadership" is the leitmotif for transatlantic relations—and, after all, President Obama, in his speech at the Brandenburg Gate in June 2013, did call for greater awareness of Germany's global political responsibility—this also means that the German federal government ought to be presenting the US administration with a clear position on issues such as spying on friends and the indiscriminate capture of personal data by the National Security Agency.

A Common European Foreign Policy for a Partnership of Equals

The Iraq issue drove a deep wedge through the EU. In a joint open letter published in the *Wall Street Journal* in late January 2003, eight European heads of state or government lined up on the side of the United States. Besides the leaders of five EU member states—Great Britain, Italy, Spain, Portugal, and Denmark—the signatories also included the leaders of three countries that were accession candidates at that time, namely the Czech Republic, Hungary, and Poland. Another ten Southern and Eastern European countries subsequently followed suit. In the opposing camp were Germany and France, which ultimately joined with Russia in delivering a joint statement in the Security Council on the negotiation of Iraqi disarmament, thereby blocking a resolution that would have legitimized the war. The divide was then further widened, partly by the attitude of the United States, which tried the carrot-and-stick approach to enforce obedience. Who can forget Donald Rumsfeld's simplistic distinction between the "old Europe" of France and Germany and "new Europe," comprising all the other countries?

The crisis highlighted how little common ground there was at that time between the governments of Europe on key international political issues and how widely their positions diverged. This is still evident today. Although the foreign-policy institutions of the EU have been further developed and the consultation mechanisms work far better now, there is still no guarantee that Europe will act together when the chips are down. This has got to change, for if Europe is to assume more responsibility in the world—which would also be in the interests of the United States—it must pool all of its resources. The example of Mali shows us the extent to which Europe is required to manage crises on its own too, without American assistance. To this end, Europe must not only act in the framework and spirit of the United Nations but must also involve local and regional entities from the outset. Unless one nation takes a strong lead, however, as France has done in this case, Europe remains unable to act.

This is why we need to continue developing the common foreign and security policy until it entirely supersedes national foreign policies in the course of time. This will be a long process, because proud nations regard their diplomatic services and armed forces as sacred cows. Yet there will be no alternative. Geopolitical challenges, combined with the state of national finances, will compel us to join forces. We would therefore do better to shape the process together than leave it at the mercy of national budget cuts. For example, the member states of the European Union should entrust their consular and visa activities to the European External Action Service. This would allow efficiency gains to be made in a relatively nonpolitical field of administrative activity. In the realm of defense policy, European capabilities and troop formations should be established for the purpose of deployment on UN peacekeeping missions. Both measures would enhance acceptance of the EU's status as a global player among the European public and among its partners in other parts of the world.

European foreign policy and the European security policy are not intended to undermine NATO. On the contrary, they should serve to strengthen NATO, for a Europe that knows what it wants is reliable, not least because it knows what it does not want. A Europe that knows what it wants is also entitled to expect trust and cooperation. A Europe that knows what it wants can set its own priorities and show global leadership on issues such as climate change and energy policy. This will make it a better partner for the United States in the quest to meet global challenges. If Europe has the self-assurance to see itself not only as a trading giant but as a force to be reckoned with in the field of security policy, and if it looks as a matter of course to the United States as its first and natural ally in the world, transatlantic relations can be further consolidated and made unshakeable, and a strong partnership can be made even stronger in future.

Kerstin Müller (Alliance 90/The Greens) was a member of the German Bundestag from 1994 to 2013. During that time, she was chairperson of the party's parliamentary group (1994–2002), state minister in the Federal Foreign Office (2002–2005), and spokesperson of her parliamentary group for foreign policy (2005–2013).

Capacity for Adaptation:
The Munich Conference and
European Security

Javier Solana

Compiling fifty years of snapshots from the Munich Security Conference would yield an exceptional historical flipbook. The conference is an event I have been attending for nearly two decades now, in three different roles, and one I never fail to appreciate. What has truly stricken me during my time with the organization—which is in fact only a fraction of its fifty-year history—is its enormous capacity for adaptation. This adaptability is what keeps the conference relevant, in fact, more so every year.

While moving through the subsequent editions of the conference in my roles as NATO secretary general, European Union high representative for the Common Foreign and Security Policy, and in my current noninstitutional role, I have seen the face of international security change. During my first lustrum with the conference, in the final years of the twentieth century, participants focused on reinforcing international security following the end of the Cold War. Europe and its borders, in particular, formed a fragile scene. It was absolutely critical that we discover ways to heal wounds and find a

Javier Solana (left) and Frank-Walter Steinmeier at the 2013 MSC proper place for the new pieces in the European and transatlantic security order. This difficult exercise found great backing in the Munich Security Conference. Throughout, the participation of ministers and heads of state, even when the situation was particularly tense, was crucial. Discussions were open and sometimes fraught, but always useful.

Later, during the first decade of the twenty-first century, I was professionally dedicated to the construction of a common EU foreign and security policy. Again, the Munich Security Conference was a place where many tensions found their outlet and expression, an unconventional venue in which to truly assess the state of affairs—and to find a constructive way forward. In working to enhance the defense dimension of Europe's foreign policy, the initial paths led through the North Atlantic Treaty Organization, the Munich Security Conference's traditional axis. It was through the European Security and Defense Identity (ESDI) pillar within NATO and the Berlin agreement, followed by the lessons learned during the brutal events in the Balkans, that the EU finally understood the need for hard security as one of its dimensions. Berlin Plus, signed in 2002 not so far from Munich, was a key step in the gradual construction of the European Security and Defence Policy and later Common Security and Defence Policy.

In recent years, the conference has again proven its unique adaptability to the circumstances, geographically diversifying to reflect changes on the world scene. As economic weight shifts across the globe and particularly pools in Asia, security interests and ties follow. Each country or bloc of countries must adapt to these changes, designing foreign policies to operate intelligently within the new panorama. Indeed, we are seeing this wave of adaptation the world over, in the form of pivots, rebalancing, and other shifts. Here again, the Munich Security Conference has a critical role to play, and it has not remained blind to its environment. By including participants with an active role in the incipient Asian century, it has provided a critical forum for dialogue and information sharing.

The Strength of the Transatlantic Axis

When Ewald-Heinrich von Kleist founded the *Internationale Wehrkunde-Begegnung* in 1963, he was driven by his profound experiences as a soldier during World War II. He believed that openly addressing security concerns between the United States and Europe was vital, and from this base he created the most important independent forum worldwide for the exchange of views by security policy decision-makers.

This transatlantic security connection constituted the centerpiece from which we worked in the nineties, when Europe, the former Soviet states, and Russia found themselves suddenly staring across the space where an Iron Curtain had once hung. Before the fall of the Berlin Wall, Europe was essentially at war. The East-West divide, which had spawned proxy wars elsewhere, was gaping painfully in continental Europe. Where NATO, a bloc of capitalist countries led by the US, once represented the natural opponent to the USSR-led Warsaw Pact, after the Cold War it uniquely became the guarantor of political stability in Europe.

This was no easy feat. It required carefully putting into place building blocks capable of bridging enormous differences without antagonizing the smarting, distrustful parties. Following the formal dissolution of the USSR in 1991, the newborn Eastern European nations rapidly expressed their will to join NATO. I remember very well the multiple debates we had on the eastward enlargement of the Alliance at the Munich Security Conference. The enlargement was a recipe for the stability that was sorely needed but not a self-evident one for all sides: Russia's reluctance was obvious and understandable. At the conference, nevertheless, the support for the stabilizing enlargement of the Alliance was overwhelming.

The architecture and connecting mechanisms ultimately put into place during that last decade of the twentieth century were intricate but effective. They secured the distinct parties into dynamics based on dialogue and cooperation rather than strain and antagonism. A key piece of the puzzle was the Euro-Atlantic Partnership Council (EAPC), the successor to the North Atlantic Cooperation Council (NACC) that had jump-started NATO's cooperation with Eastern Europe right after the fall of the Wall. The NACC and later EAPC, which currently holds fifty member states (twenty-eight NATO members and twenty-two partners), provided the multilateral forum to build the overall framework for cooperation between NATO and its partners. Tailored bilateral relationships, on the other hand, are sculpted within the individual Partnerships for Peace (PfP) signed by the Alliance and individual partner countries. By simultaneously strengthening the web in its entirety and the ties between the individual nodes, avenues for essential trust building were opened. These would later serve as a fundamental base for further cooperation.

Before NATO could formally expand to include Poland, the Czech Republic, and Hungary as formal members, however, another hurdle had to be taken. I was convinced, as were many others, that this step could not be taken without having Russia on board. To do so would have created tensions that far surpassed the stabilizing benefits of the eastward integration.

Consequently, the moment when Russia and the Alliance signed the Founding Act (on Mutual Relations, Cooperation and Security) at the Élysée in 1997 was truly a great one. The participants of the Munich Security Conference lent a strong backing to this rapprochement, which I recall with great fondness. While the newly established relations were tested only a few years later during the NATO-led Kosovo operation, Russian troops did later take part in the Kosovo Force (KFOR) peacekeeping mission. The warming of relations ultimately opened the door for the accession of the three new NATO members in 1999.

Europe Takes Up Its Role

The stabilizing measures taken within the NATO framework satisfied an immediate and initial need for defense and security structures in the new Eastern European nations. Once these prerequisites were in place, a layer of political stabilization was added as these countries integrated into the European Union's Nobel Peace Prize-winning structures. The conflict in the Balkans, however, opened Europe's eyes. After the fall of the Berlin Wall, Europe's geostrategic panorama had changed completely: Europe's nations found themselves staring at a world which, for them, had remained frozen behind that barrier for decades. As described above, Europe adapted at first mainly through its NATO channels. But the need for a truly European foreign policy and defense policy became painfully clear when the EU's members found themselves unable to respond to the crisis in the Balkans.

In the pursuit of a Common Foreign and Security Policy (CFSP), the transatlantic connection once again proved vital, and ideas for novel constructions sprouted and grew from the conference rooms and halls of the Munich Security Conference. The transatlantic defense foundation was already sound. The 1996 Berlin agreement had established a strong European pillar within NATO, the ESDI. But the EU's foreign policy structures were still very young and immature. When I inherited a new post with the mission to construct the CFSP, the first tasks were those of an architect. A few years and many blueprints later, the EU was empowered with an ambassadorial-level Political and Security Committee, an EU Military Committee and Military Staff, a Joint Situation Centre, and a nascent European Defence Agency (EDA).

Endowing the European Union with true capacity to act on the ground, however, took further steps: a tricky recalibration of EU-NATO relations, passing through the decades-old structure of the Western European Union.

The keystone for this effort was laid in 2003, with the upgrade to the 1996 EU-NATO agreement: Berlin Plus finally gave the Union the essential capacity to launch EU missions with NATO capabilities and assets, using NATO's communication channels and headquarters. Following the St. Malo declarations, with the Helsinki Headline Goals set and the EDA in action from 2004, the EU was institutionally and materially ready to take up its international role in crisis management.

Of course, even with all elements in place, the machine cannot move forward without a common will to act and a common voice. As I always say, the European Union started as all institutions do, as all humans do: by learning to speak. The first steps were the statements it issued. The Union then learned to write, publishing documents. And finally, it learned how to take action. Let it be clear: there have been and always will be many struggles within the EU before foreign action can be taken. A common voice has never been easy to find. In 2002–03, for example, the moments leading up to the Iraq invasion were excruciatingly tense—both inter- and intracontinentally. The strong words and sharp debate between German Foreign Minister Joschka Fischer and American Secretary of Defense Donald Rumsfeld at the Munich Security Conference in 2003 were one of the clearest signs of the degree of acrimony that marked the times.

Nevertheless, when the member states' voices join, EU action can be swift and effective. ESDP missions started shortly after the institutional and material bases were put into place. The range of missions and their geographical scope clearly exhibit the need that existed for European actorship on the global security scene. Drawing from the strength of its idiosyncrasies, the EU launched its first police mission in Bosnia and Herzegovina in 2003, closely followed by its first military operation, Concordia, in the former Yugoslav Republic of Macedonia. Very rapidly, the European Union moved beyond its continental borders and into Africa, launching Operation Artemis to stabilize security conditions and improve the humanitarian situation in Bunia—this time, without recourse to NATO. A few years later, the EU was able to put the rich lessons of its troubled history to use in Asia, through the peacekeeping mission in Banda Aceh (the Aceh Monitoring Mission). In less than fifteen years of the ESDP, built nearly from scratch in 1999, the EU has executed or is executing no less than twenty-eight civilian and military missions worldwide.

Of late, European defense has come across harder times after the world economy took a fall it is still reeling from. European member states, in the clutches of a formidable and multifaceted crisis, have made strong cuts in defense spending. According to Stockholm International Peace Research

Institute statistics, twenty of the thirty-seven Western and Central European states cut their military spending by more than 10 percent in real terms in the period from 2008 to 2012. The twenty-seven NATO members have cut their budgets by 7.5 percent since the start of the crisis. If we are not careful, Europe will turn inward—a hazardous development for a continent with a highly inflammable neighborhood. Recent events to Europe's south only highlight this danger. Given today's geopolitical panorama and the eastward proclivity of the world's traditional security providers, it is clear that Europe cannot rely on others to douse the fires at its doorstep.

This topic has been high on the agenda in recent editions of the Munich Security Conference. The collection of twenty-eight ESDP missions is a clear reflection of the need for a European security presence in the world, one that builds from Europe's unique strengths and experiences. Now is not the time for Europe to retreat or to endanger its security role. Quite the contrary: Europe's defense industries remain an economic motor for many of its countries. With improved coordination, numerous economically and strategically beneficial synergies lay waiting to be reaped.

The Value of a Meeting Place

The strong transatlantic roots of the original *Internationale Wehrkunde-Begegnung* have fed a multitude of discussions and ideas on transatlantic and European security. The conference has truly been a place where ideas grow, especially on Europe's security dimension. The debates have not remained restricted to this geographic axis, however. The conference has always been open to international developments, and it has been a critical meeting spot for leaders involved in some of the most pressing international issues of the time, increasingly so in recent years.

This is, in my opinion, one of the forum's most important roles. Recent editions of the Munich Security Conference have brought Chinese scholars and public figures to speak, granting perspective on security issues in a strategically important and perpetually strained continent. Closer to home, no matter how rocky bilateral relations may be, both Russia and the United States are always well represented. The presence of senior Russian ministers such as Igor Ivanov, Sergei Ivanov, and Sergei Lavrov, and the attendance of such prominent American figures as Hillary Clinton and John McCain are very important ingredients; the United States Congress is consistently well represented as well. Discussions and speeches are frank and sometimes downright provocative, but the channels of dialogue are open.

The same holds for the participation in recent years of top Iranian nuclear negotiators such as Ali Larijani: while the conference may not lead opponents to see eye to eye, it does provide an opportunity for leading negotiators to meet outside of the traditional circuit. These encounters can be difficult, heated, enlightening, and/or enabling. But they are always informative, shedding some light on the prospects for dialogue and negotiated solutions. Meanwhile, on the sidelines, there is room for exchanges on such significant matters as the New Strategic Arms Reduction Treaty.

Conclusion

The Munich Security Conference is not a place where treaties are signed or where war and peace are formally made. It is, however, a place where decision-makers in international security can meet and speak openly, outside of the sometimes constricted arteries provided by traditional bilateral and multilateral channels. Throughout my career in international security, I have found it to be a highly constructive bypass, a channel that can provide insights beyond posturing into true interests—and thus into creative solutions. The conference has been a place where I have found support for many projects of institutional engineering that were necessary for the construction of international security and thus peace—through dialogue. These three last words, inscribed on the Ewald von Kleist Award I was most graciously granted in 2009, are truly the key to the Munich proceedings and the Munich moments. At age fifty, the organization is flexible yet and will doubtlessly continue to play a useful role in international security in the future.

Dr. Javier Solana was secretary general of NATO (1995–99) and high representative of the European Union for foreign affairs and security policy (1999–2009). Today, he is Distinguished Fellow in Foreign Policy at the Brookings Institution and president of the ESADE Center for Global Economy and Geopolitics.

Euro-Atlantic Security in a Globalized World

Transatlantic Ties That Must Still Bind

John Kerry

On July 4, 1962, President John F. Kennedy set forth a bold vision for transatlantic cooperation. The president was unequivocal about the mission. He said simply, the Atlantic partnership "must look outward to cooperate with all nations in meeting their common concern." Half a century later, the transatlantic partnership has become an unrivaled source of strength in the world. When I was chairman of the Senate Foreign Relations Committee, I saw that strength firsthand as a participant in the Munich Security Conference—and I have seen that strength throughout my life.

My father moved our family to Berlin in the early fifties to take on a new posting as legal advisor to the US high commissioner to Germany. Even as a twelve-year-old boy, I became aware of postwar reconstruction efforts. Walking into a building in downtown Berlin, I could not miss a plaque that declared: "This building was rebuilt with help from the Marshall Plan." And that, of course, only reinforced my belief that the United States and Europe are strongest when we stand behind our common values—and when we stand together as partners in defense of our common security.

With more than seventy countries and organizations represented this year, the Munich Security Conference has become a truly global security

John Kerry, debating at the 2010 Munich Security Conference

policy forum—and we need that kind of thoughtful, creative, nonpartisan input on tough issues now more than ever. We face tremendous foreign policy and national security challenges worldwide—from helping countries manage peaceful, democratic transitions in the Middle East and preventing violence, conflict, and terrorism from engulfing key partners to leading humanitarian responses to forestall drought, famine, and natural disasters.

We need a strong, prosperous, and confident Europe to meet these challenges—and Europe needs our unwavering commitment and support. As we look to the future demands that will define our alliance, we must continue to adapt to meet new threats and push forward a transatlantic renaissance to seize the common possibilities that lie ahead of us.

The United States has committed to deepen its engagement in the Asia-Pacific. But make no mistake: President Obama's plan to rebalance our interests and investments in this region does not diminish in any way our close and continuing partnership with Europe. On the contrary, changes to the US force posture in Europe—from the deployment of missile defense assets to the investment in shared NATO capabilities—are yielding a more capable, more modern US presence that will allow us to partner with our European allies and respond to future contingencies.

NATO is and will remain the cornerstone of transatlantic security, and our European allies will continue to be our partners of first resort for dealing with the full range of global security concerns. Even after we complete our new force structure, more than 60,000 US service members will remain in Europe, supporting US, NATO, and coalition-led operations globally.

Our partnership has underwritten the peace, stability, and prosperity of the world for decades. But we can break new ground in how we keep our countries safe, help our economies grow, and sustain global leadership now and for future generations. The launch of negotiations for a Transatlantic Trade and Investment Partnership (T-TIP) is just one example. T-TIP will add to the more than 13 million American and European jobs now supported by nearly $4 trillion in two-way investment and the $2.6 billion dollars worth of goods and services traded between us each day. It will promote economic growth, strengthen our competitiveness, create hundreds of thousands of jobs on both sides of the Atlantic, and set the global gold standard for free and open societies.

Strong economic growth will allow us to move forward on one of the greatest responsibilities that we share: combating global climate change. Smart investments in a cleaner climate create good jobs, new infrastructure, and entire new industries. Europeans have made important progress in diversifying their energy markets, with Germany ranking as the world's leader in installed solar photovoltaic panels. So we have the technology, we have the innovation, we have the investments, and together we are shaping the global direction of clean energy.

We are also working in partnership to finish the job of a Europe whole, free, and at peace by addressing remaining challenges in the Balkans and the frozen conflicts further east. We continue to support efforts under United Nations auspices toward the reunification of Cyprus as a bizonal, bicommunal federation. We also remain firmly committed to an independent, sovereign, and multiethnic Kosovo. We commend Serbia and Kosovo for undertaking commitments toward long-term reconciliation, and we must continue to reinforce their European integration path.

Our commitment to universal rights and freedoms does not end at Europe's borders. In too many countries, governments continue to crack down on dissent, stifle free expression, and limit civil society. Journalists are harassed and intimidated. Online activists are prosecuted for investigating corruption, and lesbian, gay, bisexual, and transgender individuals are faced with discrimination, abuse, violence, and even execution. If we are to lead a transatlantic renaissance, we must remain vigilant and stand tall for our democratic values when these rights are threatened or denied.

The United States and Europe share a global partnership based on common values and common approaches to regional and global challenges. From Afghanistan and Iran to Libya and Mali, we are working together to advance our shared security and prosperity. Over the past year alone, we have provided humanitarian assistance to displaced Syrians, supported civil society in Egypt, and sustained a democratic opening in Burma. In partnership with Russia, the UN Security Council, and the Organisation for the Prohibition of Chemical Weapons, we are making great strides in eliminating Bashar al-Assad's chemical weapons stockpile.

We cannot—and need not—allow our differences with Russia to define our relations. We will stand up for principle when we have disagreements, whether on Syria policy or the treatment of nongovernmental organizations, civil society, political activists, and journalists. Even as we stand for the values that we believe make all nations stronger, we must work together on the regional and global challenges we share. When the United States and Russia work in common purpose, we are each stronger and the whole world benefits.

Take the New START Treaty, an enormously significant agreement that sets the stage for greater nonproliferation and disarmament progress. The United States and Russia have fulfilled the annual quotas of eighteen on-site inspections of our respective strategic nuclear facilities and exchanged more than five thousand notifications on the numbers, locations, and movements of our strategic nuclear forces. Accurate and timely knowledge of our respective nuclear forces dampens the risks of misunderstanding, mistrust, and worst-case analysis and decision-making.

In the long history of our partnership, the United States and Europe have made our peoples stronger, and we have made the world more stable, prosperous, and secure. We celebrate those accomplishments, but rather than rest on our laurels we are working together as allies and partners to look outward and meet the common concerns of the twenty-first century. That is the charge of the Munich Security Conference, and that is how we will live up to our global responsibilities not only to our own citizens but to citizens around the world who aspire to liberty, economic opportunity, and peace.

John Kerry, who for twenty-eight years represented Massachusetts in the United States Senate, is the sixty-eighth US secretary of state. As chairman of the Senate Foreign Relations Committee from 2009 to 2013, Mr. Kerry attended the Munich Security Conference in 2010 and 2012.

Peace and Security in Germany, Europe, and the World

Guido Westerwelle

Few international conferences reach their fiftieth year. Even fewer manage always to keep a finger on the pulse of their times. The *Internationale Wehrkunde-Begegnung*, as it was dubbed when Ewald-Heinrich von Kleist founded it and shaped its early decades, would appear to be undisputed as the most important forum for peace and security policy in today's globalized world. The first weekend in February is a fixed date in the calendars of more and more heads of state and government, foreign and defense ministers, members of parliament, security experts, and journalists. Over three days, possible solutions are tested and differences resolved in a constant dialogue. The Munich Security Conference is an arena of practical diplomacy and international understanding. Many people have contributed to that success. First among them are the conference's guiding spirit, Ewald-Heinrich von Kleist, and his two successors in the role of chairman, Horst Teltschik and Wolfgang Ischinger.

Apart from the official sessions, days are filled with diplomatic negotiations and confidential dialogue on the crises of the moment. The world comes together in Munich in a way that is only matched by the opening week of the United Nations General Assembly in New York every September.

Guido Westerwelle, Hillary Clinton, Leon Panetta, and Anders Fogh Rasmussen at the 2012 MSC

The world has not stood still since the first *Wehrkunde* conference. Great changes in the political sphere and their implications for security policy have shaped and altered Germany and Europe. In 1963, many people's hopes centered on overcoming the division splitting the country and the continent. Success did not seem very likely, especially after the Berlin Wall was built. Half a century later, not only can we look back with joy and pride on Germany's unification, we are now living in a largely united Europe, sharing peace and security with more than five hundred million citizens of the European Union. It would not have been possible to peacefully attain that goal without the resilience and steadfast support of the United States. We in Germany, and across Europe, owe our unity and freedom to the political wisdom of the US and to the millions of personal ties that have grown across the Atlantic over the decades. The Munich Security Conference, with its traditionally large, high-powered, and always enthusiastic US delegation, has contributed significantly to that strong network. On the other side of the pond, the MSC has become synonymous with the strength of transatlantic cooperation.

We have achieved a great deal in Europe over the last fifty years. Not only can people here now benefit from the economic and monetary union and the largest single market in the world; they also share common values and enjoy the protection of the rule of law, which is fostered and upheld across the EU by shared laws and institutions, not least the European Parliament. For all the challenges it is facing domestically, the European Union has proved a convincing and exemplary solution to the security dilemma that plagued our continent for centuries. Germany is enjoying the longest period of peace it has ever known. Nevertheless, we are not living in a peaceful world.

One of the most far-reaching changes currently sweeping international politics is the rise of new markets and new powers. Countries like China, India, and Brazil are not only visibly increasing their wealth and prosperity; their economic success is also giving them increasing political clout and self-confidence. It is our challenge to integrate them as new players shaping the way world affairs are run, without giving up our values and principles. If we want to remain able to shape globalization, we need to complement our traditional alliances with new partnerships. The United States has already recognized this and begun rebalancing toward Asia. This is just as fundamentally significant for our own security arrangements in Europe as the rapid changes in trade and investment flows.

Another groundbreaking development has been the triumph of digital interconnectivity. This technological force is making its transformative impact felt in every major area of politics, be it liberty, security, or the generation of wealth. The transformation is reflected in debates about Internet freedom and counterterrorism, cyber security and data protection, indus-trial espionage and the fourth industrial revolution. Here, too, huge oppor-tunities are accompanied by considerable risks. The de facto elimination of distance in time and space in the digital world has consequences for in-ternational politics, which we can probably best circumscribe as "growing fragility."

Add to that the political and social upheaval taking place in Europe's im-mediate neighborhood. What started around three years ago as the Arab Spring continues to effect fundamental change in the region and is still transforming the inward and outward structures of these societies and states. We are witnessing developments of historic proportions that will affect our own security in ways that are still impossible to predict.

Some of the countries in question have weapons of mass destruction. The region's missile arsenals are also a threat, with Europe within range of some of the weapons. Were these states to fall apart, it would be practically im-possible to keep tabs on where those armaments ended up—such as in the hands of terrorists. That is one of the chief reasons why disarmament and arms control have to play a key role in our approach to security. They help promote civilian-centered conflict management and prevention. If we want a stable Euro-Atlantic security architecture, we need to place our energies in disarmament and arms control.

Our influence may be limited, but we have to support the transformation of the countries south of the Mediterranean and deal as best we can with the challenges and opportunities with which Europe finds itself confronted as a result. Europe will need to assume greater responsibility for its own and its neighborhood's security in the future.

In view of the upheaval in international politics, Germany is only going to be able to hold its own in collaboration with its allies and partners in Europe and North America. Like any other EU member state, Germany could not stand alone. While relatively large within Europe, Germany is too small in global terms to defend its interests without strong partners at its side. The European Union remains the primary arena of Germany's foreign and se-curity policy. And the transatlantic alliance remains indispensable to safe-guarding our interests in defense and security policy. Whether or not the European Union can function as a global player in tomorrow's world will critically depend on our ability to further unify Europe in terms of foreign and security policy.

We have made incremental progress in recent decades by establish-ing and developing the Common Foreign and Security Policy (CFSP) and the Common Security and Defence Policy (CSDP). We now have effective instruments at our disposal with which to give weight to Europe's concerns on the world stage. Establishing the European External Action Service (EEAS) was a particular innovation in that regard. The idea anchored in the Lisbon Treaty has flourished within a short time into a globally operational, highly capable service with 3,400 staff members manning 140 delegations around the world. We need to keep working to make it more and more of a voice for Europe in the international arena. We saw in the Western Balkans in spring 2013 just how much we can achieve if we work together and stand united. The agreement achieved between Serbia and Kosovo should be appreciated as a success for European diplomacy, with the high representative and the EEAS at the helm.

Indeed, the EU is already making a considerable contribution to security and stability in the world, as evidenced by the thirty-odd missions and operations deployed around the globe under the auspices of the CSDP. They are under way all over the world, whether, for instance, combating piracy off the coast of Somalia (EU Naval Force Somalia—Operation Atalanta), training police officers in Afghanistan (EU Police Mission), or helping institutionalize the rule of law in Kosovo (EU Rule of Law Mission). That said, the above-mentioned developments confront us with new challenges that urgently call for not only closer European integration more generally but also expanded and restructured European foreign and security policy. The upheaval in North Africa and Syria and the rise of Islamist terrorist groups in the Sahel in particular have direct implications for Europe. What we need more than ever in the light of such developments is a capable EU that is in a position to exert an influence in favor of stability and peace through a smart mix of foreign, security, defense, development cooperation, and economic policy.

We cannot expect to see budgets for this purpose grow at the moment, neither in foreign policy nor in defense. Instead, we need to make our cooperation more efficient. This is all the more essential in times of economic crisis and tough public finances. The 22 EU states that are also members of NATO spent around $269 billion on defense in 2010. That is more than China, Japan, Saudi Arabia, Brazil, and Australia combined. However, a good part of those vast resources is lost by splitting it between twenty-two sovereign, independent defense budgets. We need to be more decisive about pooling resources, improving coordination, and generating gains in efficiency. This will mean changing the way we do things in order to retain the capabilities that we need to ensure our political conflict resolution has military backing.

Germany has been pushing for increased coordination and more robust synergy with our European partners for some years. The intention of EU pooling and sharing initiatives and smart defense projects within NATO is not only to safeguard existing capabilities but also to enable closely coordinated and cost-efficient ways of developing the capabilities that are lacking. Where we commit to a division of labor, specialization, close coordination, and shared systems being developed and made available, a great deal will depend on partners having dependable access to the capabilities they require when these are held by others or maintained jointly. For this approach to work, the political will to integrate military capabilities will have to be there—and only successful harmonization of European security and defense policy can make that will grow. Besides encouraging cooperative and integrative steps in our armed forces, we also need more effective use of the European Defence Agency to harmonize planning processes with respect to the development of capabilities, improve coordination on arms procurement, and link these elements with the integration of the armed forces.

The European heads of state and government addressed these issues at the European Council in December 2013 and agreed on concrete measures that now have to be implemented. The idea is to make CSDP more effective and visible, as a complement to the North Atlantic alliance, intensifying the development of our defense capability and strengthening Europe's defense industry.

None of this will be easy at a time when Europe is very much looking inward. The debt crisis and the crisis of confidence has absorbed an enormous amount of strength and energy and raised fundamental questions about the continuation of European integration. There is still much to be done to return Europe and the euro to the path of sustained success—but the ambitious reforms are starting to bear fruit. Closer collaboration in finance, fiscal, and economic policy is needed with a view to achieving a new quality of European unification. As part of that, the three strands of solidarity, consolidation, and growth combine to help boost Europe's competitiveness on the world stage. Only by retaining its competitive edge will Europe maintain its position of influence in the shaping of globalization.

In light of all the discussions about reform within the European Union, we must not forget that Europe has plenty more to offer in international competition than its economic might and instruments of foreign and security policy. Europe has always been more than simply a single market and a free trade zone. It is, as ever, far more than a single currency. Above all else, Europe is a community of shared culture and common values. The values we share are the foundations that underpin Europe. What we in the EU have built on them has massive international appeal. The important thing now is to uphold and strengthen our fundamental values and the rule of law within the EU too. If we can live up to our own standards, we have every reason to enter this contest over values and social, economic, and political systems with our heads held high. They are our strongest card in this globalized world. That explicitly also applies to the protection of privacy. Data protection is part of our Western value system.

These values also form the basis of our decades of friendship with the United States. This is a strategic partnership whose special status has grown historically but continues to be entirely relevant. The United States' strategic turn toward the Asia-Pacific region is not a turn away from Europe. Europe remains America's closest and most vital partner—politically, economically, and in terms of security. With its unique capacity to unite the armed forces of twenty-eight nations in joint action, and its many partnerships in Eastern Europe, Central Asia, the Arab world, and right into the Pacific region, the North Atlantic alliance remains the cornerstone of our security and defense policy.

Europe and the United States need one another if their actions are to be effective in a more complex, less readily manageable world. Together we can play our part in shaping a peaceful, flourishing world—through joint efforts in pursuit of disarmament and nonproliferation, more determined action to combat climate change, and fresh economic impetus that can set standards at the global level.

Creating a Transatlantic Trade and Investment Partnership (TTIP) would not only generate an estimated gain in prosperity in the hundred billions for the transatlantic economic area. What make the project so attractive are above all the strategic advantages. A transatlantic agreement that covers investments, services, norms and standards, as well as trade issues would constitute an important building block for the future of a liberal international order. Tomorrow's norms and standards would be set by us and in our countries. Together we have a chance of making our mark on the way globalization turns out. What is more, such an agreement should be conceived as nonexclusive, so that it can constitute an incentive for worldwide free trade in the long term.

There is a long list of areas requiring urgent action in German and European security policy. It can but continue to grow in a world becoming ever more closely interconnected. Cyber security, demographic developments, climate change, refugees, energy security, food security, and water scarcity are only some of the subjects that security policy needs to address these days. At the same time, the number of players is rising too. Balancing interests internationally is becoming significantly more complicated. That is yet another reason why we need to rethink security policy, including our own structures. Nowadays, security policy based on prevention encompasses a whole range of measures from the most diverse policy areas. Increasingly, it is a combination of diplomacy, development cooperation, and elements of military, economic, and environment policy. The EU and its institutions provide a unique platform for integrating these components into sensible and operational policy.

For the foreseeable future, German and European security policy is going to be caught between two very different perspectives: on the one hand, our own continent and immediate neighborhood with a historically unprecedented degree of stability and prosperity; on the other, an unsettled world to which we are more connected than ever and in which upheaval and transformation take place at unprecedented speeds. Given these competing perspectives it is therefore hardly surprising for experts to come up with vastly different assessments of the risks and opportunities arising from our environs and of the strengths and weaknesses inherent in Europe. Lively and critical debate about the future shape of European foreign affairs and security remains essential. While open to new ideas, that discussion should, however, never lose sight of the fact that over the last fifty years, peace, freedom, and prosperity have depended on European unification.

The Munich Security Conference has never taken its eyes off those foundations, nor has it forgotten its transatlantic roots. At the same time, it has always kept an open outlook toward the horizons of the future. It is thus that the conference has become a hallmark of Germany's globally networked foreign and security policy—and yet capable of a fresh look at new challenges each and every year.

*Dr. **Guido Westerwelle** has been German foreign minister in the CDU/CSU-FDP coalition government (since 2009). He was a member of the German Bundestag from 1996 to 2013, and from 2001 to 2011 chairman of the Free Democratic Party.*

The Transatlantic Partnership—
The Foundation of German Security Policy

Thomas de Maizière

The Munich Security Conference first took place from November 30 to December 1, 1963, at the initiative of Ewald-Heinrich von Kleist. It was known at the time as the *Internationale Wehrkunde-Begegnung*. Ewald-Heinrich von Kleist was a remarkable man who passed away on March 8, 2013, at the age of ninety. He initiated this meeting of leading representatives from both sides of the Atlantic as a forum for open and honest talks on pressing issues of foreign and security policy. Transatlantic relations are thus the key element of the Munich Security Conference, which will be taking place for the fiftieth time in 2014. While other conferences focus on other topics, the Munich Security Conference traditionally focuses on the transatlantic dialogue.

Europe and the United States

The end of the Cold War marked a turning point in transatlantic relations. These relations are now different than how they were during the Cold War, but they remain just as important. To Germany, the United States is

▲
Thomas de Maizière delivering his opening address to the 2013 MSC

no longer just a power that protects the Western world; in the twenty-first century, Europe itself has become a partner of the United States and a producer of security. The transatlantic partnership has evolved from a defense alliance to a security factor at the global level. Both sides are aware of their common responsibility. The United States has developed a new relationship with Europe. It supports European integration and enhanced cooperation. "America will stand with Europe as you strengthen your union,"[1] President Barack Obama said during his visit to Berlin in June 2013.

Invoking common ground or history does not suffice, however. Actively shaping and maintaining relations is as necessary today as it was fifty years ago. It must be taken into account that not all interests are identical all the time and that occasionally this leads to disagreements. In addition, identical interests may sometimes lead to different approaches.

Relations between Europe and the United States are characterized by great stability because they are special. They are based on common values and common interests. They are distinguished by close political, social, cultural, and economic exchanges at various levels. Many examples could be given, but a few will suffice: in addition to the various contacts at governmental and ministerial levels, there is the exchange of personnel between the German Bundestag and the US Congress, there is active cooperation between the armed forces of both nations, and there are numerous political organizations and non-governmental actors such as the German Marshall Fund of the United States, the *Atlantik-Brücke*, and the American Academy. Thanks to German-American clubs and associations as well as twinned cities and schools, there is a multifaceted and intense cultural exchange at the regional level as well. In Baden-Württemberg alone—its capital, Stuttgart, is the seat of the US European Command and the US Africa Command—there are more than three hundred German-American organizations. The transatlantic dialogue is thus stimulated and shaped not by politics alone, but it is characterized by its deep roots in society and its complexity.

Europe and the United States are also closely connected in economic terms. A few facts impressively demonstrate this: the European Union is the largest trade partner of the United States, which in turn is the largest trade partner of the EU.[2] The United States is also the EU's largest export market. The aspired conclusion of a transatlantic free trade agreement (Transatlantic Trade and Investment Partnership) promises to provide sustainable incentives for growth and employment in numerous economic fields. This agreement will allow us to tap the potential of a true transatlantic market and to add a new dimension to our partnership.

NATO

The set of values established in the North Atlantic Treaty of 1949 has not lost any of its significance. It was then and still is our common "desire to live in peace with all peoples and all governments."[3] We are still "determined to safeguard the freedom, common heritage and civilization of [our] peoples, founded on the principles of democracy, individual liberty and the rule of law."[4]

This foundation of our transatlantic relations remains intact and will continue to do so. Over sixty years after its foundation, NATO remains the only multilateral organization that is able to conduct rapid military interventions and that is committed to the principles of the United Nations Charter. In military terms, it is stronger than any other power, and it threatens no one. In the words of President Barack Obama: "Our alliance is the foundation of global security."[5]

Like no other mission before, Afghanistan has fostered a common leadership and mission orientation within the Alliance. This has led to a new level of confidence of American soldiers in the abilities of their European as well as their fellow German soldiers. Our soldiers can rely on one another—especially in operations.

The security situation, however, is characterized more than ever before by strategic imponderables. Crises and conflicts can arise at any time and at short notice.

In the recent past, major changes have taken place about every ten years: the end of the division of Europe in 1989/90, the terrorist attack that took place on September 11, 2001, and the upheavals in the Arab world in 2011. The highly developed industrial and service-oriented societies of the West are also threatened in a new way by attacks on our vital infrastructure. This is due to the vulnerability of and the possibility of attacks through the Internet, and the vulnerability of trade routes. The financial and economic crisis has had a major impact on security in the transatlantic region. In addition, there is the rise of new regional powers in Asia and South America, demographic changes, and the repercussions of migration.

Traditional military superiority is no longer a guarantee for the long-term stabilization of conflicts. Neither does money alone buy security. The process of building and creating sustainable peacekeeping structures, especially the build-up of security structures, is a highly complex matter. This is also one of the lessons we have learned in Afghanistan. Europeans can draw on steadily increasing experience in long-term stabilization, reconstruction, and humanitarian operations. The challenge is to improve the dovetailing and coordination of available political, economic, and military instruments. In the future, Europeans should make contributions that cannot be made by others, for instance by NATO, in the same way. The Alliance's structures must not be duplicated, however. For this reason, special emphasis should be placed on the development and the provision of nonmilitary capabilities. NATO and the EU must cooperate closely and complement each other by means of intelligent task sharing.

The same approach is also appropriate for increased cooperation with those partners who are not part of Western alliances and institutions. In Afghanistan, Germany is the third-largest troop contributor and has successfully worked together with several partner nations. Without them, the Alliance could not fulfill its task there. The fight against piracy at the Horn of Africa also shows that multinational cooperation can be effective outside the usual institutional structures and with a large number of actors. With its partnership policy, NATO has shown that it offers opportunities and forms of cooperation besides full membership, which will enable it to develop into a global security network.

The further development of this network will be an important task, especially after the year 2015 and the termination of the current International Security Assistance Force mission in Afghanistan. The question arises how operational readiness and solidarity—within the Alliance but also with partner nations—can be maintained at a high level in the future. Within the framework of its Connected Forces Initiative, the Alliance is working on a concept that relies on extended education and training programs, more exercises, and an increased use of modern technology. The Munich Security Conference, which brings together participants from around the world every year, also provides a valuable forum for the build-up and maintenance of relations with partner nations and other actors. It should nurture and develop the special role it plays.

Reliability

Europeans and Americans can rely on each other—now and in the future. Europe may not be the best conceivable partner for the United States, but it certainly is the best possible partner. This is also true the other way around. No other region is as stable, as capable of taking action, and as predictable as Europe. From a military point of view, Europeans are not (yet) good enough, but they are better than any other conceivable partner of the United States.

It is often forgotten how much Europe contributed to transforming Eastern

Europe after the radical changes of 1989 and 1990 and to stabilizing the Western Balkans. Conventional arms control within the framework of the Organization for Security and Co-operation in Europe led to an unparalleled and orderly reduction of potential military threats from the Cold War and contributed to the implementation of the Dayton peace agreement. In many regions of the world, such as South America, West Africa, and Southeast Asia, Europe is considered a role model for regional integration and understanding. Furthermore, the EU is a—if not *the*—outstanding success story of regional peace and reconciliation efforts. This provides the EU with international recognition and political credibility, which is symbolized by the Nobel Peace Prize it was awarded in 2012.

Today as well, the EU's focus is on its neighbors. The challenges faced by the EU's neighboring states have long become challenges faced by the EU and the transatlantic community. Whether it is refugees from crises-stricken northern Africa, organized crime in the Western Balkans, or tensions along the Turkish-Syrian border—targeted cooperation with neighboring states is essential if we are to contain and overcome crises and conflicts at an early stage that pose a threat to the security of Germany and its allies and partners.

The EU also attaches great importance to cooperation with key countries such as Russia. Owing to their geostrategic location, their size, and their regional influence, these countries are not only directly affected by developments in the EU's immediate neighborhood, they also have the political, economic, and military resources to decisively shape such developments. Close relations between the EU and its neighbors create an anchor of stability that has a positive effect far beyond the region. Europe cannot assume the role of a mediator in the difficult relationship between the United States and Russia, but it is willing to help in certain situations.

The ability of the EU to shape security affairs will depend on two factors: civilian and military effectiveness and the political will to shape the future together. Both factors can be improved.

In the long term, the EU can increase its military effectiveness by two means: by further increasing the efficiency of national forces—we need to be able to do more things and new things—and by improving cooperation between member states—we need to be able to do more things together and new things together. This also includes closer cooperation between NATO and the EU. This is where it is important to overcome political resistance in order to facilitate cooperation.

The available financial means are limited—in all NATO and EU member states and on both sides of the Atlantic. The manner in which we deal with ever-scarcer resources will define the future of both NATO and the EU.

It is important that member states not reduce capabilities in an uncoordinated fashion. It is therefore imperative, particularly in the field of planning, that we strengthen NATO's existing instruments and cooperate more closely within the EU. The value of the Smart Defence and Pooling & Sharing initiatives consists in starting a process that could lead to the long-term consolidation of a broad European capability spectrum. Europeans do not at present need new visions or new announcements of further institutional steps; instead, they require a strategy of decisive pragmatism. The decisions that have already been made should be implemented intelligently and swiftly.

This also requires a change of mentalities. It is impossible to want Smart Defence but to refuse dependencies. The relationship between Europe and America shows that dependencies are not an expression of weakness. If designed properly, they are a sign of trust, efficiency, interoperability, and strength.

Reorientation toward the Pacific as an Opportunity

The increased strategic orientation of the United States toward Asia and the Pacific region is also the result of years of stability and peace in Europe. It is also a response to Europe's success and a symbol of the great trust Americans place in their European partners. Fears that the United States could turn away from Europe are unfounded. The United States has always been— if only because of geostrategic necessity—an Atlantic and at the same time a Pacific nation. The Pacific region has always played a significant role in American foreign policy. The increased focus on Asia is not surprising, since there is large potential for instability in this region of the globe.

Europe should consider the reorientation of the United States as an opportunity for deepening cooperation between America and Europe. An orientation toward Asia is also in the interest of Europeans. Above and beyond economics and trade, they have as great an interest in Asia as the United States, but they do not carry the same weight when it comes to security policy. Various developments in recent times have shown that this region poses substantial security challenges and will continue to do so in the future.

Europeans are well advised to deepen already existing relations in the Asian region and to expand the dialogue in an intelligent manner. This is a valuable addition to and an enhancement of transatlantic relations. Europeans and Americans should enlarge the transatlantic bridge and together consider common opportunities for cooperation in the Pacific region that could lead to a more pronounced political, diplomatic, and strategic presence for Europeans in the medium term.[6] Germany is prepared to make a substantial contribution to this goal. In Afghanistan, for example, soldiers from the United States and Europe are already working closely together with soldiers from Asia, Australia, and New Zealand.

More than ever before, Germany will be assuming responsibility in the North Atlantic alliance, the EU, and the OSCE. Due to its geography, history, and economic weight, Germany can and is willing to assume a leading role in Europe. Germany has shown its ability and its will to lead, for example during the European debt crisis.

The contribution of Germany and Europe to international security must not be reduced to military potential. One of the central lessons we have learned from the Alliance's missions over the past twenty years is that military power alone, however significant it may be, cannot bring permanent peace to conflict-ridden regions. In addition, no country is able to solve security problems on its own. Chancellor Angela Merkel emphasized that "We are like all of our partners—including the United States of America—dependent on partners and alliances."[7] Stabilizing and rebuilding societies necessitates extensive, long-term, and expensive measures and programs, such as those being successfully carried out by the EU in the Balkans. For this reason, we must in the future make more use of transatlantic relations to tackle security challenges together. Every partner must contribute his own strengths, in other words his own instruments and means.

The reorientation of the United States toward Asia and cuts to the US defense budget will have tangible consequences for Germany, such as the announced withdrawal of American troops. The importance of the remaining US soldiers will thus increase. The American forces stationed in Germany make a valuable contribution to the Alliance and represent a visible symbol of German-American friendship. Germany will remain the largest basing nation for US soldiers, even after the announced withdrawal. They are more than welcome in Germany.

The Way Ahead

We Germans know what we owe the United States of America: our freedom, our democracy, and the rule of law. America's commitment as "a European power," as Richard Holbrooke once wrote,[8] was the decisive factor that contributed to ending the cycle of violence in the western part of the European continent after 1945.

During the peaceful revolution in 1989/90 and during German reunification, nobody stood as firmly by our side as the United States. Germans know that when freedom is at stake, it must be protected and, if necessary, defended. This was a painful lesson we learned during the Cold War.

Ensuring collective defense has always been the cornerstone of transatlantic relations. This will rightly continue to be the case. The United States of America and Europe together bear responsibility for international security—this is the result of intact transatlantic relations. In the twenty-first century, our goal continues to be the shaping of security affairs together.

The Munich Security Conference can continue to make valuable contributions to this goal—just as Ewald-Heinrich von Kleist intended.

*Dr. **Thomas de Maizière** has been German defense minister since 2011. From 2009 to 2011 he was German interior minister, and from 2005 to 2009 head of the Federal Chancellary during Chancellor Merkel's first term.*

Notes

1 President Barack Obama in a speech delivered at the Brandenburg Gate, Berlin, on June 19, 2013.
2 Cf. European Union, DG Trade, *United States: EU Bilateral Trade and Trade with the World,* July 5, 2013, trade.ec.europa.eu/doclib/docs/2006/september/tradoc_113465.pdf.
3 "Preamble," *The North Atlantic Treaty,* April 4, 1949.
4 Ibid.
5 President Obama, op. cit.
6 As an organization and forum for building cooperation and security, the OSCE provides an ideal framework. It already constitutes a link between North America, Europe, and the former Soviet states and thus parts of Asia.
7 Speech delivered by Chancellor Angela Merkel in Strausberg on October 22, 2012.
8 Richard Holbrooke, "America, A European Power," *Foreign Affairs* 74 (March/April 1995), 38–51.

The Munich Security Conference at Fifty: The Challenge of Change

Chuck Hagel

Over the last half-century, the Munich Security Conference has helped shape the course of history and the transatlantic partnership. But the world has dramatically changed since the late Ewald von Kleist convened the first *Wehrkunde*. As we mark this anniversary, we should reflect upon what has sustained the conference and the transatlantic relationship over this consequential period, and consider how we can prepare this partnership to address the challenges and opportunities of the next fifty years.

Wehrkunde was born out of the aftermath of World War II, when the United States—having been captive to isolationism and protectionism after World War I—learned that its own security and prosperity was tied to its friends and allies, especially in Europe.

History, culture, and shared values have forged a special bond between our two continents. Together we helped shape the defining events of the postwar era, including Western Europe's economic recovery and integration, the Soviet Union's dissolution, Germany's reunification, and the growth of NATO and the European Union to include former Warsaw Pact countries.

Today the transatlantic partnership remains a cornerstone of both US

US Secretary of Defense Chuck Hagel

and European foreign policy—demonstrating that our mutual interests and concerns reach far beyond the Cold War. When crises break out around the world, telephones linking Washington, London, Paris, Berlin, and other European capitals are the first to ring. As Vice President Biden said at the 2013 Munich Security Conference, "Europe remains America's indispensable partner of first resort."

For me, this bond has been very personal. Every time I travel to the Hotel Bayerischer Hof to engage with world leaders and policymakers, I think of my great-grandparents, who emigrated from Germany to the United States in the late eighteen-eighties. During the years I attended *Wehrkunde* as a United States senator, I was proud to represent not only my country, but also so many Nebraskans of German descent. And I will always appreciate how the conference helped shape my perspective on global affairs.

As the world changed in the half-century since the first *Wehrkunde,* so did the conference itself, continually seeking to look beyond the horizon and address future security challenges. Conceived at a time when the most pressing threats to transatlantic security resided in the Euro-Atlantic region, the conference evolved to include Asia security issues, a summit on cyber, and a forum on energy.

Our transatlantic partnership must be equally adaptable, because this is a defining time in our history. Our world is changing at an unprecedented and incalculable rate—with the rising importance of new centers of economic influence and power, such as China, India, and Brazil; the resurgence of revolution and sectarian conflict across the Middle East and North Africa; and the role of technology in closely linking the world's people.

With these developments come opportunities to help shape a more stable and prosperous world, but also dangers, including international terrorism; weapons proliferation; energy security and resource competition; poverty and disease; ethnic strife; cyber attacks; and failed states and regional conflicts.

The world will continue to grow more complicated, interconnected, and in many cases more combustible. The challenges and choices before us will demand leadership that reaches into the future without stumbling over the present.

Meeting this "challenge of change" will not be easy. Looking back on the years following World War II, former US Secretary of State Dean Acheson recounted in his memoirs, "Only slowly did it dawn upon us that the whole world structure and order that we had inherited from the nineteenth century was gone and that the struggle to replace it would be directed from two bitterly opposed and ideologically irreconcilable power centers."

Acheson's words remind us that the realities and subtleties of historic change are not always sudden, obvious, or easy to sense or predict. Indeed, staying a step ahead of the forces of change requires an ability to foresee and appreciate the consequences of our actions, a willingness to learn the hard lessons of both history and our own experiences, and a clear understanding of the limitations of great powers.

Acheson and the Wise Men of his time—Harry Truman, Konrad Adenauer, Winston Churchill, Charles de Gaulle, and George Marshall among them—got it right. They shaped the post-World War II world order through strong and inspired leadership, a judicious use of power, and alliances and international institutions, such as the United Nations, the North Atlantic Treaty Organization, the World Bank and the IMF, and the General Agreement on Tariffs and Trade—helping establish the international rules, norms, and institutions we live by today. While they did make mistakes, as all great leaders do, they succeeded because they met the challenges of the day with leadership, vision, cooperation, and sacrifice. If we are to ensure the continued strength and relevance of the transatlantic partnership, we must do the same. In this moment of change, we must meet the great challenges of our time—and meet them together. If we do not, others will step in to fill the void.

As the world grows more complex and interconnected, a strong, cohesive, and capable transatlantic alliance will continue to be an essential component of helping preserve peace, prosperity, and freedom. And while our military power, embodied in NATO, will continue to play a vital and central role, the future success of the transatlantic partnership will be determined by our ability to deepen and expand cooperation in intelligence, law enforcement, trade, diplomacy, and humanitarian endeavors.

Our success also depends on how we respond to events occurring beyond our borders—recognizing both the great responsibilities that come with our power, and our limitations. Increasingly, we must act through new regional partnerships and coalitions of common interest—as we did in Afghanistan and Libya—to confront security threats in the greater Middle East, Central Asia, and Africa. We share many common interests with former Cold War adversaries, like Russia, and we must continue to identify areas where we can work together to advance shared interests.

We must also recognize Asia's growing role in both America's and Europe's economic and security future, given that the European Union is China's largest trading partner, the Association of Southeast Asian Nations' (ASEAN) second-largest after China, and the third- and fourth-largest trading partner of Japan and South Korea, respectively. As our economic ties increase, so must our security ties. Europe and the United States should work together to help strengthen Asian security institutions such as those being built by ASEAN, as well as broaden our defense dialogues and exchanges with the nations in the region—building upon *Wehrkunde's* recent efforts to include more Asian leaders addressing issues of mutual concern. NATO can be a model for how nations can work together to accomplish regional security and prosperity.

The transatlantic partnership is focusing on the growing threat of disruptions in space and cyberspace—an issue *Wehrkunde* is already addressing, as evidenced by its dedicated cyber security summit. This will demand continued, concerted, and sustained effort. The world depends on space and cyber in every facet of our lives—in our homes, our offices, our governments, our militaries, and our infrastructures.

For all the dangers we face beyond our borders, some of our most serious challenges come from within. At a time when budget problems are affecting defense establishments on both sides of the Atlantic, the over-dependence of our transatlantic alliance on any one country carries serious risks, and the United States cannot be expected to continue to shoulder a disproportionate share of the costs. NATO is an alliance of democracies, with leaders who are accountable to their people, and for the United States to be able to justify the commitments that we will continue to make for deterrence and defense in Europe, we must be able to show that our partners are willing to share in this burden. As NATO redefines its role in global affairs and its commitments around the world, its members must review their commitments to the alliance—ensuring that NATO maintains key operational capabilities. It is also important that we assure agility and flexibility in NATO structures and decision-making mechanisms so that when necessary we can act quickly and effectively.

The Munich Security Conference has stayed relevant for fifty years because of its ability to adapt to a constantly changing world. But no less critical to its continued success is its ability to understand how the world has changed. This conference was founded to bring people together, because people are the ones who truly change the world. Technology and institutions are instruments of change, but it is people who invest, lead, decide, inspire, and both prosper and suffer.

I am reminded of what President Gerald Ford said at the 1975 Helsinki Conference on Security and Cooperation in Europe, that America and Europe "are bound together by the most powerful of all ties, our fervent love for freedom and independence, which knows no homeland but the human heart." President Ford's words came at a time when conditions and relationships were very different, but their spirit and meaning still ring true today. As long as we understand and remember the importance of the human dimension of our transatlantic partnership, the Munich Security Conference will continue to thrive for years to come and stay relevant to the times in which we live.

Chuck Hagel is the twenty-fourth Secretary of Defense of the United States and the first enlisted combat veteran to lead the U.S. Department of Defense. He previously served as chairman of the Atlantic Council, a non-partisan institution devoted to promoting transatlantic cooperation and international security, and was a Distinguished Professor in the Practice of National Governance at Georgetown University's Edmund A. Walsh School of Foreign Service. From 1997 to 2009, he represented Nebraska in the United States Senate, where he was a senior member of the Foreign Relations and Intelligence Committees.

Keeping NATO Strong

Anders Fogh Rasmussen

When I arrived at NATO headquarters in Brussels in August 2009 to start my job as secretary general, the dates of the next Munich Security Conference were already blocked in my calendar. I was well aware of the conference's unique reputation as a focal point of the international security debate, and I was keen to contribute to that debate. So every year since 2009, I have looked forward to coming to Munich, to set out my vision for the Alliance, and to discuss new initiatives to turn that vision into reality.

Cooperative Security

I used my first speech in Munich in 2010 to argue that, faced with global security challenges, NATO must take a global perspective and develop its global network of security partnerships. That notion of NATO as the hub of a network of security partnerships became a centerpiece of the new Strategic Concept that we adopted at our Lisbon Summit later that year.

Our partners have played a vital role in the Alliance's achievements for over two decades. By engaging in dialogue and cooperation with countries

▲
Anders Fogh Rasmussen introducing NATO's
Smart Defence initiative at the 2011 MSC

all over the world, NATO has spread stability both within and beyond Europe. I firmly believe this cooperative approach to security is also critical to NATO's continued success.

Today, we hold regular discussions with all our partners on security issues of common interest. We continue to look for ways to make those consultations more frequent and focused, and to better engage certain interested partners on specific subjects of common concern.

In addition to intensifying our political dialogue, we also continue to involve interested partners in concrete cooperation, to further develop our ability to work together in operations, and to share both our skills and our resources to develop capabilities that will strengthen the security of all our nations.

I see a particular role for NATO in helping other nations to modernize their security sectors and develop their capacity to build security, so that we can project stability without the need to project forces. I also see scope for closer cooperation between NATO and regional organizations such as the Arab League, the African Union, and the Gulf Cooperation Council.

Finally, NATO must be open to explore contacts with any interested country, beyond the Euro-Atlantic area, because today's risks cross borders in a world where we are all interconnected. This does not mean that our Alliance seeks to expand its footprint or assume global responsibilities, but it does mean that NATO must be globally aware, globally connected, and globally capable.

Smart Defence

Yet in recent years, in many of our nations the modernization of our military capabilities has often taken a back seat to more pressing, operational requirements. This has been compounded by the economic crisis, which has prompted many allies to make severe cuts in their defense budgets. As a result, we no longer need some of the capabilities we have, and we do not have enough of some of the capabilities we need, such as intelligence, surveillance, and reconnaissance assets or air-to-air refueling aircraft.

That is why my speech at the 2011 Munich Security Conference introduced the notion of "Smart Defence." I urged nations to work together to deliver capabilities that would be too expensive for any of them to develop alone, and I was glad to see that notion endorsed by all allies one year later at the Chicago Summit.

We have seen some good progress in several areas. For example, many European allies are contributing together with the United States to deliver a common, integrated, and shared NATO missile defense capability. We have also agreed to develop a NATO-owned and operated Alliance Ground Surveillance system that will provide military commanders with an "eye in the sky" in future operations.

"Smart Defence" projects now cover more than thirty capability areas, from protection against improvised explosive devices, logistics, airlift and sealift, to energy efficiency. More projects are in the pipeline. They help allies to standardize requirements, pool resources, and achieve tangible gains in terms of operational effectiveness as well as cost efficiency, and we are working closely with the European Defence Agency to make sure that what we do is coherent and complementary.

It is vital that we build on these early successes. Ultimately, we need a new culture of cooperation across NATO. Multinational solutions to developing, acquiring, and maintaining capabilities should become the option of choice for all allies. Yet it is clear that achieving such a cultural shift is a big challenge, in particular for European nations.

My message to all allies in 2011 was clear, and it remains the same today: hold the line on defense spending, and gradually increase it as our economies recover. I have also urged European allies to work more closely together to develop long-term procurement and investment programs, to end the fragmentation of their defense industry, and to enhance its efficiency and competitiveness.

Connected Forces

Having the right capabilities is important, but it is not enough. As we prepare to complete our International Security Assistance Force (ISAF) mission in Afghanistan at the end of 2014, our forces—forged in over twenty years of operations—are more capable and connected than at any other time in the Alliance's history. It is vital that we maintain that readiness today so we can meet the challenges of tomorrow.

It was with this in mind that in my speech at the 2012 Munich Security Conference I launched a Connected Forces Initiative—to preserve and strengthen the skills of our forces for high-intensity joint operations, particularly through expanded military education and training, increased exercises, and the better use of technology.

At the Chicago Summit a few months later, we set ourselves the goal of NATO Forces 2020—modern, tightly connected forces that are equipped, trained, exercised, and commanded so that they can operate together, and with partner forces, in any environment. Alongside "Smart Defence" we identified "Connected Forces" as an important instrument to achieve that goal.

Education and training are at key to the implementation of the Connected Forces Initiative. We must capture the relevant lessons from our missions and operations, translate them into training and education objectives, teach them in our schools and training facilities, and practice them in demanding field exercises. All these elements are needed if we are to fulfill the core tasks identified in our Strategic Concept.

The NATO Response Force will continue to be the engine of this effort. It is a joint force of some 13,000 high-readiness troops provided by allies on a rotational basis. It demonstrates Alliance readiness and resolve and provides a "test bed" for multinational force integration and Alliance transformation more broadly.

The Steadfast Jazz exercise, a large-scale, live-fire field exercise held in the Baltic region in November 2013, showcased the NATO Response Force. We will continue to build upon that positive experience with an ambitious yet realistic exercise program that ensures our troops keep their operational edge and that demonstrates we can and will defend any ally and respond to any situation.

NATO Rebalanced

In all my speeches at the Munich Security Conference, I have looked to the future of NATO. So in 2013, I set out my long-term vision for NATO beyond the completion of our ISAF mission. I highlighted the challenge of shifting from operational engagement to operational readiness. I also stressed the need for all allies, on both sides of the Atlantic, to continue to invest in NATO—politically, militarily, and financially. For NATO to remain successful, we must all shoulder a fair share of the burden, just as we all share in the benefits.

There are growing concerns that the current balance of responsibilities and contributions within the Alliance is neither satisfactory nor sustainable. While European nations have deployed more troops than ever on NATO operations in the last twenty years, and have often also taken the lead in those operations, they continue to rely on the United States to make available key capabilities. We saw that in the NATO-led operation to protect the people of Libya in 2011, and with the French-led operation in Mali in 2013.

The increased attention the United States is paying to the Asia-Pacific region has also raised questions in Europe. For my part, I welcome it. The American focus on Asia does not come at the expense of the United States' continuing commitment to the transatlantic relationship and NATO; on the contrary, it is also in the interest of Europe's security and well-being.

In fact, the United States is constantly adjusting and modernizing its posture to the challenges of our times. For instance, although the last American nuclear submarine left Sardinia a few years ago, the first American Aegis ship deployed to the Mediterranean soon thereafter to enhance our defense against missile attacks. And while the last American tank left Germany in early 2013, the first American Brigade Combat Team deployed to Europe later that year as part of the NATO Response Force during Steadfast Jazz.

So the American commitment to modern transatlantic security remains strong. It is vital that European allies continue to try to match this commitment. A strong NATO needs a strong Europe, with strong capabilities, strong defense industries, and strong political commitment.

No single NATO ally should be expected to shoulder a disproportionate share of the common defense burden, or to fill alone the capability gaps that we have seen, time and again, in NATO missions and operations. This means we need much greater cooperation between European nations, whether within NATO, the European Union, or across smaller, regional groupings. It will help to strengthen both Europe and the transatlantic partnership. And it will help to create a new, fairer balance in NATO.

Toward NATO's Next Summit

At the end of 2014 we will complete our ISAF mission in Afghanistan, NATO's longest and biggest operational engagement. We will lead a new and different mission to train, advise, and assist Afghan security forces after 2014. We are also keeping the Alliance strong beyond our engagement in Afghanistan by building on the gains we have made in twenty years of missions and operations and by strengthening our links with partners around the world.

To do all that, I expect we will take important decisions at our next NATO summit in the United Kingdom. If our experience over the past five decades is any indication, the fiftieth Munich Security Conference will provide an excellent opportunity to help set the stage for what will be a key year for NATO. The dates have already been blocked in my calendar for many months.

Anders Fogh Rasmussen has been NATO's twelfth secretary general since August 1, 2009. From 2001 to 2009 he was prime minister of Denmark. Before that, he held numerous other positions in government and opposition, including as minister for economic affairs and as vice chairman of the parliament's foreign policy board.

NATO: Quo Vadis?

James Stavridis

The most consistent NATO question I heard over the four years I attended the Munich Security Conference while I was serving as Supreme Allied Commander Europe was very simple: "Does NATO still matter?" The clear implication was that it was a tired organization that had done a fine job in its day but was clearly long past its prime, if not headed for the knacker's yard any minute.

I disagree. Indeed, throughout my time behind the original desk of General Dwight Eisenhower, our esteemed military founder, I continued to think the North Atlantic Treaty Organization mattered deeply, and I believe that today. But there are really two parts to the question, and it is worth answering both of them to fully understand why NATO still matters.

The first question relates to the United States, and is a variant on the basic one of NATO's importance. It is whether or not NATO matters *for the United States.* The line of thought that seems to answer this question in the negative normally follows the theory that World War II and the Cold War are long since over, the Europeans have stopped trying to kill each other as they did throughout the two previous millennia, and that US interests are far more vitally engaged in other parts of the world, notably Asia. Under this theory,

Debating NATO and Afghanistan: Admiral Stavridis (center) at the 2011 MSC it seems ridiculous to still have thousands of soldiers, sailors, members of the Air Force, and marines based out of Europe; and equally ridiculous to fund a dozen or so big bases and many smaller sites across the "old continent."

It seems to me that both Europe and therefore NATO continue to matter deeply for the United States.

Let us begin at the beginning—with values. The things we cherish in the United States, and which are so deeply enshrined in our constitution and indeed our political DNA, all came from Europe: democracy, freedom of speech, freedom of religion, freedom of assembly, freedom of education, on and on. These values were evolved in the Enlightenment, tested in revolutions both in Europe and the nascent United States (and today in the Arab Spring, by the way), and remain at the core of who we are as a nation. Nowhere in the world does the United States enjoy such a reliable pool of partners who share our fundamental values than with Europe.

Second, Europe and NATO matter because of geography—something that is unlikely to change much in the coming centuries. Europe remains strategically located on an important piece of real estate from the perspective of the United States. As I have said many times, quoting a think tank report, these bases are not the "fortresses of the Cold War," as some have called them; they are truly the "forward operating bases of the twenty-first century."[1] Europe provides critical access to North Africa, the Levant (where our key ally, Israel, is located), and Central Asia. By staging forward out of the United States, we are far more capable of reaching the next crisis soon enough to have real impact. Given the events in the Arab world over the past several years, this seems particularly true today.

Third, follow the money. Europe and the United States are each other's largest trading partner, when Europe is viewed as a bloc. Each represents about 25 percent of the world's gross domestic product (GDP)—indeed, the twenty-eight nations of NATO account collectively for just over half of all the goods and services produced in the world. There are nearly four trillion dollars worth of goods moving across the north Atlantic each year, and the interconnections of the US and European economies remain profoundly important.

Fourth, Europe provides the most capable, highly trained, and battle-tested group of military operators in the world outside of the United States. Collectively, the Europeans spend nearly 300 billion dollars annually on defense; while only half of what the US spends (and I would argue not enough, as it does not represent much above an anemic 1.5 percent of their GDP), it is still the second largest pool of defense spending in the world. It is well ahead of China and Russia combined, for example. So having military partners who have stood and fought with us in the Balkans, Afghanistan, Iraq, Libya, and on piracy missions (and that is just lately) is a key strategic plus for the US.

Finally, there is the fact of the alliance itself. It is the richest and most capable in history. Today there are three million men and women under arms on active duty, and another four million or so in the reserves. We have 24,000 military aircraft, 800 ocean-going warships, 50 AWACS long-distance air surveillance airplanes, the highest technology, and the best-trained military forces after a decade of combat in Afghanistan. Most importantly and least appreciated, we have a standing command structure of about nine thousand men and women from all the nations (plus many liaisons from partners) at locations all over the Alliance. They can quickly conduct detailed planning, take command of a mission, and move out. Granted, the political tempo is not always brisk, but the fact of the standing command structure is extremely valuable in situations like Libya, for example. So this alliance remains a fundamental part of the international security backbone, and it is carefully manned by the nations with top-performing military personnel.

So when you look at that rich basket of benefits that the United States derives from our partnerships with Europe—especially through the NATO military channel—it seems to me the answer to the first question about the importance of Europe and therefore NATO to the US seems to be a strong "yes."

The second, and more interesting (and difficult) question to ponder is the one I posited at the beginning: Does NATO matter? Those who pose this question generally mean "does NATO matter in this globalized world?" given that it is essentially a regional alliance. I think it does, for a variety of important reasons.

First, just look at the footprint. This is not your grandfather's NATO, hunkered down along the Fulda Gap in Europe, awaiting a Soviet attack. NATO during my time in command had over 170,000 troops on active service across three continents—over 130,000 in Afghanistan, 20,000 in Libya, 10,000–15,000 in the Balkans, 5,000–7,000 on piracy missions, and 1,000 manning Patriot missiles in southern Turkey. We also had a training mission in Iraq, connections to the African Union, and partnership exercises literally around the world. So there seems little doubt that there is a certain amount of prima facie evidence that NATO is a global organization.

Second, from a diplomatic perspective, NATO continues to be very important in the councils of international politics. The NATO summits in Lisbon (2010) and Chicago (2012) brought together not only the twenty-eight heads of state and government from the NATO members, but also many of the state leaders from the twenty-two partners in Afghanistan and other geographic partners from the Mediterranean basin and the Gulf states. NATO Secretary General Anders Rasmussen is a fixture at high-level diplomatic conferences and discussions around the world, and he has immediate entrée to virtually any leader. He consults on security matters with the UN secretary general and the leaders of the European Union (notably with Baroness Catherine Ashton) on a routine basis. At the military level, both the chairman of the military committee (my friend and colleague, General Knud Bartels of Denmark) and the Supreme Allied Commander were part of the uniformed discussions about security issues ranging from Central Asia to the implications of global warming in the High North. NATO is fully engaged in the global conversation, and will continue to be so.

Third, NATO has a role to play in training and standardizing military operations around the world. With our Partnership for Peace program, we conduct officer and enlisted exchanges, intelligence sharing, exercises in the field and on tabletops, student courses, and many other functional engagements with nations as diverse as Russia, Mongolia, and New Zealand. NATO standards for operations are largely adopted in the militaries around the world, and NATO observers participate in virtually all of the big global war games.

Fourth, NATO has responded to natural disasters, including the Pakistani earthquake in 2005, the Haitian earthquake in 2009, and various other fires, floods, and dire events both within Europe and elsewhere in the world.

Lastly, NATO has been called upon by the UN Security Council to take on significant security operations that were beyond the reach of the UN itself—most recently and notably in Libya. While not without controversy, the Libyan operations serve as a good example of NATO's useful role when called upon by the UN to provide stability and security. All of the other operations I noted above were under UN auspices, by the way.

All of this brings us to the most interesting question of all: Quo Vadis NATO? Where is the alliance headed in this somewhat chaotic twenty-first century? Hard to say with certainty, but here are some of the vectors that make the most sense to me:

First, I think NATO will continue to be a significant part of broad global security mechanisms. That is different than being the world's policeman, an outcome that few of the nations (if any) would support. Early on in my time as Supreme Allied Commander, the columnist Roger Cohen recommended that NATO "avoid the arrogant-sounding 'global actor' in favor of 'actor in a globalized world.'"[2] That makes sense to me. It means picking and choosing causes and operations, effectively saying "yes" to Libya, "no" to Mali, and "maybe" to Syria, to give three recent examples.

Second, NATO must move out on three key technologies, and I believe we will. They are cyber, unmanned vehicles, and special forces. In terms of cyber, NATO should be setting up a separate cyber command, perhaps as a memorandum of understanding organization much like the Special Operations Command in Mons. Individual nations (as always) could decide whether and at what level to provide manning and funding. Given all the potential for cyber activity in a military and security context, it seems logical to me that there would be quite a bit of interest in this. In terms of unmanned vehicles, we are adding the Global Hawk-inspired Alliance Ground Surveillance system, which will arrive in 2015 and operate out of Sigonella. This is a start, and we should be looking to add other unmanned technologies, including small drones, undersea vehicles, and land-based vehicles (for mine-clearing, scouting, disaster relief, and the like). Finally, we have a fairly mature special operations command, headed up by an American three-star general or admiral, which is a voluntary contribution portion of the command structure. This should be brought formally into the command structure as soon as possible, and I think it will be.

A third factor to consider as we ponder the future of the alliance is the political appetite for expansion. This is of course a political decision for the civilian leadership to make, but from a military perspective, there are some reasonable candidate nations in the mix. I believe that over the next few years, Montenegro and Macedonia will become alliance members, taking total numbers to thirty. Georgia and Bosnia are both candidates, but at the moment each has political challenges that will be difficult to overcome (Bosnia has a dicey tripartite governance structure, and Georgia is occupied by Russia).

In addition to full-blown alliance members, we should be considering expanding and strengthening the numbers of partners. There are currently two fairly active partnership groups—the Mediterranean Dialogue and the Istanbul Cooperation Initiative, which includes Arabian Gulf states. Both have been useful vehicles in both counter-piracy operations and during the Arab Spring. It would be valuable to expand partnerships for NATO to Asia, perhaps including those nations who participated strongly in the Afghan mission: Australia, New Zealand, Japan, South Korea, Mongolia, and others. There may be some equivalent work that could be done both in sub-Saharan Africa (with piracy as a potential centerpiece). More difficult, but worth exploring, would be a relationship (perhaps for disaster relief or counter-narcotics) with Latin American and Caribbean nations. Colombia has considered participating in Afghanistan, for example. There are always anti-NATO strains flowing through Latin America (linked to historical anti-American feelings), but this remains worth exploration and keeping communications open. I believe this will be a growth area for the alliance.

Another area that I think will grow and become of importance to NATO will be certain high-technology missions. One will surely be in missile defense—we have already begun a controversial mission with our Russian colleagues, but it is definitely one that will expand as more unstable nations (Syria, Iran, North Korea) obtain long-range ballistic missile technology. Linked to this will be additional work involving the counter-proliferation of weapons of mass destruction, including not only nuclear but also chemical and biological weapons. As discussed above, cyber and unmanned vehicles will certainly be part of this. Over time, NATO may have a role in biological defense, both against manmade agents and against naturally occurring pandemics. All of these are expensive, high-tech applications that will require a well-resourced organization like NATO to be a leader globally.

Russia will remain problematic for the alliance while President Putin remains in power, which will probably be for a long time to come. While I do believe that over time we will fulfill the mandate of the 2010 strategic guidance with regard to Russia ("forge a true strategic partnership"), it will be difficult under the current political construct. The recent Snowden revelations, disagreements over Georgia and Syria, and a lingering sense of encirclement on the part of the Russians as they look at NATO expansion will stand in the way. Nonetheless, we should continue to seek positive zones of cooperation wherever we can—Afghanistan, piracy, narcotics, terrorism, and possibly cyber come to mind, although none of it will be easy.

A significant challenge for the Alliance going forward will be unbalanced levels of defense spending. If European spending continues to decline (it is below 1.5 percent, and falling), it will over time unhinge the Alliance's sense of balance. Burden sharing, as this is called, has been a bone of contention for many years in the Alliance, but given the ongoing European struggles with budgets and the euro it may continue to be a negative factor. While US defense spending is in decline as well, we will by almost any measure continue to outspend the European allies (and Canada) by more than two to one. That is unsustainable over the long haul, as American politicians will ultimately deride the Europeans for taking a somewhat "free ride." However, we should remember that while the Europeans have not met the NATO spending goals of 2 percent of their GDP (saving only the UK, Greece, Turkey, and several other smaller countries), they still spend in the aggregate about 300 billion dollars. The key will be ensuring we spend intelligently and use the principles of comparative advantage in what we all buy. In other words, smaller nations can purchase systems like minesweepers, helicopters, diesel submarines, and the like, somewhat freeing up other, larger nations to concentrate on super high-tech systems like nuclear submarines, aircraft carriers, or advanced fighter jets. The key is that all the nations in the alliance should be at least close to (and preferably over) the 2 percent of the GDP target we have all set for ourselves. Will this happen? I suspect we will see a moderate decline in US spending, perhaps to around 3 percent of the GDP, while our European allies will hopefully improve to around 2 percent as their economies come back. Whether that happens time will tell, but if it does not, the stress on the Alliance will be palpable.

Finally, there is a fundamental question about *where* NATO should operate in the time ahead. This is a real discussion if not a fault line in the Alliance. Generally, some of the members (US, UK, France) have an expansive view of where the alliance should operate, believing (as I do) that security threats in the twenty-first century are not bounded by geography. Dangers come from all around the world, and to meet them we cannot restrict ourselves to the borders of the alliance. Extremism, cyber, convergence, weapons of mass destruction, and so on can come from anywhere, thus we must be ready to go anywhere. Other nations believe that we should tend to our knitting in Europe, put the Alliance on a very defensive crouch inside the borders of the North Atlantic (a big area, but hardly the world), concentrate on exercising and training, and (by the way) reduce defense spending. Personally, I think the latter approach, while understandable—especially after Iraq and Afghanistan—would be a mistake and eventually doom the alliance to irrelevance.

For NATO to matter—both to the US and the world—it must be an alliance that is willing, albeit carefully, thoughtfully, and reluctantly, to intervene with military force not only within the borders of the Alliance but outside when called upon to do so and in accordance with international laws and norms.

I am proud of the many, many discussions I have had about NATO at the annual Munich Security Conference over the years. This is an alliance that has been the subject of controversy, strong opinion, and advice for decades but still holds center stage in both European security and transatlantic relations. Its determination and morale will be tested in the time ahead, but assuming NATO remains an outward-looking, inwardly cohesive organization, I believe it will continue to have an important role to play in the years to come.

*Admiral **James Stavridis** attended the MSC many times over the thirty-seven years of his career in the US Navy, the last four as Supreme Allied Commander Europe at NATO. He is now the dean of The Fletcher School of Law and Diplomacy at Tufts University, from which he earned his PhD.*

Notes

1   Luke Coffey, "Keeping America Safe: Why U.S. Bases in Europe Remain Vital," Special Report #111 on National Security and Defense, The Heritage Foundation, www.heritage.org/research/reports/2012/07/keeping-america-safe-why-us-bases-in-europe-remain-vital.
2   Roger Cohen, "Of Polish Angst and NATO," *The New York Times*, September 9, 2009.

The United States, Europe, and a Pivot to Reality

Ruprecht Polenz

Every year in early February, calendars are marked for Munich. The security conference held in Bavaria's capital is a not-to-be-missed event for policymakers, members of the armed forces, business leaders, academics, and media representatives alike. Invitations are much sought after. Over the course of five decades, the forum has established itself as a marketplace for the best ideas and as a high-level debating ground for the global security community.

The Munich Security Conference's formula for success includes a particularly open exchange of views. Opportunities for direct encounters are numerous. The famously limited size of the conference translates into almost unlimited access to the current thinking of the heavyweights from the world of foreign policy and defense. Added to this is the critical atmospheric factor owing to the narrow halls of the Hotel Bayerischer Hof. Tight seating at the plenary sessions, countless meetings on the sidelines, and casual encounters over breakfast or coffee make it easy to rub shoulders with global leaders. For parliamentarians, the MSC is an information hub that is unmatched by any other foreign policy platform.

Debating Iran: Ruprecht Polenz (left)
and Ali Akbar Salehi (second from right) at the 2013 MSC

Founded in 1963 as the *Internationale Wehrkunde-Begegnung,* the MSC concept was originally rooted in the East-West conflict. Yet, under the leadership of all three of its chairmen—Ewald von Kleist, Horst Teltschik, and now Wolfgang Ischinger—the forum has never failed to add discussions on new security challenges to the agenda. In the early years, participants' perceptions of the gravest threats to international peace were dominated by the Cold War dichotomies. Since then, panel discussions have steadily evolved beyond the traditional concept of state security and the regional limitations of the Euro-Atlantic realm, and the conference has been enhanced by new formats such as the MSC Core Group Meetings and the Munich Young Leaders Round Table. Today's list of participants encompasses all five continents.

The scope of the 49th MSC in February 2013 ranged from the euro crisis to the changing geopolitics of energy; from Syria to Mali; from cyber security and environmental degradation to human-rights violations, nuclear proliferation, terrorism, and transnational organized crime. Foreign policy experts from forty countries presented their views on future key challenges. The far-reaching approach is in line with the logics of "networked security." While conventional security thinking was rooted in the assumption that the majority of threats were of a military nature and needed to be countered using the tools of symmetric warfare, the current multifaceted conflicts call for integrated strategies. New dangers are being posed by the weakness of states rather than their strength. It is precisely the need for a comprehensive understanding of security that makes finding a common ground a prime task for the global community.

Another dominant molecule in the conference's DNA is the bolstering of transatlantic ties. The strong presence of American foreign policy leaders in Munich and the size of the congressional delegation from the United States never fail to make a deep impression.

A great deal has been said with respect to America's new "pivot to Asia"— a short formula for the strategic reorientation of the United States' global engagement. When President Barack Obama called himself a "Pacific president" in his first year of office, many observers perceived this as the beginning of America's abandonment of Europe. This interpretation was misleading in many ways.

Firstly, Washington's strategic shift was never intended to put an end to the Euro-Atlantic partnership. Rather, it aims at rebalancing resources and political attention to adapt to the profound changes that have occurred in global geopolitics. The economic significance of Asia, the rise of China, the Far East's proneness to security crises, and seriously strained defense budgets require strategic priority-setting. Europeans, too, have to adjust themselves to the increased importance of the Asia-Pacific region. Given our lack of Pacific power-projection capabilities, we have a vital interest in the United States' stabilizing presence in the region and in conflict-free cooperation between Washington and Beijing. This holds true for export-oriented Germany in particular.

Secondly, America's focus on Asia is not a recent development. In the sixties and seventies, leading German politicians, such as Willy Brandt, witnessed the growing attention paid by Washington to Southeast Asia, fueled by the United States' involvement in Vietnam and President Nixon's diplomatic initiatives with China. Germany's exposed position as a Cold War frontier state and the particular vulnerability of Berlin turned concerns about America's interest in sustaining engagement in Europe literally into a question of survival. Willy Brandt's strategic conclusion was that Europeans had to exhibit more political unity in order to reinforce ties with Washington. In a speech delivered in June 1972 at Harvard University, Chancellor Brandt not only explained the concept of *Ostpolitik* (eastern policy) but also spoke about the need for Europe to form "a common political will" and to "grow into an equal partner with whom [the United States] can share the burden of responsibility for world affairs."[1] His plea is equally valid today.

Finally, Washington's pivot to Asia comes as a healthy wake-up call. Even before the euro crisis, we Europeans were prone to focus slightly too much on ourselves and too little on our strategic role in the world. Particularly worrisome is Europe's contribution to Euro-Atlantic security. The obvious mismatch in our NATO engagement—70 percent of the costs for Washington, 30 percent for all Europeans together—is increasingly unacceptable from a US point of view. The dilemma is not only about money and capabilities; it is also a question of strategic burden-sharing.

America's clear expectation is that today's peacefully integrated Europe should play a more active role in both conflict prevention and crisis management in our own periphery. This was true for Libya and now applies for Mali. When President Obama spoke at the Brandenburg Gate in June 2013—almost exactly fifty years after John F. Kennedy's historic address to the then-divided city of Berlin—his plea to Europe and Germany in particular to resist the temptation of merely looking inward was straightforward and unambiguous.

For Europeans, it is time for a "pivot to reality"—a shift toward a more coherent, strategic, and tangible foreign and security policy that acknowledges the new geopolitical power configurations and is rooted in Europe's shared values. This includes rethinking the European Security Strategy from 2003 and its update from 2008, preferably in an inclusive process inspired by the open debate on NATO's New Strategic Concept. It requires intensifying "Pooling & Sharing" initiatives for our civilian resources, for example the more than forty thousand diplomats that the European Union member states and the European External Action Service could put to much more coherent use. Most importantly, it calls for a truly common security concept, more collective EU spending on procurement, and sincere steps toward restructuring Europe's defense industry.

The December 2013 European Council on Defense needs to set out a concrete timetable to boost European defense cooperation. Joint projects like the European Defence Agency's air-to-air refueling initiatives—a major European capability gap—mark the starting point, not the finishing line. Unmanned aerial vehicles, cyber security, and joint transport capabilities should be added to the list. More thought has to be given to the role of EU battlegroups and the use of permanent structured cooperation, as foreseen in the Lisbon Treaty.

Reaching higher levels of operational and industrial integration is beyond doubt a major challenge. No EU member state is willing to lose jobs and production facilities overnight. However, the global dynamics that made smart spending a necessity in the first place are here to stay. It is time to acknowledge that our future defense can only be effective if it is integrated and that we need a change of policies to move away from national priority-setting.

Equally important is sincere European investment in a transatlantic free trade agreement. The negotiations on the Transatlantic Trade and Investment Partnership (TTIP) will neither be easy nor run smoothly. On both sides of the Atlantic—and also among EU member states themselves—opinions on trade regulations and environmental, labor, privacy, or safety standards differ noticeably.

Our joint gain, however, promises to be considerable. The EU and the US are the world's largest economic powers, accounting together for about half of the world's gross domestic product. Our trade relationship is worth €2 billion in goods and services every day. Overall US investment in the EU is three times higher than in all of Asia, and EU investment in the US is around eight times higher than in India and China combined. The European Commission estimates that the transatlantic economy already currently supports some fifteen million jobs on both sides of the Atlantic, and that hundreds of thousands new jobs will be created as a result of the TTIP.[2] When it comes to savings for consumers, an average yearly gain of €545 for each European and of €655 for each American household is projected. In addition, the German Ifo Institute suggests that a comprehensive transatlantic agreement could lead to long-term prosperity gains in the EU of between 2.64 (France) and 9.7 percent (United Kingdom), with 4.7 percent in Germany.[3]

The idea of a free trade agreement between the European Union and the United States is far from new. Proposals have been around for decades but have never materialized due to market complexities on both sides of the Atlantic. Yet the shift of global competitiveness from industrial countries to emerging powers such as China and India, the continuing need for growth-stimulating structural reform in Europe and America, and the deadlock in the multilateral trade negotiations in the World Trade Organization make the launch of TTIP negotiations as much a macro-economic as a strategic decision.

Washington expects Germany, Europe's current powerhouse, to be a driving force in the TTIP process and to put our economic potential to good use. Given the foreseeable long way for the negotiations to go and the manifold economic interests involved, waves of concerns are certain to appear on both sides of the Atlantic. This will require political resolve and leadership.

European and American parliamentarians will be in the front line when it comes to meeting customer concerns in their constituencies and preventing the momentum from getting lost in fragmented interests and technical details. One idea to consider might be a standing MSC meeting format for the US congressional delegation and members of the Bundestag to ensure continuous dialogue on the TTIP.

Germany would be best advised to remain focused on the larger picture and to be creative and flexible in developing TTIP solutions that respond to the specific characteristics of the transatlantic economic relations. Conducting negotiations with the shortest possible list of exceptions and keeping an open mind about the opportunities rather than the problems will be of prime importance over the next few years.

It seems safe to assume that the state of TTIP negotiations will be on the agenda of the next MSC in February 2014. The conference has always been an outstanding forum for the frank—and often heated—exchange of views on policies and perceptions. Over the last decade alone, conference participants have witnessed a couple of defining moments that have gone down in history.

When, in February 2003, Foreign Minister Joschka Fischer declared that he was not convinced by Defense Secretary Donald Rumsfeld's case for military intervention against Saddam Hussein, the serious rift among members of the Atlantic alliance was physically perceptible for everyone in the hall of the MSC plenary. In 2007, President Vladimir Putin participated in the conference for the first time and sent a chill reminiscent of the

Cold War through the corridors of the Hotel Bayerischer Hof when he reminded his audience of the importance of Russia on the world stage and challenged the existing global security architecture as a formula for disaster. And only two years later, from the same podium, US Vice President Joseph Biden would convey the "reset button" message of newly elected President Obama and offer Moscow a reduction of nuclear warheads by 80 percent on either side. In February 2011, US Secretary of State Hillary Clinton and Russian Foreign Minister Sergey Lavrov deliberately chose the occasion of the 47th Security Conference to exchange the New START ratification documents.

The global agenda for participants of the 50th Munich Security Conference promises to be no less challenging, since a new and ambiguous geopolitical landscape is evolving.

Over the course of the last two decades, countries in different regions of the world have managed democratic transitions. East European countries joined the EU and NATO, and the open-door-policy of both organizations continues. In 2009, NATO welcomed Albania and Croatia to the table. With Croatia becoming the twenty-eighth EU member state this summer, the first Western Balkan country has taken Europe up on the promise of the Stability Pact Declaration made in Thessaloníki. Given the enlargement fatigue that is often perceivable in Europe, the stabilizing effects and strategic importance of both integration processes for our immediate neighborhood cannot be highlighted enough.

Other world regions, however, are increasingly characterized by the absence of order and by alarming political instability. In the Middle East, the order established after World War I along the Sykes-Picot lines is dissolving. The colonial border system has never ceased to trouble the region, and it has caused tensions in manifold ways. Yet, the current dynamics of challenging the existing territorial division through violence risk bring on a regional conflagration. What will be left of the affected countries cannot be predicted: Syria has descended into an anarchic civil war with terrifying spillover implications. Lebanon, politically split along sectarian lines that either support or oppose Bashar al-Assad's regime in Damascus, is on the tipping point and may be torn apart as violent unrest increases in the north, including Tripoli, and large numbers of Syrian refugees continue to pour into the country. Iraq is in the midst of the deadliest wave of violence since 2008. Sectarian fighting targeting both Sunnis and Shias might push the fragile country to the brink of a civil war. Jordan, seriously strained by the onslaught of Syrian refugees as well, fears spillover violence from the fighting in southern Syria and serious destabilization from within the Hashemite

Kingdom caused by jihadi militants. In this scenario, the potential for total regional disintegration is more imminent than ever, and a new balance of power is nowhere in sight.

A lasting solution can only be found and implemented by the states of the region themselves. The joint US-Russian Geneva II initiative aims at this goal. It would be utterly shortsighted not to invite all regional powers to the table, including the Kingdom of Saudi Arabia and the Islamic Republic of Iran. With President Hassan Rouhani, chances of finding solutions to both the Syrian crisis and the conflict between the international community and Tehran over the Iranian nuclear program have increased. One can only hope not to hear too much about the latter subject in the months to come. No news will be good news, as direct talks between Washington and Tehran will above all require confidentiality.

In East and South Asia, the geopolitical system is rooted in a difficult meshwork of counterbalance. The Asia-Pacific region spans two oceans, accounts for nearly half the world's population, and is home to some of the most crucial emerging economies. No less than four of the world's nuclear powers are present in the region. India, China, Pakistan, South Korea, and Singapore rank highest on the global arms import list. The divided Korean Peninsula, North Korea's nuclear program, and territorial disputes with serious destabilizing potential add to the picture. Yet, the region is still without red telephones and an overarching multilateral security architecture.

In Africa, despite the continent's enormous human and economic potential, threats to security and stability remain high—from Somalia to Mali and from the Democratic Republic of Congo to the Sahel Zone. Since 2003, the EU alone has launched fourteen civilian and military missions to African countries—more than to any other world region and, in the case of the maritime antipiracy European Union Naval Force mission in Somalia, particularly robust. In North Africa, the popular uprisings of the Arab Spring have initiated political transition processes and put an end to autocratic regimes in Tunisia, Egypt, Libya, and Yemen. However, social fragmentation along tribal, ethnic, and religious lines; political rifts between Islamists and secularists; the emergence of radical parties; grim fights over the postrevolutionary order; "winner-takes-all" mentalities; and particularly low levels of pluralism and mutual trust remain major hurdles. Political, economic, and social instabilities continue to burden the countries on the southern shores of Europe.

For more than half a century, the United States held the keys to global order. This is still indispensable today, yet parameters have changed. In the new world of the twenty-first century, Americans are neither willing nor able to play the leading role everywhere at once. The financial and economic crisis, the debt burden, ongoing political polarization in US policy-making, the strategic significance of growing energy independence, and the rise of new powers—all of these factors influence Washington's geostrategic cost-benefit analysis and need to be thoroughly understood.

For Europeans, the new global posture of the United States leads to at least three conclusions:

1. Europe needs to get its act together and take a major step forward on European security and defense integration. It would be a historic failure to allow arguments over national sovereignty and the protection of domestic jobs to prevail and create an excuse for continued military and industrial fragmentation. Quite the contrary is necessary if we want to accept responsibility for our own security and contribute to stability in our neighborhood.

2. The transatlantic partnership remains the cornerstone of Euro-Atlantic security. "Free rides" and a two-tiered NATO are unacceptable. The European contribution to NATO must be relevant if Europe wants to be a partner on an equal footing. The burdens and benefits of the Alliance's commitments need to be shared more fairly. Germany, for decades a beneficiary of NATO solidarity, has many reasons to highlight the principles and joint values that underlie NATO and to work toward strengthening the European pillar within the transatlantic alliance.

3. Among the European Union's ten strategic partnerships, the EU-Russia relationship stands out. Russia is its largest neighbor and third-largest trading partner, a UN veto power and G20 member, important to European security, and a key energy supplier to numerous EU member countries, including Germany. The relationship has seen ups and downs and European disagreements with Moscow on the rule of law and the role of civil society, and trade issues are manifold. Yet strategic concerns on the situation in Syria, the Iranian nuclear program, Afghanistan, North Korea, and the threats of terrorism and illicit drug trafficking are shared. In the case of Syria, the road to Damascus leads through Moscow, and the joint Russian-US initiative for a Geneva II conference has the European Union's full support. It will serve Europe's joint interests to work toward solving existing differences, keep Moscow engaged, and deepen and broaden the strategic scope of our cooperation wherever possible.

The 50th Munich Security Conference will be a most suitable platform to exchange views on a geopolitical landscape that is marked by power shifts and deepening interdependence. True to the forum's mission, participants from all world regions will be certain to find the main security issues of our time addressed. It is precisely the mix of global strategic thinking and the striving for the best ideas that makes the Munich Security Conference an indispensable forum.

Ruprecht Polenz (Christian Democratic Union, CDU) was a member of the German parliament from 1994 to 2013. From 2005 to 2013, he was chairman of the Committee on Foreign Affairs. In 2000, he was secretary general of the CDU.

Notes

1 Willy Brandt, "Thanking America: Twenty-Five Years after the Announcement of the Marshall Plan" (speech, Harvard University, Cambridge, MA, June 5, 1972), www.gmfus. org/thanking-america-willy-brandts-marshall-memorial-convocation-speech/ (accessed August 28, 2013).
2 European Commission – IP/13/548: Transatlantic Trade and Investment Partnership: Commissioner Karel De Gucht Welcomes Member States' GreenLight to Start Negotiations, 14/06/2013 europa.eu/rapid/press-release_IP-13-548_en.htm (accessed August 28, 2013).
3 Gabriel Felbermayr, Benedikt Heid, Sybille Lehwald (2013): Transatlantic Trade and Investment Partnership (TTIP): Who Benefits from a Free Trade Deal? Bertelsmann Stiftung, 2013, 24, www.bfna.org/sites/default/files/TTIP-GED%20study%2017June%20 2013.pdf (accessed August 28, 2013).

Indispensable Partners in an Uncertain World

Constanze Stelzenmüller

US Vice President Joseph Biden is not the man to leave an audience in doubt of his message. "Europe remains America's indispensable partner of first resort," he said in a keynote speech at the 2013 Munich Security Conference. He added: "And, if you'll forgive some presumptuousness, I believe we remain your indispensable partner."

What a difference ten years make. A decade earlier, in the same buttery-yellow ballroom of the Bayerischer Hof (and with much the same audience), with Afghanistan seething and another, much larger war looming in Iraq, US Secretary of Defense Donald Rumsfeld had dismissed the doubts and fears of many of America's long-standing NATO partners with cheerful contempt as "so Old Europe." German Foreign Minister Joschka Fischer, a Green transatlanticist, his face even more agonizingly crumpled than usual, spat back: "Sorry, I am not convinced!" Then, the tension in the ballroom had been palpable. Biden's remarks, delivered with the vice president's customary geniality, were received with smiles all round. So, is the transatlantic relationship back to business as usual?

Hardly—and not just because US-European relations appear to be enter-

▲
Constanze Stelzenmüller (center) and Eric Gujer (left)

ing a new stormy phase due to allegations of National Security Agency spying on European (and especially German) institutions, businesses, and ordinary citizens. The past ten years have taught us all sharp lessons about the limitations of Western power, influence, and legitimacy. And the shape of the current strategic landscape gives no cause for complacency on either side of the Atlantic.

Seen in retrospect, 2003 marked an apogee of hubris and hysteria in the transatlantic relationship: illusions of global hegemony based on hard power on the American side, delusions of a counter-utopia based on moral superiority and soft power on the European side. As we now know, things went swiftly downhill from there. American-led forces left Iraq in 2011; the country remains riven with sectarian violence. NATO, battered and humbled, is preparing to leave a brittle Afghanistan in 2014; meanwhile, the Taliban have opened an embassy for the "Islamic Emirate of Afghanistan" in Doha. In Libya, where a coalition of European NATO members (with the US "leading from behind") intervened to depose Muammar al-Gaddafi in 2011, Islamist militias continue to spread terror. There are many legitimate reasons for American and European reluctance to intervene militarily in the unfolding Syrian catastrophe—despite the use of chemical weapons by the regime against its own people. But it is undeniably also informed by a profound sense of failure in all but a few (the Balkans, East Timor) of the previous two decades of intervention.

The global economic crisis, now in its fifth year, has morphed from a financial market crisis and global recession into a full-blown economic and political crisis. America appears to be showing some green shoots of recovery, and a number of European economies, notably the Baltic countries, have successfully undergone wrenching austerity programs. Yet Europe is now split into Northern creditor and Southern debtor nations with an alarming youth unemployment rate. An end to the crisis is still not in sight. Perhaps the most alarming revelation the crisis has produced is the vulnerability of our supposedly robust and confident market economies, our social contracts, and our institutions of representative democracy.

Finally, take the Arab rebellions, Russian civil society protests, demonstrations against government corruption in Brazil, the hyperactive Chinese blogosphere: around the world, movements are afoot that assert the rights of human dignity and citizenship against authoritarian or corrupt governments—rights that form the very core of Western values. Western governments appear to have understood that their past support for authoritarian rulers exposed them to justified accusations of hypocrisy and double standards. President Obama's speech of May 2011, in which he compared the

Tunisian fruit vendor Mohamed Bouazizi (whose self-immolation sparked off the North African uprisings) with the American civil rights icon Rosa Parks, remains the most eloquent articulation of this insight. But American or European governments have little influence, let alone leverage—indeed, little credibility—with the protesters. The reason is simple: because they have done little, far too little, to support their aspirations.

Ten years on, the global strategic landscape has undergone profound changes: globalization and economic interdependence, the empowerment of individuals, the erosion of state power, the rise of non-Western powers. Some observers maintain that these changes mark the end of the postwar liberal world order created by the West, and with it the end of the trans-atlantic relationship.

This situation, the argument goes, is a welcome and long-overdue opportunity to throw off the fetters of outdated alliances and universal normative frameworks such as the United Nations and its sub-organizations, NATO, even the European Union. In a fluid and uncertain environment, coalitions of the willing and non-binding codes of conduct are as good as it will ever get again. Decline? Face it! Embrace it! (Note: Europeans usually make this particular recommendation to Americans. And, occasionally, vice versa.) Anyway, if you are not comfortable with decline quite yet, get used to the idea that growth and income can only ever be found in commerce with the new powers, and on their terms. And if China, Russia, and others play zero-sum games—particularly where access to scarce resources is concerned—then so must we; only better, of course. Oh, and as for the "commons": well, that is just what we used to call spaces we could not conquer, dominate, control, or exploit; technology has changed all that. Multilateralism is so postwar; but multipolarity is good for business! Meanwhile, we had better make sure our borders are secured; in a zero-sum world, others are going to want what we have, and we had better protect our goods against the have-nots. Caricature? Perhaps. But surely one that is easily recognizable, and with good reason.

For like all caricatures, this one contains no small degree of truth. Ad-hoc coalitions and informal workarounds have become common currency even within multilateral frameworks; the Libya intervention split NATO down the middle. What is "commercial foreign policy" (as espoused explicitly by the United Kingdom and Canada, and implicitly by many others) if not license to make deals with Russia or China, regardless of their human rights record? "Helping others help themselves" (Robert Gates) through security sector development: sounds plausible but looks a lot less great if it is about—by way of actual example—Germany selling tanks to authoritarian regimes like Saudi Arabia, who might well be tempted to use them not for tank warfare but for crowd control (as its neighbor Bahrain did in 2011). China's determined worldwide push for access to rare earths has found not just resistance but imitators; a country like Mongolia—possessor of significant rare earth deposits—is finding itself wooed assiduously by European nations (again, including Germany) who not long ago treated it as a strategically irrelevant former Soviet backwater. Climate change and/or technological advances are turning the Arctic, the deep sea, and outer space itself into contested domains. Immigration reform in the US comes at the price of massive new fortifications at the Mexican border. And the Schengen Treaty, a milestone of European integration that abolished passport controls among twenty-six European countries, is increasingly subject to reservations and opt-outs—not just because of migrants trying to enter the EU but also because of migration *within* the territory of the European Union. The proposed Transatlantic Trade and Investment Partnership is already being called into question by special interests on both sides of the Atlantic. Last but not least, populist politicians (in Europe, France's Marine le Pen or the UK's Nigel Farage come to mind) have gained ground by ruthlessly playing on voters' fears in the economic crisis. No need to look abroad for zero-sum thinking.

So why bother with the transatlantic relationship? Simple: because under the circumstances just described, the United States and Europe *need each other* as they have never done before in the history of their alliance. Throughout the Cold War, the relationship was about the traumatic shared experience of a world war and the deterrence and containment of a common threat. It was never free from distrust and conflict, but it worked—perhaps more than either side ever expected. After the velvet revolutions and the fall of the Berlin Wall in 1989, and finally the dissolution of the Warsaw Pact and the Soviet Union itself, the *raison d'être* of the relationship shifted to completing "Europe whole and free"—a continent-wide zone of peace, freedom, and prosperity that some hoped might someday include Russia. That task was only partially accomplished. Still, the crisis-defying queue for EU and euro membership bears testimony to the continued attraction of the European model; and in July 2013, a former Soviet Republic—Lithuania—took over the rotating EU Presidency for the first time. Increasingly, Washington also looked to Europe to help solve larger problems: stabilizing the Balkans, containing the Iranian nuclear threat, Middle East peace.

Then, in response to the atrocities perpetrated by al Qaeda on September 11, 2001, a "global war on terror" was declared (and ordained as NATO's new overarching mission at the 2002 Prague Summit): a state of permanent worldwide war against an asymmetric enemy as the new paradigm for transatlantic relations. As a military strategy, this concept foundered first in Afghanistan and then, even more disastrously, in Iraq; al Qaeda was disbanded and its successor franchises kept at bay, mainly by patient police and intelligence work. Yet its most decisive and lasting impact was felt elsewhere: in the ramping up of transatlantic intelligence cooperation and of the intelligence apparatus and executive powers in the United States, as well as in some of its allies—with consequences that became visible in the NSA spying scandal. Inasmuch as it eroded Western influence and legitimacy, however, it may well have contributed to the "rise of the rest."

So the new paradigm for transatlantic relations is exactly what Vice President Biden said it was in Munich: in today's global strategic landscape the United States and Europe are now *indispensable to each other*. Not because we are in terminal decline, as some critics have suggested; flawed and vulnerable our polities may be, our liberal values and our pluralist and participatory polities allow us to innovate and adapt in ways that will forever elude authoritarian countries. But our power—hard and soft—is relatively diminished by our own actions and omissions as well as by the rise of the emerging powers. We need each other to leverage our influence and legitimacy, and because, as Joseph Nye has noted, we provide the largest pool worldwide of resources for dealing with common transnational problems. And we are still each other's largest trading partners and military allies.

Above all, however, we share a broad set of values and interests, first among them an existential common interest in preserving a free, peaceful, and rule-based global order—because that enables us to reap the benefits of globalization in the form of free movement of people, goods, data, and ideas. Western nations will have to accommodate rising powers within this order by sharing both wealth and power in international forums with them. And indeed, there are many rising powers with burgeoning middle classes who, if they do not share all of our values, often share an interest in the preservation and adaptation of this order, and are quite likely to become what Robert Zoellick once called "responsible stakeholders." The double conundrum for the transatlantic relationship in this context is how to turn challengers into stakeholders without compromising on Western liberal principles, and how to contain or deter spoilers. But here, too, we are and will be indispensable for each other. One thing, at any rate, is certain: we will fail at this task if we do not set out to achieve it together.

Constanze Stelzenmüller is Senior Transatlantic Fellow at The German Marshall Fund of the United States.

Euro-Atlantic Security:
Before and after the "Reset"

Frank-Walter Steinmeier

The history of the transatlantic partnership was and is closely linked with the Munich Security Conference, which celebrates its fiftieth anniversary this year. For decades, the Hotel Bayerischer Hof in the heart of Munich has provided the setting for speeches and discussions and—probably much more important and formative—for informal talks and contacts on the fringes of the conference events.

Secure Areas for Discussing Foreign Policy

In the beginning, in the sixties and seventies, it was a very manageable group of politicians, military officers, and civilian security experts who met under the conference leadership of the legendary Ewald-Heinrich von Kleist. The Munich Security Conference has tried to maintain a certain degree of exclusivity to the present day, even though the circle of participants has gradually expanded and broadened from year to year.

Today, the hustle and bustle in the corridors of the Bayerischer Hof, which

Frank-Walter Steinmeier on the panel during the 2013 conference the tradition-conscious organizers unwaveringly and rightly continue to use, sometimes resembles that at a London underground station during the rush hour rather than that of a sober meeting of experts. The invitations are much sought after, and anyone allowed in may count themselves as part of the select club of one of the most influential groups of security policy experts in the world.

Now in its fiftieth year, the Munich Security Conference is also—and possibly more than ever before—a magnet for politicians and security experts from all over the world. Quite rightly so and with good reason, as it is one of those increasingly rare places where an open exchange on the burning foreign and security policy issues of the age can take place beyond and independently of the straitjacket of protocol and summit rhetoric. These are the spaces that politics so urgently needs in order to provide an impetus for new political initiatives and also to test their acceptance and viability in a battle of intellects away from the public spotlight.

From Cynical Certainties to New Complexity

At the center of the discussions in the early years there was, of course, that conflict that had influenced, reshaped, and structured the general security policy situation in practically all parts of the world for over four decades. The East-West conflict was the unalterable fixed point of security policy debates until late into the eighties.

The threat of massive nuclear overkill capability was of vital significance and ever present. In retrospect, however, it was at the same time calculable, settled, and clearly identifiable in a cynical way. The security policy debates, including those taking place in Munich each year, in essence revolved around the same old questions: the latest developments in military potential, various strategic operational options, and first- and second-strike capabilities. Yet they also revolved around questions regarding the sharing of the military burden within the defense alliance and a fair share of the work in ensuring security for the free world.

This situation, which remained more or less stable for the first twenty-five years of the history of the Munich Security Conference, came to a rapid end with the collapse of the Warsaw Pact; an end, moreover, that taught the security policy community, and not just those who assembled at the Bayerischer Hof, modesty and realism when assessing their own limited analysis and forecasting capabilities. No one had the epoch-making change on their radar, and no one had the blueprints in their pocket for dealing with the new security policy challenges and the new threats looming on the horizon.

The Western defense alliance was facing new tasks. NATO had lost the fundamental basis for its existence in a positive sense. Was it still really needed, when many were already enthusing about the end of history? What would a future European security strategy look like now that the division of Europe had been overcome?

There was ample material for discussions and for developing visions and concepts. Those were challenging and exciting years. At the Bayerischer Hof too, where former opponents were suddenly greeted as new and welcome guests and the debates became more and more animated, fresh, and diverse but at the same time clearly more complex and less clear-cut.

Talking with Rather than about Each Other

I myself had been a keen observer for many years before I came to Munich as a speaker and participant for the first time in 2006 as the newly appointed foreign minister of the Federal Republic of Germany.

By then, the epoch-making change of 1989/90 was already quite a long way in the past. While the new order in Europe was almost complete, the new order in the world was by no means complete. Numerous crises and conflicts kept foreign and security policymakers busy throughout the world. The resolving of the conflict surrounding the Iranian nuclear program, a lasting peace in the Middle East, the stabilization of Afghanistan: these were the issues that were reflected in my speech and also shaped the agenda of the Munich Security Conference.

Together with Igor Ivanov, secretary of Russia's Security Council, and Bob Zoellick, president of the World Bank, we discussed the future of NATO on that afternoon in Munich. In my speech I had carefully attached partic-ular importance to the fact that we were conducting the discussions on the future tasks and the shape of NATO not as a monologue among its members but as part of a greater task: namely, to ensure security, in cooperation with other influential powers, in a world that had become more complex.

My core argument then was that the European Union, the United States, and Russia are indispensable strategic partners for each other. Indispens-able because only by joining forces can they solve the global problems. I was convinced that that applied to Iran just as much as to the Middle East and Afghanistan and—right at the top of the agenda at that time—to the solution to the Kosovo question.

To this day—unfortunately, it should be said, in view of the still unresolved conflicts—all that sounds very topical. And the list of crises awaiting a solution can be extended effortlessly, for new trouble spots have not waited for old ones to be resolved. Developments in Egypt and the tragedy in Syria have further increased the complexity and lack of transparency of the international security situation—and made the need for cooperation even across ideological boundaries more urgent than ever.

In 2006 this view was by no means universally accepted, not even among the experts and decision-makers who had gathered in Munich. The discussions that we had to have at that time, particularly with the transatlantic partners, concerning the role of and the appropriate way of dealing with Russia were at times difficult and laborious.

Old and New Cold War Warriors

Unmistakably, the thought process in many minds was still caught in those thought patterns of bloc confrontation that had been practiced over decades. Above all, discussions were still about instead of with Russia. People still thought in terms of rivalry and opposition, spheres of influence, and containment.

That was true of the close circle of the Munich Security Conference. However, it also applied beyond there. Russian offers of talks and initiatives on issues of European security and on closer economic cooperation were regarded as scarcely worthy of examination and, unfortunately, Russia often enough made it easier to adopt this attitude. The inclination to align mutual security interests was less marked. For example, the missile defense project was pushed ahead without particular consideration for Russian sensibilities.

All that contributed to a situation in which the Russian-American climate clearly cooled further in the Bush era, instead of at least falling into line with the mood of business-like, responsible mutual cooperation. The whispering about an approaching new phase of the Cold War that was doing the rounds in parts of the United States security establishment had the nature of a self-fulfilling prophecy in the end.

The first appearance of a Russian president at the Munich Security Conference, which no one who was there will ever forget, fell into this context.

Vladimir Putin's participation was, as such, already a special event. His speech itself should hold a firm place in the history of the conference. The frankness with which the Russian president expressed his displeasure and frustration regarding the lack of willingness on the part of the Western community, and particularly the US, to cooperate and enter into a dialogue caused a sensation. A great deal was pointed and exaggerated, even aggressive. But it was also the angry reaction to a policy of wasted opportunities and a lack of awareness regarding a still important power that was looking for its place in an emerging new world order—and, what is more, still is.

End of the Leaden Times

For everyone who was and is convinced that we are fated to cooperate and that today's and tomorrow's crises and conflicts cannot be overcome with yesterday's political categories and perceptions, the electoral victory of Barack Obama in November 2008 was a hopeful signal.

In fact, the leaden times in the Russian-American relationship came to an end surprisingly quickly when the new president took office. The symbolic reset button, pressed jointly by Secretary of State Hillary Clinton and Foreign Minister Sergey Lavrov in March 2009 with such high public impact, introduced a phase of productive cooperation that produced lasting results.

In this respect, everyone thinks first of all of the significant successes regarding disarmament and arms control. And, in fact, it was and is to Obama's lasting credit that he brought this issue back onto the security policy agenda.

Still, in February 2008, when I spoke at the Bayerischer Hof about the need for further nuclear disarmament, I got a great many frowns and, above all, condescending smiles from the old MSC bucks. Many regarded this as an issue of the last century; some found the call for a reduction in the nuclear arsenal very naïve and dangerous.

The fact that, in this general atmosphere, Obama adopted no less than the vision of a "Global Zero" barely a year later was courageous and pioneering, and it opened the door to the greatest success in disarmament policy of the last few years. The New START agreement was, without doubt, the most striking and tangible result of the reset, and its significance extends far beyond its actual content. Disarmament and arms control have again become a firm foundation of American-Russian cooperation, a foundation that has the potential to maintain lines of communication, even during phases of political cooling-off, and stop them being broken off completely. For this reason alone, it was a good thing and right that President Obama, in his speech before the Brandenburg Gate in summer 2013, announced that he would strive for a further reduction in strategic and substrategic arsenals.

However, as is well known, the reset had by no means reached an end with the considerable negotiating successes regarding disarmament and arms control. Cooperation on security policy between the United States and Russia blossomed in a way hardly ever known in the past. There were cooperation agreements relating to Afghanistan, joint initiatives on combating terrorism and on cyber security, and, at the least, a new culture of discussion with regard to missile defense. In addition, there were numerous initiatives for closer cooperation beyond traditional security policy, in the field of economics and innovation, in the promotion of dialogue in civil society, in cultural exchange. All this remained somewhat below the general threshold of perception, but it was an important component of the efforts to establish firm ties between the former rivals.

In many aspects, the new alignment of the American-Russian policy resembled the modernization partnership that Germany had offered the Russian partners during my period as foreign minister and which had become a fundamental guideline of EU-Russian policy. The reset strategy and the modernization partnership are based on a similar philosophy, which focuses on identifying areas of joint interest, organizing joint successes in cooperation, and also providing incentives for the internal modernization of Russia on the way to cooperation and exchange.

Disappointment, Hardening of Attitudes, Estrangement

The American-Russian reset also brought some notable collateral results, which were not necessarily part of the actual agenda. The fact that, in 2012, Russia finally ended up in the World Trade Organization after nineteen years of negotiations can with some justification be ascribed, at least indirectly, to the improved Russian-American relations. In addition, the improved climate between the former rivals may have played a part in the fact that Russia did not make use of its right of veto at a decisive point in the vote on a Libya resolution in the Security Council in spring 2011, to the surprise of many.

Many observers see in what followed an important reason why, after a phase of prolific and fruitful cooperation, the American-Russian relationship has clearly deteriorated again.

It has been shown that the military activities of France, Britain, the United States, and other allies in Libya were regarded by Russia as a breach of resolutions and agreements. And it must be accepted as plausible to some extent that the Libya experience is also influencing Russia's behavior in the Syria conflict.

It is difficult to determine the deeper reasons for the insidious estrangement that has occurred since the successes of the reset in the second half of

President Obama's first term of office, and this has overshadowed the beginning of his second term in such a way that whisperings have recently started of a new ice age, a new Cold War.

In any case, it is not enough to look for the reasons for this only in disappointment and mistrust on the Russian side. The domestic hardening of attitudes in Russia has been followed with some concern not only in the US but also in Europe and in Germany. The restrictive, sometimes violent action against opposition movements in Russia; the legal measures to limit the freedom of action of foreign nongovernmental organizations; the irregularities confirmed by independent observers in connection with the 2012 presidential elections; a series of dubious—by our legal standards—court proceedings and judgments; the internationally much criticized, discriminatory legislation against homosexuals; the dispute regarding the so-called Magnitsky Act—all of these impacted Russian-American relations, as did the pointed admission of Richard Snowden, sought by the US for prosecution for betraying secrets, who had asked for asylum in Moscow.

Fated to Cooperate

Has the American reset strategy foundered? Was the attempt to establish a strategic partnership through dialogue and cooperation and, at the same time, to provide incentives for internal change in Russia too naïve?

The truth is: it is a recurring dilemma, to which a policy aimed at change through cooperation is exposed. How far such cooperation can go without becoming, at least by omission, complicit in domestic as well as foreign policy developments that cannot be reconciled with our own fundamental political principles—that is the crucial question of any foreign policy in states founded on democracy and the rule of law.

Meanwhile, the debates in Germany, Europe, and the United States on these issues are all very similar. They may sometimes be rather more simplistic in the US because of the particular view of the last six decades, the deep-rooted enmity and rivalry of earlier years, and also the greater geographical distance with respect to Russia. Here, like there, however, it is soon a question of something quite fundamental. Here, like there, a policy of willingness to talk and openness to cooperation must defend itself against suspicion of abandoning values and of opportunism.

No one who has to deal with Russia these days will be able to close their eyes to the political deficiencies, the fundamentally divergent ideas of rule of law, democracy, and civil rights. Russia is visibly oscillating between economic modernization and relapses in the political modernization and opening-up of the country. The former superpower is clearly looking for its place in an emerging world order.

Which way Russia will ultimately go, strategically and domestically, is undecided. However, one thing is entirely certain in the foreseeable future and cannot be denied: we will remain reliant on cooperation with Russia. This cooperation is for our own security, and so it is in the own interests of Germany, the European Union, and also the United States—and in Russia's interest, too.

A European security architecture designed for the long term is inconceivable without Russia. In particular, we in Germany and Europe will not be able to guarantee lasting energy security without Russian participation. The energy superpower Russia will have to play a central role in fighting climate change. And we need Russia, as stated in the introduction, in order to resolve virtually all the security policy crises and conflicts of our age, from "frozen conflicts" on the fringes of Europe via the Middle East and Iran to Syria and Afghanistan.

It is impossible without Russia. However, how can this absolute necessity for cooperation be combined with resolute principles and a policy that stands up for democracy, free market economy, the validity of international law, as well as the recognition and implementation of universal human rights on the international stage?

I am firmly convinced that in the end it simply remains for us to assert our interests in a way that also opens up scope and opportunities to support and promote the modernization of Russian society. There is a narrow dividing line between condemnation and refusal of dialogue on the one hand, and policies of pure self-interest without principles on the other.

Anyone who does not want to cross this dividing line will ultimately have to answer the question of how policy is to retain its freedom of action. In any case, indignation is not a foreign policy and is all too often ineffective. Sometimes it can even lead to serious harm.

The first requirement for ensuring security in a Euro-Atlantic perspective in the future is, of course, consolidation of the transatlantic partnership in political, economic, foreign policy, and defense respects. As with the consolidation of European integration in the security and defense field, there are a number of major projects here awaiting implementation, from a transatlantic free-trade zone to a European army.

However, this is not the end of the policy; it is possible that the really difficult part only starts here: anyone wanting to take on responsibility for foreign and security policy will not be able to confine themselves to interacting with partners and like-minded people. Dealing with difficult partners will be unavoidable. It is a question of responsibility, not abandoning principles. Places such as the Munich Security Conference serve an important purpose in this respect—as a forum for confidential dialogue and for developing and fostering informal channels for discussion, which have already prevented many a conflict from further escalation. For that reason I wish the Munich Security Conference many more successful years of existence.

Dr. Frank-Walter Steinmeier is chairman of the Social Democratic Party's parliamentary group in the German Bundestag. From 2005 to 2009, he was German foreign minister, and, from 2007 to 2009, vice chancellor. Before that, he was the head of the Federal Chancellery under Chancellor Gerhard Schröder (1999 to 2005).

The Munich Security Conference and the Russia-NATO Relationship

Igor S. Ivanov

When Ewald-Heinrich von Kleist incepted the Munich Security Conference, he realized that the division of Europe that had resulted from the outcome of World War II was a temporary phenomenon that did not reflect the long-term interests of Europeans in the East and in the West of our continent. The whole idea behind the Munich conference was to create a locus for an open dialogue between politicians, military leaders, and independent experts on how to build a new Europe that enjoyed democracy, security, and prosperity for all Europeans.

Today, this vision of the Munich Security Conference remains as compelling as ever. The Cold War ended more than twenty years ago, but Europe is not yet united. Democracy, security, and prosperity for all Europeans remain a dream, and on top of the numerous residual problems inherited from the second half of the twentieth century, European nations are now being confronted by many new challenges and threats that question our common future. The Munich conference has not outlived its purpose; on the contrary, as time passes this forum gains more stature and more prominence within global political and intellectual communities.

▲
Igor Ivanov (left) with Turki al-Faisal at the 2013 MSC

One of the central issues discussed at the Munich conference has always been the question of the Russia-NATO relationship and how it affects prospects for a common Euro-Atlantic security system. Twenty years ago, after the end of the Cold War, there were a great deal of elevated expectations about the future of Russia-NATO relations. Some politicians and experts on both sides went so far as to propose Russian membership in NATO. Participants at the conference in the early nineties heard numerous interpretations of this bold idea. But the idea has remained a pipe dream; it has never been seriously considered in either Moscow or Brussels. Furthermore, we have to confess that mistrust, mutual suspicion, misperceptions, and fears have survived through the best years of our relations.

It would no doubt be wrong to say that in twenty years we have accomplished absolutely nothing. That would not be fair to the numerous politicians, uniformed men, and academics on both sides who desperately tried to build a common Euro-Atlantic security space. In late May 2002 we formed the NATO-Russia Council. Over time, it has become an important interface between the two sides, helping us to compare notes, to exchange views on international and security matters, and sometimes to discuss possible cooperation in various fields. However, the council could not change the fundamentals of the relationship; it does not have either the authority or the resources to make strategic decisions, and its meetings are quite often limited to mostly formal procedures.

The Russian side tried more than once to launch a meaningful partnership between NATO and the Collective Security Treaty Organization, uniting most of the post-Soviet states. Unfortunately, the NATO side expressed very little enthusiasm about this opportunity. Likewise, our suggestions to discuss a new European Security Treaty were almost completely ignored by the Atlantic alliance. Russian proposals on joint efforts in developing a European missile defense system were met with a great deal of skepticism. I recall sessions of the Munich conference during which Russian and NATO officials seemed to experience major communication gaps trying to reconcile their approaches to the institutional and legal foundations of the Euro-Atlantic security system.

Today it appears evident that twenty years ago, the West—primarily the United States—succumbed to triumphalist moods. They fell into the trap of illusions such as the "end of history," a "unipolar world," and the universality of liberal values. If you go through the records of the conferences in the nineties and the first decade of the twenty-first century, you can find any number of statements by US politicians and intellectuals saturated with such ideas. Triumphalism prevented a sober assessment of the scale of unsolved problems that gave rise to the illusory idea that the international system would regain stability almost automatically—without strenuous effort, without large-scale political and material investment, and without compromise with old-time foes and new opponents. This triumphalism would have to be paid for dearly—not just with a host of international crises and long-term foreign policy challenges, but also with missed historical opportunities.

What about Russia? Looking back, we must acknowledge that we were not always able to avoid illusions and foreign policy blunders. Far from it. The main Russian illusion in the nineties was probably a romantic vision of the world after the end of the Cold War. Our early presentations in Munich were filled with this romantic approach to the world at large and to the West in particular. Then we thought that there was a reserved place for Russia in the changing system, and that partners would easily understand our current difficulties and help us address the outstanding issues. In fact, we had hoped—though no one uttered it out loud—that someone would do our work for us just because Russia had unilaterally ended the Cold War and renounced much of the Soviet heritage. We significantly underestimated the harshness, even cruelty of modern politics and overestimated the willingness of our partners for a strategic vision and ambitious solutions. The realization of this came after a long while and was very painful.

In the West there has been much talk about "Putin's U-turn" in Russian foreign policy and frequent comparisons of his pragmatism and the romanticism of the previous period. The famous "Munich speech" made by President Vladimir Putin at the Munich Security Conference in 2007 is regarded as a borderline between "old" and "new" Russian policy. But we should not forget that the early years of Putin's presidency saw a distinct "integrationist" trend in foreign policy. It was then that firm efforts were exerted to bring our relations with the European Union to a qualitatively new level. Russia agreed to a US military presence in Central Asia to support the anti-Taliban operation in Afghanistan, the NATO-Russia Council was established, and there was a breakthrough in relations with the World Trade Organization.

It would not be an exaggeration to say that in the early years of the twenty-first century, the Western track was a priority of Russia's foreign policy. Moscow repeatedly demonstrated its readiness for very serious political investment. I want to stress this: Russia did not take a single step, it did not take any decision, nor did it come out with any international initiative that the Western partners might interpret as unfriendly or harmful to their legitimate interests.

And what did we get in response to the desire for strategic partnership with the West? NATO's enlargement continued—in defiance of persistent objections from Moscow and of the obvious doubts over the feasibility of the Alliance's strategy of geographic expansion from the military point of view. The United States unilaterally withdrew from the Soviet-US Anti-Ballistic Missile Treaty, thereby undermining the system of strategic balance between Moscow and Washington that had taken decades to establish. The beginning of the US-led allied military operation in Iraq once again raised questions about the rule of law in world politics. The West exerted great efforts in terms of political penetration into the territory of the Commonwealth of Independent States countries to weaken Russian positions there.

All this could not but cause disappointment. Therefore, "Putin's U-turn," which culminated with the famous "Munich speech," was obviously to some extent inevitable. A significant part of the responsibility for it lies with our Western partners. The very logic of development in the early twenty-first century brought Russian politicians to the disappointing conclusion that in this world only strength enjoys respect, that nobody will ever guarantee Russia anything, and that one's interests must be defended firmly and resolutely. That U-turn was based on the recognition of the fact that Russia had passed the point of its maximum weakness, the resource base for an active foreign policy got stronger with each year, and therefore Moscow was able to, and should talk to, the West in the language of an equitable partner.

Perhaps historians will keep arguing to what extent "Putin's U-turn" increased or decreased the effectiveness of Russia's foreign policy. One can enter into polemics about whether it was proportionate to the circumstances, or redundant and excessive. However, probably both the firmest supporters and the irreconcilable critics will agree on one thing: today it is extremely important not to repeat the mistakes made by the United States in the recent past. And that means steering clear of the euphoria over the past decade of growth in the capabilities of Russia's foreign policy, not succumbing to the temptations of unilateralism, not abusing tough rhetoric, and not pinning all hopes on comparative advantages—whether in terms of military strength or energy resources.

When speaking about the relationship between Russia and NATO, it sometimes looks like an arranged marriage. The parties are supposed to form a happy couple, and in theory they should make a perfect fit. But in reality the chemistry simply does not work, and both sides are working against the arranged marriage. If so, do we really need to insist on this marriage? Do we need closer cooperation between Russia and NATO? Is there anything wrong about both sides minding their own business?

The answer to these questions depends on how we assess the current security situation in Europe in general. Are we happy with the current state of Euro-Atlantic security? Is it something that we would like to preserve in the future? Will all of us be proud to pass the current state of affairs on to our children and grandchildren? My answer to all these questions is a resolute "no." The current state of affairs is not acceptable and has to be changed. The change depends largely on positions taken by NATO and Russia *vis-à-vis* each other.

In my view, the initial step in building trust between Russia and NATO is to take a sober and unbiased look at the current security situation in Europe. The Munich Security Conference might be an ideal platform to do so. If we do not try to hide problems behind nice words and diplomatic protocol, we should recognize that today, twenty years after the end of the Cold War, we do not have an integrated Euro-Atlantic security system. We still have the West and the East; the borderline between the two has moved eastward, but it has not disappeared. True, we no longer have an Iron Curtain. Our citizens now travel all over Europe; Internet reaches out to remote corners of our continent. And, even more importantly, there are no ideological contradictions that could explain and justify a protracted political conflict. But mistrust and mutual suspicion are still with us; our attempts to create a common Euro-Atlantic security space have failed in the most spectacular and unambiguous way.

I tend to believe that Russia and NATO failed because neither side has even considered a strategic partnership in a serious way. We never really learned the lessons from 9/11. Neither did we make proper conclusions from subsequent terrorist attacks in Spain and in the United Kingdom. The United States continued to pursue its unilateral world domination strategy, having missed a chance to lead the international community to a new world order. Russia initially fought for mere survival and later on enjoyed unprecedented energy-based wealth. Europe was too busy managing its geographical expansion and then had to confront a chain of constitutional, political, and economic difficulties. In sum, everyone was busy minding his own business, and the concept of the Euro-Atlantic security system remained a concept shared only by a few idealists.

The paradox of the NATO-Russia relations today is that unlike in the past, we do not have any significant disputes in how we define regional or global security challenges and needs. We can disagree on specific questions, on how particular institutions should work, or on what issues should get our immediate attention. But when you talk to responsible politicians in Moscow or in Brussels, in Washington or in Berlin, you are likely to get mostly the same assessments and the same conclusions on the majority of security matters. However, the common NATO-Russian security system remains probably as far away from us as it was in late eighties.

Today, the NATO-Russian security agenda has two distinctly different sets of problems. On the one hand, we have the "unfinished business" of the Cold War. The old notions of the twentieth century—deterrence, balance of power, mutual assured destruction, verification procedures—are still with us. Many of the conflict situations in various corners of the European continent and territorial disputes can be traced back to the Cold War era, or even prior to that. On the other hand, we have new challenges to Euro-Atlantic security that became particularly visible only recently—energy security, migration, international terrorism, communications security, and so on. The Euro-Atlantic zone is by no means immune to numerous destabilization impulses coming from other regions of the world.

The reality is that the "unfinished business" of the Cold War seriously diminishes our abilities to deal with the "new" agenda. If we have no trust between us, if we still stick to the dogmas of the twentieth century, how can we find solutions to much more comprehensive and sensitive problems of today and tomorrow? We cannot simply bypass old problems; we need to resolve them—once and for all.

One of the essential preconditions for building trust in relations between Russia and NATO is a common vision of our preferred future relations. Can we agree on an ideal model of this relationship? What might such a model look like? To be a visionary does not mean to be an idle dreamer; visions do not exclude realism and pragmatism. For instance, a realist should recognize that full Russian membership in NATO is not the goal that we can pursue in the foreseeable future. However, why do we not consider Russian membership in political institutions of the Atlantic alliance? After all, for a long time France did not participate in the military organization of NATO without leaving the political dimension of the Alliance. This political engagement became an important anchor linking France to the rest of the Euro-Atlantic and prevented Paris from becoming a loose cannon in global politics.

I would venture to say that Russia should become part of key NATO institutions to learn more about the Alliance—its basic principles, values, procedures, and aspirations. For its part, NATO should provide more opportunities for Russian participation. We must make sure that our communications are not limited to a small group of top-level bureaucrats or generals—only very broad and diverse contacts can really change public attitudes and bring us to a new level of trust and mutual understanding.

The year 2009 saw the creation of the unique process called the Euro-Atlantic Security Initiative. This project brought together former policymakers, diplomats, generals, and business leaders from Russia, North America, and Europe to look at options for addressing the region's faltering security system and to chart a roadmap of practical action that would lead to a more secure future.

As a result of our discussions and studies, we concluded that the only means to assure the long-term security of our peoples lie in building an inclusive, undivided, functioning Euro-Atlantic security community—a community without barriers in which all would expect the resolution of disputes exclusively by diplomatic, legal, or other nonviolent means without recourse to military force or the threat of its use. Governments within this community would share a common strategy and understanding in the face of common threats and a commitment to the proposition that the best and most efficient way to tackle threats, both internal and external, is through cooperation.

Following up on this initiative, in 2013 the report "Building Mutual Security in the Euro-Atlantic Region" was prepared and presented at the Munich Security Conference. It consists of concrete proposals, and its realization can reduce the chances of conflict in the years ahead and build a more secure and promising future for all our citizens.

This is a challenge for all of us, including those who are trying to turn the Munich Security Conference into the most inclusive, most dynamic, and most innovative global forum on security matters. The conference should continue to serve as a critical source of out-of-the-box thinking, unorthodox ideas, and frank and mutually respectful discussions. The legacy of Ewald-Heinrich von Kleist should be developed further.

Igor S. Ivanov is president of the Russian International Affairs Council (RIAC) and professor at the Moscow State Institute for International Relations. He served as minister of foreign affairs from 1998 to 2004, and was the secretary of the Security Council of the Russian Federation from 2004 to 2007.

Enter the Arab People:
The Munich Security Conference,
the Middle East, and the Arab Revolts

Volker Perthes

The Middle East, here understood as the region comprising the Arab states, Israel, and Iran, has not been much of an issue at *Wehrkunde,* now the Munich Security Conference, over the first four decades of its fifty-year history. Regional conflicts and potential or actual threats that were emanating from the region—terrorism in particular—have figured in various debates about European, transatlantic, and global security, especially since the end of the Cold War. Following the 9/11 attacks, the 2002 conference was naturally centered on international terrorism. However, special panels focusing on the Middle East or parts thereof only became a more or less regular feature of the conference from 2003 onwards. Notably, both the Asia-Pacific region and "rising powers" had entered the conference agenda as regularly scheduled items some years prior to that.

The year 2003, of course, was the year of the US-led Iraq war. The MSC, in February as usual, came just six weeks before the invasion began. However, it was not the scheduled panel on Future Developments in the Middle

Debating the Egyptian revolution: Perthes (second from right) and
Kenneth Roth of Human Rights Watch (left) at the 2011 MSC

East and the Persian Gulf that made international headlines but the dispute between US Secretary of Defense Donald Rumsfeld and German Foreign Minister Joschka Fischer. The argument highlighted what was to become a major political conflict between the United States and some of its most important European allies—or arguably even the deepest crisis ever in the history of the transatlantic alliance, and US-German relations in particular. Obviously, not only Fischer was "not convinced" by Rumsfeld's rationale for war against Iraq.

Little wonder that the Middle East has remained a regular, almost unavoidable topic for transatlantic partners and for the MSC since then, not only in panels explicitly dedicated to the region. Given the increasing relevance of the region for European and global security and the fact that Middle East policies were often controversial, top US and European policymakers who addressed the conference regularly used their speeches to also outline their approaches to or their visions of the Middle East. Israel and Palestine as well as the Gulf region remained the main issues. The conference did not only talk *about* the region, though, but began to more regularly invite high-ranking representatives from the Middle East to present their view of things.

A few examples may suffice here. In 2004, when Rumsfeld outlined President George W. Bush's so-called "forward strategy for freedom in the Middle East," King Abdullah of Jordan reminded the audience of what he called the core challenge of the Middle East, namely the Israel-Palestinian conflict, requesting American leadership particularly (or rather) on this subject. In 2006, then US Deputy Secretary of State Robert Zoellick struck a conciliatory note toward European critics of US Middle East policies. It was necessary, he said, to understand the interests of countries we deal with: "We didn't do that so well with Iraq," he added, and, "probably, we don't do it so well with Iran." Quarrels over the wisdom of the Iraq war had by now become spilled milk, while discussions about how to deal with Iran and its nuclear program gained importance, and also became more constructive. In 2009, for example, the then-head of the International Atomic Energy Agency (IAEA), Muhammad al-Baradei, proposed to resolve the dispute over the Iranian nuclear program by multinationalizing it: this would allow Iran to maintain the fuel cycle, but to do so—and only to do so—in cooperation with other regional or international powers, thus creating an element of mutual dependence and control. Baradei's idea had few takers at the time but may reappear if negotiations between Iran and international powers at some point become more solution-oriented.

Also in 2009, US Vice President Joe Biden outlined the Obama administration's approaches: to Russia, to Europe, and to the Middle East. To the relief of many Europeans, he underlined the "centrality of diplomacy" in US national security, and explained to the audience that the new administration would work for a secure, fair, lasting peace between Israel and the Palestinians; that it intended to draw down its forces from Iraq; and that it was willing to talk to Iran but also prepared to use pressure if Iran was not prepared to change its course. One day earlier, Iran's speaker of parliament, Ali Larijani, had addressed the conference, as he had already done two years earlier when he was Iran's chief nuclear negotiator. Larijani's speech and the ensuing discussion were not exactly an MSC highlight. They rather epitomized the difficulty of talking to each other: the difficulty of an Iranian policymaker to find the right language for a Western audience on the one hand, and that of understanding the fine print, as it were, in the presentation of one of the more sophisticated Iranian politicians on the other: thus, the Iranian speaker's refusal to publicly and in foreign lands distance himself from the country's president, as well as his reiteration of accusations and historical grievances against the United States, which are standard fare of Iranian rhetoric but not what most US policymakers are accustomed to hearing, made a constructive exchange almost impossible. And Larijani's invitation to the United States to engage in "playing chess, not boxing" was largely lost in transcultural misunderstanding.

Occasionally, but all too rarely, policymakers from the Middle East have used the conference to send confidence-building messages into their regional environment. There was one such remarkable moment at the 2010 meeting, when Prince Turki bin Faisal from Saudi Arabia not only kept his cool in the face of unfounded personal accusations from an Israeli deputy minister, but also expressly stated that "Israeli security fears have to be taken seriously."

Not astonishingly perhaps, the more typical pattern for representatives from the Middle East (and often from other regions too, as has to be said in fairness) has been to utilize the Munich platform to address a Western audience in order to enlighten it about the misdeeds of their respective neighbors or regional competitors. This specific discursive pattern may have supported the understanding—up to 2011 at least—that the problems of the region were mainly of a geopolitical nature. For most MSC panelists and participants, domestic conflicts, socioeconomic challenges, or public opinion in the Arab or other Middle Eastern states were negligible, at least from an international-security perspective.

This changed with the eruption of the uprisings against Tunisian President Zein al-Abidine Ben Ali and Egyptian President Husni Mubarak. The 2011 conference, with no Arab leader present, was captured, as it were, by the unfolding Arab revolts. History was "on the move," as EU Council President Herman Van Rompuy put it, right on Europe's southern borders, and policymakers and pundits present in Munich tried to make sense of it. German Chancellor Angela Merkel and quite a number of Eastern Europeans saw reflections of the revolutions their countries had undergone two decades earlier. Merkel, referring to her own experience from the peaceful revolution in East Germany, pointedly warned the West against patronizing attitudes: "Egyptians," she said, "are certainly not just sitting there now and waiting for our advice." US Secretary of State Hillary Clinton warned that governments all over the Middle East could face a perfect storm if they did not respond to the demands of their people.

A special panel was introduced at the last minute in order not to miss the unexpected developments. Quite unusual for the MSC, the panel title consisted of only a question: "What's happening in the Arab world?" It was becoming clear that to understand the dynamics in the region, one needed to develop insights beyond just geography, armaments, oil, and the personality of individual leaders.

As could be expected, the panelists came up with quite different answers that did not divert too much from their respective earlier approaches. US diplomat Frank Wisner expressed that Washington still hoped to work, and achieve progress, with Husni Mubarak. For most of us on the panel, however, the Egyptian president had already become history. Javier Solana and this author were fairly optimistic as to the course of change in the Arab world, asking for new, positive approaches of Europe to its southern neighborhood while at the same time stressing that the necessary political and socioeconomic transformation process in these countries would be a long-term, generational effort. Uzi Arad from Israel was much more skeptical, assuming—rightly—that free elections in Egypt would likely lead to a Muslim Brotherhood victory. While he would not expect a Brotherhood-led government in Egypt to revoke the peace treaty with Israel, Israel would still need to prepare for the worst, strengthening its defenses rather than—as some of us others suggested—using the opportunity to make a major peace gesture towards the Palestinians and the Arabs in general.

While assumptions and policy recommendations differed, everybody seemed to sense that what had happened in Tunis and was unfolding in Cairo was not a one-time event. These developments would likely not be restricted to two countries in North Africa, but rather envelop the entire region. Different countries would feel the storm in different ways, but no country between the Maghreb and the Persian Gulf would remain unaffected. Clearly the Arab world and the Middle East were no longer being shaped by governments or regimes only but also by people making history. Future Munich conferences would have to deal with the better known geopolitical conflicts of the region and with the popular revolts and their effects. And as it comes, some things at least would go wrong, and domestic upheavals would impact the regional geopolitical dynamics.

In 2012, consequently, the MSC saw the largest number ever of speakers from the Arab world and the Middle East. This included people, and also encounters between people with very specific worldviews, that one would not have expected at a Munich conference in earlier years. In one remarkable conference moment, one could see Tunisia's then-prime minister, Hamadi Jebali, a member of al-Nahda, the Tunisian sister party of the Muslim Brotherhood, pledging Western support for moderate Islamic movements in a very warm exchange with US Senator Joe Lieberman, who in his turn explained the need to distinguish between different forms of political Islam, comparing Jabali's al-Nahda with European Christian-democratic parties. Lieberman asked everybody to "invest" in Tunisian democracy; both the US senator and the Tunisian prime minister underlined the need for value-oriented international policies. Later, conference participants were captured by a rather atypical kind of charisma: who would have expected an Arab woman in tight Islamic headscarf who spoke in Arabic make the largely male crowd of international security experts burst into repeated applause? Nobel Peace Prize laureate Tawakkol Karman, one of the leaders of the peaceful protests in Yemen, spoke mainly about Syria. And in her own ways she brought to the Bayerischer Hof a bit of that constructive lack of respect that had characterized the Arab revolts, particularly the gatherings on Tahrir Square in Cairo, Taghyyir (Change) Square in Sanaa, or Pearl Square in Manama: "In the name of the Arab youth," Karman exclaimed, "we condemn Russia and China for supporting the Assad regime." She then warned the West against expecting any stability in the Middle East as long as dictatorship and corruption prevailed and as long as the Palestinian people had to wait for justice.

Syria was even more in the focus at the 2013 MSC. UN and Arab League Special Envoy Lakhdar Brahimi gave a very sobering account of "one of the situations where the parties can't solve their problems by themselves," calling on the UN Security Council to eventually "do its job." Moaz Khattib, then leader of Syria's National Coalition, expressed his preparedness to talk to regime representatives if that was a way to begin a transition process. He also urgently called on the international community to at least prevent Syrian air force planes from bombarding opposition-held territory, a call that was emphatically seconded by Senator John McCain.

The 2013 conference also highlighted some of the region's own geo-political dynamics: in a different but no less remarkable moment, Israel's outgoing defense minister Ehud Barak used the Munich platform for a long statement about his concerns and a kind of political testament: the Middle East, he explained was witnessing "a geopolitical earthquake like the fall of the Ottoman Empire." A two-state solution, that is, the establishment of a Palestinian state at the side of Israel, was not a "favor for the Palestinians" but in Israel's own interest. And, with a clear hint to Iran and Tehran's nuclear program, Israel would never outsource its own security, not even to its "most trusted allies."

Developments in the Gulf region and in the Levante were obviously again becoming closely interconnected, not least so with Iran as a main supporter of the Assad regime. Iran's Foreign Minister Ali Akbar Salehi tried to convince the audience as well as the Syrian opposition, whose leader he met during the conference, that Tehran wanted to be part of the solution, that it could not be ignored, and that it wanted both to solve the nuclear dispute and "to change enemies into friends." Obviously, this did not succeed. Rather, the 2013 conference seemed to repeat an already established pattern whereby American and Iranian speakers declared that the respective other side would have to move first. Thus, according to Salehi, there were "no red lines for negotiations." But Iran needed to be sure that Washington came "with real, authentic intentions." Or, in the words of US Vice President Joe Biden: direct negotiations with Tehran were possible—but only "when the Iranian leadership is serious."

Insights from Munich

Where does all this leave us? The fact that developments in the Middle East and the Arab world have become an indispensable theme at the Munich Security Conference does not offer many lessons by itself, but it certainly allows a few insights. Among other things, and despite a number of unsuccessful or half-hearted attempts at starting a dialogue as the one just mentioned, the MSC remains a good venue for representatives from the Middle East to make their views heard to a mainly Western security policy community and meet with people they otherwise would not interact with. Such a place is definitely needed. Beyond that, "Munich" is also an appropriate format to exchange and develop ideas about what external actors—Europe, the United States, but also Russia, China, or India—could and should do to resolve geopolitical and domestic conflicts in the Middle East and support its people in what seems like a complex but necessary process of change.

The Middle East will no doubt continue to force itself on the Munich conference schedule. We can safely assume that the main geopolitical issues of the region will not be resolved within the next five years or so. At the very best, domestic upheavals in various countries of the region, the Israeli-Palestinian conflict, and security issues in the Gulf region can be managed, brought closer to a solution, or contained, but they will certainly remain on the global agenda even by the end of the decade. The turbulences unleashed by the Arab revolts are not just a seasonal phenomenon—as the somewhat misleading expression "Arab Spring" suggests—but will likely continue for a decade or two. Sadly, we also have to expect that the struggle for Syria will drag on. This struggle began as, and it still is, an uprising against a brutal dictatorship. But it has also become a regionalized, partly internationalized geopolitical contest over future influence in Syria, after the expected end of the Assad dynasty, over the reach of Iran into the Levante, and generally over regional hegemony. We cannot tell, while these lines are being written, how deep the international involvement in the conflict eventually will be. In particular since the massive use of chemical arms in August 2013, however, the conflict has attained an additional dimension that reaches beyond Syria and the Middle East. Syria, in a way, has become a test for whether and how the international community will cooperate to uphold the ban on the use of chemical arms. Add to that that the war in Syria, even before, has tested the meaning of the Responsibility to Protect that the international community had adopted as a principle in 2005.

Developments in Syria will definitely impact the future of the entire region. The conflict is already fuelling an extremely dangerous confessional Sunni-Shiite polarization. If Syria was to fragment—which is at least a plausible scenario—it will be very difficult to maintain the unity of other multi-confessional and multiethnic states in the Middle East, and we may indeed witness the end of the post-Ottoman (or "Sykes-Picot") order in the Middle East, as Ehud Barak suggested at the 2013 MSC. From today's perspective, it does not seem very likely that any combination of regional and international powers would then put the pieces together again or establish a more viable, new order for the Middle East any time soon.

Neither the regional players nor Europe, as the region's closest neighbor, seem able to resolve any of the geopolitical and domestic conflicts in the region; US involvement in the region seems to have peaked, and emerging powers with an undeniable interest in—at least—secure resource flows from the Middle East are not yet ready to assume any significant role in regional security affairs. While further developments will eventually be determined by local and regional actors, international powers need to be aware of their influence and use it properly.

Europe is good at supporting political and economic transformation where countries have chosen that path, and it has substantial experience in furthering and institutionalizing regional cooperation. It will have to make a greater effort to demonstrate that it sees the societies of these countries as partners, not as a threat, and it needs to do so without ignoring or denying the risks that emanate from the region. Europe is still not well equipped to deal with violent conflicts in its neighborhood. It will need to improve its conflict resolution and conflict management capabilities, and it will also need to step up its security involvement in the Mediterranean region.

The United States, even if it reduces its power projection into the region, is still the most sought-after ally for any state in the region that feels threatened by its neighbors. Washington has to use this leverage to push for a viable Israeli-Palestinian peace agreement, without which there are few prospects for wider regional cooperation. It also needs to lean on its Arab allies in the Gulf to reform domestically and refrain from further attempts to heighten the confessional polarization in the region. This would make it much easier to enter into a meaningful dialogue with Iran, which remains a necessary condition—not necessarily a sufficient one—to resolve the nuclear dispute between Iran and the international community.

Russia and the emerging powers, China in particular, will have to appreciate that security and peace in the Middle East will be even more closely linked to questions of governance and sociopolitical transformation. It would be helpful if these countries would change their attitude to deal with the domestic conflicts of the region from the time-honored principle of noninterference to the more challenging one of nonindifference (which has been promoted by Brazil).

These domestic conflicts, and our way of responding to them, will remain on the MSC agenda as long as struggles for dignity, better governance, participation, and justice continue across the region. If Europeans and other external actors have learned anything from the Arab revolts, it is certainly that security issues in, or emanating from, the Middle East can no longer be understood by focusing on the state or government level alone. This also means that gatherings like the MSC need to develop an understanding for public opinion and its differentiations in Arab and other Middle Eastern societies. The times when it was enough to invite a president or a member of a royal family from one of the countries to learn what "the Arabs" think are definitely over.

*Dr. **Volker Perthes** is director of the German Institute for International and Security Affairs (Stiftung Wissenschaft und Politik) in Berlin, a think tank that advises the German parliament and government. He is a frequent commentator on German foreign policy, international relations, and developments in the Middle East.*

Not the Whole Picture:
The History of the Incomplete Answer
to Iran's Nuclear Threat

Omid Nouripour

The Munich Security Conference is undoubtedly a major stage of world politics. And as with any other stage, from the opera houses of the Scala or the Met to theaters like the Viennese Burg, one part of the performance takes place on the stage itself and another in the hallways, loges, and foyers before, during, and after the show.

All the major topics are discussed at the conference, people mingle quite regardless of their backgrounds (provided, of course, they have been accepted into the elite circle of the invited), and odd diplomatic constellations evolve.

For all these reasons, the Iranian nuclear program has very frequently been the center of attention at the MSC, especially in the last few years. As Iran continues to be a major topic of international political discourse and a pariah in large parts of international diplomacy, Munich is the ideal place for informal dialogue to take place, especially between the United States and Iran, who do not maintain diplomatic relationships. It is thus a vital

▲
Foreign Minister Manouchehr Mottaki of Iran (right),
Stefan Kornelius, and Carl Bildt (left) at the 2010 MSC

institution to international politics, and not only concerning Iranian nuclear issues.

But as Munich is also a stage in the proper sense, Iranian diplomats and politicians have often managed to put on their farcical dramas with high-ranking representatives from all over the world watching. As the master of ceremonies, Ambassador Wolfgang Ischinger more often than not had to apply all his diplomatic tact to accommodate the special necessities of dealing with Iran. The delegation from Tehran usually fails to let the public know exactly when they wish to make their *entrée en scène*, and the organizers need to make room at the very last minute, enabling a dialogue—however ephemeral—but still avoiding the impression of an all too special treatment of the country. This culminated in 2010 when Manouchehr Mottaki, foreign minister of Iran, reigned over one day of the conference without issuing a single proposition of any substance.

How Could It Come to This?

The Iranian nuclear program dates back to the days of Mohammad Reza Shah Pahlavi. The autocratic ruler tried to modernize his country at all costs. Unfortunately, this did not involve a bottom-up approach that would have started by improving the living conditions and education of all citizens. It stood primarily for shiny new technology and arms imported from his Western allies (and for a cruel oppression of political opposition and a shameless display of wealth on the part of a privileged elite, for that matter). Part of this program was the construction of nuclear power plants. In 1968, Iran signed the Nuclear Non-Proliferation Treaty (NPT), giving it the right to use nuclear energy for civilian purposes and having access to certain technology while obliging it to play by the rules of the international community, which in particular meant not pursuing nuclear weapons and opening all its facilities to inspectors from the International Atomic Energy Agency (IAEA), the United Nations body designated to implement the treaty. In 1974, Iran started the planning of the power plant in Bushehr, eventually relying mostly on German technology. The plant was not finished when the 1979 revolution toppled the old dictator and eventually replaced him with a new one, Ayatollah Khomeini, at the head of the Islamic Republic.

The revolutionary forces originally held most of the Shah's technological innovations to be part of the corruptive Western influence. Khomeini refused nuclear energy and declared weapons of mass destruction—among them the atomic bomb—to be un-Islamic. The fatwa issued in that sense is theoretically still valid today. The ambitious project at Bushehr, already more than half completed, fell into decay, besides suffering Iraqi attacks during the First Gulf War.

Khomeini's refusal did not hold very long. At the end of the eighties, after the war with Iraq, the country's leadership decided to resume construction of the nuclear reactor in Bushehr, this time drawing on Russian technology. This was still basically in accordance with the NPT signed a little more than two decades earlier. Yet to our best knowledge, this was not the only decision made at that point in Tehran. The Islamic Republic of Iran also broke its vow to both its stated principles and the NPT by acquiring plans for nuclear weapons. They came from a well-known source: Abdul Qadeer Khan, the "father of Pakistan's nuclear bomb," sold the information to Iran.

The news about this broke at the beginning of the next decade. In 2002, the discovery that Iran was building a nuclear enrichment facility in Natanz, which had not been declared to the IAEA, arose suspicion among world leaders as to the peaceful nature of the country's nuclear program.

The nuclear issue became the dominant factor in the relationship between Iran, the European Union, and the United States at a point in time in which closer ties seemed within reach for the first time since the revolution of 1979. The liberalization of the first years of Mohammad Khatami's presidency bore fruit. The late nineties brought an unprecedented slurry of newspapers and magazines, and intellectual and cultural life in Iran flourished. Of course, this did not occur without opposition from the conservatives around the spiritual leader. They used all the powers granted to them by the constitution, soon closed many of the newly opened publications, and arrested activists, journalists, and intellectuals. The West should have realized at this point that in dealing with the Islamic Republic of Iran one was not dealing with one state but with many conflicting groups and interests within one state, which as a consequence could not be expected to act coherently in international politics.

And yet despite all these problems, 2001 brought two promising signs: the European Commission brought a proposition before the European Parliament in which both Iran's access to the World Trade Organization and a dialogue on human rights were defined as feasible goals. And, seemingly paradoxically, it was the great tragedy of the attacks on 9/11 that also brought the US and Iran closer together. The sympathy for the victims within the Iranian civil society was overwhelming. And Tehran offered the United States and its allies a constructive contribution to its efforts to topple the Afghan regime that harbored al Qaeda and reconstruct Iran's war-torn neighbor to the southeast. This was a particularly precious offer, as the country had very good connections to the Northern Alliance, who governed the northeastern part of the country and was a major partner of the US and NATO in rebuilding the country.

The engagement on Iran's side was not rewarded. In January 2002, President George W. Bush presented Iran as part of the "axis of evil." This came as a shock to many in Iran, especially the liberals, who were instead seeking international recognition of their difficult endeavors to modernize the country.

Obviously, the lesson from the dynamics of the early Khatami years had not been learned. The US administration did not play on the differences within Iranian society. It did not try to cautiously lure Iranian public opinion to their side, discreetly strengthening the forces within the country eager for change. Instead, they managed to move the opposing groups closer together in their irritation over President Bush's statements.

The Nuclear Issue Cannot Be Singled Out

It is not clear whether the nuclear issue was originally part of the conflicts between the different factions in Iranian politics. However, it became very clear in the years of the Khatami government that some parts of the regime had discovered it as a tool in their internal debates. It was the beginning of a decade that was frustrating both for the international community and the people in Iran.

It was consequential and yet tragic that the news about Iran's nuclear enrichment program abruptly ended trade talks between the EU and Iran in early 2003. At this point, the Khatami presidency seemed to have completely failed. The liberals were frustrated both because the hardliners inside Iran cracked down on them and because they did not feel taken seriously by the people outside the country, whom they regarded as their natural allies. This played into the hands of the conservatives in Iran, who won a sweeping victory in the 2003 parliamentary elections, making progress even harder. The United States and the European Union were by now too absorbed with the nuclear conflict to even seriously notice the human rights implications of this development.

The negotiations on the nuclear issue continued despite all the resistance. Khatami and his negotiator, Hassan Rouhani, on the Iranian side had to navigate between the nuclear plans of the basically hostile hardliners on their own side and the legitimate demands of the international community. After all, the country could not account for Natanz. It did sign the NPT's additional protocol but did not ratify it. With the initial negotiators, Khatami and Rouhani, there was still a base of trust in the talks. The Iranian side seemed to comprehend that the changed landscape of international politics after 9/11, and the diffuse threat of international terrorism raised a legitimate fear of a spread of weapons of mass destruction. Both parties agreed on a framework for future negotiations. Yet the beginning shift of power inside Iran almost made diplomacy impossible before it had even had a real chance.

A letter from 2004 from the IAEA demanding full disclosure of all nuclear plans went unanswered. The conservative majority in the Iranian parliament, together with the spiritual leader Ali Khamenei, who eventually has to sign off on all international arrangements, found Khatami's stance too soft.

When Mahmoud Ahmadinejad, the populist mayor of Tehran, was elected president in the summer of 2005, things turned even worse. Only two weeks after the beginning of his term he replaced Rouhani with the more conservative and nationalist Ali Laridjani as new chief negotiator. The nuclear issue became even more a matter of internal Iranian politics. Ahmadinejad cleverly connected the question to patriotic and nationalist sentiments in his aim to use the widespread disillusion over the perceived failure of the reformist government.

In January 2006, in an act of unprecedented contempt for the negotiating process, he broke the seals of the nuclear enrichment facilities put in place by the IAEA. This set in motion the wheels of international politics in an escalation that began with the IAEA resolution of February 2006. The level of trust was finally abandoned. Even though negotiations continued (it would, of course, have been irresponsible to do otherwise), they seemed to be less and less about the issue itself. New accusations and findings by the international community—some well founded, others not—were met by some concessions, none of which seemed sincere but were instead a way of gaining time.

The sanctions themselves did not seem very painful at the outset. Rather than decisively targeting those inside the system who were well known to control both the nuclear program and the repressive forces that brought down the freedoms of the Khatami era, they rather ineffectively seemed to be set to weaken the economy as a whole. Admittedly, this was due also to the difficult dealings inside the UN Security Council but also in part to a miscalculation in the general diplomacy toward Iran. Economic interests on the part of numerous EU countries and the willingness of many of Iran's neighbors to help circumvent the rules completed the picture of a rather inconsequential endeavor.

The 2009 Turn

Yet all these rather grim circumstances did not manage to suffocate the Iranians' aspirations for change. Before the 2009 presidential elections, an unexpected atmosphere of change and reform revived the country. The "green" movement was born, selecting the candidates Mehdi Karroubi and Mir Hossein Mousavi as their horses in the presidential race. Even though neither of them openly differed from Ahmadinejad in their stance toward the nuclear issue, for neither of them did it seem as central as it did to the then president and his conservative allies.

This might have contributed to the unprecedented manipulations in the election results. With the Iranian authorities usually limiting their influence to preselecting candidates that fit into their political schemes, thereby keeping the outward appearance of a democratic process, the rigging that took place to ensure Ahmadinejad's second term came as a surprise to many.

The demonstrations that followed the elections were further proof of the people's urgent demand for freedom and change. Tehran and the other major cities had not seen such a display of popular discontent since 1978/79. Yet, after a brief moment of uncertainty, the regime applied violent repression in full force. Peaceful demonstrators were attacked, arrested, and many of them tortured and raped in jail. With most of the international media banned from reporting from the country, the whole world anxiously watched the shaky amateur Internet videos that were the main source of information about the ongoing confrontations.

The hardliners now transferred their desperate plot to the international stage. A pattern evolved: each time the authorities expected another wave of demonstrations, they tried (quite successfully) to divert attention to the nuclear dossier taking either a step forward or backward, offering concessions only to take them back a few days later.

The masterpiece of this charade was Foreign Minister Mottaki's monologue on the big Munich stage in 2010. Literally the whole world—representatives from all walks of international politics—was listening. He managed to speak without saying anything. He took existing proposals that had already been discarded, twisted them here, modified them there—to no avail. Everyone was eager to find a phrase with substantial meaning. The stage, the audience demanded great drama, but it was only robbed of its precious time. While the speech was still going on, possible interpretations were already being discussed in subdued voices, and after it ended the philological debate was in full swing. The few questions about the demonstrations and the ongoing repression were moved aside by Mottaki with the negligence we have unfortunately come to expect from the Iranian government.

To me and some fellow spectators, this did not seem like a play worth considering but an actor to throw a shoe at. I did not perform this radical act of criticism literally, but I got my feeling transmitted to some of the journalists, who then transported it to their readers—these short channels of communication are another feat of the Munich Security Conference.

Of course, this feeling was not a reproach to those who were listening. It is infinitely valuable to talk and listen in international relations and diplomacy—this even constitutes the nature of these relations themselves. And thus the Munich Security Conference embodies the best of what diplomacy can be: a forum for dialogue that in the worst case might come to no avail, but which so often is the key ingredient in the "process" of peace, the nonviolent "way of solving problems," as John F. Kennedy once put it.

However, the past thirty years of dealing with Iran have shown that to acquire a peaceful coexistence despite differing worldviews, we need to look at the whole picture. The nuclear debate was never an isolated phenomenon. It resulted partly from a lack of understanding of the country's internal situation, of the vastly complex political and cultural legacy of a revolution that did not stem from the ideology of fundamentalist religion alone. Pointing not only to the ideology of Iran's nuclear program but also singling out the perpetrators of the massive human rights abuses in the country would have made our policy more credible and effective—both by demonstrating to the Iranian people that we are on their side and by fostering exchange, dialogue, and trade, which might have put those who sought to advance their cause by playing with the nuclear fire into their rightful place inside Iranian society: at the margins. This is not to say that sanctions and pressure were not adequate responses once we found out that Iran was making moves to acquire nuclear weapons and seriously damage the Nuclear Non-Proliferation Treaty, that precious political achievement whose vital aim is to eventually rid the world of this deadliest of threats—nuclear war.

Of course, this lack of communication and earnest debate was to be found on both sides. As Sylke Tempel, editor-in-chief of the journal *Internationale Politik*, remarked in a very pertinent Tweet on the occasion of the 2013 MSC debate with Mottaki's successor as foreign minister, Ali Akbar Salehi, his way of playing chess was to turn to another player as soon as the one he was currently playing against made a move. This elegant way of escaping a serious debate is a quality often found in the dealings of Iranian representatives on the international stage. It is a consequential form of outward appearance of a political system based not on transparency and debate but on the repression of its own people, corruption, and on the often unscrupulous readiness to use whatever means necessary to stay in power.

After the 2013 elections, which put Khatami's negotiator, Hassan Rouhani, at the helm of the government, there is reason for hope. The country elected the candidate that promised to leave behind resistance and pursue meaningful collaboration and coexistence with the rest of the world and its institutions. It seems that by letting the moderate cleric win at the ballots in July, Khamenei and the hardliners might have understood that a head-on confrontation would not be in their best interest either. That also applies for the "Western" world. Solving the nuclear problem is feasible if we reestablish trust. For that we need to begin the talk anew, expanding our dialogue to more than just this one issue, applying pressure where necessary, and relieving it where it has lost its *raison d'être*.

What would be a worthier way to celebrate the fiftieth anniversary of the Munich Security Conference than to fulfill its promise of a truly meaningful dialogue beyond all ideological divisions, also in the case of our dealings with Iran?

Omid Nouripour is the spokesperson for security policy of the Alliance 90/The Greens parliamentary group in the German Bundestag. He has been a member of parliament since 2006.

Europe, the United States, and the Rise of the Asia-Pacific

Kevin Rudd

My experiences with the Munich Security Conference have always provided me with renewed faith in the power of international dialogue to address the world's challenges. I am delighted to have been asked to contribute to this anthology marking the very special occasion of the conference's fiftieth anniversary.

When I last attended the Munich Security Conference in 2012, I had the honor of participating in a discussion panel on "America, Europe, and the Rise of Asia" chaired by former United States Secretary of State Dr. Henry Kissinger. The panel's theme reflected the increasing focus of thinkers and decision-makers in Europe on the implications of the Asia-Pacific's rise for the rest of the world. The engagement between the Chinese vice foreign minister and Senator John McCain was memorable because we saw two countries talking past each other.

Without doubt, the increasing economic and strategic importance of the Asia-Pacific is one of the defining trends of this century. It is an economic and demographic change that will affect not only Australia's region but Europe and the wider world. Australia's geographic location and our

▲
Kevin Rudd (second from right) at the 2012 panel on the "rise of Asia"

longstanding engagement with the region means we are well placed to provide a unique perspective on the challenges and opportunities presented by the rise of the Asia-Pacific.

From the outset, I would like to emphasize that the rise of Asia is not a zero-sum game. To borrow an allusion from the former British prime minister Harold MacMillan, it is not a case of the West playing Athens to Asia's Rome. Europe and the United States will continue to play major roles in shaping the twenty-first century, just as they did in the century before. We should not, either, neglect the important economic developments in Africa and Latin America.

But the extraordinary growth in the economies of the Asia-Pacific means that the economic center of gravity that has for the past two centuries found its focal point in first Europe and then the United States is shifting back toward Asia.

The increasing importance of Asian economies and societies is clear. The share of world output generated in Asia has doubled over the past half century. It now accounts for more than a third of all global economic output. By 2030, this will have risen to around half of all global output. By then, four of the world's ten largest economies will be in Asia. Within a few years, Asia is set to become home to most of the world's middle class.

China is the most well known part of this story, and it is easy to see why: China's trajectory over the past three decades is a compelling narrative. Its gross domestic product has grown at an average rate of almost 10 percent since Deng Xiaoping's economic reforms in 1979. I think it is always helpful to consider the human consequences of these impressive numbers: 500 million Chinese have been people lifted out of poverty to date. This is a monumental achievement and a powerful illustration of the true effect of economic growth.

If we expand our scope to look at China and India together, in the past two decades they have almost tripled their share of the global economy. That trend continues. The Organisation for Economic Cooperation and Development (OECD) has predicted that by 2060, India and China's combined share of the global GDP will be larger than that of the entire current OECD membership.

Two hundred years ago, China and India were the world's two largest economies and had been for nearly two millennia. In the two centuries since, the defining feature of the world economy has been the gap between the living standards, wealth, and productivity of the industrialized West and the developing East.

Samuel Huntington called the separation of these two economic hemispheres the "Great Divergence." Now, the trends that have prevailed for most of human history are reasserting themselves. Today, we are living through the "Great *Con*vergence."

Within a few years, Asia will be not only the world's largest producer of goods and services but also the world's largest consumer of them. This is not a historical anomaly. And the rise of Asia goes beyond the success stories of China and India. Japan remains the world's third-largest economy, while Indonesia, South Korea, and Australia (Asia's fourth-largest economy) continue to see strong growth. The economic success stories of Singapore, Hong Kong, and Taiwan are by now well established, and the newly industrializing economies of Thailand, Malaysia, and Vietnam are all expected to experience continued strong growth over the next decade.

As mature economies grapple with the aftermath of the global financial crisis, Asia has become the primary driver for global growth and prosperity. For Australia, as an Asia-Pacific country, this is an immediate reality. We have seized the opportunity to build upon the connections we have in the region and to forge new ones. Australia now has sophisticated bilateral architecture with all the region's powers, including China, India, Indonesia, the Republic of Korea, and Japan.

But developments in Asia do not only matter to Australia and other regional countries; the economics and politics of the region are now inextricably linked to the world at large. For that reason, all of us have a collective interest in ensuring that Asia's prosperity continues. Policymakers on both sides of the Atlantic need to work hard to understand the characteristics of Asia's rise in order to better understand the direction it is likely to take in the future.

The foundation for this extraordinary prosperity has been a decades-long period of relative peace and stability. But ongoing stability cannot be taken for granted. Even as investment and trade bring the economies of Asia closer together, nationalism and competing territorial claims continue to threaten regional cohesion. The notion that extensive economic ties can guarantee peace is a fallacy disproved by history, not least the early twentieth-century history of Europe.

There are the three regional flashpoints that have historically preoccupied the region: the Taiwan Strait, Kashmir, and the Korean Peninsula. Of these, cross-strait relations are arguably in a better state than they have been at any point since 1949, with both sides committed to strengthening economic ties and ongoing dialogue. Similarly, India and Pakistan are showing a welcome determination to improving ties, though Kashmir and the scourge of fundamentalist terrorism remain potent destabilizers.

Tensions on the Korean Peninsula remain high, with North Korea reacting provocatively to the strong United Nations Security Council resolutions condemning its December 2012 missile launch and February 2013 nuclear test. The region, and the world, are justifiably concerned by the threat to international peace and security posed by North Korea's nuclear weapons and missile development.

To these tensions we should now add two more: conflicting territorial claims in the South China Sea and the East China Sea. This is a concern not just to the countries immediately involved but also to their neighbors in the region and the international community, including Europe, as Asia is a maritime domain where access to the sea's resources and transport routes is paramount. By way of example, the movement of most of Europe's $ 860 billion trade with Northeast Asia passes through the South China Sea. In fact, half of the world's maritime merchant traffic traverses this highly strategic sea (including 48 percent of Australia's merchandise trade). A serious conflict could interrupt the movement of oil inward or goods outward, resulting in staggering implications for Europe, indeed for the entire world.

Of course, the above is by no means an exhaustive list of current regional tensions, but these points of friction do represent a serious threat to regional harmony. Encouragingly, there is broad recognition of this fact among policymakers in most Asian nations. Leaders and thinkers in Asia realize that continued prosperity depends upon regional stability and that Asia's rise is not preordained, but rather something that must be worked at, cultivated, and protected.

Although there are many important relationships in Asia, the relationship between the United States and China is the critical axis around which much of the ongoing security and stability of the region revolves. For the past six decades, US power—including its guarantee of the safe provision of seaborne trade around the world—has provided the bedrock for regional stability, allowing others, including China, to grow and prosper. The Obama administration's "rebalance" to Asia is a welcome progression of this structural cooperation, though it should be acknowledged that China views this renewed American focus on Asia and the attendant increased bilateral engagement in the region with some wariness.

I have written in more detail elsewhere of the possible paths for the US-China relationship (most recently for the March/April 2013 edition of *Foreign Affairs* magazine), and I will not restate that thesis in its entirety here, but I will offer a *précis*. My own personal view is that the most productive path for Asia would involve a new framework for cooperation between the US and China that accepts the reality of competition, the importance of cooperation, and the fact that these are not mutually exclusive propositions.

I continue to argue against the skeptical position that trust must be built before the United States and China can engage in significant strategic co-operation. In fact, I believe that the opposite is true: trust is built on the basis of real success in cooperative projects.

A solid, functional relationship between the United States and China is both essential and achievable. Despite some tensions, both sides have demonstrated a longstanding commitment to strengthening ties and mutual understanding. This commitment was evident in the summit between presidents Obama and Xi at the Sunnylands Estate in California in June of 2013, but extends much further than that to incorporate a large array of bilateral mechanisms between the two governments. The fifth round of the biennial US-China Strategic and Economic Dialogue took place this July, with the US and China agreeing to work cooperatively on issues ranging from climate change and global energy security to cyberspace. The United States and China have also established a Strategic Security Dialogue to facilitate more robust military-to-military ties. In addition, the United States and China have a wide range of other bilateral ministerial and officials'-level structures to discuss specific issues.

From the United States' perspective, having built and sustained much of the postwar order that has enabled global economic prosperity, the logic of effectively integrating a reinvigorated Chinese power into that order is sound. The world, moreover, has a strong stake in China engaging in the international system. No major international problem can be solved without the active engagement of China, from climate change to global development, from nuclear proliferation to the peaceful resolution of conflicts that threaten global peace and security.

What, then, can we infer of China's perspective and intent? Does China intend to use its international influence to reform the current system, and if so in what direction?

The Chinese have long argued that modern China must operate within the international system, rather than outside it. For China this is important both for the strategic benefits facilitated by participation in this system (World Trade Organization accession, et cetera) and to facilitate the successful reestablishment of what it sees as its rightful position as a respected global power. At the same time, China has been consistent in its call for reform of the international system and the "democratization of international relations." A constant corollary to this position has been its resentment of any attempt to use the international system to export what it considers Western values and ideology.

China's worldview is shaped by the continuing central role of the Chinese Communist Party, and one of the core tasks for the party and the government over the decade ahead is to transform China's economic model to more balanced consumption-led growth. This will involve much needed structural reforms that address the income inequality that currently divides city and country, tackles unregulated "shadow" lending in the financial sector, and provides better access to social welfare and healthcare for China's people.

The Communist Party will aim to complete this task while lifting more Chinese citizens out of poverty, providing jobs to China's youth, and raising the living standards of its workers. Thus far, China's economic transformation has depended on internationalization of the Chinese economy and access to global markets. Chinese policymakers recognize the fact that a stable international system is essential to continued growth and the successful transformation of the country's economic model.

A stable international order is also integral to the fulfillment of the deeply held Chinese desire to restore the nation's international prestige. The value that China places on continuing economic growth as a means of lifting living standards at home and validating the country's importance abroad makes it clear that it will remain in its strategic national interest to continue to support a form of the multilateral rules-based order that has served it so well in the past.

While relations between the US and China remain central to peace and prosperity in the Asia-Pacific, many other countries and institutions will also play important roles in determining the region's future. The Association of Southeast Asian Nations (ASEAN) remains at the core of regional architecture and has played an important role in socializing regional norms and shaping states' behavior. But more will be required of it—and expected of it—as regional states gain more economic and strategic weight.

A focus on economic community-building in the region will remain important but ultimately inadequate to preserve peace. An effective multilateral order requires the active participation of most, if not all, of the region's states. As it stands, our region lacks the well-developed institutions required to support regional security in the face of what we have seen are a considerable number of potential flashpoints that could provoke political crises that degenerate quickly into regional instability.

The comparison between postwar Europe and modern-day Asia has been raised by those who wonder if Asia can learn from Europe without repeating its mistakes. This comparison is far from exact, but Europe's invaluable experience in establishing and building the architecture required to manage conflict is instructive; it has informed and will continue to inform the Asia-Pacific in our ongoing efforts at securing a stable and cooperative regional environment.

The Asia-Europe Meeting (ASEM) provides a forum to exchange ideas on shaping such an environment. We should see ASEM as an opportunity for dialogue and relationship-building between Asian and European leaders and ministers who might not otherwise regularly cross each other's paths. In this vein, ASEM can be used as an arena to share experiences and lessons about our respective security and economic circumstances in an open and nonconfrontational setting.

Regional mechanisms in Asia are still evolving, and there is reason to be optimistic about the progress on this front. The ASEAN-centered East Asia Summit (EAS), for example, is beginning to take shape as a key institution for helping to manage regional relations. Its members include all of the region's major powers. EAS also counts eight members of the G20 and three permanent members of the UN Security Council. Most importantly, it has the remit to incorporate economic as well as security dialogues, and facilitates discussion between the US and China in the company of those who are directly affected by the outcomes of these discussions. As a practical matter, the EAS could be strengthened through the development of a stronger secretariat function, including a policy support unit, within the ASEAN Secretariat. Again, although the analogy is not a direct one, Europe's experience and remarkable success in taming nationalism is a valuable resource for Asia to draw upon.

It is still early, but the EAS offers an opportunity to make important headway on the development of the regional norms that will underpin peace in the region and sustain Asia's prosperity—a *Pax Pacifica*—in coming decades.

Along with the development of the necessary institutions, I believe a number of core principles would need to be collectively acknowledged for a *Pax Pacifica* to function effectively. One of these is that China's peaceful rise should be accommodated and its national security interests acknowledged. Another is Chinese acceptance of a continuing US presence in the region and a respect for America's alliances in Asia. A further basic principle is that the US and China need to accept that other states have major equities in Asia's future and must have an equitable voice in the region's management.

Temporary periods of peace can be created by the dominance of one power over other states, but for true regional stability we must seek empowerment rather than submission. I use the adjective "Pacifica" rather than "Americana" or "Sinica" precisely because this is a peace that must be delivered in the region, by the region as a collective.

Of course, even if these mechanisms were successfully put in place there would still be tensions. Tensions over values like democracy, human rights, and noninterventionism are accompanied by tensions over resources and territory as well as tensions that are based in longstanding ethnic and religious acrimony. Overcoming these will be a challenge, but informed self-interest in national growth and a shared awareness of the role of regional stability in fostering that growth are strong starting points for collaboration.

Finally, the communal nature of the challenges that we face requires a shared responsibility for the path we choose to follow in confronting them. This shared responsibility means our policy responses will be deeper and more robust if they reflect a genuine understanding of the relationships that connect our region and our world.

We are best served in this regard if we remember that economics and security, while primary, do not describe the entirety of our international relations; culture must be linked to this discussion as well. Cultural rifts within Asia cannot be papered over; they have to be worked through slowly, and the iterative process of structured dialogue is a key part of developing the trust necessary to achieve this at the leaders' level. People-to-people links and the intimate contact facilitated by international travel and modern communications technology also have a part to play in establishing a secure regional environment.

In Australia we are taking concrete steps to develop our knowledge of regional actors, our skills in regional languages, and our people-to-people links with our Asian neighbors. Asia's place in the global economy and its growing strategic importance mean this should not be the endeavor solely of those of us located in the region, but also a concerted undertaking for our partners in Europe and elsewhere who have their own strong connections to Asia and who share with us a deep and abiding interest in Asia's future.

Kevin Rudd served as Australia's twenty-sixth prime minister from 2007 to 2010, then as foreign minister from 2010 to 2012, before returning to the prime ministership in 2013. From 1998 to 2013, he was a member of the parliament of Australia. He is a proficient speaker of Mandarin Chinese and a visiting professor at Tsinghua University in Beijing.

Asia's Rise and Asia's Risks

Eberhard Sandschneider

Since its initiation fifty years ago, the Munich Security Conference has established an impressive tradition. Once a year, major issues of world politics are on the agenda of foreign policy elites from the United States, Europe, and increasingly from other parts of the world as well. But the focus on traditional transatlantic security issues, for which the MSC became famous, is shifting rapidly. Since the end of the Cold War two-and-a-half decades ago, some of the issues (and even some of the speakers) have remained on the scene. However, new ones are not only changing the agenda of Munich debates, they are also defining challenges for the future relevance of the MSC. The challenge itself is not new.

Existing world orders broke down three times during the twentieth century. After the first and second breakdowns (1918 and 1945), the world sought new institutional arrangements (the League of Nations, the United Nations). The Munich Security Conference itself was born out of the necessity to come to terms with new security challenges due to the effects of the breakdown of world order after World War II. Forty-five years later and after the third collapse of the world order in 1989/90, however, major institutions did not change. Thus, institutional perseverance is increasingly challenged

▲
Officials from Singapore, Brazil, India, and China debating global governance at the 2013 MSC

by rules that have kept changing beneath the surface of world politics ever since. And many "of the institutions that have been critical over the last decades will likely prove to be unfit, ineffective, and lacking legitimacy, at least in their current state and setup."[1] In Munich, those who rightly or wrongly believed to have won the Cold War could come together and celebrate—inviting some of their former opponents to join the party while others (mainly from Asia) were already standing outside in the February cold and asked for admission.

Even twenty-five years later, this challenge can still be felt almost physically: while the audience snuggling together in the ballroom of the Bayerischer Hof (closely watched by those who are banned as observers to the balconies on the second floor) still mostly reflects the transatlantic security community, the topics debated on the panels have already become globalized. Apart from traditional security issues dominated by NATO, homeland security and concerns about the respective bad guys in world politics, financial stability, access to resources, cyber security, and even developments in parts of Africa (such as Mali) have made it onto the agenda. Perhaps it is this tension between participants and topics that is responsible for the impression of helplessness that has been attributed to recent conferences.[2]

While most Western participants in the Munich Security Conference still seem to assume that they have come to Munich to debate solutions to global problems, Asian participants openly criticize that the West has become part of the problem. Hesitant European self-criticism is meanwhile matched by open admonitions to adapt to change. One of the most prominent voices in this debate, Singapore's former top diplomat Kishore Mahbubani, puts it this way: "The Middle East, nuclear proliferation, stalled trade liberalization, and global warming are all challenges that the West is essentially failing to address. And this failure suggests that a systemic problem is emerging in the West's stewardship of the international order—one that Western minds are reluctant to analyze or confront openly. After having enjoyed centuries of global domination, the West has to learn to share power and responsibility for the management of global issues with the rest of the world."[3] Similar voices are coming from China. In March 2011, China's deputy foreign minister, Mme. Fu Ying, echoed Mahbubani's criticism and simply admonished Europe "to learn to learn again."[4]

While the world is changing rapidly, change is also slowly but recognizably coming to the Munich Security Conference. A conference that used to be dominated by representatives of Western countries and by topics that define security risks in a more or less strictly transatlantic way has to face the fact that bipolarity is gone. Enter what most people would describe as multipolarity onto the Munich stage of world politics? Certainly not in a hurried way. But one of the trends among many is clear: Asia's rise will be one of Munich's most important challenges.

During the first fifty years, Asia remained mostly on the sidelines. But that will have to change and already is changing. In 2010, the honor of opening the 46th Munich Security Conference was given to the foreign minister of China for the first time ever. And in 2013, a panel on "Rising Powers and Global Governance" was organized for speakers from Australia, China, India, Brazil, and Singapore—without one representative of the West or NATO among them. This trend will continue. In a few years time, if not earlier, developments in Asia might well turn out to be the defining issues at the MSC. Since the conference not only addresses the long-term trends in security and international cooperation but also the current hotspots of global affairs, Asia is offering an irritatingly high number of such hotspots, which might turn up on the MSC agenda at any time. Those who are impressed by Asia's rise should be careful not to overlook its risks, which are similarly impressive: the situation on the Korean Peninsula, conflicts between China and Japan over islands in the East China Sea and with all neighboring countries in the South China Sea, the dormant conflict between China and Taiwan, the effects of China's military modernization (for example, the so-called string of pearls around the Indian Ocean), cooperation and conflict potentials in Central Asia, reactions by India, Pakistan and Russia to China's rise—the list is long and could be easily extended in detail. In addition to these short-term risks, the long-term trend is clear: the rise of Asia is a harbinger for the growing influence of emerging powers on a global scale.

There is, however, another and even more important change in the deep structure of global affairs that might add enormously to these shifts in power and risks. Almost all of these emerging new powers demonstrate that global power currencies are undergoing dramatic shifts and changes as well: military capacities are still important, yet while the United States is still the only remaining military superpower, it becomes ever more visible how little any US government can achieve with all its military preponderance, because others are effectively using the new currencies of global power: economic strength and growth (including financial stability), access to resources and growing technological capacities, but also social cohesion and political stability (even in autocratic structures) convey more efficiency to political actors than the simple command of the gun. The setup of power currencies is radically changing to the disadvantage of the West, because the simple fact becomes visible that others take an increasing share in defining the rules of the game. In a strictly Western perspective one might argue that the game is still ours but the rules are theirs—unless we find ways to effectively and peacefully accommodate new powerbrokers in global affairs. Future conferences will have to address these issues, even if a majority of participants might not like the results.

Let us pause for a moment and ask what this will mean for traditional transatlantic relations. The most important consequence becomes more and more obvious: old-style transatlanticism, as it has been celebrated by the first fifty Munich conferences, is gone. It is not only the fact that the United States is strategically rebalancing toward Asia, but also the tribute to Europe's predominantly economic pivot to Asia that keeps changing the fundamentals of transatlantic vows. Most political elites in Europe would still subscribe to Hillary Clinton's 2010 whitewashing of a "strategic partnership between Europe and the United States that has never been stronger,"[5] but the effects of Asia's rise are increasingly being felt, even in this most sensitive issue.

Whenever transatlantic partners meet to discuss the rise of China, they agree on the importance of the issue and on the necessity for a continuous transatlantic dialogue, but they almost never agree on substance issues. The US perspective is fundamentally different from European attitudes—not to mention the cacophony of European positions. But while the European Union is in general concentrating on Asia and China as economic partners, the US is taking a much more conflict-oriented attitude toward China as potentially the next major military opponent.

Thus, both for Europe and the US, hope does not come automatically from the other side of the Atlantic, although transatlantic relations still are the indispensable point of reference for many political speeches. Swearing on transatlantic cooperation, praising common values, and insisting on common interests, strategies, and institutions has become an essential exercise for politicians on both sides of the Atlantic. The reality, however, is different. The transatlantic disconnect is growing while the transatlantic world is falling apart. With a common threat gone after the end of the Cold War, divergent geopolitical interests, different threat perceptions, and even divergent value and belief systems have added to a process of transatlantic disengagement and competition, which will be decisive for the shaping of a new world order. The tension that has risen over the euro crisis is a harbinger of more friction to come.

Is this the end of the West? Most probably not! Stepping aside and inviting others to take their share of global responsibility—albeit according to their own definitions of responsibility—is not equivalent to loss, decay, and ultimate destruction. The global community of the twenty-first century has to outlive zero-sum mentalities. We in the West have proposed a world of rule-based competition. Now it is time to live up to it. While we congratulate the Munich Security Conference on the occasion of its fiftieth anniversary, we know that acknowledging change and exploring options for dealing with the uncertain rise of Asia will be the major task of conferences in the decades to come. The meeting on the first weekend in February will be as important in the future as it has been in the past.

Eberhard Sandschneider is Otto Wolff Director of the Research Institute of the German Council on Foreign Relations.

Notes

1 MSC Booklet 2013, 47.
2 Stefan Kornelius, "Die Ohnmacht des Westens," *Süddeutsche Zeitung,* February 5/6, 2011, 4.
3 Kishore Mahbubani, "The Case Against the West: America and Europe in the Asian Century," *Foreign Affairs* 87, no. 3 (May/June 2008), 121.
4 Fu Ying, "Europa muss das Lernen lernen," *Handelsblatt,* March 30, 2011, 63.
5 Secretary of State Hillary Rodham Clinton's remarks at the Munich Security Conference plenary session, February 5, 2011.

Climate Change and Its Impact on Security

Nikolaus von Bomhard

Recent decades have seen a dramatic rise in the frequency and severity of weather-related natural catastrophes throughout the world and mounting economic and insured losses. One sensible approach would start with efforts to research the causes of this development, as only in this way is it possible to determine whether and to what extent we are already dealing with immediate consequences of climate change, for example the observable changes in the distributions of extreme values in meteorological parameters such as temperature and precipitation. At least equally important are efforts to evaluate the economic consequences of climate change, the resulting droughts and floods, but also the rise in sea level to be expected.

The indirect consequences of climate change—a deterioration in the bases of life resulting from inadequate food supply or withdrawal from flooded coastal regions—have been on the research agenda for many years, but only a few aspects have thus far found their way onto the agenda of political decision-makers. Regrettably, this is true especially of recent years, in which financial and economic topics have dominated political discussion.

This contribution on the occasion of the 50th Munich Security Conference is a plea for an earnest exchange, in particular within the context of this

Nikolaus von Bomhard (center) with Georg Mascolo (left)
at the MSC's 2010 Moscow Core Group Meeting

important political forum, on long-term changes in our environment. We must soon find solutions that make it possible for people to live together securely in spite of these foreseeable challenges.

Migration as a Strategy for Adapting to Environmental Changes

Regardless of how they are organized socially, human beings confronted with deteriorating environmental conditions have only two basic options to respond: either to correct the causes of the deterioration or to adapt continually as the situation changes. In practice, efforts to respond often turn into a twofold strategy involving a combination of elements from both options. What will be the most probable response in cases where changes in environmental conditions can be influenced at best over a very long period and exceed social groups' ability to adapt or continually exacerbate disparities in the distribution of prosperity? That they shift the focus of their existence to geographic areas offering actually or supposedly better living conditions. From a historical perspective, migration has always been a strategy for surviving by escaping from desperate situations. So it is also plausible today that a severe, lasting deterioration of environmental conditions—particularly in regions with growing populations—will give rise to growing migratory pressure. This, in turn, has the potential to threaten other societies.

Climate Change and Security Issues

In the discussion regarding climate change, it is the task of the natural sciences to inform political decision-makers about the changing probabilities of meteorological parameters and shed light on their causes. Most recently, for example, the first part of the Fifth Assessment Report (AR5) by the Intergovernmental Panel on Climate Change (IPCC),[1] published in September 2013, again confirmed the substance of existing knowledge regarding the physical science basis of climate change, also addressing scientists' understanding of the causes of the pronounced slowing in the rise in atmospheric temperature that has been observed since the end of the nineties. Analyzing the reasons for this is the aim of further research activities. The IPCC AR5 report offers an interim result consisting of three main factors: short-term, internal fluctuations in the climate system; a minimum in the eleven-year solar cycle; and a strengthening of the cooling effect produced by aerosols from several minor volcanic eruptions. However, the report also points to climate-change-induced developments, in evidence of which observable environmental changes can now be better quantified thanks to the improved data situation. This includes first and foremost recognizing the accelerated rise in the global average sea level over recent decades and observations of altered weather patterns, such as increased precipitation in wet regions of the tropics and in temperate latitudes of the northern hemisphere, and decreased precipitation in dry regions of the subtropics.

The World Meteorological Organisation also describes findings similar to those of the IPCC in its status report "The Global Climate 2001–2010: A Decade of Climate Extremes."[2] Climate-model-based scenario simulations conducted in earlier decades had already indicated that an increase in the concentration of greenhouse gases in the atmosphere could lead to regionally varying changes in weather extremes due to the gases' direct and indirect radiative forcing.

Working on this basis, initial studies[3] from as far back as the seventies pointed to global security issues as a possible new consequence of anthropogenic climate change. The subject of climate change and security was elevated to the official political agenda in Toronto in 1988 as part of an international scientific and political conference supported by the then prime minister of Canada, Brian Mulroney: "The Changing Atmosphere: Implications for Global Security." In the ensuing years, this issue was repeatedly the object of interdisciplinary research and also taken up in political discussions and consultations.[4]

Socioeconomic Effects in Developing/Emerging Countries

In a special report published in 2012, the Intergovernmental Panel on Climate Change summarized the current state of knowledge regarding climate change as follows: "A changing climate leads to changes in the frequency, intensity, spatial extent, duration, and timing of extreme weather and climate events, and can result in unprecedented extreme weather and climate events."[5]

In order to develop measures that will be effective responses to these prognosticated consequences of anthropogenic climate change in both humanitarian and economic terms, it would make sense to review the catastrophes that have resulted from extreme weather events in recent decades. Studies conducted by the World Bank[6] and other supranational organizations as well as loss databases of research institutions[7] and the insurance industry[8] provide relevant information for a conclusive picture of the development of natural catastrophes worldwide and thus also valuable and necessary bases for the analysis of possible future scenarios.

As regards the question of how global warming is affecting security, special importance must be placed on information that makes it possible to measure how severely societies are affected by natural catastrophes resulting from severe weather events in relation to their economic means to take adequate adaptation measures. For example, the World Bank classifies the world's countries into four income groups (high-income, upper-middle-income, lower-middle, and low-income economies):

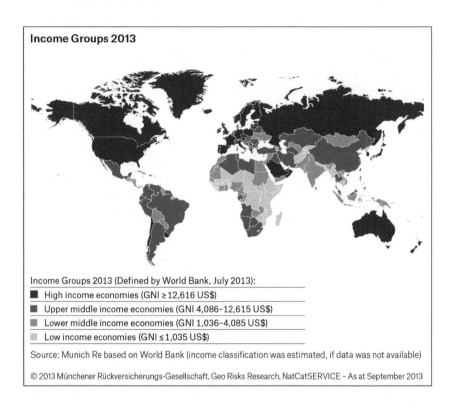

Income Groups 2013

Income Groups 2013 (Defined by World Bank, July 2013):

■ High income economies (GNI ≥ 12,616 US$)

■ Upper middle income economies (GNI 4,086–12,615 US$)

■ Lower middle income economies (GNI 1,036–4,085 US$)

▨ Low income economies (GNI ≤ 1,035 US$)

Source: Munich Re based on World Bank (income classification was estimated, if data was not available)

© 2013 Münchener Rückversicherungs-Gesellschaft, Geo Risks Research, NatCatSERVICE – As at September 2013

Combining the World Bank's income classification with loss figures from the global natural catastrophe database of Munich Re's NatCatService generates a data set of about 19,500 weather loss events during the period from 1980 to 2012 and yields the following picture:

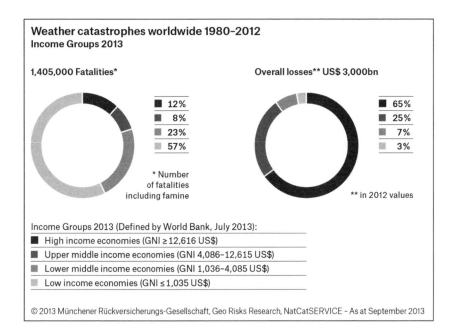

Weather catastrophes worldwide 1980-2012
Income Groups 2013

1,405,000 Fatalities*

- 12%
- 8%
- 23%
- 57%

* Number
of fatalities
including famine

Overall losses** US$ 3,000bn

- 65%
- 25%
- 7%
- 3%

** in 2012 values

Income Groups 2013 (Defined by World Bank, July 2013):
- High income economies (GNI ≥ 12,616 US$)
- Upper middle income economies (GNI 4,086–12,615 US$)
- Lower middle income economies (GNI 1,036–4,085 US$)
- Low income economies (GNI ≤ 1,035 US$)

© 2013 Münchener Rückversicherungs-Gesellschaft, Geo Risks Research, NatCatSERVICE – As at September 2013

These statistics can be boiled down to two statements:
- In recent decades, the number of fatalities attributable to weather catastrophes has been considerably higher in low-income regions than in industrial regions with higher incomes.
- Overall losses are highest in high-income economies, but such losses have
  a more powerful effect on countries in the lower income-classes, as these
  losses represent a greater proportion of their GDP.[9]

Regardless of whether event-driven or imperceptibly gradual, a climate-
change-induced deterioration in many people's livelihoods makes it highly
probable that migratory pressure will continue to rise in the coming decades. This applies particularly to developing and emerging countries that,
because of their already relatively weak economic situation, are unable to
adapt adequately to degradation of the food supply or a problem such as the
rising sea level, as they lack the strength to adapt.

The office of the UN High Commissioner for Refugees estimated that
about twenty-four million people around the globe had fled from their
homes due to flooding, famine, and other environmental catastrophes in
2005.[10] The International Organisation for Migration in Geneva expects that
the number of climate-related migrants could grow to 200 million by the

year 2050.[11] Since the term "climate-related migrants" has not yet been precisely defined, the figures cited above may be considered merely an indication, yet they do convey an impression of the scope of disaster-related migrations. This impression is confirmed by data from Germany's Federal Office for Migration and Refugees: in 2010, flooding caused fifteen million people to flee their homes in China alone, as well as another eleven million people in Pakistan.

After analyzing numerous scenarios for climate-related migration up to 2009, a European Union-funded study[12] concluded that "environmental impacts will undoubtedly affect an increasing number of communities and become a major push factor for displacement. Therefore it is important to rapidly address, at the policy level, the issue of environmental migrants/refugees."

Since streams of refugees have multiple causes, often resulting from a wide variety of economic, political, and ecological challenges, categorizing them by cause ranges from difficult to impossible. At the present time, it is probably still safe to assume that economic and political constraints dominate the push-and-pull factors determining worldwide refugee streams. For how much longer?

Unresolved Liability Issues as a Potential Security Risk

What is to be expected in the future when, based on the results of scientific research and societal and political developments, the responsibility for the direct and indirect consequences of climate change becomes a pressing international issue? Even a bilateral scenario involving the potential liability of country A, which has high CO_2 emissions, *vis-à-vis* country B, which has low emissions but has been hard hit by the rise in sea level, is complex enough. Things become even more difficult in scenarios involving possible claims by a third country C, which has suffered no direct losses as a result of climate change but has had to shoulder burdens as a consequence of migration from country B.

To date, the issue of liability under international or private law for the consequences of climate change has not been conclusively resolved. Attempts by individuals and groups of people to sue industrial groups have hitherto met with failure. Of course, the insurance industry is following trends in court decisions in this area with the keenest attention. Thus far, there has been no case that has really tested whether and how international liability claims based on the consequences of climate change would be settled. The lodging of a liability claim based on the impairment of a country's security interests due to migratory movements resulting from climate change would in any case open up entirely new dimensions.

Potential Disputes over Energy and Food Resources in and between Industrialized Countries

As outlined above, potential changes in the global security architecture—particularly between countries with high prosperity gradients—resulting from climate change have been the object of scientific research for years. Considerably more recent, on the other hand, are studies regarding the effects of climatic changes on the energy and/or food security sectors among industrialized countries.[13] How will industrialized countries with inadequate adaptation options conduct themselves in order to successfully counteract a deteriorating supply situation? Will political agreements regarding the protection of Arctic regions against massive incursions to exploit raw materials continue to be upheld without conflict even when further diminution of the North Polar ice cap makes exploiting oil and gas deposits there economically attractive?[14] Any attempt to offer reliable answers to these security issues at present would be premature. The important thing, however, is that the international community of nations sets these issues on the political agenda at the appropriate time. Yet it is equally important that researchers prepare the relevant information and scenarios in the form needed by political decision-makers and develop solution options.

Global Challenges Demand Perseverance— and Sometimes Approaches that Allow Nations to Work toward a Shared Objective at Different Speeds

Recent history offers good examples of how worldwide agreements have been achieved regarding both environmental and security issues. In 1987, for example, the International Conference for the Protection of the Ozone Layer set the stage for the signing of the *Montreal Protocol on Substances that Deplete the Ozone Layer*. This first worldwide environmental protection protocol entered into force in 1989, regulating the emission of chlorofluorohydrocarbons to protect the ozone layer in the upper atmosphere. Just a few years later, measurements started to show that the global agreement was having the desired effect.

As regards issues associated with climate change and its effects, the search for solutions is pursuing many avenues, with these efforts being coordinated globally under the mandate of the United Nations and its subsidiary organizations. Here, a significant role is played by the United Nations Framework Convention on Climate Change (UNFCCC), which was resolved in 1992 at the UN Conference for Environment and Development with the principal aim of creating rules governing the emission of greenhouse gases that would be binding throughout the world. Another objective set within the framework of political negotiations conducted under the auspices of the annual Conference of the Parties (COP) is the development of multilateral solutions for climate-impact adaptation, including international financing systems. That policymakers, particularly those at the global level, need perseverance and shared values becomes evident when one considers the results of the nineteen COP negotiations conducted thus far: following initially promising steps and the resolution of the Kyoto Protocol regulating emissions of carbon dioxide and other greenhouse gases, the UNFCCC process faltered and for some years now has progressed only in very small increments. At the present time, there is little indication that the nations of the world share the resolve to find a global solution to the challenges posed by climate change.

The negotiations on reducing anthropogenic impact on the climate and adapting to the consequences of climate change have now revealed a "world of different speeds." At first glance, this may seem to be an unsatisfactory approach toward solving a global problem, as many countries—particularly industrial nations with high per-capita CO_2 emissions—have joined the group of "slow movers." Yet in a world with a continually growing population and mounting competition for successful models of economic growth, it is becoming ever less likely that all nations will undertake to achieve a joint CO_2 target in the coming years. So it is not simply just the second-best solution, but perhaps even a global opportunity that nations are moving at different speeds—which are often attributable not only to different prosperity levels but also to different strategies for generating sustainable growth—to reduce the carbon footprint of their economies.

Of relevance for the cause of global climate protection, however, is that there be a vision shared by all UN signatory countries. By officially recognizing the "two-degree goal,"[15] the community of nations agreed on such a vision in 2010 at the COP16 World Climate Conference in Cancún.

Is Protecting Human Rights a Foundation for Global Solutions?

In a world marked by growing population and increasing economic and eco-logical disparities, there will over the long term have to be a foundation of values shared and supported by all peoples that will serve as a basis for build-ing solutions to global challenges.

Working on such a foundation, it should be possible to identify ways of escaping from the dilemma of having to bring about a hard-to-achieve con-sensus on answers to global issues such as "climate change and security." For example, acceptance of the principle of "climate justice" could be a shared point of departure for negotiations between industrial, emerging, and de-veloping countries. This approach relies essentially on recalling the founda-tion of the Human Rights Convention resolved by all nations in 1948 and the shared values formulated therein.

The year 2015 will therefore be an important one for the community of nations:

– It is hoped that the nations participating in the world climate summit in Paris (COP21) will pass far-reaching resolutions regarding climate pro-tection (mitigation and adaptation) that will also affect further develop-ment in the area of "climate change and security."
– The World Conference on Disaster Risk Reduction to be held in Sendai, Japan, will devise solutions for adapting to extreme natural events—also with a view to climate change.

The hope remains that the world community will respond to complex global challenges with shared solutions. Securing a peaceful future is a goal wor-thy of every effort, as national or international conflicts are no acceptable alternative.

Nikolaus von Bomhard is chairman of the Board of Management of Munich Re.

Notes

1 Intergovernmental Panel on Climate Change (IPCC), "Summary for Policymakers," in *Climate Change 2013: The Physical Science Basis* [Stocker, T. F., D. Quin, G.-K. Plattner, M. Tignor, S. K. Allen, J. Boschung, A. Nauels, Y. Xia, V. Bex and P. M. Midgley (eds.)], Working Group I Contribution to the IPCC Fifth Assessment Report (Cambridge and New York: Cambridge University Press, 2013).
2 World Meteorological Organization (WMO), Summary report, WMO No. 1119. Geneva, Switzerland, 2013.

3   Lester R. Brown, *Redefining National Security,* Worldwatch Paper No. 14 (Washington, DC: Worldwatch Institute, 1977).

4   German Advisory Council on Global Change (WBGU), *World in Transition: Climate Change as a Security Risk; Summary for Policymakers* (Berlin: WBGU, 2007).

5   Intergovernmental Panel on Climate Change (IPCC), "Summary for Policymakers," in *Managing the Risks of Extreme Events and Disasters to Advance Climate Change Adaptation* [Field, C.B., V. Barros, T.F. Stocker, D. Quin, D.J. Dokken, K.L. Ebi, M.D. Mastrandrea, K.J. Mach, G.-K. Plattner, S.K. Allen, M. Tignor, and P.M. Midgley (eds.)], Special Report of the Intergovernmental Panel on Climate Change (Cambridge et al.: Cambridge University Press, 2012), 3–21.

6   The World Bank, *Turn Down the Heat: Why a 4°C Warmer World Must be Avoided,* Report for the World Bank by the Potsdam Institute for Climate Impact Research and Climate Analytics (Washington, DC: The World Bank, 2012).

7   EM-DAT: OFDA/CRED International Disaster Database. Brussels: www.emdat.be, Université Catholique de Louvain, 2013, accessed August 24, 2013.

8   NatCatSERVICE: Natural Catastrophe Database, Munich: www.munichre.com/touch/naturalhazards/en/natcatservice/default.aspx, Munich Re, 2013, accessed August 26, 2013.

9   Eduardo Cavallo and Ilan Noy, *The Economics of Natural Disasters: A Survey,* IDB Working Papers No. IDB-WP-124, May 2010.

10 Koko Warner et al., *Human Security, Climate Change and Environmentally Induced Migration* (Bonn: United Nations University, Institute for Environment and Human Security, 2008).

11 IOM International Organisation for Migration, *Migration and Climate Change,* IOM Migration Research Series No. 31 (Geneva: IOM, 2008).

12 EACH-FOR Environmental Change and Forced Migration Scenarios, D.3.4. Synthesis Report, 2009, www.each-for.eu, accessed August 12, 2013.

13 International Energy Agency (IEA), *Redrawing the Energy-Climate Map,* World Energy Outlook Special Report (Paris: OECD/IEA, 2013).

14 Interagency Arctic Research Policy Committee (IARPC), *Working Together to Understand and Predict Arctic Change (Arctic Research Plan, 2013–2017)* (Washington, DC: Office of Science and Technology Policy, 2013).

15 Limitation of global warming to no more than 2°C above pre-industrial levels.

The Shifting Geopolitics of Energy—
The Green and Shale Revolution

Friedbert Pflüger

The world is more dependent on energy today than at any previous time in history. Energy is the lifeblood of the modern economy and is a vital input to nearly all goods and services, from essentials like food, clothing, and heating to manufacturing, transportation, and health care. Thus, critical questions revolving around the supply and demand of energy as well as its sustainability will continue to represent one of the biggest and most important challenges of the twenty-first century. Several mega-trends in particular will in all likelihood determine the global energy landscape and energy policy agenda in the coming decades.

Diminished Salience of Global Climate Change Policy

On September 23, 2013, government representatives and scientists opened a meeting of the Intergovernmental Panel on Climate Change (IPCC) in Stockholm to finalize the *Fifth Assessment Report* evaluating the evidence for climate change and its causes.[1] The report shows that there is

The panel on "The Changing Geopolitics of Energy" at the 2013 MSC overwhelming consensus among the scientific community that the earth's climate is warming due to human influence. At the same time, it also includes data that indicates that the rate of warming from 1998 to 2012 has slowed to about half the average rate since 1951, citing natural variability in the climate system as well as cooling effects from heat absorption by the oceans, volcanic eruptions, and a downward phase in solar activity.[2] This development is not likely to bode well for the ongoing fight against global warming.

The topic of climate change has long taken a back seat to economic priorities ever since the financial crisis of 2008. According to a GlobeScan multi-country poll, environmental concerns among citizens around the world have been falling since 2009 and have now reached twenty-year lows.[3] The recent IPCC report will likely reinforce this trend. Many governments are now demanding a clearer explanation of the pause in temperature increases over the past fifteen years despite higher global CO_2 emissions, while climate skeptics are using the data as fodder for their argument that emissions do not increase the temperatures of the planet in the first place. In Australia, the new government led by Tony Abbott has shut down the country's climate commission, which had been established to provide public information on the effects of and potential solutions to global warming.[4]

Nevertheless, this paradigm shift does not mean that climate change will disappear from the global agenda. The fact that millions of people in developing countries continue to face unbearable living conditions in cities across the globe as well as the recurrence of major floods and tropical storms with a certain degree of regularity will prevent the climate issue from being forgotten altogether. Moreover, climate-induced natural disasters continue to exact a heavy economic toll. Therefore, the climate change topic will remain on the agenda but with diminished significance relative to other energy policy objectives.

Rising Energy Demand

Another mega-trend that is sure to be a fundamental driver of global energy policy is rising energy demand. The International Energy Agency (IEA) estimates that global energy demand will grow by more than one third over the period to 2035, with China, India, and the Middle East accounting for 60 percent of the increase.[5] Energy demand in Organisation for Economic Co-operation and Development (OECD) countries, on the other hand, will barely rise.[6] Three primary long-run trends will drive global energy demand over the short to medium term: population growth, economic expansion, and urbanization.

By 2030, there will be about 8.4 billion people on the planet, up from some 7 billion today.[7] Particularly non-OECD regions like India and the Middle East will see steep growth in their populations and working-age groups,[8] while OECD countries will experience low birth rates and a shrinking working-age population.

This trend in emerging economies will help them grow significantly faster than developed countries. By 2030, non-OECD countries are expected to account for 51 percent of the world's gross domestic product, up from about 35 percent today.[9] In addition, up to three billion people could join the middle class in the coming decades. To illustrate how quickly wealth is increasing in emerging economies, consider this: it has taken China just six years to double its gross national income, compared to twenty-two years for the US.[10] As living standards rise, so too will the demand for energy, as it will not only be needed for lighting, cooking, and heating but increasingly also for more energy-intensive activities like manufacturing, large-scale construction, and transportation.

Rising urbanization rates will also continue to play a key role in increasing future energy demand. The share of the world's population living in cities has increased from about 30 percent in 1950 to 50 percent today and is expected to climb to nearly 70 percent by 2050.[11] The number of so-called mega-cities (cities with over ten million inhabitants) is also on the rise. Forty years ago there were only two cities with over ten million inhabitants; today there are twenty-three, and this figure is expected to increase to thirty-seven by 2025.[12]

Governments around the world are deliberately pursuing a policy of urbanization as a means of efficiently delivering more goods and services to their citizens. This trend will increase future energy demand as it leads to more household appliance and motor vehicle ownership, as well as the need to construct additional housing, public transportation, highways, and water systems to accommodate the rise in urban populations.

A Green Revolution Is Underway ...

An increasing share of energy stemming from renewable sources is expected to meet this rising global demand. The Green Revolution that we have experienced over the last decade will continue. Between 2005 and 2012, the total global capacity of renewable energy (excluding hydropower) increased by 200 percent.[13] According to the IEA, the share of nonhydro sources such as wind, solar, bioenergy, and geothermal in total power generation will double in this decade.[14]

This development has been underpinned by governmental policy measures to facilitate the expansion of renewables. Countries with strong political support and subsidy schemes like the United States, Germany, and China are leading the pack. However, the promotion of renewable energy is not just confined to these countries—it is spreading to more and more regions around the world. Today, about 140 countries have renewable energy targets, up from 55 in 2005.[15] This is also driving job growth. Direct and indirect jobs in the sector have more than doubled in the same period from some two million to over five million globally.[16] Developing countries in particular, which already represent more than half of all countries with policy targets and renewable support policies, will play an increasingly important role in expanding renewable energy generation in the coming years.[17]

And yet despite this expansion in global renewable energy capacity, we will still be far away from a so-called age of renewables for at least the next two decades. It is true that the dominance of traditional fossil fuels will wane due to the rise of renewable energy sources, but not by much. Since total energy demand by 2035 is expected to increase by over 30 percent, the consumption of and demand for fossil fuels are also set to increase.

… But Fossils Remain Strong!

In 2035, fossil fuels will still account for about 75 percent of the world's primary energy mix,[18] even if all current policy commitments to tackle climate change and other energy-related challenges are met.[19]

Global oil consumption, excluding biofuels, is set to increase from about eighty-seven million barrels a day in 2012 to nearly one hundred million barrels a day in 2035.[20] Most of the demand will come from the transportation sector, 90 percent of which will still run on liquid petroleum-based products in 2040, only slightly down from about 95 percent today.[21]

According to the IEA, coal use is projected to increase 65 percent (!) by 2035 if no policy measures are undertaken to curb consumption, thus making it the fastest growing fossil fuel.

Alongside coal, natural gas is one of the fastest growing fossil fuels, and demand is set to increase by nearly 50 percent to 2035.[22] Moreover, its share is expected to reach near-parity with oil and coal in the global primary energy mix in the next two decades.

Much of this demand for fossil fuels will be driven by strong economic growth in developing countries as well as subsidies, which amounted to half a trillion dollars in 2011, up almost 30 percent on 2010.[23] The Arab Spring has strongly contributed to this substantial increase. Several states in the Middle East and North Africa have boosted subsidies and abandoned existing subsidy reform plans in order to appease their citizens and prevent domestic unrest. The trend is likely to continue, because the underlying causes for turmoil in the region, including high unemployment, corruption, and lack of political freedoms, have not yet been properly addressed.

What is more, the widespread belief that we are quickly running out of fossil fuels despite the growth in consumption is not reflected in the data. We have added nearly a trillion additional barrels to our proved conventional oil reserves, from 680 billion barrels in 1980 to about 1.6 trillion barrels today, through new finds, enhanced recovery techniques, and technological improvements.[24] This is more than all of the oil in the Middle East and enough to meet global demand for the next fifty years, given current consumption levels. Similarly, proved conventional natural gas reserves are up from about 70 trillion cubic meters to almost 190 trillion cubic meters during the same period—enough to last for about sixty years.[25]

In light of these developments it is clear that even as the deployment of "green technologies" continues to progress, it will still be the fossil fuels that sate the bulk of rising global energy demand in the foreseeable future. Even today, local populations and governments in most regions throughout the world consider it a blessing whenever new hydrocarbon discoveries are made in their respective countries; they are generally far removed from sharing the concerns associated with fossil fuel production and consumption common in some developed countries. In general, the sometimes observable "demonization" of fossil fuels that seems to be more common in developed countries like Germany is markedly absent in many other societies. Hence, those who hope that the effects of climate change will spur greater international awareness for the environment to the detriment of coal, natural gas, and oil will in all likelihood be disappointed.

Shale Revolution

The supply of fossil fuels is set to rise even more dramatically due to a fairly recent development, namely the shale revolution. The use of hydraulic fracturing to release vast untapped supplies of unconventional hydrocarbons like shale oil and shale gas trapped in rock formations is redrawing the global energy map. The IEA estimates that there are some 400 billion barrels of unconventional oil and 220 trillion cubic meters of unconventional gas.[26] When combined, this amounts to approximately 70 percent of the world's current proved oil and gas reserves. More interestingly, for the first time, the bulk of the supplies are not concentrated in a few, often volatile, regions of the world, but are rather widely dispersed in countries like the United States, Russia, Argentina, and China.

The US is currently the frontrunner in unconventional fossil fuel production. Spurred by elevated oil and gas prices in the early to mid-first decade of the twenty-first century, many smaller and mid-sized energy companies in the US began utilizing horizontal drilling and hydraulic fracturing techniques to exploit shale resources, which has led to a downright revolution in US oil and gas production. Over the past decade, the country has added almost four billion barrels of crude oil and lease condensate proved reserves, an increase of 15 percent, and the greatest volume increase since the US Energy Information Administration (EIA) began publishing proved reserves estimates in 1977.[27] Likewise, shale gas reserves now constitute almost a third of American natural gas reserves. This has several important geopolitical implications.

Firstly, the US shale boom is driving down energy costs and has sparked a revival in American manufacturing. Companies operating in the US can now purchase energy at a significantly lower cost than their counterparts in Europe and Asia, thus giving them a clear competitive edge. As a result, more and more energy-intensive companies are building plants and factories in the US, which, in turn, is leading to the creation of thousands of new jobs.

Secondly, with natural gas production outpacing domestic consumption, the US is poised to become a major liquefied natural gas (LNG) exporter in the next few years. The US Department of Energy has already begun approving some LNG export projects, and federal policymakers are deliberating the merits of a free trade agreement with Europe, which would in effect give gas producers the green light to export. The flow of new LNG supplies from the US to world markets would likely provide economic benefits to gas-importing countries by placing downward pressure on international gas prices. Gas exporting states, on the other hand, could suffer a decline in revenues due to price decreases and supply displacement. Moreover, this would also pressure traditional natural gas suppliers using long-term, oil-indexed contracts to adopt market-based prices or revise their contracts, as was the case when Russia's Gazprom had to renegotiate the terms of its contracts with German utility giants RWE and E.ON.

Thirdly, the rapid increase in shale oil production is prompting many analysts to suggest that the US could become wholly energy independent by 2020. While this may not fully be the case, as the US will still be tied to international oil markets, it is certainly taking big steps to diversify its supply portfolio by reducing its dependence on foreign supplies. Since 2007, US oil imports have declined by some 15 percent.[28] This adds an element of uncertainty regarding the degree and willingness of the US to continue to secure vital oil routes. It seems increasingly likely that major energy importers and exporters will have to take on more responsibility in securing their own supplies and markets, respectively.

Fourthly, the added supply of US shale oil will most likely also exert downward pressure on global oil prices. While this may be a welcome development for consumers, it could prove to be very problematic for a number of Middle Eastern producers whose budgets primarily rely on oil revenues. Major producers like Saudi Arabia, Iraq, and Libya, for instance, need an oil price per barrel of at least eighty-five dollars to balance their budgets.[29]

Rising Energy Nationalism and Imperialism

The continued dependence on fossil fuels also bears important geopolitical and security implications. We are currently experiencing a precipitous rise in energy nationalism and imperialism where governments with substantial natural resources are securing greater economic benefits from their exploitation or are utilizing them for political gain. The cases of Argentinian President Cristina Fernández de Kirchner deciding to nationalize the Spanish-owned oil company Yacimientos Petrolíferos Fiscales or Bolivian President Evo Morales seizing control of the Spanish electric company Red Eléctrica de España underscores this trend. But this phenomenon is by no means confined to South America. Today, nationally owned oil companies control over 80 percent of the globe's total oil reserves. To compare, the largest of the private supermajor oil companies—ExxonMobil—only ranks fourteenth in terms of reserve holdings! This is hardly different in the case of natural gas. Some of the largest conventional natural gas reserves in the world are located in countries with nationally owned energy companies, such as the Russian Federation, Qatar, and Iran, just to name a few. This implies that the risk of energy being used as a political and foreign policy tool by resource-rich states could increase due to the diverging objectives of nationally owned energy companies from purely commercial ones. Here, regional markets dependent on a few external energy suppliers and with low grades of diversification are particularly vulnerable.

What is more, energy-hungry states like China are active on all fronts when it comes to securing the natural resources needed for their rapidly growing economy. Since 2007, China's imports of crude oil have increased by some 65 percent.[30] Consumption of other commodities has also dramatically risen over the past two decades. Between 1990 and 2010, China's shares of global steel consumption rose from 8 to 45 percent, copper from 6 to 29 percent, and aluminum from 5 to 40 percent.[31] A gas pipeline that is currently being constructed from Turkmenistan to China not only has an economic purpose, it is also concurrently a projection of political power. The same certainly goes for the Russian South Stream pipeline project.

Geopolitics always plays a role. It does so when Russia plants its national flag on the seabed at the North Pole during a submarine expedition, Canada reacts with a military maneuver in the Arctic, or the United States drills for oil in West Africa in order to secure their influence in the region with a greater military presence. It is quite likely that the intensified quest to secure the finite natural resources of this world will eventually lead to serious interstate disputes, imperialism, and even outright war.

The Hope—Technological Innovation and a Well-Functioning Market Economy

Diminished importance of global climate change, increasing energy demand, the persistent dominance of fossil fuels, and energy imperialism— is there any positive news? Are there no options available to cope with these daunting developments?

The hope lies in the strength of technological innovation and a well-functioning market economy. More energy efficiency, the economic and controlled use of carbon capture and storage (CCS), new storage technologies, dramatic efficiency gains in conventional and unconventional energy use, substitution of oil with natural gas or hydrogen in the transport sector, and smart grids coupled with the ability to market these technologies—these could be the solutions, not wishful thinking or the ability of nations to compromise. Perhaps the only chance that the planet has is the hope of a more efficient and economic utilization of energy in the future.

Friedbert Pflüger is professor and director of the European Centre for Energy and Resource Security (EUCERS) at King's College London and non-resident senior fellow of the Atlantic Council of the United States. He served as a German member of parliament from 1990 to 2006 and was deputy minister of defense in the first Merkel government.

Notes

1 United Nations Environment Programme, UNEP News Center, "IPCC Starts Meeting to Finalize Working Group," September 24, 2013, unep.org/newscentre/default.aspx?DocumentID=2726&ArticleID=9629#sthash.MqKl6T5s.dpuf, accessed October 2, 2013.

2 CBS News, "Controversy Over U.N. Report on Climate Change as Warming Appears to Slow," September 19, 2013, www.cbsnews.com/8301-205_162-57603772/controversy-over-u.n-report-on-climate-change-as-warming-appears-to-slow/, accessed October 2, 2013.

3 Globescan, "Environmental Concerns 'At Record Lows': Global Poll," February 25, 2013, www.globescan.com/news-and-analysis/press-releases/press-releases-2013/261-environmental-concerns-at-record-lows-global-poll.html, accessed October 2, 2013.

4 Tom Arup, "Abbott Shuts Down Climate Commission," The Sydney Morning Herald, September 19, 2013, www.smh.com.au/federal-politics/political-news/abbott-shuts-down-climate-commission-20130919-2u185.html#ixzz2g6LLuWen, accessed October 2, 2013.

5 International Energy Agency, World Energy Outlook 2012, November 12, 2012, www.worldenergyoutlook.org/media/weowebsite/2012/factsheets.pdf, accessed October 2, 2013.

6 Ibid.

7 United Nations, Department of Economic and Social Affairs, Population Division, Population Estimates and Projections Section, "World Population Prospects: The 2012 Revision," medium variant, June 13, 2013.

8 People fifteen to sixty-four years old.

9 Organisation for Economic Co-operation and Development, "Looking to 2060: Long-term Growth Prospects for the World," November 9, 2012, www.oecd.org/eco/outlook/lookingto2060.htm, accessed October 2, 2013.

10 Based on purchasing power parity. See The World Bank, "GNI Per Capita, PPP (Current International $)," data.worldbank.org/indicator/NY.GNP.PCAP.PP.CD?page=4, accessed October 2, 013.

11 Deutsche Bank Research, "Globalisation 2011: Investing in the Global Megatrends," June 21, 2011, 4.

12 United Nations, Department of Economic and Social Affairs 2013, op. cit.

13 Ren21, "Renewables 2013 Global Status Report"; Ren21, "Renewables 2005 Global Status Report." Increased from 160 GW of installed capacity in 2005 to 480 GW today.

14 International Energy Agency, "Renewables to Surpass Gas by 2016 in the Global Power Mix," June 26, 2013. It will reach 8 percent by 2018, up from 4 percent in 2011 and just 2 percent in 2006. www.iea.org/newsroomandevents/pressreleases/2013/june/name,39156,en.html, accessed October 2, 2013.

15 Ren21 2013, Ren21 2005, op cit.

16 Ibid.

17 Ren21, "Renewables 2011 Global Status Report," 7.

18 With fairly even distribution between oil, coal, and natural gas.

19 International Energy Agency, "Reserves to Resources," 2013, www.iea.org/Textbase/npsum/resources2013SUM.pdf, accessed October 2, 2013.

20 International Energy Agency 2012, op. cit.

21 ExxonMobil, The Outlook for Energy: A View to 2040, 17, www.exxonmobil.com/Corporate/files/news_pub_eo.pdf, accessed October 2, 2013.

22 International Energy Agency 2012, op. cit.

23 Ibid.

24 BP Statistical Review of World Energy, June 2013, www.bp.com/content/dam/bp/pdf/statistical-review/statistical_review_of_world_energy_2013.pdf, accessed October 2, 2013.

25 Ibid.
26 International Energy Agency 2013, op. cit. www.iea.org/Textbase/npsum/resources 2013SUM.pdf
27 EIA, 2013. www.eia.gov/naturalgas/crudeoilreserves/
28 BP Statistical Review of World Energy 2013, op. cit.
29 International Monetary Fund, Regional Economic Outlook: Middle East and Central Asia, World Economic and Financial Surveys, November 2012, www.imf.org/external/pubs/ft/reo/2012/mcd/eng/pdf/mreo1112.pdf, accessed October 2, 2013.
30 BP Statistical Review of World Energy 2013, op. cit.
31 Division Resources and Sustainability, Federal Ministry of Education and Research (BMBF), ed., Raw Materials of Strategic Economic Importance for High-Tech Made in Germany (Bonn: BMBF, 2013), www.fona.de/mediathek/pdf/Strategische_Rohstoffe_EN.pdf, accessed October 2, 2013.

Moving the Conversation Forward on Nuclear Disarmament

Jane Harman

One of the hallmarks of the Munich Security Conference is that it is a forum for discussing tough issues like nuclear nonproliferation and arms control. Every year, the event gathers the top leaders and thinkers on issues that matter—like keeping the world safe from nuclear terrorism and thinking about how we must address and prevent the new and emerging threats facing our world.

Learning from the Elders

Last year, I had the honor of paying tribute to one of the forum's elders, former US Senator Sam Nunn. At the forty-ninth conference, we honored Nunn's life-long contributions to security issues—a blueprint for what top-notch work in this field should be.

As coauthor of the highly successful Nunn-Lugar legislation, Nunn had the foresight to envision—and the political savvy to bring to life—a program to make sure the former Soviet Union's most dangerous weapons would be

Jane Harman (center) with Estonian President Toomas Ilves and Dora Bakoyannis at the 2009 MSC safeguarded from accidents or theft, to help find peaceful employment for former Soviet weapons experts, and to begin the complex and difficult process of dismantlement. That program, Cooperative Threat Reduction, has now expanded to two new continents and evolved into a strategic effort to cooperate with foreign governments to prevent weapons-of-mass-destruction (WMD) terrorism—on our soil and theirs.

The numbers speak for themselves: more than 7,500 warheads have been deactivated or destroyed, over 1,000 ballistic missiles and launchers have been eliminated, and sensitive facilities storing nuclear, radiological, chemical, and biological materials have been better secured. The continued success of the Defense Threat Reduction Agency in supporting nonproliferation efforts around the world is the living legacy of that legislation.

Sam Nunn's genius was to realize just how important it is to seize these nonproliferation opportunities as they arise—something that we ought to have in mind as we hear continued reminders that Syria's chemical weapons stockpiles are at risk of getting lost in the chaos of its civil war. Part of the role of forums like the Munich Security Conference is to ensure that we understand proliferation risks as they evolve and that policymakers are ready and willing to act when moments of opportunity emerge. That is a difficult, often thankless job, but the MSC is at the heart of that vital dialogue.

Lasting Memories

It is the knowledge and expertise of great leaders like former Senator Nunn that make the Munich Security Conference so successful and so meaningful. To hear Nunn talk about his first trip to Europe as a young man—to Berlin, during the Cuban missile crisis—is a lesson in how close our world came to nuclear war. Never before had nuclear conflict seemed so plausible, and if the crisis had escalated, Berlin would have been ground zero.

Sam Nunn is not just a friend but also a personal mentor. He took an interest in me during my time in Congress and helped me develop a passion for security issues, which continues to be my focus. As the "Older Guard" moves out of leadership roles and the next generation takes their places, I worry that memories of the Cold War, and its lessons, may be forgotten. The rising generation of policymakers were babies during the Cold War. They do not remember what it was like to live under the shadow of mutually assured destruction. But here is a news flash: as more states seem intent on advancing their destructive capabilities, nuclear weapons and other WMDs still pose a clear and present danger, with the growing possibility that any one of them could provide a terror group with the means to murder on a catastrophic scale. Since the end of the Cold War, North Korea has developed a nuclear program, Iran has amassed a vast stockpile of potentially weaponizable material, and India and Pakistan have crossed the nuclear Rubicon. Yet we are still failing, globally, to secure nuclear, radiological, chemical, and biological materials to the standards we need; we are still struggling to reduce existing stockpiles further; and the threat of WMD terrorism looms.

We face real dangers, but we cannot just play the fear card. Our challenge is to educate, to build a better understanding of the threats and the best ways to manage the risk. That is exactly what the Munich Security Conference— and its participants—aims to do. We are all partners in this effort to achieve the goals of disarmament, and the conference has been an essential place for that project throughout its now fifty-year history.

Moving the Conversation Forward

The Munich Security Conference has also been an invaluable forum for dialogue that moves the policy conversation forward—a space to swap proposals that address tomorrow's problems and get us beyond yesterday's solutions. For example, the global nuclear nonproliferation regime still hinges upon a "basic bargain" enshrined in the 1968 Non-Proliferation Treaty (NPT), a deal that commits the five treaty-acknowledged nuclear weapons states to reducing their arsenals while confirming the universal right to peaceful enrichment, which in the wrong hands may come dangerously close to the threshold of building a bomb. Although the NPT's Additional Protocol provides much-needed supplementary inspection and transparency measures to ensure that nuclear programs remain peaceful, some states of grave concern have not yet signed, and others comply inconsistently or not at all.

Since the end of the Cold War, a new nuclear power has emerged roughly every ten years, not a single one becoming a NPT signatory in good standing. Of nine states with nuclear weapons, four of them—India, Pakistan, North Korea, and Israel—are nonparties to the treaty. And Iran remains in blatant noncompliance with its responsibilities under the NPT and the Additional Protocol. If Iran ultimately develops a nuclear weapon, it will tip the balance among known nuclear powers to five that played by the rules and five that did not—fifty-fifty is not a record to be proud of where Armageddon is concerned. Nor does this record offer much incentive for rising powers to follow the path of NPT compliance and peaceful nuclear development.

I know personally just how tough this work can be. In 2008, I watched with concern as Congress quietly endorsed India's nuclear activities with the US-India Civil Nuclear Cooperation Agreement. I worried that we were sending a dangerously inconsistent message on proliferation. I was hardly reassured when India, with its eyes on China, tested its new long-range Agni 5 missile in 2012. I am equally concerned about US and Russian plans to invest billions of dollars over the coming decades in developing or refining nuclear weapons and delivery systems, despite both sides' stated commitment to eliminating their entire stockpiles. I am also troubled by the reluctance of governments to engage seriously on proposals to create a verifiable and internationally guaranteed nuclear-weapon–free zone in the Middle East. The Munich Security Conference is a place to air these concerns and tackle these difficult questions. And more importantly, it is a place where discussion leads to action, where words can become deeds.

The Conference and the New START

For proof, look to the conference's central role in the story of the New Strategia Arms Reduction Treaty, one of the greater nonproliferation success stories of recent years. Secretary of State Hillary Clinton and Russian Foreign Minister Sergey Lavrov chose the Munich Security Conference as the venue to seal the deal in 2011, exchanging the instruments of ratification with which the treaty entered into force.

I remember my friend Congresswoman Ellen Tauscher's speech to the conference in February of 2009, just a few months before the United States and Russia started work on drafting the treaty. In her role as chairwoman of the Strategic Forces Subcommittee of the House Arms Services Committee, she spoke of the critical importance of ensuring that the expiration of START not be allowed to unravel the verification regime at the heart of cooperative disarmament. I also remember Vice President Joe Biden's declaration of the "reset" of US-Russian relations, which laid the groundwork for the agreement to come, likewise announced at the conference.

To borrow from Congresswoman Tauscher, a strong nonproliferation regime is not a "nice-to-have"; it is a "have-to-have." The conference has been invaluable in communicating that message. When Secretary Clinton said in her 2011 remarks at Munich that the proliferation of ballistic missiles was the most pressing security threat of the day, she also testified to the MSC's remarkable success in advancing the nonproliferation dialogue.

The Future: New Ideas for Old Problems

The Munich Security Conference has always been a space to share ideas that make a difference. It was there that I first heard the suggestion for an international nuclear fuel bank, for example.

As nuclear energy becomes more attractive, we will need to watch carefully for nations making a run for the atomic bomb under the guise of civilian research and design. In a 2006 contribution to the *Wall Street Journal*, I encouraged the development of a nuclear fuel bank by a consortium of private-sector companies providing end-to-end oversight of nuclear material. By operating enrichment facilities and providing fuel according to market demand, an international consortium would reassure nations seeking civilian nuclear energy of a consistent fuel supply. By agreeing not to pursue independent enrichment or reprocessing, participating nations would inspirit the international community that their aims were peaceful.

This is a new twist on an old idea. Back in 1946, Bernard Baruch called on aspiring nuclear nations to turn over civilian activities and resources to the international community. Senators Richard Lugar and Evan Bayh proposed a similar public-sector initiative, the International Nuclear Fuel Authority. What these proposals share is a belief that a better roadmap for nuclear security means reckoning with the reality that more and more states will express civilian nuclear ambitions. We need a system that provides comprehensive regulatory oversight for civilian activities while reducing the incentives for states to go it alone on enrichment and reprocessing. Otherwise, we can look forward to more debacles like Iran, more guessing games, and less nuclear security. We all benefit from dialogue that brings to light ideas like this. Our challenges are substantial, and we must answer them together.

Conclusion

This is the nature and magnitude of the task ahead of us and ahead of the Munich Security Conference: to build on past successes in counter-proliferation, to educate a new wave of policymakers on evolving proliferation risks around the world, and to combat at every turn the temptation to let nuclear security needs be crowded out by other "pressing" concerns.

My generation understands just how important the nonproliferation imperative is. We lived under the shadow of these weapons. We know the incredible risk they pose to international security. There are good ideas out there for managing that risk, but too often they get lost in the political noise.

It is the continued responsibility of institutions like the MSC, former Senator Sam Nunn's Nuclear Threat Initiative, and the Wilson Center to support informed dialogue that informs good policy. Those of us who experienced the fear of the Cold War know that this responsibility is a sacred one, and we need to communicate as much to our leaders and our constituencies.

In case I sounded too grim about our younger generation's engagement with nuclear security, let me inject a note of optimism. The summer of 2012, I had an extraordinary young intern named Harrison Monsky working in my office who cares deeply about these issues. A student at Yale, he decided to bring Global Zero to his campus for a summit bringing together more than three hundred students from around the world, along with activists and experts in the field of nonproliferation. That is a good start, a new start.

Our work must be to nurture a generation of policymakers to tackle the thorny issues of nuclear security and disarmament—and to make certain that the public in Europe, the US, and other relevant countries supports them. The Munich Security Conference will continue to be an invaluable part of this effort. I look forward to playing a small role as the dialogue continues.

Jane Harman is director, president, and CEO of the Woodrow Wilson International Center for Scholars in Washington, DC. She represented California's 36th District in Congress for sixteen years, and served on the Armed Services, the Intelligence, and the Homeland Security Committees.

To Tweet or Not to Tweet?
The Impact of Social Media
on Global Politics

Anne-Marie Slaughter

It started with the "Twitter revolutions," first in Moldova, then in Iran: political opposition movements connected both to each other and to the outside world through lightning-fast short messages that allowed their senders to stay one step ahead of the police at home and one post ahead of the news cycle abroad. Then came the revolutions in Tunisia and Egypt, where Facebook groups of hundreds of thousands of young people had incubated collective determination to transform street demonstrations into regime change.

Then came the counter-narrative. It was insulting to the millions of people who ultimately participated in these movements—people who were willing to face tear gas, beatings, and bullets to stand up for their principles and make change—to suggest that "social media" were the decisive factor in tipping the balance against the government. Calling for demonstrations via Facebook or Twitter messages was no different from using Xeroxed or faxed materials in earlier revolutions, or indeed Tom Payne's pamphlets and Paul Revere's and William Dawes' famous rides in 1775. As technology changes,

▲
Anne-Marie Slaughter at the MSC Core Group Meeting 2013 in Washington

so do forms of communication, but the substance and impact stay the same.

Dissertations and books will be written seeking to mine the truth about the precise role of social media in all these cases; data will be analyzed and regressions run. For now, evidence from activists on the ground supports several key roles for Twitter, Facebook, and similar platforms in the social and political upheaval across the Middle East and North Africa. These include speed, coordination, the creation of global and diverse communities, and collective psychology.

The importance of speed cannot be overestimated. According to Mahmood Salem, an Egyptian activist and blogger who played an important role in the original 2011 revolution, previous efforts to organize the Egyptian opposition in schools, factories, and other worksites had foundered because the amount of time it took to communicate with people in one institution was so long that security forces were inevitably alerted and could shut the process down. With social media the recruitment was fast and simultaneous across multiple institutions at once, giving the activists an advantage.

Once the revolution moved from physical and virtual meetings to street protests, social media enabled mass coordination in ways that appeared anonymous, in the sense that a Facebook page would announce meeting points and times that could be instantly spread through the Facebook and Twitter networks of tens of thousands of people, all of whom could also coordinate their friends and families by word of mouth. Once the demonstrations began, Twitter also proved a valuable way of instantly communicating where security forces were gathering and what was happening at different sites.

Social media also kept the outside world informed. Even though a relatively small percentage of the Egyptian elite actually uses Twitter, those who do are well connected to friends and contacts abroad. The most striking example of the power of social media is the saga of Mona Eltahawy, a well-known Egyptian-American blogger with 60,000 Twitter followers, who went to Cairo to cover and participate in public demonstrations against the military government in November 2011. The night before Thanksgiving in the United States, she was arrested and beaten in the Egyptian Interior Ministry in Cairo. Somehow she managed to tweet five chilling words: "Beaten arrested in interior ministry." She tweeted those words at 8:44 p.m. Egyptian time. At 6:05 p.m. EST, I got a direct message on Twitter from Andy Carvin, National Public Radio strategist and top English-language curator of tweets from Arab protesters on the ground in multiple countries, telling me of Mona's tweet. I responded to him and immediately sent an email to my former colleagues at the State Department. Within another ten minutes I had heard back and was able to send out a general tweet that the US Embassy in Cairo was on top of the case.

New York Times columnist Nick Kristof also used his contacts and sent out a similar message to his over one million followers. By then #FreeMona was trending on Twitter, and a few hours later Mona was free, although with two broken bones and a traumatic story of sexual assault to tell. Maged Butter, an Egyptian blogger who was arrested with Eltahawy, was also released.

Writing about this incident, University of North Carolina sociology professor Zeynep Tufekci observed that social media did not itself "cause" Eltahawy's release. But it certainly played a part, perhaps an indispensable one.[1] In addition to the speed element, it allowed "complex, diverse, ad hoc networks to come together." It took a range of different people, from activists on the ground and journalists to former government officials, to provide the necessary information and mobilize the right contacts to help free Eltahawy. As Tufekci points out, without instant communication across a very wide range of people even the most basic tasks can be difficult to organize, such as "Who will call the embassy? What's her date of birth? Who's arranging the lawyer?"

More broadly, Tufekci credits social media with creating an "increasingly global, networked, public sphere": a mass of diverse people across continents who are watching, listening to, and talking to one another about the same things. It has been possible to build a community of global constituents around specific issues, such as human rights, landmines, or an International Criminal Court, without social media. But today many people are part of that sphere by virtue of whatever issues they happen to be most interested in rather than having to be identified and mobilized by activists. Social media allow them to build their own news networks and communities dedicated to specific issues, and to browse each other's interests the way friends might look across a table or over a shoulder to see what other friends are reading.

A final dimension of the impact of social media on global politics is the enormous power of changing collective psychology. Psychologists have demonstrated that individuals are systematically prone to assume that they are in the minority when in fact they are in the majority. Consider the impact of that assumption. It means that an individual who is opposed to her government would like to demonstrate against it, but assumes that the majority of her fellow citizens support the government. Once she realizes that in fact she is in the majority, she is far more likely to be emboldened enough to take action. The celebrated Facebook page that helped to launch the original

Egyptian revolution in February 2011, "We are all Khaled Said," a thirty-one-year-old Egyptian man who died in custody after being arrested by Egyptian police and savagely beaten, allowed Egyptians who were outraged by his death to see that hundreds of thousands of others shared their views. It also made going out and demonstrating seem more like a social event, such that peer pressure operated in favor of rather than against going out and demonstrating.

Still, revolutions have happened throughout history when the principal mode of rapid communication was a quill and rag paper, or, in the case of the Counter-Reformation, the limited edition printing press. In this context, social media may only play a critical role in contemporary revolutions because oppressive governments have already learned how to manipulate and suppress more traditional forms of communication. Twitter and Facebook and more local forms of social media are thus only the latest technological innovations in the centuries-long cat-and-mouse game between governments and their opponents, in which governments always catch up and learn how to turn the technology in question to their own purposes.

That pattern is already evident with social media and information and communication technologies more generally. The Chinese government advises other countries in censorship and surveillance techniques. These governments are often aided by Western firms. According to Ronan Farrow and Shamila Chaudhary, relying on information provided by the OpenNet Initiative, a company owned by Intel provides filter technology used for censoring purposes to Saudi Arabia, the United Arab Emirates, Bahrain, Oman, and Tunisia, while a Canadian content-filtering company helps Qatar, the United Arab Emirates, Yemen, and Pakistan block websites based on political content.[2]

Moreover, neither social media nor any other form of communication are any match for a government determined to crush the opposition by any means, as Libya, Syria, and indeed Russia demonstrate. Twitter could not have saved Benghazi without NATO intervention. The tens of thousands of videos uploaded to Facebook over the course of the opposition's increasingly desperate struggle against the regime could not stop the reduction of Syrian cities to rubble. And the popularity of Moscow mayoral candidate Alex Navalny's blog could not prevent his arrest and prosecution, even though his followers remain a continuing thorn in the Russian government's side.

The deeper significance of social media is less their use than their existence. They give a literal face to millions of individuals and make visible personal and professional relationships among citizens, groups, and enterprises that together comprise the great abstract mass of "society." We talk of "state-society relations," of global public opinion, of social movements and civil society. But only "states" have international personality: leaders, embassies, flags, armies, and seats in international institutions. "Society" has long remained a vague, inchoate entity. Specific parts of society are represented officially on the international stage: chambers of commerce and councils of executives for business, labor unions, nongovernmental organizations, charities, foundations, and political parties. And as Tom Friedman told us in the late nineties, "super-empowered individuals," from Bill Gates to Osama bin Laden, have certainly been making their presence known.[3] But the mass has been just that: an undifferentiated mass of people, groups, networks, and organizations that could be referred to and engaged only in the aggregate.

No longer. Diplomatic historians and political scientists looking back on the Obama administration will recognize that one of its most important foreign policy legacies was to see "society" as an independent actor on the international stage, one worthy of recognition and protection. In his 2013 address to the UN General Assembly, President Obama signaled a new role for the United Nations, telling the world that "a just and lasting peace," in the Middle East or anywhere else, "cannot be measured only by agreements between nations. It must also be measured by our ability to resolve conflict and promote justice within nations." Resolving conflict and promoting justice within nations means directly engaging both governments and the societies they rule.

Secretary of State Hillary Clinton put this perspective into practice. She created an entire set of ambassadors and special representatives to different segments of national and global society. These included women, youth, business, civil society, entrepreneurs, Muslim communities, and technologists. These offices were small, but the work they did extended far beyond traditional public diplomacy, developing strategies to engage these constituencies, connect them to one another, and help them grow and develop. Social media are a useful tool in these efforts, but it is national and global society that is the real emerging phenomenon.

The Munich Security Conference was founded as a closed-shop meeting of defense officials and a few experts, the ultimate affirmation of Charles Tilly's famous aphorism "the state makes war and war makes the state." Fifty years later, participants at the MSC can live-tweet proceedings to a global audience of scholars, foreign policy experts, nongovernmental organizations, and simply interested individuals. Fifty years from now, some ministers will still be here. But so will be many more representatives of global society. Social media are but the symptom of far larger forces at work.

*Professor **Anne-Marie Slaughter** is the president and CEO of the New America Foundation. From 2009 to 2011 she served as director of policy planning for the United States Department of State. She has over 80,000 followers on Twitter.*

Notes

1 Zeynep Tufekci, "The #freemona Perfect Storm: Dissent and the Networked Public Sphere," *Technosociology,* technosociology.org/?p=566INSERT (accessed October 20, 2013).
2 Ronan Farrow and Shamila N. Chaudhary, "Censuring the Censors," *Foreign Policy* (July 16, 2013), www.foreignpolicy.com/articles/2013/07/16/censuring_the_censors_technology_companies_internet?page=0,0 (accessed October 20, 2013).
3 Thomas Friedman, *The Lexus and the Olive Tree* (New York: Farrar, Straus and Giroux, 1999).

The content of the sign in the image:

Munich Security msc
Conference
Münchner Sicherheitskonferenz

13.00 – 15.00   Lunch Break
                 6th Floor Restaurant, Hotel Bayerischer Hof
COMING UP NEXT
15.00 – 16.30   Breakout Session
                 CYBER SECURITY: CRIME PREVENTION
                 OR WARFARE?
                 Venue: Königssaal
15.00 – 16.30   Breakout Session
                 SECURITY AND STABILITY IN SOUTH-
                 EASTERN EUROPE AND THE CAUCASUS
                 Venue: Kleine Komödie

The New Frontier:
Cyberspace and International Security

Keith B. Alexander

For more than half a century, the Munich Security Conference has provided an independent forum to address international security issues. It has helped leaders debate and analyze major questions and problems confronting them now and in the future. These leaders have included heads of state, ministers, legislators, jurists, commanders, and experts from many fields. Just as important, the conference helps leaders work together, for we are stronger working as a team. This is especially true in cyberspace, a domain unimagined by the conference's founders—but one that urgently needs our attention. The Munich Security Conference will serve its participants and the global community well by discussing issues related to cyberspace, and in particular how to secure the virtual space that we all inhabit together.

How Has International Security Changed since 1963?

The Munich conference convened at the height of the Cold War. International security debates at that time revolved around the bipolar ideological competition between East and West. Savvy leaders knew in 1963 that a host of other issues—such as decolonization, development, and trade—had their own importance and dynamics independent of the superpower competition. But there was no escaping the overwhelming salience of the nuclear stand-off for the first three decades of the conference's discussions. The end of the Cold War allowed, and even forced, new issues to come to the fore, such as the economic, social, demographic, and environmental aspects of international security. Yet since its inception, the conference has had a consistent focus on the quality of governance. Where governance is repressive, unstable, or lacking altogether, sooner or later it becomes a topic for consideration at the Munich Security Conference.

This consistency reaches even to the one security domain that post-dates the creation of the conference half a century ago. I am delighted to see growing attention to the many issues related to cyberspace. Ten years ago, the US Department of Defense called cyberspace a "domain," and for good reason. People the world over use cyberspace for social, economic, and governmental interactions; they create value and store wealth in cyberspace; and they engage in malicious behavior there to gain illicit use of one another's assets and to diminish the freedom of action of targeted people and nations. Cyberspace has become a risky environment where actors exploit gaps in governance, which threatens to jeopardize the free flow of information and ideas so vital to healthy, dynamic, and innovative digitally enabled societies.

We all have much at stake. Technological convergence creates social, economic, and political interdependence, which must be defended against those tempted to wreck it. In the United States, US Cyber Command was created to enhance that defense. Other nations have set up (or are in the process of setting up) their own cyber defense institutions. As in the other domains, the first job of defenders is to prevent aggression in the first place. This means deterring potential adversaries by convincing them they have little to gain—that aggression will be too costly and time-consuming—and that they risk losing far more than they could potentially win. That task is a whole-of-government responsibility and a multinational one as well. Doing it the right way is especially urgent, given the rising tide of threats in cyberspace and the vulnerabilities that accompany our interdependence. Those vulnerabilities have their roots in the global information infrastructure that began to emerge two centuries ago.

The Roots of Interdependence

In 1863 the American West was still sparsely populated with little modern infrastructure, but in historical terms that wilderness vanished almost in an instant. By the time historian Frederick Jackson Turner recognized the passing of the "Frontier" in 1893, the American West was already networked and modernized with railroad lines and telegraph wires. The order and functioning of modern societies, economies, and militaries today has come to depend on social structures that barely existed 150 years ago and which underpin the reliability of timing and flow of logistics and operations. This synchronization rested then and rests now upon an infrastructure that allows communication, transport, finance, commerce, power, and utilities to serve policymakers, managers, commanders, and ordinary citizens in an efficient and reliable manner. Efficiency and dependability make realistic planning and effective operations possible across whole societies. Yet such intricate ties in the mesh of infrastructure systems also represent a significant vulnerability for modern societies. Disrupt the synchronization, and the whole system of systems becomes unreliable—thus diminishing the nation's power and influence, reducing expected and real returns on investments, and eroding the political and social options available to all.

This unprecedented degree of exposure to disruption was first anticipated over a century ago when British cabinet ministers and business leaders contemplated the potential for disruption to their entire economy if French armored cruisers even temporarily interrupted the Empire's overseas trade in the eighteen-nineties. Britain realized it was vulnerable to disruption of its commerce and sabotage of its war-fighting capabilities. At nearly the same time, however, London also contemplated exploiting those same vulnerabilities to cause economic disruption in Germany. The coming of World War I gave the British the opportunity to test these ideas on "live opposition"— but that test proved sobering. British leaders recoiled from such economic warfare measures upon witnessing how a global financial panic on the eve of war in July 1914 was affecting world trade. Citizen and business confidence in economic institutions collapsed, traders withdrew from markets, world trade ebbed, commodity exchanges closed their doors, banks recalled loans, and global liquidity dried up. The scale of disruption in 1914 was greater than that of 1929. In an increasingly globalized and interconnected world, moreover, many of the unintended victims of economic warfare were British.

The century-old dream and nightmare of crippling a modern society by wrecking its infrastructure—or even just by disturbing its synchronization of functions—is now a reality. Cyberspace has become vital for the functioning of modern nations in the digital age. Our national digital infrastructures not only facilitate the movement of commodities and information; they also store our wealth in virtual form. We now use cyberspace to synchronize those critical infrastructure systems that coordinated economies and militaries a century ago. The features that allow all these infrastructure sectors to link together in cyberspace also make them accessible to intruders from almost anywhere at a comparative minimum of cost and risk.

Cyber capabilities are now being "normalized," following a traditional path from commercial innovations to war-fighting forces and systems (much like that of aviation in the last century). Nations have been pondering cyber doctrine for years at senior military schools and think tanks, and the cyber attacks against Georgia in 2008 demonstrated how network warfare could be employed alongside conventional military forces to produce operational effects. Lessons learned from such operations are now being turned into tactics and planning by militaries and nonstate actors. This normalization of cyber effects and their integration with conventional forces will not diminish the power of cyber—on the contrary, it will magnify it.

Cyber conflict occurs on a second level as well. Three times over the previous millennium, military revolutions allowed forces to conquer huge territories and forcibly transfer riches from losers to winners (for example, the Mongol conquests of China, Russia, and Baghdad; the Spanish conquest of the Americas; and the European empires in the nineteenth century). Remote cyber exploitation now facilitates the systematic pillaging of a rival state without military conquest and the ruin of the losing power. Across the international community there has been a staggering number of intrusions into major corporations in the communications, financial, information technology, defense, and natural resource sectors. The intellectual property stolen to date can be counted in the tens to hundreds of thousands of terabytes. We are witnessing another global shift of wealth by means of cyber theft.

What Should Be Done?

Our reliance on cyberspace yields significant social, economic, and strategic benefits but also poses grave risks to our nations and peoples. The very nature of cyberspace is one of convergence—of networks, devices, and people—combining and interacting in new and increasingly complex ways. Communications that moved in separate channels now travel in one, global network—the Internet. Nations and peoples across the globe must be able to operate securely in this convergent space and to protect the social, political, and economic developments that the digital age has brought. The things we value—personal wealth, national economic prosperity, intellectual property, defense secrets, and even our way of life—reside in cyberspace and are targets for malicious actors. The vulnerability of critical infrastructure and the power of cyber weapons is serious cause for concern about the resiliency of modern, networked economies and societies.

We must meet these challenges in common because the most open, connected and prosperous societies are also the most lucrative targets for malicious actors in cyberspace. All leaders should chart the course of their nations based on a sound understanding of the opportunities, threats, and expectations that underpin the choices comprising leadership and governance. But to a large extent, cyberspace does not respect national borders; nearly every significant problem has a cross-border dimension. It is striking how similar the challenges are for our nations attempting to put in place workable systems to protect our networks with their diversity of users, purposes, and requirements.

Some of the practical challenges we face include improving system and network security, especially for critical infrastructure, to protect public safety and preserve the economic and societal benefits that being connected can provide. We at US Cyber Command have five major focus areas that we believe are essential to reduce our vulnerability to malicious actors in cyberspace: a defensible architecture; trained and ready cyber forces; concepts for operations and for command and control; global situational awareness to enable action; and authorities, policies, and rules of engagement to defend the nation in cyberspace.

The first of these is building a defensible architecture. We in the Department of Defense need to collapse our thousands of networked enclaves into a number that is much more manageable to improve our ability to defend them. We need to leverage automation to reduce the manpower currently required to operate networks and perform information assurance functions so that we can vector that manpower into a more active defense role. As events have shown, we need to secure our systems inside and out—we have seen breaches from both sides, and they will only grow worse. We need to think of security at the front end rather than added as an afterthought. We must build it into the hardware and software, and then into training and processes. In contrast to today's legacy architecture, cloud technology offers the opportunity to build a much more defensible network. The cloud enables us to "see" our own networks using automated tools, to exercise centralized configuration control, and to patch our systems in real time.

Another major focus area is trained and ready cyber forces. We are working to establish one common joint training standard for our cyber forces. Our combatant commanders need to know that when they ask for a cyber capability, it does not matter whether the US Army, Navy, Air Force, or Marine Corps responds—they will get the capability that they require. We need cyber forces that are detailed to our combatant commanders focusing on their critical requirements, around the clock. Individual training is necessary but not sufficient to create a trained and ready cyber force. We must also establish training and certification standards for teams that are capable of operating, defending, and, when authorized, conducting full-spectrum cyber operations.

We need to continue to refine our operational concepts and set up clear command and control for cyber operations. Because a cyber exploit or attack often crosses many geographical boundaries or areas of responsibility (AORs), the traditional model of a geographic combatant commander taking responsibility for activities within a particular AOR does not always work. US Cyber Command provides cyber support elements to every combatant command today.

Fourth, we need shared situational awareness that enables operators and decision-makers to understand their environment, recognize early indications of an intrusion, and act on that information. Defenders cannot defend against what they cannot see. We must also raise awareness about the threat and its evolution; that is, how the Internet works, the growth of convergence, and how this makes us all vulnerable.

Last but not least, while authorities exist within the executive branch, we continue to work on how and when to best implement cyber capabilities in defense of the nation. We are working to assist the government in establishing clear roles and responsibilities across departments and agencies to enable timely, coordinated action. Clear rules of engagement must also be established so that operators can act quickly within their authorities to neutralize an adversary intrusion.

We believe addressing these five areas will help the United States govern its portion of the Internet in ways that will leave it open to innovation, interoperable for users the world over, secure enough to earn people's trust, and reliable enough to support their work. It will also make the United States a better international partner. America's security is linked to the security of our allies around the world, in Europe, Asia, Africa, and the Americas—in many respects and particularly in cyber. International cooperation involving the pooling of information, technology, and expertise is critical to the success of each of our nations. We must work together as partners to create incentives for, and build consensus around, an international environment in which all act as responsible stakeholders.

One area of consensus revolves around a shared recognition that governments cannot defend their nations in cyberspace without a partnership with industry. The private sector figures in one of the central challenges to effective cyber security, namely the fact that the baseline of security across US enterprise networks is below the level required to minimize disruptions from international cyber attack. Firms spend enough to ensure their networks securely support business functions but not enough to gird them from catastrophic attack. The simple fact is that there will always be more vulnerabilities than the private sector can address cost effectively. In the United States, much of our critical infrastructure is owned and operated by the private sector, and our government is often unaware of malicious activity targeting it. These blind spots prevent the government from being positioned to help critical infrastructure defend itself or to defend the nation from an attack, if necessary.

Government partnership with the private sector is a critical component of a resilient and flexible national strategy. The information technology sector (for example, telecommunications, security, infrastructure firms), with its visibility of networks across the globe, has the capability to mitigate threats across a swath of those networks quickly. The government, for its part, can improve companies' ability to detect threats by rapidly sharing relevant threat information that has been collected in accordance with foreign intelligence missions, with oversight by Congress, the courts and the administration, and in support of national intelligence priorities. With threat intelligence and early warning information provided by government, private sector entities can analyze and identify malicious traffic at the perimeters, better protect their networks and our critical infrastructure, and guard against intellectual property theft.

The US government and the private sector need to be able to share cyber threat indicators and counter-measures in near real time, and it is essential that such sharing be done with robust safeguards for privacy and civil liberties. From the voluntary approaches we have stood up in some sectors, we have learned that the US government can define precisely which attributes of malware are of national security significance and what information coming back from the private sector can improve our analysis. We are committed to using technologies and policies that protect individual privacy by making it difficult to link reported data to individuals, minimizing the amount of data the government receives, setting and enforcing use and sharing restrictions, and maintaining continuous oversight and compliance auditing. The US government has no need to receive the private communications of our citizenry in order to protect the nation. However, the government can better help industry if apprised of the malware buried in those communications.

Information sharing, by itself, will not address all the vulnerabilities to our nation's critical infrastructure. In the United States, we are partnering with the owners and operators to ensure that infrastructure is sufficiently hardened and resilient. The US government has an obligation to ensure that owners and operators of our core critical infrastructure understand the nature of the threat and the extent of their vulnerability. It is also the policy of the United States to enhance the security and resilience of the nation's critical infrastructure and to maintain a cyber environment that encourages efficiency, innovation, and economic prosperity while promoting safety, security, business confidentiality, privacy, and civil liberties. This needs to be a team effort. Just as we would not expect the private sector to have to defend against certain physical assaults on the nation's critical infrastructure on its own, core critical infrastructure operators and owners should not be expected to unilaterally shoulder all the responsibility and liability for certain cyber threats to their networks. It is important that security standards be collaboratively developed with industry and that there are reasonable, risk mitigation measures. Adoption of security standards should be encouraged through incentives such as appropriate insurance benefits, rate recovery, or liability protection.

We are just beginning to address the roles of government in protecting our nation's cyber security; how government and the private sector get valuable information to those who must protect our critical systems; and how to do it all at cyber speed. No single public or private entity has all the required knowledge, resources, authorities, or capabilities to handle the myriad issues stemming from the growing pervasiveness of this technology in all that we do. We must address these issues as a team, sharing unique insights across governments, research institutions, industry, and civil society. Above all, we must ensure that protecting civil liberties and instituting effective network protections are seen as co-equal priorities for democratic societies.

Conclusion

The Munich Security Conference is correct in viewing problems as both international and in some way related to governance—and insisting that solutions be collective. This is especially so in cyberspace. Cyberspace is a global domain and it is in all nations' best interest to protect it. All governments and organizations should secure and defend their own networks. All governments and organizations should take actions against hackers and cyber criminals within their own borders and jurisdictions. Nations should share information and cooperate to prevent cyber crime and data theft; their security organizations should participate in international and regional forums on the shared use of cyberspace and cyber security. With such steps, and the Munich Security Conference's help, we will make real progress that should be obvious long before the centennial in 2064.

*General **Keith B. Alexander** is commander of US Cyber Command and director of the National Security Agency and the Central Security Service.*

Cyberspace and International Security

Toomas Hendrik Ilves

The 2011 Munich Security Conference included for the first time a special session on cyber security. "This may be the first time," I then predicted, "but it will not be the last." And indeed, today we can see that cyber is actually at the core of discussions on security policy, overtaking terrorism.

If terrorism emerged in the first decade of the twenty-first century as a new threat to Western security, then cyber attacks rose to the fore in the second decade. Neither, of course, was new; major terrorist as well as cyber attacks had taken place earlier (the latter in my country, for example), yet awareness came with the dramatic escalation of the size and impact of the attacks.

I keep no tally of cyber attacks, hacking, and espionage, but from a subjective reading of the temperature in cyber space it is quite clear: the issue has come to concern the highest levels of political leadership in the West to an unprecedented degree. General Keith Alexander, director of the National Security Agency and the United States Cyber Command, stated last July that there had been a seventeen-fold increase in cyber attacks on American infrastructure from 2009 to 2011, initiated by criminal gangs, hackers, and nations. In December 2012, the US Department of Homeland Security revealed

▲
Toomas Hendrik Ilves (left) with Hillary Clinton and Leon Panetta at the 2012 MSC

an "alarming rate" of increase in attacks against power, water, and nuclear systems in the fiscal year 2012. The destruction of files in some twenty thousand Aramco computers, the *Mandiant Annual Threat Report on Advanced Targeted Attacks*, the "distributed denial of service" attacks on the New York Stock Exchange last year, hacking during the missile attacks against Israel, as well as countless other episodes—all indicate a rise in frustration and tensions that we have not seen before.

A country like Estonia, which is small and on many scales different from the United States, has been facing these problems for a long time. Praised by the United Nations e-Annual Report system as the "best of the best" e-government application of the past decade, ranked by Freedom House as first in Internet freedom for the third year in a row, Estonia is primarily remembered in the cyber literature as the first publicly known target of politically motivated cyber attacks in April 2007. These disruptive attacks inundated the websites of the government, parliament, banks, ministries, newspapers, television stations, and other organizations. However, by today's standards they were primitive, essentially overloading servers with signals from hijacked, hacker-controlled personal computers. Six years later, as computing power and informational technology dependency have increased enormously, cyber attacks are far more sophisticated, and our vulnerabilities are far greater.

At the same time, the visibility that resulted from the 2007 cyber attack in Estonia was also a blessing—as a result, we took cyber security seriously earlier than many others, and our allies took notice. In 2008, NATO opened its Cooperative Cyber Defence Centre of Excellence in Tallinn to enhance the Alliance's cyber defense capability. It serves as a valuable source of expertise for both its sponsoring nations and NATO. The center's interdisciplinary approach to cyber defense is unique: experts from different fields work together and share their knowledge, giving the center and its work a broader perspective. It published the so-called *Tallinn Manual*, groundbreaking research into the murky world of the applicability of international law *vis-à-vis* cyber warfare.

Estonia is extensively computerized in the fundamental operations of society and as well as our citizens' day-to-day lives. We have continued to push the envelope in developing e-governance to levels that few countries have been willing to follow up to now. 25 percent of the Estonian electorate votes online, over 95 percent of prescriptions are filled online. A recent report by the European Commission and the Organisation for Economic Co-operation and Development rated Estonia as the most advanced European country in offering e-health services. Up to 98 percent of tax returns are filed online and have been since the beginning of the millennium, and almost all banking is done online. In December 2012, Estonia passed the one hundred million mark for digital signatures. Adding to this near 100 percent broadband coverage and countrywide Wi-Fi, Estonia is one of the most wired countries in overall terms, both with respect to services as well as to physical infrastructure.

Also, as a country so dependent on the digital world, we cannot help being a proverbial canary in the coalmine. Today, almost everything we do depends on a digitized system of one kind or another. Our critical infrastructure—our electricity, water, or energy production systems and traffic management—essentially interacts with, and cannot be separated from, our critical information infrastructure—private Internet providers, lines of telecommunications, and the supervisory control and data acquisition (SCADA) systems that run everything from nuclear power plants to traffic lights and the delivery of milk to our supermarkets. As systems become more complex, threats become more sophisticated. Yet, as people's and society's technological dependence and the automatization of processes *increases,* our security consciousness *decreases.*

However, in reality, in a modern digitalized world it is possible to paralyze a country without attacking its defense forces: the country can be ruined by simply bringing its SCADA systems to a halt. To impoverish a country one can erase its banking records. Even the most sophisticated military technology can be rendered irrelevant. In cyberspace, no country is an island.

Cyber security therefore means defending our societies as a whole. The entire information and communication technologies (ICT) infrastructure must be regarded as an "ecosystem" in which everything is interconnected and functions in toto. We believe that today, both the input (that is, the data) as well as the process must be authenticated. In cyber defense, we no longer need to defend merely stored data but the integrity of the digitized process.

The more we automatize processes, the more we allow machines to make decisions, the more we need to ensure that automatized processes operate on trustworthy data. If our power generation is run automatically on SCADA systems, we had better insure that those automatized decisions are made based on true, uncorrupted data. Feeding an automatic process bad or corrupted data is one sure way to create a disaster, since, after all, an automatic decision is based *only* on the information it receives. This is precisely the underlying idea behind the Stuxnet virus that made Iranian uranium enrichment centrifuges run out of control.

The rapid change of digitized society, and the security challenges that follow, compel us to rethink some of our core philosophical notions of modern society, such as privacy and identity as well as the relations between the public and private spheres. We in liberal democracies insist on two fundamental values that often come into conflict, and will increasingly do so the more we live in a digitized world. These two core values are privacy and transparency.

Unfortunately, despite the digital revolution of the last decade, the standard view of privacy and ethics in a majority of countries has not changed. It is the "Big Brother is watching" paradigm that rules the thinking, and it goes back to the age of totalitarianism when the idea of an all-powerful state following your every move became a standard metaphor. It is also known as the Orwellian nightmare, *them,* generally the vaguely governmental or a conspiracy that followed your every more.

However, it is dangerous to remain fixed on the idea of Big Brother at a time when the greatest threats to our privacy and the security of our data come from criminal hackers and foreign countries (often working together). In an age of digital technology, it is not necessarily the government we should fear most, at least in the democratic parts of the world. This fear may have been more justified in the past, when only national governments had the ability to monitor citizens. Today, as we know, a single hacker can access the most intimate details of your digital and nondigital life, your finances, and your correspondence. Therefore, the question is "follow the money." Big Data has replaced Big Brother Government as the one who knows most about you—perhaps we should talk about the "Little Sister" who knows all your secrets and tells everyone who knows how to ask. So even in the light of ongoing heated debates on online privacy, it is first of all the Big Data we should be worried about.

Intelligence agencies collect information on various people at home and abroad—that is what they have to do. As long as this takes place legally and morally, ensuring oversight and transparency, it is a necessary activity to prevent crime and terrorism. The problem today appears to be that intelligence agencies act like a child in a candy store, because most individuals' cyber behavior is so naïve.

So the real issue with Big Brother is not so much the state collecting our data as our own behavior: we all have all kinds of applications on our iPads and smartphones. If we think all those free apps we download and the personal data we upload are really free, then we are very misguided indeed. These data are monetized. Our personal information and preferences in social media are monetized. There is no such thing as a free app. Still, we make our personal data available voluntarily—and then wonder when it is being used in ways that we failed to foresee.

Here again we touch upon automatized processes, because those data collected on us by browsers, cookies, search engines, or heart-rate and exercise apps are collected automatically, without our knowing how they are used, by companies just making money or by cyber criminals. Virtually all breaches of computer security involve a fake identity, be it stealing a credit card number or accessing internal documents. Therefore, secure identity lies at the core of security online. A three-digit security code on the back of a credit card does not provide you with a secure identity, nor does an ordinary computer password. The fundamental question is whether you can be sure the person you interact with online is who he or she claims to be.

The key to all online security is a secure online identification system, but the nebulous fear of an imagined Big Brother prevents citizens in many places from adopting a smart-chip-based access key that would afford them secure online transactions. Yet as we have seen, the real question is not whether our data is secure when we have government e-services, but rather what is being done with our data, period, in any format.

In Estonia, all citizens are issued a highly encrypted, chipped identification card that allows users to cryptographically sign digital documents and access hundreds of public and private e-services. At the same time, citizens are the legal owners of their own data. People can see what their data are being used for and by whom. This is where transparency meets privacy: we all have the right to see what data the state possesses on us and, far more importantly, how these data are used and by whom, and when they are accessed.

Eventually, countries will adopt a two-factor authentication system in one form or another, because it is the only thing that is currently secure. It will have to use a binary key code system, because that is the only one that has been proven to work this far. Many countries in Europe have adopted similar systems; however, they do not have the range of services behind them that we already have in Estonia. We just try to put as much online as possible.

In the future, Estonia hopes to connect its digital services and make them interoperable with its neighbors in northern Europe. In the longer run, we are looking toward uniting systems in all of Europe. Ultimately, government data will move across borders as freely as email and Facebook and follow the international flows of commerce and trade.

This all has an effect on our economy, both in Europe and beyond. The job of cyber security is to enable a globalized economy based on the free movement of people, goods, services, capital, and ideas. This can only be accomplished if online identities are secure.

Undoubtedly, the most effective means by which our societies could be safeguarded from cyber attacks would be to roll back the clock—to go back to the pen, typewriter, paper, and mechanical switch. We should give up on mobile phones, iPads, online banking, social media, Google searches— everything we have become accustomed to in the modern world. Yet that is not likely to happen, nor is it what we want. It is therefore crucial to understand that cyber security is not just a matter of blocking the bad things a cyber attack can do; it is one of protecting all the good things that *cyber insecurity* can prevent us from doing. Genuine cyber security should not be seen as an additional cost but as an enabler, guarding our entire digital way of life.

Toomas Hendrik Ilves is president of the Republic of Estonia. His previous positions have included serving as Estonia's ambassador to the United States, foreign minister, and member of the European Parliament.

Spotlights on the Conference

A Constant Reminder of the Transatlantic Alliance's Strategic and Moral Imperative

Joseph I. Lieberman

The world has undergone sweeping and unimaginable changes—geopolitical, technological, and social—in the fifty years since the Munich Security Conference was established. From the collapse of the Soviet Union to the explosive growth of China, and from the rise of the Internet to the Arab Spring, tectonic transformations have taken place in virtually every corner of our planet and across most aspects of our lives. Yet through it all, the annual meetings in Munich have provided an indispensable forum for decision-makers to discuss and debate the issues of the day—a living history that I have been grateful for the opportunity to be a part of. Even more profoundly, the conference is a constant reminder of the continued strategic and moral imperative of the transatlantic alliance, and the values for which we stand.

I first learned of the Munich Security Conference—or *Wehrkunde*, as it was known back in those days—as a first-term senator in the early nineties, when Senator John Glenn (D-OH) graciously invited me join the US

▲
Joseph Lieberman (center), receiving the MSC's
Ewald von Kleist Award 2012 from Ewald von Kleist (right)

congressional delegation that he led every year. When Republicans took over the Senate after the 1994 midterm elections, responsibility for that delegation shifted to Senator Bill Cohen (R-ME), who continued to invite me on the trip. When Cohen was nominated by President Clinton to be his secretary of defense in 1997, leadership of the US congressional delegation next fell to my dear friend Senator John McCain (R-AZ). McCain surprised me by proposing that we lead the trip together—he as the Republican co-chair, me as the Democrat. He felt that—whatever the disagreements and divisions that separated our two parties in Congress—it was important for us to make clear that we stood united in our commitment to the transatlantic alliance. For the remainder of my time in the Senate, I am proud to say that John and I maintained that tradition.

Although the Munich Security Conference has developed over the past twenty years into a truly global forum, its roots remain in the Euro-Atlantic community of democratic nations and the strategic questions it confronts, including the expansion of NATO, the stabilization and recovery of the Balkans, and our relationship with Russia. Particularly in the years after 2001, when the focus of US foreign policy shifted toward the Middle East and then to Asia, the conference has provided an invaluable mechanism for focusing American minds and attention on the continuing centrality and indispensability of Europe.

For me, Munich is synonymous with many unforgettable moments—from the tense exchanges on the eve of the Iraq War in 2003 to President Vladimir Putin's memorable and objectionable speech in 2007, for which Senator McCain and I had front-row seats. But in my experience, some of the most important discussions at Munich have unfolded off-stage, in the bilateral meeting rooms above the conference hall or in the quiet corners of Hotel Bayerischer Hof after hours.

These conversations always reinforce another lesson for me: that, regardless of the particular challenges confronting us in the world, it is critical for the United States to develop a common approach in partnership with our European allies, with whom we share an unparalleled alignment of both interests and values. And as daunting as the domestic and foreign challenges we face are, the conference also reminds us to draw confidence from the remarkable successes we have accomplished as allies, not only in protecting our own freedom, prosperity, and security against enormous dangers but in expanding its frontiers to include millions of people previously trapped in tyranny and terror.

From the war in Bosnia in the mid-nineties to the worsening crisis in Syria now, I have repeatedly returned from Munich with new ideas and a more developed understanding about how the US and Europe could work together to tackle the problems of the day. In other instances, through dynamic debate, the conference helped shine a light on problems and tensions in the Alliance that were not receiving sufficient attention back in the United States.

In addition to helping to forge common ground in the transatlantic context, the Munich conference has become an important venue for strengthening US bipartisanship too. In fact, there are far too few opportunities for members of Congress to spend time together and genuinely get to know each other as individuals. Traveling to Munich thus provides one of the best opportunities for Democrats and Republicans to step back from the political trenches on Capitol Hill. Even setting aside international considerations, the conference would be worthwhile simply for the cooperation it fosters on the American side. Indeed, my own close friendship with my Senate "amigos" John McCain and Lindsey Graham—which defined so much of the legislative and foreign policy work we did together—was deepened with every visit we took together to Munich.

Participating in the Munich Security Conference also carried a deeper, personal significance for me. The truth is that my first visit to the conference was also my first-ever visit to Germany—a prospect that, as a Jewish American born in the early forties and as the husband of a woman whose parents survived the Holocaust, provoked a set of mixed emotions. The experience of attending the Munich Security Conference—and through it, developing close friendships with countless German officials, legislators, foreign policy thinkers, business executives, and citizens—has proven deeply meaningful and personally transformational for me.

As it happens, the conference falls over the Jewish Sabbath, which begins at sundown on Friday and lasts until sundown on Saturday. As a result, part of my Munich ritual has been to celebrate Shabbat there. No matter how many times I have done this, I am always deeply moved by the extraordinary hospitality extended to accommodate the observance of my faith by the conference organizers, the US Consulate, and the Munich Jewish community.

A final association for me with the Munich meeting is its founder, Ewald-Heinrich von Kleist, who was still presiding over the conference when I first began attending it. During my last visit to Munich as a sitting senator, in February 2012, I was given an award from the conference in his name, and he spoke movingly at the ceremony. This was the last time I saw him before he passed away in early 2013. Receiving this award from the Munich Security Conference in Ewald von Kleist's name is one of the greatest honors of my life.

Kleist was and remains among the most inspiring men I have ever been privileged to meet. His life story is a testament to the human capacity for heroism in the face of overwhelming odds and against unspeakable horror. It is also a reminder that the moral trajectory of our universe is not preordained. Rather, it is made, for better or for worse, by the choices of individuals.

It is deeply fitting that Ewald von Kleist—having risked his life to bring an end to one of the most monstrous evils in the history of the world—went on to devote his life to the creation and survival of something so profoundly decent and honorable: a postwar alliance founded on freedom, human rights, and rule of law. That is the mission and mandate that was at the heart of *Wehrkunde* when it was established fifty years ago—and it is one for which the Munich Security Conference continues to serve as an essential bulwark today.

Joseph I. Lieberman represented Connecticut in the US Senate from 1989 to 2013. He was chairman of the Homeland Security and Governmental Affairs Committee. For many years he led, together with Senator John McCain, the congressional delegation to the Munich Security Conference. In 2012, he received the conference's Ewald von Kleist Award.

Good Arguments Are What Matters

Hans-Ulrich Klose

I took part in the Munich Security Conference for the first time in February 1993, its thirtieth edition. As chairman of the Social Democratic Party of Germany's parliamentary group at the Bundestag, I was one of the German speakers. The brief was clear, however: I was to speak about the foreign and security policy positions of the Social Democratic opposition in the German Bundestag, but no longer than fifteen minutes. I kept to this brief by writing a longer speech and having it translated into English, which I subsequently distributed to the participants. I then used the fifteen minutes to deliver an unscripted talk on what I would have addressed had I been allowed to talk for longer, and it was received and discussed positively. The discussion centered mainly on the military role of a reunited Germany. All of the participants in the discussion, except one, were Germans. The exception was Senator William Cohen, a Republican from Maine. I met him again later, when he was secretary of defense under the Democratic president Bill Clinton.

Cohen was not the only United States senator to travel to Munich. Over the years, numerous senators came—surprisingly, more senators than members of the House of Representatives. Senators Joe Lieberman and John

▲

The conference hall during Vice President Biden's speech at the 2013 MSC

McCain—the latter is still a member of the Senate today—were regularly involved as guests to and organizers of the conference, which I have continued to attend since 1993. However, personal contacts beyond a "How are you?" and "Good to see you" did not develop with these two regular guests, which was rarely the case with other US colleagues who were there on occasion: Evan Bayh, Bob Corker, John Kerry, Jon L. Kyl, or House members Jeffrey Flake and Loretta Sanchez. One time, if I remember correctly, Senator Hillary Clinton came to Munich. At any rate, it was the Americans, particularly the regular participants Lieberman and McCain, who were the stars of the conference; they sat on stage as panel members and were the most sought-after interlocutors, especially among Eastern Europeans, who were seeking to develop a close relationship with America or—as was sometimes the case with the Russians—wanted to boost their prestige through opposition to America. We, as German members of parliament, played a rather modest role as co-organizers; we took part in the smaller formats, and we observed and participated in small talk in the lobby, at breakfast, or at lunch. As the years went by, however, this changed: our role actually became clearer the more the security conference developed into an event and major "happening" for governments and heads of government.

Major events of this type are necessary; they are useful, because they provide an opportunity to meet politicians from very diverse countries and with very diverse policies, to study the way they present themselves and their argumentation, and to draw conclusions: about Donald Rumsfeld in his famous skirmish with Joschka Fischer ("Sorry, I am not convinced"); about French President Sarkozy, Russian President Putin and his foreign minister, Igor Ivanov, and later Sergey Lavrov; about successful appearances by Chinese Foreign Minister Yang Jiechi, for example, or unsuccessful ones like that of Iranian Foreign Minister Mottakki. I was able to learn a great deal by observing and listening.

Yet, at every conference, it was equally important for me to have meetings with people like Dr. Jack Janes, president of the American Institute for Contemporary German Studies (AICGS); Fiona Hill, who has worked at the Brookings Institution for many years; or Julie Smith, who went on to become deputy security adviser to Vice President Joe Biden. I also look back with pleasure at discussions with top American diplomat Dan Fried, who decisively influenced US policy toward Russia after the end of the East-West bloc confrontation before endeavoring—unsuccessfully—to (dis)solve the Guantanamo problem, for which he sought German support. Meetings of this kind, with people from various countries whom one met first in Munich and then on various occasions later, whom one still encounters today or can contact by phone, are the most useful to a German foreign policymaker and have greatly enriched my understanding of this work.

Highlights? Yes. There were and still are highlights: meetings with the great Henry Kissinger, whom I met at a preparatory conference in Washington, DC, where there were discussions on security in times of budget constraints and on demographic problems in Russia. Or Zbigniew Brzezinski, who participated in a discussion at a MSC Core Group Meeting in Moscow on the future of nuclear energy, a subject which I have been interested in since my time as mayor of Hamburg. I mention these preparatory conferences (unfortunately, for personal reasons I was unable to attend the one that took place in China), because I view this format, with around fifty participants, as particularly suitable for hearing arguments, exchanging opinions, and engaging in mutual analysis—after all, that is what it is really all about. Decisions guaranteed to turn out right do not exist in foreign and security policy. There are only decisions underpinned by good, or fairly good, arguments. And that is what matters: good arguments—at the fiftieth Munich Security Conference as elsewhere.

Hans-Ulrich Klose (Social Democratic Party) was a member of the German Bundestag from 1983 to 2013. From 1998 to 2002, he was chairman of the Committee on Foreign Affairs.

Little Patience for Frivolous Speeches— A Personal Remembrance of *Wehrkunde* and Ewald-Heinrich von Kleist

William S. Cohen

After President Harry Truman led America through the end of World War II, he tried to settle an age-old debate. While some had declared that humans are but flotsam on the uncontrollable currents of history, Truman said no, "Individuals make history, and not the other way around. Progress occurs when courageous, skillful leaders seize the opportunity to change things for the better."

It was his belief in this principle that led Ewald-Heinrich von Kleist, as a twenty-two-year-old lieutenant in the German army, to risk his life in attempts to assassinate Adolf Hitler—acts that were rewarded with arrest and detention in a concentration camp. And it was his belief in this principle that led him to found the Munich Security Conference in 1963.

At *Wehrkunde,* as it was then known, Kleist brought together courageous, skillful leaders from across the North Atlantic alliance, individuals ready to seize opportunities to make history. And make history they did—from the dawn of the Cold War to its peaceful conclusion; from the reunification of

William Cohen (left) with German Chancellor Helmut Kohl at the 1998 conference

Germany to the enlargement of the Alliance; from NATO's historic deployments in the Balkans to the first invocation of Article V and the Alliance's first mission outside of Europe following the attacks of September 11, 2001.

These events might have seemed unimaginable to Ewald von Kleist when he sat shivering in the concentration camp barracks. But even as a prisoner of the Nazi regime, he never lost his faith in the power of individuals to shape history. And today, *Wehrkunde* stands as an enduring testament to this faith.

I first attended the conference in 1979 under the leadership and tutelage of United States Senator John Tower of Texas. I was a newly minted member of the Senate Armed Services Committee, and Tower said that if I was serious about wanting to understand the security issues confronting the United States and our European allies, then my attendance at the conference was mandatory. (The compelling nature of the conference was reinforced by John McCain, who was serving as the US Navy's Senate liaison officer.)

First impressions are usually lasting, and on occasion quite wrong. When I walked into the exquisite Hotel Bayerischer Hof in Munich, the first thought I had was that I had simply entered an exclusive club that catered to political and military elites who were out to share a weekend of bonhomie and back-slapping camaraderie with like-minded friends.

Kleist shattered that false impression quickly when he insisted that the frenetic buzz that accompanies the renewal of friendships come to order. It became quickly clear that this conference was no social club (although the early years tended to coincide with *Fasching*, a wondrous Mardi-Gras sort of celebration that inflicted a temporary attention deficit disorder on some American delegates).

Although conference chairman Kleist said little, his impassive face and silence spoke volumes about his determination to preserve the freedom of the German people and to strengthen the transatlantic link between the United States and Western European democracies. He made it clear that he had little patience for frivolous speeches or political posturing during the conference.

The serious and somber tone was reinforced by Manfred Wörner, Germany's defense minister, who would later become the secretary general of NATO. I found Wörner to be a gifted and inspirational speaker who displayed the confidence and swagger of a combat pilot. He offered passionate arguments on the need to build and sustain a strong, unified defense capability and to resist the Soviet Union's psychologically manipulative and intimidating tactics to drive a wedge between America and its European allies.

While most shared Kleist and Wörner's stated goals, there were those who disagreed with both the strategy and tactics to be employed. Egon Bahr, a pipe-smoking member of the SPD, the Social Democratic Party of Germany, was a regular at the conference who often crossed verbal swords with his German colleagues and members of the US delegation. Bahr's comments would in turn provoke a vigorous response from former Under Secretary of Defense for Policy Robert Komer, who was known (not always affectionately) as "Blowtorch Bob." Henry Cabot Lodge, America's ambassador to Vietnam during the height of that war, said that arguing with Komer was the equivalent of having a flamethrower aimed at one's posterior. I was singed on a few occasions in my psyche and physique for challenging Komer's convictions on a given issue.

But that was precisely the point of the conference itself: to engage in open and vigorous debate, to challenge comfortable assumptions or misguided policies, and to help shape public opinion about security threats and requirements.

I was proud to serve as the head of the American delegation from 1985 to 1996. There were no shortage of issues to debate: the collapse of the Soviet Union, the reunification of Germany, the deployment of Pershing II missiles and ground-launched cruise missiles on German soil, the Intermediate-Range Nuclear Forces Treaty, the implementation of a European Self Defense Initiative, greater burden sharing among the NATO members, the enlargement of NATO, and NATO's role in Bosnia and Kosovo.

Over the years, it was common to question whether NATO would collapse or simply wither away. But it has held firm throughout, prompting changes in Germany's traditional interpretation of what role it could play outside of its geographical boundaries, and recalibrating in the mission of NATO itself in order to meet new security challenges.

As the threat once posed by the Soviet Union began to ease, the Munich Security Conference itself adapted to focus on the changing nature and complexity of the new threats. Under the leadership of Horst Teltschik, the conference also began to focus on economic issues. Those invited to attend represented nations from all over the world and not just Western Europe and North America. And when Ambassador Wolfgang Ischinger took over as chairman of the Munich Security Conference, diplomats joined businessmen and -women along with traditional military experts.

What Ewald von Kleist began so many years ago remains the premier gathering forum to discuss how free people can work to secure peace and prosperity in a world that has become increasingly integrated and interdependent. The challenges we face today are far different from those we faced five decades ago. In the twenty-first century, the world is vulnerable not to Soviet domination but to economic imbalances, energy shortages, food and water insecurity, nuclear proliferation, climate change, cyber threats, terrorism, and new technologies in the hands of the radical and discontented elements of our respective countries. In the information age, these threats are changing and evolving at unprecedented speeds.

The poet W. H. Auden reminded us that we "all sway forward on the dangerous flood of history, which never sleeps or dies and, held one moment, burns the hand." Despite the dangerous challenges we face, our hands need not be burned again—because thanks to Ewald von Kleist's vision we have a place where skillful leaders can gather to shape history's course: *Wehrkunde*.

William S. Cohen served as US secretary of defense from 1997 to 2001. Before that, he was a US senator from 1979 to 1997 and a member of Congress from 1973 to 1979. Currently, he is chairman of The Cohen Group, an international business consulting firm based in Washington, DC, that provides global business consulting services and advice on tactical and strategic opportunities in virtually every market around the world.

The Munich Security Conference: A British Perspective

Charles Powell

The Munich Security Conference and I grew up together, so to speak. The first *Wehrkunde-Begegnung,* as it was originally billed, was held in 1963, the year I joined the British Foreign Office. We still meet each other once a year.

I did not attend the early meetings. I was not nearly senior or important enough for that. But I quite often heard it discussed by my elders and betters with a mixture of admiration and, it has to be said, exasperation. The latter stemmed from a sense that the Germans had rather impertinently intruded on a hitherto British-administered zone in Europe, namely defense and security policy.

This rather grudging attitude was no obstacle to *Wehrkunde's* success. Over the ensuing half-century it captured the brand and the agenda for collective discussion of European defense and security issues. In Britain, we still have a respectable claim to intellectual ownership of these issues through the International Institute for Strategic Studies founded by Alastair Buchan and the Royal United Services Institute, though swamped over time in quantitative terms, at least by the myriad American think tanks. But as an

▲
British Prime Minister David Cameron speaking at the 2011 MSC

event bringing together policymakers, practitioners, and parliamentarians there was, and still is, nothing to equal Munich.

The Munich conference used to be credited by the more extreme left as a mini-Evil Empire in its own right, a hotbed of militarism, aggression, and nuclear strategy. That much was apparent from the noisy and sometimes violent demonstrations that were for many years the regular backdrop to its meetings. Their having subsided in more recent times makes one wonder whether the conference's failure any longer to provoke means it has lost relevance!

The reality is both more mundane and much more constructive. Munich is a first-class forum for hearing views, developing contacts, expanding horizons. Over the years, it has produced some outstanding political theater. One thinks of the visceral verbal battle between Donald Rumsfeld and Joschka Fischer on Iraq at the thirty-ninth conference in 2003, where Fischer responded to the priorities presented by Rumsfeld by saying: "Sorry, I am not convinced." Or President Putin dripping scorn for NATO and Europe, and being ironically thanked by an East European minister for reminding everyone how Soviet policies still survived. Or the transparent deceits of Iranian spokesmen about their country's nuclear intentions, robustly challenged from the floor. One of the MSC's greatest strengths is to be able to absorb heated exchanges without lasting harm to relationships, to the forum itself, or its standing.

It is also the tribal gathering of the transatlantic defense community where contacts are made and maintained, an unmissable date in the appointment calendars of important political and military figures in NATO, and increasingly beyond. More than anything else, it is the key event that brings the United States defense community—senators, cabinet secretaries, congressmen and -women, generals, and academics—to Europe at least once a year.

Indeed, it is the regular presence of senior representatives of the US Congress that makes Munich unique. There are plenty of international conferences where journalists and academics talk to each other, and plenty of international gatherings where ministers meet other ministers. But no other event in the world—not the UN, not Davos—has attracted senators and members of Congress in the way that Munich over the years has. They have never been shy in warning their European allies about pulling their weight or facing up to tough choices. And rightly so. But they have listened as well. And they have shown by their consistency in attending that they attach importance to what Munich symbolizes—an Alliance that is more than just a treaty of self-interest between governments but a genuine community of democratic values.

One result is the creation of a remarkable *esprit de corps* among the conference's regular participants, in no way undermined by leavening the mix with new invitees. That has saved the MSC from the rigor mortis that often afflicts similar organizations after early success.

It has to be said that Britain's participation over the years has not been as consistently substantial and high-level as that of Germany and the US, or possibly even France. Perhaps that is because it is not quite our sort of event. As Margaret Thatcher once remarked in a different context about concerted action: "This German talking shop works because it consists of Germans." Perhaps it is a sense that the Munich conference is basically a US-German love-in where Britain is as welcome as your average mother-in-law. Perhaps a perception, too, that we enjoy a special relationship with the United States and do not need the Munich event to burnish our credentials. There has also been a feeling that the most coveted platform speaking slots have not been as readily offered to British ministers as to others, reflecting Britain's hesitant approach to Europe.

One could cite yet other reasons, for instance a lack of intellectual confidence on the part of British ministers for participation in multinational, multilingual discussions of this sort, though one would certainly exempt Denis Healey, Peter Carrington, and George Robertson from any such failing. Or the fact that British ministers with their heavy parliamentary obligations like to devote their weekends to their parliamentary constituencies more than to international gabfests.

One must not overdo lament about Britain's lack of prominence at the Munich conference: numerous British defense ministers have attended, and there is a regular corps of senior officials, including in the past some of our most outstanding defense policy experts, such as Sir Michael Quinlan and Sir Arthur Hockaday. But only one British prime minister, David Cameron, has so far taken part, though that is not for want of trying on the part of the MSC's organizers.

Reviewing the great events of the last thirty years with security and defense policy implications—the deployment of intermediate-range nuclear forces, the shift from détente to winning the Cold War, the future of short-range nuclear weapons, the fall of the Wall and German reunification, Bosnia, faltering attempts at European defense cooperation—one cannot say that discussions at the Munich conference played a decisive role, certainly from a British perspective. I have no recollection of sitting in 10 Downing Street in the eighties as a foreign affairs and defense adviser and reflecting that discussions at the Munich conference had moved the agenda on these issues decisively forward. Nor have regular commitments by European ministers at Munich to mend their ways been able to prevent the steady erosion of Europe's defense capabilities.

But of course Munich is not there to take specific decisions. There are other institutions aplenty for that: NATO defense ministers' meetings, summits, and so on. Rather, its role is to facilitate decisions, identify longer-term trends, build relationships, and signal future intentions.

In these areas, its achievements have been notable. Most important has been the part that it has played in locking the United States into Europe even when it has been distracted by non-European events like the wars in Vietnam and Iraq. That ability to maintain transatlantic unity will be tested once more by the American "pivot" or, as they prefer to call it, rebalancing toward Asia. It was significant that Vice President Biden chose the 2013 MSC as the best place to deliver powerful reassurance to Europe: "The bad news is the United States isn't going anywhere. The good news is the United States isn't going anywhere."

In the same category I would put the Munich Conference's role in maintaining wide political support in Germany for NATO, even when, in the context of reunification, a more neutral position between NATO and the Warsaw Pact could have had attractions. Regular high-level attendance from France compensated to a degree for that country's self-exclusion from NATO's military structure. In more recent times, the MSC framework offered a welcome for the countries of East and Central Europe as they transitioned between the Warsaw Pact and NATO. Discussions at Munich helped create the necessary resolve in NATO to dispatch Slobodan Milošević. All these are achievements of which any nonofficial, nongovernmental conference can be proud.

I would add two other invaluable services that Munich has provided. First, it has acted as an early warning radar for changes in thinking and policy. As examples over the years I would cite the switch from the policy of modernizing NATO's short-range nuclear weapons to abolishing them altogether, the first stirrings of a European defense and security identity separate from NATO, and the implications of the extreme cuts mandated by the US Congress in American defense spending. All these and others had their first, or at least an early, outing on the Munich stage. Second, Munich debates have enabled congressional participants from the United States to pick up a sense of developing European views on a wide range of issues, so that as new policies emerge they do not come as a shock to the Washington establishment. The same applies in reverse: Europe gets a chance to pick up signals of new trends in administration and congressional thinking before they become cast in concrete. And in recent years, both Europe and the US have heard directly from participants in the Middle East and Asia how views on current issues are evolving in those regions. "You first heard it here" is a boast that Munich can often justifiably make.

Retirement ages are being extended across Europe, and I hope that will apply equally to the Munich Security Conference as it passes fifty. No organization can be free from criticism, and Munich has undeniably lost some of the intimacy of earlier decades, extended its geographic scope almost to the breaking point, become too platform-oriented at the expense of real discussion, and risks being swept up into the celebrity culture that plagues the World Economic Forum in Davos.

But the two great Atlanticists, Horst Teltschik and Wolfgang Ischinger, who have taken forward the Munich conference from its founder, Ewald von Kleist, have shown ingenuity and adaptability, which should ensure its future relevance. Recognizing how Europe itself has changed and how new security challenges lie more outside our continent, they have brought in the new world of the Middle East and Asia to redress the balance of the old, they have involved a younger generation of activists, and they have initiated more specialized conferences during the year to supplement the main event. That convinces me that Munich can hang on to its crown and continue to be a model of informed debate and partnership between nations.

*Lord **Powell** was private secretary and advisor on foreign affairs and defense (1983 to 1990) to Lady Thatcher when she was prime minister, and held the same position in the early part of John Major's time as prime minister (until 1991). He is now an independent member of the House of Lords and a member of its Select Committee on the Constitution.*

The German-American Relationship Remains at the Conference's Heart

Jim Hoagland

Talk shops, gabfests, even BOGSATs: these are some of the slightly derisive terms that journalists use among themselves to describe the biggest and best-known annual international conferences that assemble the good and the great of current world affairs. We want to deflate any balloons of self-importance we (or others) might puff up after being invited to participate in, or assigned to cover, these meetings of experts, policymakers, business sultans, politicians and statesmen (a distinction with a true difference), and others. (The acronym, if you haven't guessed, stands for Bunch of Guys/Gals Sitting around a Table.)

But the reality is that for scribes and chroniclers, many of these gatherings are welcome interludes in the year's chaotic chase of events, personalities, and the dramatic change we call news. It is an efficient way of seeing a wide variety of that most valuable of commodities in the world of journalism—well-informed, well-placed sources brought together from disparate locations to one point on the map to interact and explain, and the ideas they develop. In my experience, none of these gatherings has been more useful than the meeting previously known as the *Wehrkunde-Begegnung,* or simply *Wehrkunde.*

▲

Robert Gates (left) and Franz-Josef Jung signing
a defense agreement during the 2008 conference

Conferences have cultures of their own, for better and occasionally for worse. An organized discussion that continues to attract attentive audiences and knowledgeable speakers over five years and longer inevitably develops its own personality and what crime-novel detectives call an M.O.—a distinctive *modus operandi* that distinguishes it from others of its kind.

The oh-so Anglo-bucolic atmosphere of Ditchley Park; the Dutch-centric business and power amassing of Bilderberg; the Yankee brashness of the Trilateral Commission (see its early and innovative outreach to Japan decades before President Obama's "pivot" to Asia); the earnest and eponymous USA-Italy Council's Venice gathering where intellectual jousting is encouraged; the deceptively named Shangri-la meeting of Pacific defense ministers that submerges Singapore's gardens under visions of battleships and marching armies; the global grandeur of France's ambitious, bicultural World Policy Conference conducting its business as much in English as in French; and the reproaches and resentment toward the rest of the world felt by American visitors at Russia's Valdai Club are examples of cumulative, manifest culture drawn from my own four decades of conference-going.

The Munich Security Conference has—perhaps more nimbly than any other major conclave—redefined and adapted its culture and mission in the changing world it attempts to analyze, explain, and influence. It has moved from the Cold War era to the time of globalization by extending its scope, reach, and vision. And like the transatlantic community as a whole, it still faces significant challenges in this still uneven transition.

Throughout my forty-plus years at *The Washington Post,* the meeting in Munich has usually been the most important annual barometer of the vitality and solidity of the German-American relationship. That is its M.O.

Yes, more actual business gets done at bilateral leadership summits when it comes to the two nations' formal agendas. Yes, the Munich meeting is more intellectual and conceptual than transactional. And yes, it has become increasingly diffuse in subject matter, geographical focus, and even the makeup of delegations as the world has moved from Cold War bipolar and Bushian unipolar to Euro multipolar and what French Foreign Minister Laurent Fabius calls the present "nonpolar" disorderly distribution of economic and military power. Yet, because of its conciseness and painstaking preparation, Munich has through the years provided the most telling glimpses of the state of the overall German-American relationship, the key link on which NATO's Cold War strategy was founded and maintained.

It has taken a lot of work to maintain in good order the set of bonds that lash together World War II's main conquering nation and that conflict's principle conquered (and divided) country. It could have worked out differently, and a lot worse for all.

But pragmatist met pragmatist when Germans and Americans began to work for reconstruction and reconciliation. And early on, *Wehrkunde* played a significant conceptual role in the process of consultation, cajoling, bargaining, and seeking common ground, which came to form the habits of transatlanticism.

Other countries certainly contributed to, participated in, and benefited from the NATO strategy that helped end the Soviet empire—and from the constant debating of that strategy in Munich. My point is that the nature of German-American cooperation had to be thought out by both sides in much greater detail than was the case with, say, US-British cooperation, which was fairly automatic, or US-French cooperation, which was anything but automatic. (US differences with France were more theological and political than strategic, meaning they could be left unresolved.)

The heavy lifting of consensus-building on strategy was left to the Germans, who faced particular dangers from the potential use of nuclear weapons on their soil to halt the feared Warsaw Pact invasion, and to the Americans, to whom the nuclear weapons stationed in Germany belonged.

The different responsibilities and dangers each of the two nations faced could be discussed in confidence and great detail by the relatively small group of strategic planners and academics who attended the first *Wehrkunde* meetings. By gradually broadening the circle of participants to policymakers, parliamentarians, and journalists, the Munich meeting became a major media event that provided a barometer on the Cold War at large as well as the German-American relationship.

A good example of that change came in 1985, when Chancellor Helmut Kohl voiced full support at Munich for President Ronald Reagan's Strategic Defense Initiative—a stance Kohl could not get his coalition partners to adopt as the official German position but which he presented at Munich while surrounded by key members of his cabinet and pleased US officials. This strengthened Reagan's hand in the nuclear arms negotiations with Mikhail Gorbachev taking shape at the time.[1]

As the public visibility of the Munich meeting increased, so did its attraction to key members of the House of Representatives and the Senate, who traveled on US military transports as members of an official congressional delegation. They had space to invite along a handful of Washington-based journalists, who eagerly accepted because of the simplified logistics of a direct flight to Munich, the savings brought to their organizations by the reasonable fares the Air Force charged, and most of all the chance to schmooze about big issues with Joe Lieberman, John McCain, Jane Harman, Lindsey Graham, Loretta Sanchez, Tom Udall, and others while flying across the Atlantic. Munich was a favorite stop for Joe Biden, who continued to find his way to the conference after he became vice president, and for Hillary Clinton, who attended as senator and then as secretary of state.

In becoming larger, more public, and more political, the meeting also inevitably became more formulaic. The congressional delegations devoted inordinate amounts of time both in the public sessions and the "CoDel" (congressional delegation) private briefings begging, blasting, and/or bullying NATO's European allies to maintain or increase defense spending, particularly after the Cold War and the Warsaw Pact had been tossed onto history's ash heap. It became such an established routine with so little to show for it that I concluded that the American participants feared that an absence of such rhetoric would be seen as a weakening of US resolve on the issue.

But if the public sessions became more predictable, remaining constant was the tremendous value of what I call the "bilaterals" that occur between journalists and policymakers in the hallways or over a lunch or a beer in the basement tavern in the Hotel Bayerischer Hof, where complicated policy wrinkles could be explained or defended and sensitive information conveyed in nuanced terms to scribes not working on a deadline. There have been times when I learned as much about France, Poland, or Russia as I would have by spending a day each in Paris, Warsaw, or Moscow.

However much I might wish it to be the case, nobody is going to run a conference just to simplify the lives of journalists. So *Wehrkunde* faced an existential challenge with the end of the Cold War. Without the threat of Soviet tanks charging through the Fulda Gap, was there still a reason for the gathering? It fell to Horst Teltschik and Wolfgang Ischinger, the two successors of the conference's founder Ewald-Heinrich von Kleist, to update and broaden it not just geographically but substantively—in journalistic shorthand: to go global.

It seems to me that the German-American relationship remains at the heart of the annual meeting, even if that is not proclaimed from the dias. No country's support is more important to America's continued leadership in transatlantic and global affairs than is Germany's. The implicit message of Munich is that Washington and Berlin must cooperate now on global problems, not just European ones. The mission of the alliance—and the conference—in linking US and German action abides.

It was to Munich that Secretary of State Hillary Clinton and Secretary of Defense Leon Panetta both came in 2012 to reassure the Europeans that the Obama administration was still fully committed to the transatlantic partnership. Until then, I had not fully realized how worried Washington had become about the doubts that the "pivot" to Asia and other Obama moves were stirring among Europeans.

The fact that in recent years Germany and the US have not always been able to find the common ground they once shared has simply made that reality all the more obvious. Consider the way in which American and German power and motives were united in the Balkans crises of the nineties, and the positive results achieved there.

Yet the most compelling moments of the first thirteen Munich meetings of this millennium have been ones in which German-American unity came under pressure. I have four moments in mind that to me illustrate how the combination of high stakes, compressed schedules, and the organizers' sixth sense of who has something important to say make Munich such a valuable barometer in establishing trends in international affairs.

The memory of Foreign Minister Joschka Fischer and Defense Secretary Donald Rumsfeld glaring at each other and then shouting in anger across the stage of the 2003 Munich Security Conference in a wounding dispute over Iraq will remain the unforgettable image of the kind of disunity that our two countries—and the world—can ill afford. No one can be pleased with the way the Iraq experience turned out.

In 2007, Russian President Vladimir Putin chose the Munich Security Conference as the forum in which to express his increasingly bitter disillusionment with the United States, which he accused of having "overstepped its national borders in every way. … Who likes this? Who is happy about this?" He was not, clearly.

It was an unusually belligerent declaration that surprised and disappointed John McCain, whom I spoke with as Putin was leaving the stage. "But we have to find a way to work with Russia, even so," McCain added, voicing a sentiment that infused US and German decisions not to overreact to Putin in the months and years ahead.

Munich was also the scene of an important declaration of Chinese intentions that shaped events deep into 2010. Having known Yang Jiechi when he was the soft-spoken and affable Chinese ambassador in Washington before becoming foreign minister in Beijing, I was immediately struck by the on-edge assertiveness with which he delivered his talk to the Munich conference, and said as much to him in a question from the audience. Yang did not back away: "We also deserve a hearing. … One country or a few countries definitely cannot decide the future of the world."

I was not the only one to notice the change in tone. Secretary of State Clinton soon traveled to Hanoi and elsewhere in Southeast Asia to push back against what the administration perceived to be a suddenly assertive Chinese foreign policy, provoking ever more warnings from Beijing. Eventually, Washington and Beijing backed away from the diplomatic duel that had begun in Munich.

Equally revealing I felt was the way in which Hamid Karzai, president of Afghanistan, conducted his private and public dialogues with US officials at the 2011 Munich Security Conference. Behind closed doors I later learned that the Americans had made heavy demands on Karzai, and those demands were still on his mind when he delivered his speech to the plenary. When a red light went on to remind him that the time allotted to his speech had expired, Karzai hardly paused, noting that he was the president of Afghanistan and that he would continue speaking as he pleased. On finishing, he breezed past the row of US officials who had been hammering him with glances so disdainful that I concluded the US would always have its hands full in trying to manage the Afghan leader.

History has frequently been made or at least foretold at the Munich Security Conference meetings over the past half-century. I am fully confident that this will continue to be the case in the years to come.

Jim Hoagland is a two-time winner of the Pulitzer Prize for The Washington Post, *where he has spent four decades as a reporter, editor, senior foreign correspondent, and syndicated columnist. He is now a contributing editor, writing occasional opinion articles for the paper.*

Notes

1   See also W. R. Smyser, *From Yalta to Berlin: The Cold War Struggle Over Germany* (New York: St. Martin's Press, 2000), 302–303.

Talking Points

The Conference between Genuine Debate, Catwalk, and Public Ambiguity

Stefan Kornelius

When Ewald-Heinrich von Kleist founded the *Internationale Wehrkunde-Begegnung,* although he wanted to conduct discussions openly within a small group, they were nevertheless to be absolutely secret. For him it was a question of openness, and this meant not only establishing trust but a sense of confidentiality as well. Von Kleist wanted honest talking. Anyone who experienced him in the final years of his life, ill at ease against the powerful backdrop of the Munich Security Conference, suspected how much he struggled with the catwalk nature of the modern meeting.

But fifty years is a long time, and as much as diplomacy needs confidentiality, so have the rules of the game for back-room politics changed. The world has seen several revolutions, unleashing not only the freedom movement in Eastern Europe or powerful new forces in the Arab world. None of that would have been thinkable without the rise of communications technology, the need for more transparency and information. The world is now reduced to the digits 0 and 1—the binary code has overthrown more regimes

Talking Points | **383**

and caused more wars than wordy dispatches. Globalized patterns of trade are inconceivable without globalized communication.

Communication is now the heart of security policy. Nothing threatens authoritarian structures and totalitarian systems more than the need for exchange and intellectual freedom. A television show about a liberal Muslim, middle-class marriage arouses more needs in Egypt than any Friday sermon. A season of *Homeland* on American cable TV jolts the self-confidence of the nation more strongly than any state of the union address by the president. Edward Snowden's files are torturing the intelligence community, which by nature hates to be in the limelight. More than anything else, Snowden has revealed the virtues and dangers of communication 3.0.

The Internet and digital globalization have triggered a wave of enlightenment that is currently sweeping through China via Sina Weibo, that flooded Tahrir Square in Cairo, and that is leading the white-clad opposition through the streets of Moscow. The instant availability of information, images, and evidence does not permit secret drone wars; it exposes corrupt party officials with luxury watches on their wrists, and within hours of a toxic gas attack, such as the one that occurred in Syria, it causes outrage that leaves no scope for neutrality.

Is it therefore no longer possible to have back rooms? Are emissaries and ambassadors no longer needed? Wrong. It is precisely in the delicate dealings among nations that diplomacy must have the chance to waste a few words in private without immediately antagonizing neighbors with the force of sovereign power. Foreign policy is perception and evaluation, the right word at the right time. People ultimately want to assert their interests. Those who upload the collected embassy dispatches of the United States onto a server use transparency with destructive intent. Who is thinking what about whom? Who is protecting whom? What does the one know about the other? Not even a marriage can endure that much transparency.

Klemens von Metternich, who in his political dealings saw himself as an "actor on a stage," understood only too well how important it is to have a fixed order in relations between states. He was confident that freedom can flourish only when there is order. Today he would recognize that no order is secure in the face of the tremendous force of modern communication—which does not always have to be detrimental.

So what, in the second decade of the new digital age, are the mechanics of a conference on foreign and security policy that at one time began in a back room and at which any number of modern Metternichs (or those who would like to be) take to the stage as much as they live by the confidential word?

Perhaps this is the key problem of an event that is rumored to be too much Bismarck and too little Assange.

Yet it cannot even be claimed that the meeting in the heart of Munich operates according to the rules of a secret lodge, as the friends of conspiracy time and again murmur. Even decades ago, the Bayerischer Rundfunk broadcast every word via radio. The television station Phoenix later took over, and today everything is tweeted, blogged, and streamed. In any event, secret agreements are not concluded.

Today, more media people are accredited than there are participants at the Munich Security Conference. The boundary between inside and outside in the hall has long since been eliminated. There are as many journalists among the participants as members of parliament. They benefit from direct access to political players, and anyone who is serious about their journalistic craft leaves the conference with a thick notebook full of ideas and assessments. There has never been so much communication.

It is worth noting that the sheer news value of the conference has not really increased—paradoxically, thanks to the digital age. In the years *ante retem* (before the Internet), the conference provided a condensed version of security policy and players that no reporter could escape. Today, the Internet provides for permanent compression. Munich may supply one or the other turn of phrase for connoisseurs, but big news is more the exception.

Vladimir Putin's appearance in 2007 still causes a shudder today—just as Nikita Khrushchev once thumped the United Nations lectern with his shoe, the Russian president ranted against the domination of the United States in the world order. Likewise, the duel between Joschka Fischer and Donald Rumsfeld from 2003 is remembered with a thrill. Nowadays, speeches and interventions have to be closely scrutinized to ensure their validity.

So why is it that the conference has so much trouble escaping from the clouds of secrecy? Perhaps it is the speech code that makes the reunion of foreign and security policy experts look like a closed event. Diplomats are accustomed to a formal language that only had a chance of being printed in *Foreign Affairs* without prior translation. This might be a reason that for the television audience, Munich is reduced to the arrival and departure of big limousines and the enormous security precautions that conferences of this size now entail. Foreign policy as a celebrity event—not even von Kleist would have imagined that to be possible.

Also, the sealing-off of the area to observers on the other side of the police cordon underscores the impression of a closed event, notwithstanding the live streaming on the Internet and all other communication efforts. Thus, the wildest ideas flourish about the—take your choice—NATO conference, warmongers' conference, arms fair, or the submission-to-the-imperialistic-US-system conference. Stripped of all ideology, there remains just this truth: of course government-level men and women naturally take advantage of the opportunity for back-room discussions, which they would otherwise conduct in their ministries or on the phone. However: what is reprehensible about that? Why the outrage?

The Munich Security Conference polarizes because the subject polarizes—precisely in Germany, where for good historical and poor political reasons it cannot be taken for granted that a nation might have interests and, yes, might also exercise power. Security policy in Germany is one of the niche products in the public marketplace—hard to find, and even harder to sell.

The political class of the major parties has reached agreement on a silent consensus: the country cultivates its alliances, acts defensively in military matters, does not talk much about the difficult alternatives, and hopes to be spared the famous cup when the Western world struggles to act responsibly, such as in Libya or, most recently, in Syria. Apart from that, we make our small contribution to arms exports because there is an industry, and the others do it too.

Like under a magnifying glass, the Munich Security Conference exposes that this fair-weather treatment of security policy is not enough; indeed, that it may even be dangerous if the political dispute in matters of war and peace is conducted on a quagmire.

Munich is a singular major event; there is not another date on the calendar when the political class in Germany is forced to discuss the unwelcome topic in such an exposed way. They meet in a hall, filled for the most part with alliance partners, in which a basic tenor of political realism is fostered. Dealings concerning their relations are conducted in the same language and currency.

This could be the perfect opportunity to talk openly about gauging conflicts, new threats, and old enmities. This would be the ideal moment for communication and building trust. But the German political class is acting as if not much has changed since the first meeting fifty years ago.

And yet a great deal has: the country senses that something new is expected of it. Germany has to explain what it proposes to do with its strength at the center of Europe—or whether it may even be instrumentalizing its past in order to be able to avoid engaging in current conflicts. This is how the German president, Joachim Gauck, expressed it. In his speeches, he voices a central theme on German foreign and security policy where he has identified a gulf: the world attaches new meaning to Germany, yet the country persists in its self-ordained abstinence. Gauck even quotes Hannah Arendt, who gave pause to the new republic only five years after the collapse of the National Socialist regime and the end of World War II: "It looks as if, having been denied world domination, the Germans have fallen in love with powerlessness."

Gauck uses the quotation to dramatically condense his argument. Today, speechlessness might be a more suitable word than powerlessness, since nothing better characterizes the relations between the players at the conference and their opponents outside. Speechlessness occurs when nothing is said. And too little was said in Germany about the responsibilities of the most populous country in Europe and the fourth biggest national economy in the world.

This leads to a tangible conflict between those who conduct foreign and security policy on the stage (and sometimes in the back room) and those in front of the cordon, who believe that the world would be a better place if people would just leave it well alone. Because the moral cudgel is quickly used to conduct this debate in Germany, the one side has to compare Srebrenica with Auschwitz, and the other side has to execute arms exporters as merchants of death.

However, it would aid the matter if Germany were to be aware of its influence to shape events—in the Balkans, just to mention a tiny issue, where it could help to bring Greece and Macedonia closer together in the name dispute. In the delicate issue of arms exports, for example, it would help to point out that a Leopard tank in Indonesia—coupled with a training agreement for tank commanders at the Bundeswehr Command and Staff College and close supervision in the country—can do more for the rule of law than a Chinese-manufactured tank. The argument is multilayered, but moral zero-sum games are rare.

Hence, Ewald-Heinrich von Kleist's back-room circle designed to build up trust has become a mirror for the state of affairs of the Federal Republic. What better can happen to a conference? It is therefore worth taking a look, decoding the language, listening in front of and behind the cordons: it all boils down to a question of communication. And of trust. Just like fifty years ago.

Stefan Kornelius is foreign editor of the Süddeutsche Zeitung, *a leading German daily newspaper. In previous assignments he served as national correspondent in Bonn and Berlin and as the paper's Washington bureau chief. He is a regular participant of the Munich conference, reporting on it for almost twenty years.*

From Munich to the World:
Broadcasting the MSC

Ulrich Wilhelm

The Munich Security Conference adopts no resolutions or decisions. However, more than any other international conference, it facilitates personal encounters that create trust. And trust may be the crucial drop of oil when the ritualized gearing of international politics is stuck.

Fifty years down the road, the conference has come a long way—from quite modest beginnings as a small, genuinely private round of talks to the major media event we see today. The television archive of the Bayerischer Rundfunk (Bavarian Broadcasting Service) contains the oldest report on the *Internationale Wehrkunde-Begegnung* (as it was then known) from 1967. It was ten minutes long. And radio colleagues remember how, in the seventies and early eighties, they still took a small tape recorder with them to the conference at midday in order to produce a short report for the evening. Today, over seven hundred journalists from all over the world are accredited. Reporting is almost uninterrupted. The Munich Security Conference is therefore a logistical challenge for the media too. Radio and television prepare for it weeks in advance, for outdoor broadcast vehicles with satellite dishes have to be put in place, kilometers of cables laid, and cameras set up.

The Bayerischer Rundfunk, with almost eighty journalists and technicians, is the MSC's media partner and broadcasting host and supplies television images throughout the world. Altogether, some thirty to forty television stations in Germany, Europe, and worldwide make use of its services each year. The few minutes of reporting in the initial years have expanded to almost round-the-clock transmission. Until two years ago, the Phoenix television station, the event-based public broadcasting channel in Germany, transmitted the conference live in its entirety. Today, Phoenix broadcasts compilations lasting several hours. Bayerisches Fernsehen (Bavarian Television) transmits the opening session on Saturday morning. Year after year, the conference is, for one weekend, the top story on television news programs and radio news stations. And now the Internet is also a channel of communication between the conference and the public. At Bayerischer Rundfunk, we are working on linking television, radio, and Internet more closely, and so for the last two years we have transmitted the security conference as a live stream on our website, supplemented during the conference breaks by looks behind the scenes and by analyses, assessments, and interviews by specialist journalists. There is a live conference blog in which interested members of the public can also participate.

Within the narrowest of confines, the press has the opportunity to talk to politicians and experts with the most diverse specialisms. Thus, going beyond topical reporting, the conference contributes to providing the public with a picture of the state of affairs and the approaches shaping future developments. Year after year, it offers facts and ideas for public discourse on questions of security policy.

The Munich Security Conference, with its range of topics and with new participants, reflects the shift from a bipolar to a multipolar world. To some extent, it regularly takes the pulse of the world and records the changes. Media reports allow the general public to participate in this annual checkup. Thus, the MSC makes an important contribution to public debate on security policy. It is no longer merely a question of the strength of armed forces and armaments but also of many other questions, such as energy reserves, access to clean drinking water, demographics, and targeted hacking of the World Wide Web, to name a few.

The list of "new" subjects is much longer. It reflects a new, interconnected understanding of policy. And so, just as the World Economic Forum in Davos has expanded the concept of "economics" rather than shrinking it, so the Munich Security Conference has adopted a comprehensive understanding of "security."

The Munich Security Conference: fifty years. Leaving aside the developments in confidential talks, there have been remarkable occurrences in the public sessions. There is no forgetting the historic moment in 2003 when the then German Foreign Minister Joschka Fischer responded "Sorry, I am not convinced" to the speech by the United States Secretary of Defense Donald Rumsfeld—a brief and pithy expression by Fischer of the deep skepticism of the German Red-Green coalition toward American policy, which foresaw war against Iraq. It was a discussion, a dispute, that split Europe and, with Fischer's five words, laid bare the deep rift in the Western alliance, the solidarity of which had continually been pledged at the MSC.

Shortly before that, in Washington, Rumsfeld himself had coined the terms "old" and "new" Europe, and in the conference chamber that distinction was all too clear from the American point of view. The tension was palpable. On one side the wish not to give up on the solidarity of the alliance, but on the other the wish not to allow ourselves to be drawn by our more powerful American partner into a war the justification for which we did not share and whose consequences were unforeseeable.

Bavarian Minister-President Edmund Stoiber, whose party, the Christian Social Union, was in the opposition camp, was the first to respond to the speech by Secretary Rumsfeld setting out the reasons why war was inevitable. While other representatives of the German opposition agreed unreservedly with the American position, Stoiber stressed that Rumsfeld's analysis was not shared to that extent by the majority in Germany and in Europe. And, presumably also with an eye to the 30,000 people demonstrating at that moment in downtown Munich against a war in Iraq, Stoiber declared that politicians were under a substantial moral obligation to convey the threat from Saddam Hussein and the necessity for war to the public.

There is a wealth of such notable events at the Munich Security Conference. One, in 2007, was the speech by Russian President Vladimir Putin, who started by saying that the conference's structure allowed him to avoid "excessive politeness." "We are constantly being taught about democracy," said Putin, "but for some reason, those who teach us do not want to learn themselves." There followed sharp criticism of the US and of a "unipolar world" dominated by it. In retrospect, this speech by Putin is a good example of the Munich Security Conference and its character as a private and yet public gathering. "This conference's format," said Putin, "will allow me to say what I really think about international security problems." Four months later, at the G8 summit in Germany in the Baltic spa of Heiligendamm, Putin had presumably not changed his position on the matter, but the tone of his discourse in the official context was much more moderate.

High points in the recent past were the appearances by US Vice President Joe Biden. He had previously attended the Munich Security Conference as a senator. In 2009, Munich was his first international appearance as vice president. At the conference, Biden virtually gave a government statement from the new Obama administration aimed at the international public; something similar happened again in 2013 following the reelection of President Obama.

I also remember the sobering moment in 2010 when Iranian Foreign Minister Manouchehr Mottaki first raised hopes of a solution to the nuclear conflict and then completely shattered them. The fact that Mottaki had come to the MSC and President Mahmoud Ahmadinejad had, shortly before the conference, expressed Iran's willingness to cooperate on the nuclear issue gave many participants cause for hope. When the Iranian minister once more merely reiterated the country's well-known position, the realization of another Iranian refusal became all the more clear to everyone.

I am thinking, too, of the most recent conference, in 2013, when a Syrian student who had fled her home took the floor, saying that her people were suffering under the brutality of the regime and the rebels. Why, asked the young woman, was the world standing by doing nothing? She called for more action and fewer conferences.

As a place of reflection, the Munich Security Conference has earned worldwide esteem. In character it stands out from many other conferences. The venue in Munich offers participants direct proximity, specifically fosters unplanned encounters, and opens up interesting dialogues. The interweaving of the international stage with a wide range of confidential, bilateral talks produces the intense atmosphere on which the Security Conference thrives.

Ulrich Wilhelm is director general of the Bavarian Broadcasting Corporation (BR). The public-service radio and television broadcaster has more than six million viewers and listeners daily. From 2005 to 2010, Wilhelm was spokesman of the German government and director of the Press and Information Office of the German government.

"I Didn't Know They Were Letting Girls Go to *Wehrkunde*"

Catherine McArdle Kelleher

In the late eighties, when the word spread that I had an invitation to "Munich," a jealous American think-tank colleague snarled, "I didn't know they were letting girls go to *Wehrkunde*." I smiled as sweetly as I could and promised to debrief him when I was back.

He was right to be jealous. The Munich Security Conference is, and always has been, a great opportunity for those engaged in security policy at the national and global level. It stands almost alone as a wide-ranging policy review and annual conference, a mixture of political conference and intimate discussions, involving superstars of today, supporting staffers hoping to be the stars of the future, and featuring interchange with friends and occasional adversaries. It is always interesting and challenging, a reflection of crucial debates past, crises present, and risks future. I have attended in a number of capacities: official in the Department of Defense and at NATO, accompanying staffer, student of Russian-American-European relations in general and German security policy in particular, and interested policy critic. I have always learned a great deal and left with a whetted appetite for more.

Tawakkol Karman, Charlotte Knobloch, and Claudia Roth at the 2012 conference

What stand out most, though, are the almost unique opportunities for serious discussion that Munich provides. Some have seen it as the security twin of Davos: a type of mid-winter blood pressure check for the great and the good and a chance to catch up between formal organizational meetings. Munich, however, has always seemed more than that to me, especially in the ratio of serious participants to hangers-on or "wannabes." As Ewald-Heinrich von Kleist intended from the first, it is a place for critical conversations, for launching and testing out new ideas or new compromises, for corridor conversations of moment. There have been a number of significant co-located negotiations. One of my strongest memories indeed is of the late Richard Holbrooke energetically striding through the lobby of the Hotel Bayerischer Hof with a number of Bosnian political figures in tow. Their destination was a major meeting in a hotel conference room to carry on the search for consensus late into the night.

There are also clear memories of the many "bilateral" meetings when I worked as a Defense Department official, particularly those I did in support of Secretary William Perry and Secretary William Cohen. Each used these meetings on the sidelines of the general conference to explore both broad issues and specific agreements, with "deliverables" always in view. The process is almost invariably the same. At the appointed hour, a small delegation from each side exits the main hall and sweeps into small associated rooms, there to be shielded both from other participants and the increasing number of global press Munich has attracted. Most of these meetings were productive and civil, but a few during the Yugoslav wars in particular were exercises in frozen hostility, lightened only somewhat by Munich's mid-winter warmth. One or two even featured unscripted exchanges, as when Perry and NATO Secretary General Javier Solana, both by then security stars, fell into comparing their starts in science and reminiscing about their respective career paths.

For Americans, Munich has also been unique because of the strong representation of both the executive branch and Congress at the same discussion table. The secretaries of defense have almost always come; in recent years secretaries of state have increasingly joined them. But the simultaneous and almost "equal" presence of congressional figures, giving and receiving messages directly, is novel for all sides. Powers such as John McCain, Joe Lieberman, Ellen Tauscher, Susan Collins, Jane Harman, and earlier, John Tower and Les Aspin, have been regular attendees and have often taken the floor to advance their own ideas. The Vladimir Putin-John McCain exchanges in the last decade were particularly memorable. But for many lesser lights, this has been a special experience, and an invitation to join the congressional "delegation" has been eagerly sought after. The lure is the chance to meet European and Asian leaders, to observe the policy interactions directly, and to connect with a range of scholars and critics they would otherwise never encounter, let alone debate. I am told that the congressional breakfast that is always held is remarkably open and cordial. Given the recent regrettable narrowing of America's global vision and individual international experience, as well as its off-and-on political stalemate, these achievements take on new significance.

As a research scholar myself, I have also witnessed or been a small part of the many "test balloons" and policy suggestions that transnational groups have launched at the Munich Security Conference. Of particular note were the side meetings and discussions of scholars in the nineties who first began the work of untangling the individual and conjoined nuclear histories of Great Britain, France, Germany, and the United States. Led by Uwe Nerlich of the Stiftung Wissenschaft und Politik and Ernest May of Harvard, and supported by the MacArthur and other foundations, these represented a distinct break with the past and led to the training of a whole new cohort of men and women interested in these issues on both sides of the Atlantic.

A more recent example and one perhaps more central to the core Munich discussions was the presentation of the results of two years of study and discussion by the Euro-Atlantic Security Initiative (EASI) that was co-chaired by Munich's Wolfgang Ischinger, Senator Sam Nunn, and former Russian Foreign Minister Igor Ivanov. To me as an EASI commissioner, Munich presented a remarkable opportunity to broadcast the findings and to attract attention for EASI's ideas from precisely the people we called upon to act. Beyond the formal recommendations, EASI's successful trilateral approach had a considerable impact on its two dozen elite participants, was well received by the Munich conference participants, and has already given rise to a number of follow-on efforts and imitators.

I have also enjoyed the continuing professional and personal contacts Munich allows in a compressed time and space. I always see and interact with friends, colleagues from past posts, and officials I have interviewed and tracked over my own career. Sometimes, especially in earlier days, this tested the limits of protocol. An older member of the conference staff once reminded a small reminiscing group of us (younger then and perhaps more unruly in the hotel lobby than we should have been) that the real Munich conference was happening behind the closed doors of the conference hall. We meekly followed him back into the hall, but even then, I found some of the informal experiences close in just as valuable as some of the prepared speeches.

That assessment certainly holds true for conversations I have had with the women I have been privileged to meet and cooperate with at the Munich meetings. In recent years, this has become easier as more and more women have risen to levels of authority that command their presence at Munich. The Munich Security Conference now surpasses most other security conferences (for example, the annual International Institute for Security Studies meetings) in the number of women and the conference roles they have been accorded, formally and informally. Women politicians from Germany and Europe always came and spoke from the floor: among them Uta Zapf, Claudia Roth, Ilse Aigner, Brigitte Schulte, and Susanne Kastner. Moreover, the addresses by Chancellor Angela Merkel, Secretary of State Hillary Clinton, and the European Union's Lady Catherine Ashton alone have set a high standard both substantively and as an encouragement to younger women—and men.

But the relative ease of exchanges today can also be attributed to a stimulating development, the associated meeting of a "women's breakfast" organized for the past three years by the Bavarian state government under State Secretary Emilia Müller, the Hanns Seidel Foundation, and Women in International Security Germany (WIIS.de), led by Constanze Stelzenmüller. Brief but focused, these meetings have attracted, among others, Hillary Clinton, Michele Flournoy, a remarkable group of American congresswomen, several European Union commissioners, defense officials, ambassadors, journalists, and scholars. Held at the Prinz-Carl-Palais, the gathering has had more than forty women in attendance in the past two years and attracted considerable press attention. It is without question a tradition to be continued and extended.

Even in earlier days, when the number of women formally invited to *Wehrkunde* was far smaller, there were interesting and challenging contributions from women—if not always from the podium, then certainly in numerous questions from the floor and in published commentaries by researchers and journalists. One of those who was always larger than life was the *International Herald Tribune's* Flora Lewis, who attended regularly and always wrote two or three thoughtful commentaries on speeches or issues that came up at the conference. When these were reprinted in the *New York Times*, many American foreign policy watchers got their first taste of what had happened at Munich. Other notable English-language journalists known for their reporting on Munich meetings over the years include Elizabeth Pond and Judy Dempsey.

Not all were fans of the conference method. I am reminded of distinctly wry comments from a German colleague about whether military transformation and Bundeswehr reform would succumb to the "conference approach." In earlier days, reflecting realities in both the academic and the think-tank world, most of the researchers were from the United States, from the United Kingdom, and from northern Europe. I vividly recall some sharp interventions from the floor, for example by now Dame Pauline Neville-Jones of the UK.

Once the post-Cold War transformation began, there was an influx of journalists and researchers from Eastern and Central Europe—and especially the former Yugoslavia, which was then being torn apart by civil war. In their case, intentionally or not, the meetings were part of a broader socialization effort, an attempt to integrate women in the new democracies into a broader international level of debate and discourse. Several later went on to hold high posts in the security establishments of their countries. In the past the same was true as well for women from a number of West European states.

As the Munich Security Conference meetings continue to expand their parameters to take in Asian and Middle Eastern security issues and balances, the inclusion of women from these areas will be a challenge; their present numbers are small. This is the spirit of United Nations Security Council Resolution 1325: to multiply the opportunities for women to lead in all aspects of security decision-making. I am sure this will be an item on the conference's agenda of outreach and engagement.

My last comments on Munich's "socialization" function reveal part of my answer to the now somewhat musty question: why does the participation of women in the Munich meetings matter? My own experience is certainly one indicator. "Girls," to use the word of my past colleague, not only get invited; they even star at Munich. Over a span approaching three decades as a participant in the Munich Security Conference, I have seen the number and influence of women grow in the security sectors of government, the military, business, and intellectual life. They not only deserve a voice; they unquestionably enrich the dialogue and the debate, as the experience at Munich has underscored time and time again.

More women will appear at the podium as this trend continues. But more may well have to be done in targeted invitations or within the Munich Young Leaders group to ensure the trend continues in all categories. Now that security is defined globally, women in some areas may need disproportionally greater opportunities for socialization and exposure to the domain of defense than their male colleagues do to be fully effective as leaders or even analysts. Munich provides one opportunity. Women in International Security or WIIS, a global network I helped found, is another. Still others should be created and extended to reach the goal of equal treatment and advancement—in political and military life, in journalism and diplomacy, in civilian life and in combat. I confidently predict that the women who emerge as leaders from these broader programs will not do any worse than the 50 percent of the population that has up to now held sway.

Women are increasingly present as both actors and subjects in the security enterprise, and they should be involved fully and prominently in the global security interchange as well as in their domestic political frameworks. Especially at more recent meetings, the Munich conferences have made persistent, observable contributions to advancing women's participation in all conference categories. These conferences and the women who have contributed to them are the better for it.

Catherine McArdle Kelleher is College Park Professor of Public Policy at the University of Maryland and professor emeritus for strategic research at the Naval War College. She has served in numerous US government positions, including as US defense advisor to NATO and deputy assistant secretary of defense for Russia, Ukraine, and Eurasia.

The Munich Young Leaders

Klaus Wehmeier and Thomas Paulsen

There was absolute silence—a rare moment in the otherwise bustling large hall of the Hotel Bayerischer Hof. Only the spotlights aimed at the stage of the 49th Munich Security Conference hummed softly as Kholoud Mansour spoke about the tragedy in her home country of Syria. The emotional statement by the young Syrian journalist, who was attending the conference as one of twenty-five young professionals in the field of security policy, the Munich Young Leaders, was not really going to fit in with the otherwise so sober, analytical conference discussion. Her people were suffering, and the international community was standing by and watching, argued the political scientist, who has since fled from Syria, in front of the international security policy elite gathered together in Munich. "We need more *action* and fewer conferences"—Kholoud Mansour's appeal was an expression of rage and despair not only at the passivity of the international community but also at the disunity of the Syrian opposition. No, she did not expect any decisive moves to resolve the Syrian crisis, said Kholoud Mansour after her appearance—even though some observers rated the first meeting between Russian Foreign Minister Lavrov and the head of the Syrian opposition, Moaz Al-Khatib (who has since resigned), on the margins of the 49th Munich Security

Henry Kissinger with two Munich Young Leaders at the 2009 MSC

Conference as a positive sign. Rather, she had traveled to Munich to rouse the representatives of politics, administration, and business who were attending and to make them aware of the views of young Syrians, who were suffering under the brutality of the Assad regime but also under the increasing radicalization of the rebels.

Listen to the New Generation

Give the young security-policy professionals a voice—Kholoud Mansour's example provides a particularly vivid explanation of the declared aim of the Munich Young Leaders. Since 2009, when twenty-five young security-policy specialists from all over the world took part in the Munich Security Conference for the first time, the Munich Young Leaders have become an established part of the conference. More than that: the young professionals were listened to. This was also Kholoud Mansour's experience. Following her passionate call for decisive action and greater commitment by the international community in the Syrian crisis, all manner of conference participants tried to talk with her, sought her opinion, and listened to her. Even in the Munich Young Leaders group, which in 2013 included a Turkish member of parliament, a staff member from the US Department of Defense, and a Russian government adviser, there was an extremely controversial discussion on the question of the "right" Syrian policy. Should the rebels be supported against the Assad regime, possibly with supplies of weapons as well? What can Syria's neighboring states do to prepare themselves for the conflict spilling over onto them? And what could a political solution of the Syria crisis look like?

Innovative Ability Is the Key

The Syrian conflict makes one thing very clear: the international system is becoming more and more complex, diffuse, and confusing. Regional and international processes are forever being influenced by new players—increasingly nonstate. The age of a conflict-ridden but nevertheless transparent bipolar world order in which the acute threats of the Cold War were debated at the annual *Internationale Wehrkunde-Begegnung* is long gone. Ever new creative solutions must be found to adapt international structures to the challenges of increasing multipolarity in the twenty-first century. That is why innovative skills are more important than ever, particularly in foreign and security policy. The ideas of the next generation represent an invaluable resource in this. Encouraging them is a worthwhile investment in the foreign and security policy landscape of the future—this belief is shared by the Munich Security Conference and the Körber Foundation, which together created the Munich Young Leaders in late 2008.

Involving New Players

The unique experience of being able to take part in the Munich Security Conference bound the Munich Young Leaders together as a group. The gradual emergence of an *esprit de corps* is a part of the concept. This should not be taken for granted, bearing in mind that the individual classes of the Munich Young Leaders bring together participants from up to twenty different countries. It is not only the personal qualifications of the candidates that matter in the selection of the Munich Young Leaders. New players from outside the Euro-Atlantic area should be specifically identified and included in the debate on security policy. Therefore, the Munich Security Conference and the Körber Foundation invite not only participants from NATO states to Munich but also and in particular young leaders from other strategically important regions of the world: from the Middle East, the Commonwealth of Independent States, and Asia. What is true for "high politics" is also reflected in the make-up of the Munich Young Leaders: in a world that is more and more closely integrated, no one player can develop solutions for urgent problems on their own. "The new challenges in foreign and security policy need to be discussed on a global level," is also the opinion of the Indian security expert Ambika Vishwanath, who was present in Munich in 2011. "In this respect the Munich Young Leaders are the ideal platform."

Communication Instead of Confrontation

Naturally, these discussions do not always proceed without tension. This is because the Munich Young Leaders also bring together young leaders from states that have tense relations with each other—or in extreme cases, no relations at all. From the Syrian conflict and the Iranian nuclear program to China's role in Southeast Asia, the list of controversial subjects is long. However lively the culture of debate may be: even the Munich Young Leaders cannot get by without rules. Fairness and confidentiality are indispensable principles, and without them there can be no constructive dialogue. In Munich, the young politicians, diplomats, journalists, and scholars are meant to meet on an equal footing and discuss openly with one another—without speaking notes, talking points, and press communiqués. Loyalty to the team, respect for the position of others, and the certainty that the content of all discussions will be treated confidentially are basic prerequisites—even if the general political climate makes dialogue difficult. Only in this way can it ultimately succeed in establishing trust. "It took a bit of time before we warmed to each other," reports Sawsan Chebli, a German participant with Palestinian roots, about her meeting with a Munich Young Leader from Israel. "But then we actually talked about the situation in the Middle East for hours."

Maintaining Networks

Since then, 150 participants from six classes have helped to carry on this spirit of the Munich Young Leaders. Many of the young people attending Munich remain in contact—even after the end of the conference. Networking via Twitter and Facebook? For most of the Munich Young Leaders this has since become a matter of course. But even in the social media age, the best technology cannot replace personal exchange. Once a year, therefore, all Munich Young Leaders meet at a "reunion." The participants take on the preparation and organization themselves. The last meeting was held in Rabat at the invitation of the Moroccan foreign minister. It is hardly surprising that the meeting in Morocco was concerned above all with the upheavals in the Arab world and the civil war in Syria. Only a few days after the meeting of the Munich Young Leaders in Rabat, the Friends of Syria group met in Marrakesh to discuss ways out of the crisis. Kholoud Mansour remains skeptical regarding the role of the international community: "No matter how the situation develops: in the end only the Syrians themselves can free themselves from decades of oppression and autocracy."

*Dr. **Klaus Wehmeier** is the vice chairman of the executive board of Körber Foundation. Along with Ambassador Wolfgang Ischinger, chairman of the Munich Security Conference, he serves as a patron of the Munich Young Leaders.*

*Dr. **Thomas Paulsen** is the executive director international affairs of the Körber Foundation and chairman of the Munich Young Leaders.*

Fasching, Family Reunions, and Hard Power

The Munich Security Conference, the Alliance,
and International Security—A Very Personal Remembrance

Josef Joffe

Above all, the Munich Security Conference, née *Wehrkunde,* has been a family reunion of the Western strategic community, though it expanded in the nineties to bring in the entire world: presidents and prime ministers, princes and potentates from the Near to the Far East.

Yet in the beginning, it was strictly "family"—NATO, the West. Membership in this august grouping was not easy. I remember my botched attempt to break into the *Wehrkunde* Conference as a young graduate student. My colleague Dieter Mahncke and I had both studied with Robert E. Osgood, one of the greats of the strategic craft, at the School of Advanced International Studies in Washington, DC. To see our mentor and teacher again, we resolved to crash the 1968 *Wehrkunde* at the Regina Hotel, an enchanted place that is no more.

The two of us at least got a bit farther than anyone would today, when security at the Bayerischer Hof, the new venue, is tighter than in the Kremlin or the White House. Today, interlopers would not even manage to breach

▲

the perimeter, about four hundred meters out. In those days, though, *Wehrkunde* was a bit more intimate, with perhaps sixty participants, and it had to share cramped quarters with the *Fasching* (carnival, mardi gras) crowd carousing into the wee hours of the morning.

So we made it into the hall, but that was the end of the foray. Lowly graduate students rubbing shoulders with the Great and the Good? Good-bye, boys. We huffed and we puffed, but then we realized: why bother with the masters of missiles and munitions when a *Fasching* party was swirling all around us? We grabbed bits of the decoration here and there to fake a costume and repaired to the bar, where we were privy to a little vignette that could no longer unfold today.

There, at the bar, was another great of the field, Morton Kaplan of Chicago: huge horn-rimmed glasses, a crew cut, flood pants, and a tie as thin as a shoestring. "Great *Fasching* disguise," we needled him, "you dressed up as an American." Today, Americans and Europeans dress and look alike, and the gravitas of today's security conference forbids the intrusion of scantily clad young women and their inebriated beaus.

Today, what with 400 participants, 200 observers, and 700 reporters guarded by 3,500 police, the "family reunion" has lost some of its intimacy. An iron law of conferencing has again claimed its due: the more successful the gathering, the more it will expand into a highly ritualized and highly "hierarchized" assembly. As a result, the more informal contacts take place elsewhere: during coffee breaks, in the upstairs suites of the Bayerischer Hof, in dinners around town. The World Economic Forum started out with some thirty thinkers in the snowy seclusion of Davos, now it has expanded to three thousand who meet at "private dinners" and invitation-only cocktail parties.

No history of the conference could be written without putting its chairman of more than three decades, Ewald von Kleist, into the limelight; indeed, there would be no such confab without this Prussian officer who entered German history as a twenty-two-year-old would-be assassin of Adolf Hitler (as part of the July 20th plot). It was a suicide mission—a man in a dynamite vest who would blow himself up next to *Der Fuhrer*. Postponed several times, the meeting was finally cancelled. Von Kleist survived the Gestapo, concentration camp, and the Eastern front. After the war, he published a defense-policy magazine appropriately called *Wehrkunde* (an archaic German term for "military science") and then, in 1963, founded the eponymous conference.

It was a bold, perhaps slightly crazed venture. Bringing the luminaries of Western strategy—academics, officials, politicos—to a country still eyed with suspicion, even disdain? This man with the bearing of a Prussian noble right out of central casting, with the clipped speech and the stand-offish demeanor? There was a lot more to him. First of all, von Kleist was a man who had been ready to save German honor; as a convener he had impeccable credentials. Second, behind the façade of diffident hauteur, there lurked a brilliant mind, a wondrously wry wit, and an incorruptible character. Third, he was a uniquely gifted impresario who picked the right participants and then prevailed on them to make the Munich trek. Each fall, he made the rounds on Capitol Hill first and then went off to hunt bear in Alaska.

When Ewald von Kleist retired as chairman of the conference in 1998, eight defense ministers showed up, showering him with half a dozen medals. In due time, his gaze fell on me, who found favor in his eyes and, now equipped with the proper credentials, was allowed to join the august assembly. I have attended almost every *Wehrkunde*/MSC meeting since the eighties. As board member of the American Academy in Berlin, I was fortunate to be able nominate Ewald von Kleist as recipient of the Henry A. Kissinger Prize in 2013 (previously bestowed on Kissinger himself, Helmut Schmidt, Richard von Weizsäcker, and Helmut Kohl). To everybody's dismay, von Kleist died just before the ceremony at the age of ninety. His daughter accepted the prize in his name.

Von Kleist was followed as chairman by Horst Teltschik (1999–2008), formerly Kohl's national security adviser, and Wolfgang Ischinger, previously state secretary in the German Foreign Office in Washington and London. Ischinger has been running the conference since 2009.

Let us dwell above all on the "family-reunion" theme. Today, the Munich Security Conference is the world's most important meeting on international security. The once secluded gathering has burgeoned into a happening in front of the klieg lights—complete with the obligatory demonstrations against the "warmongers" and "conspirators." But its original function remains what von Kleist had wanted and safeguarded.

Like a NATO summit, the MSC offers those set-piece speeches by premiers, presidents, and ministers which are carefully vetted by their advisers to evade diplomatic imbroglios. These speeches lay out familiar talking points or unassailable principles like "peace" and "cooperation." But the confab is informal enough to let trial balloons drift through the ballroom—a new proposal, a new idea. More important is the fairly free-floating discussion, which will occasionally transcend the "let's keep it civil" confines of the conference choreography. As in a real family, familiarity does not necessarily breed consent. Often enough, it is "let the brickbats fly!"

One of the most deliciously dramatic moments is owed to German Foreign Minister Joschka Fischer at the thirty-ninth conference in 2003. Having listened to Donald Rumsfeld, the US secretary of defense, lay out what he believed to be compelling reasons for the Second Iraq War, Fischer burst out: "Sorry, I am not convinced." A lively discussion ensued, and Fischer had made history.

It got tougher as the alienation between Germany and the America of George W. Bush progressed. In 2005, Peter Struck, Chancellor Gerhard Schröder's defense minister, practically committed blasphemy when he decreed: NATO "is no longer the primary venue where the transatlantic partners consult about and coordinate their strategic conceptions." So, no more family? To add insolence to injury, Schröder's *Kanzleramt* had leaked Struck's speech to the *Süddeutsche Zeitung*. Promptly, the Munich paper regaled the conference on the first full day with what Schröder had in mind for the longest-lived coalition of free nations. That was too much even for his foreign minister, who tried to pour a little oil on the roiling waters. Fischer was not amused, because his foreign office minions had provided the usual soothing boilerplate for Struck's speech.

Donald Rumsfeld was not shy, either, repeating a classic shibboleth: "Of course, the mission determines the coalition." Different speaker, same message: NATO is no longer the *Una Sancta* of Western defense. In the previous year, Fischer had flung a clear "no" at the Americans. No, the Germans would "not dispatch troops" to Iraq. But, he added diplomatically, if the alliance so decided, Germany would not "defy the consensus." Thus, the security conference delivered what it has done since the early von Kleist days: to serve as a sounding board and to provide the kind of "kitchen table" where family members occasionally slug it out.

After the demise of the Soviet Union, Russia has been invited as a kind of distant cousin. In 1999, Vice Foreign Minister Gusarov insisted that Moscow would not just look on if NATO enlarged eastward and so crossed a "red line." Yet, at this point, the Munich family had *already* expanded to the East. And so, the assembled Ukrainians, Romanians, and Georgians furiously protested. Gusarov pedaled back. "Esteemed NATO members," he wheedled, please respect "our sensitivities."

President Putin would not be socialized so quickly. In 2007 he showed up at Munich, delivering a speech in the tradition of Nikita ("We shall bury you") Khrushchev. Whereupon I got up to ask politely whether Putin had just declared a "new Cold War." Let history record that the Cold War remains safely buried.

The nineties belonged to what used to be called "out-of-area" engagements. The Cold War was over; the great strategic threat was gone. Now, "small wars" moved in on the West, or what later came to be known as "responsibility to protect." It was also a time of growing up for Germany, now safely reunited and facing no serious enemy as far as the eye (and the satellites) could see. It was the decade of the Balkan wars, or the war of the Yugoslav succession, to use the vocabulary of the seventeenth and eighteenth century.

It was also the decade of hand-wringing: the United States did not want to intervene while Germany suffered paroxysms of pacifism. It had lost two wars, and now it was "never again." Naturally, the conference was given to endless debates over what moral duty demanded and cold-hearted interest defied. The 1993 meeting stood out. Here were Chancellor Kohl and the Social Democrats' foreign policy spokesman Hans-Ulrich Klose both proclaiming "without us!" A grand coalition of abstentionism unfolded. One German participant cried out: "You have robbed me of a democratic human right. I don't know for whom to vote anymore."

Both Kohl and Klose were for "peace-establishing measures" (that is, intervention) in general. But not in the Balkans! Kohl demurred. Why not? In so many words, the chancellor defined a "Kohl Doctrine": German troops could not tread where the *Wehrmacht* had once raged. I meekly interjected: "But that doesn't leave us any place to go except for Switzerland, Portugal, and Sweden." We stayed on good terms nonetheless, and in 1999, Joschka Fischer courted the revolt of his pacifist Greens by belting out "Never again Auschwitz" and taking Germany into the air war against Serbia.

The eighties were overshadowed by *Nachrüstung*—the 572 US Pershing II and cruise missiles the Alliance had decided to deploy in response to the Soviet SS-20 missiles and Backfire bombers. These were systems that could hit European targets but not the United States. Chancellor Helmut Schmidt had raised the "separate threat" in his fabled 1979 speech before the International Institute for Strategic Studies, but it was so carefully hedged that it could not be used in evidence for a German call for compensatory deployments. NATO gave the Soviets a way out by offering the "dual-track" decision of 1979: if you go to zero, we will not deploy. Moscow chose to unleash a full-press propaganda campaign playing on Europe's, especially West Germany's, nuclear angst.

While the Social Democrats preached abstention, détente, and cooperation, Christian Democrat Werner Marx, a member of the Bundestag's defense committee, cringed at the 1981 *Wehrkunde*: "The supporters of *Nachrüstung* are caught in a difficult psychological situation"; there was a lack of "spiritual readiness and courage." Frank Carlucci, the US defense secretary, orated: "We want to be able to say at home that a new consensus has arisen in Europe that endows the defense of freedom with the highest priority." It was not an easy victory. The war for Europe's soul contributed to Schmidt's fall in 1982. Nonetheless, Helmut Kohl won the 1983 election, and the deployment began on schedule. We know how this story ended. Gorbachev relented, and the Euromissiles are history.

Were these battles fought and won during the Munich *Fasching*? No; the decisions were made elsewhere, as befits representative government. Yet while the conference allowed for grandstanding and well-worn formulas, it also made for deliberation in tough times. *Die Zeit* once wrote: "The conflicts between Europe and America have rarely been sharper." That was during the 1981 gathering, but it could have been written at almost any time since the *Wehrkunde's* lowly beginnings in 1963.

A family that fights together stays together—that is the moral of this tale. As its members hash it out, thinking improves. It is a learning experience above all: this is how *they* think, this is how *we* think. In Munich, "they" were often enough members of one's own national camp who thought for themselves, as befits a liberal democracy. Just to know that Americans and Europeans also argue among themselves breaks up monolithic positions on both sides while increasing the supply of insight all round. Upon his retirement in 1998, Ewald von Kleist had it right: "It would be shortsighted to neglect the [European-American] relationship. We have to mend it continually because we will be confronting problems that we can only solve together." Good advice for the next fifty years.

Josef Joffe is editor of Die Zeit *and Fellow of the Freeman-Spogli Institute for International Studies and the Hoover Institution, both at Stanford, where he also teaches international relations.*

Mutual Security in
the Twenty-First Century

The Future of Power in
the Twenty-First Century

Joseph S. Nye, Jr.

Recent books have proclaimed "the end of power," "the end of big," and "a G-Zero world."[1] There is great uncertainty about how to think about power in today's world. It helps to start with a simple definition. Power is the ability to affect others to produce the outcomes one wants, and that can be accomplished with the hard power of coercion and payment or the soft power of attraction and persuasion. While it is sometimes difficult to measure, the exercise of power is as old as human history.

But what will it mean to wield power in the global information age of the twenty-first century? What resources will produce power? In the sixteenth century, control of colonies and gold bullion gave Spain the edge; seventeenth-century Netherlands profited from trade and finance; eighteenth-century France gained from its larger population and armies; while nineteenth-century British power rested on its primacy in the industrial revolution and its navy. American primacy in the second half of the twentieth century rested on a combination of economic scale, military investment, and cultural resources.

Conventional wisdom has always held that the state with the largest military prevails, but in an information age it may be the state (or nonstates) with

Joseph Nye with Eugene Kaspersky at the 2012 MSC

the best narrative that wins. Today, it is far from clear how we measure a balance of power, much less how to develop smart power strategies to survive in this new world. Most current projections of a shift in the global balance of power are based primarily on one factor—projections of growth in the gross national product of different countries. They ignore the other dimensions of power, including both hard military power and the soft power of narrative, not to mention the policy-related difficulties of combining them into successful strategies. For example, it is plausible that in the next decade, China will surpass the United States in the total size of its gross domestic product, but that will not mean China has surpassed the US in overall power. It will still lag far behind the US in per capita income, in the vulnerability of its economy to external factors (such as energy), as well as in soft power, global military capacity, and in alliances.

As I argued a few years ago in my book *The Future of Power,* two great power shifts are occurring in this century—power transition and power diffusion. Power transition from one dominant state to another is a familiar historical process, and many analysts try to explain it with a narrative of supposed American decline and facile historical analogies to Britain and Rome. But Rome remained dominant for more than three centuries after its apogee; even then, it did not succumb to the rise of another state but died a death of a thousand cuts inflicted by internecine conflict and external attacks by barbarian tribes. With its lead in twenty-first-century technologies such as bio, nano, and information technology, its leading universities, and its capacity to attract and assimilate talented immigrants, the United States does not fit the caricature of absolute decline. Indeed, for all the fashionable predictions of China, India, or Brazil surpassing the United States in the next decades, the greater threats may come from modern barbarians and nonstate actors. In an information-based world of cyber insecurity, power diffusion may be a greater threat than power transition. More things are happening outside the control of even the most powerful states.

States will remain the dominant actors on the world stage, but they will find the stage far more crowded and difficult to control. A much larger part of the population both within and among countries has access to the power that comes from information. Governments have always worried about the flow and control of information, and the current period is not the first to be strongly affected by dramatic changes in information technology. Information revolutions are not new—think of Gutenberg and movable type five centuries ago—nor is transnational contagion, nor nonstate actors. What is new—and what we see manifested in the Middle East and elsewhere today— is the speed and reduction in cost of communications and the technological empowerment of a wider range of actors. In addition to the reduction of costs that followed Moore's law in the sixties—halving the cost of computing power approximately every two years—is the growth of an urban middle class with a diminished deference to traditional authority and government.

What this means is that world politics will not be the sole province of governments. As the cost of computing and communication decline, so do barriers to entry. Both individuals and private organizations, ranging from corporations and NGOs to terrorists, are empowered to play direct roles in world politics. The spread of information means that power will be more widely distributed and that informal networks will undercut the monopoly of governmental bureaucracy. The speed of Internet time means all governments have less control over their agendas. Political leaders will enjoy fewer degrees of freedom before they have to respond to events, and then they will have to share the stage with more actors. Some of those actors may be individuals who take it upon themselves to divulge classified information that has been a source of government power.

Today, power in world affairs is distributed in a pattern that resembles a complex three-dimensional chess game. On the top chessboard, military power is largely unipolar, and the United States is likely to remain supreme for some time. But on the middle chessboard, economic power has been multipolar for more than a decade, with the US, Europe, Japan, and China as the major players and others gaining in importance—Europe's economy is larger than America's. The bottom chessboard is the realm of transnational relations that cross borders outside of government control, and it includes nonstate actors as diverse as corporations electronically transferring sums larger than many national budgets at one extreme, and terrorists transferring weapons or hackers threatening cyber security at the other. It also includes new challenges like pandemics and climate change. On this bottom board, power is widely diffused, and it makes no sense to speak of unipolarity, multipolarity, hegemony, empire, or other terms commonly used by academics, politicians, and pundits.

In transnational politics—the bottom chessboard—the information revolution is dramatically reducing the costs of computing and communication. Forty years ago, instantaneous global communication was possible but costly and restricted to governments and corporations. Today, it is virtually free on Skype. In the seventies, the US and the Soviet Union spent billions on secret satellite photographs with a resolution of one meter. Today, anyone can download better pictures from Google Earth for free. In 2001, a nonstate group killed more Americans than the government of Japan killed at Pearl Harbor in 1941. A pandemic spread by birds or travelers on jet aircraft could kill more people than perished in World War I or II. And increasingly, power will be exercised in the diffuse domain of cyber interactions.

In its forty-seventh year, the Munich Security Conference convened a special session on cyber security for the first time, and the president of a small European country told the assembled dignitaries that "this may be the first time, but it will not be the last." Until recently, the issue of cyber security was largely the domain of computer specialists. When the Internet was created forty years ago, this small community was like a virtual village of people who knew each other, and they designed a system with little attention to security. Even the commercial Web is only two decades old, but it has exploded since then, and the burgeoning interdependence has created great opportunities and great vulnerabilities. The largest powers are unlikely to be able to dominate this domain as much as they have others such as sea, air, or space. While they have greater resources, they also have greater vulnerabilities, and at this stage in the development of the technology, offense dominates defense in cyberspace. The United States, Russia, Britain, France, and China have greater capacity than other state and nonstate actors, but it makes little sense to speak of dominance in cyberspace. If anything, dependence on complex cyber systems for support of military and economic activities creates new vulnerabilities in large states that can be exploited by nonstate actors. While governments have the computing power to make use of "big data," so do a number of private corporations as well.

Under the influence of the information revolution and globalization, world politics is changing in a way that means even the largest countries cannot achieve all their international goals acting alone. For example, international financial stability is vital to the prosperity of Americans, but the United States needs the cooperation of China, Europe, and Japan to ensure it. Global climate change will affect the quality of life, but no country can manage the problem alone. And in a world where borders are becoming more porous than ever to everything from drugs to infectious diseases to terrorism, nations must use soft power to develop networks and build institutions to address shared threats and challenges. In this sense, power becomes a positive sum game. It is not enough to think in terms of power *over* others. One must also think in terms of power to accomplish goals, which involves power *with* others. On many transnational issues, empowering others can help us to accomplish our own goals. In this world, networks and connectedness become an important source of relevant power.

In the community of people who think about international security, our tendency to focus on the hard power of coercion and payment alone rather than to include the soft power of attraction and persuasion is outdated. In the US, Congress finds it easier to boost the budget of the Pentagon than the State Department. That bias has been reinforced by the prevailing academic theories. The dominant approach to international affairs has been called "realism," and its lineage stretches back to such great thinkers as Thucydides and Machiavelli. Realism assumes that in the anarchic conditions of world politics, where there is no higher international government authority above states, they must rely on their own devices to preserve their independence, and that when push comes to shove, the *ultima ratio* is the use of force. Realism portrays the world in terms of sovereign states aiming to preserve their security with military force as their ultimate instrument. Thus, war has been a constant aspect of international affairs over the centuries. Realists come in many sizes and shapes, but all tend to argue that global politics is power politics. In this they are right, but some limit their understanding by conceiving of power too narrowly. A pragmatic or common-sense realist takes into account the full spectrum of power resources, including ideas, persuasion, and attraction.

Realism represents the best first cut at portraying some aspects of international relations. But as we have seen, states are no longer the only important actors in global affairs, security is not the only major outcome that they seek, and force is not the only or always the best instrument available to achieve those outcomes. Indeed, these conditions of complex interdependence are typical of relations among advanced postindustrial countries such as the United States, Canada, the European states, Australia, and Japan. Mutual democracy, liberal culture, and a deep network of transnational ties mean that anarchy has very different effects in such contexts than realism predicts.

It is not solely in relations among advanced countries, however, that soft power plays an important role. In an information age, communications strategies become more important, and outcomes are shaped not merely by whose army wins but also by whose story wins. In combating terrorism, for example, it is essential to have a narrative that appeals to the mainstream and prevents their recruitment by the radicals. It was necessary to use hard military force against Osama Bin Laden. We could not attract him, but soft power instruments are necessary to shape the preferences ("win the hearts and minds") of the majority of the population and diminish the flow of new recruits.

Smart power strategies must include an information and communications component. States struggle over the power to define norms, and the framing of issues grows in importance. For instance, while CNN and the BBC framed the issues of the First Gulf War in 1991, by 2003 Al Jazeera played a large role in shaping the narrative in the Iraq War. Similarly, if one thinks of international institutions it makes a difference if economic agendas are set in a Group of 8 with a few invited guests or a Group of 20 equal invitees. China and other governments are spending billions of dollars annually to increase their soft power, but much of a country's soft power is generated by its civil society and nonstate actors. Government propaganda is generally mistrusted and rarely an effective source of lasting soft power.

If power is the ability to affect others to get the outcomes we want, we will have to realize the importance of exercising power *with* others as well as the traditional power *over* others. Smart power strategies will require combining the hard power of coercion and payment with the soft power of attraction and persuasion. It will no longer be adequate to define a "great power" as a country able to prevail in war (in the words of the famous Oxford historian A. J. P. Taylor). In an information age, success will depend not only on whose army wins but also on whose narrative wins. In 2012, the National Intelligence Council (which I once headed) issued an estimate of the condition of world politics in 2030. It will not be a "post-American world" or a "G-Zero world." The United States will still have more power than other countries, but it will have to contend with the "rise of the rest"—both state and nonstate actors—and will have to form networks and institutions to deal with the security problems it will face. Many political leaders and scholars have not yet adjusted to this greater complexity of power in the twenty-first century, yet for all countries that will be the key to creating smart power strategies.

Joseph S. Nye, Jr., is University Distinguished Service Professor at Harvard and the author most recently of Presidential Leadership and the Creation of the American Era *(Princeton: Princeton University Press, 2013).*

Notes

1   Moisés Naím, *The End of Power: From Boardrooms to Battlefields and Churches to States, Why Being in Charge Isn't What It Used to Be* (New York: Basic Books, 2013); Nicco Mele, *The End of Big: How the Internet Makes David the New Goliath* (New York: St. Martin's Press, 2013); Ian Bremmer, *Every Nation for Itself: Winners and Losers in a G-Zero World* (New York: Portfolio, 2012).

Atlanticism in the Era of Globalization

Strobe Talbott

In the last century, when the term "Atlanticism" came into common usage, it was associated with the global and seemingly permanent challenge of keeping at bay a giant adversary sprawled across the Eurasian landmass—from Vilnius on the Baltic to Vladivostok on the Pacific. Why, then, make the Atlantic the focal point of grand strategy? And why the Greek suffix, suggesting not a military doctrine but a school of thought and a code of behavior? In fact, though, that was precisely what the word was meant to evoke: a philosophy of cooperation that would bind the fates of two continents on either side of the world's second largest ocean. Allies in North America and Western Europe felt close enough to nickname the three thousand miles of open water between them "the pond." Hence, Atlanticism was key to the vocabulary, mission, and vision of the founders of the *Internationale Wehrkunde-Begegnung*.

Fifty years later, the concept and goals of Atlanticism are still valid, but they have taken on new dimensions, including expanded geographical scope. "Western Europe" has extended eastward, and North America is an increasingly integrated economic space that includes Mexico in a way that was unforeseen in the sixties.

▲
Strobe Talbott (right) with Caroline Atkinson and Wolfgang Ischinger
at the 2013 MSC Core Group Meeting in Washington

The Munich conference originally focused on "defense studies" (*Wehrkunde*), thus giving priority to the overarching task of the era. What John F. Kennedy called "the long twilight struggle" with the Soviet Union was dangerous and preoccupying to a degree without precedent, and, we can only hope, never to be repeated. But deterring and preparing to defend against a monolithic enemy every hour of every day for decades was, in its own way, starkly simple and ultimately effective: a suicide pact between two parties who were determined to survive.

The menace to peace today is less apocalyptic but kaleidoscopically more complex and diffuse, therefore harder to thwart. The principal sources of danger today are rogue states and nonstate actors, often in cahoots with each other. Attacks can come literally out of the blue. Many of the perpetrators are determined to acquire weapons of mass destruction and are already deploying warriors who have made a suicide pact very different from the one that kept the nuclear peace between the superpowers.

It was against that backdrop that the organizers of the Munich conference eventually dropped *Wehrkunde* from its name and substituted *Sicherheitspolitik,* meaning "security policy." The German word goes well beyond the strictly martial connotation of the one it replaced. The name change reflected a game change. As the twentieth century gave way to the twenty-first, it became apparent that the danger to international peace and order would increasingly come not from the build-up of military-industrial complexes but from the breakdown of societies; not from expansionist policies of national governments but from sectarian and tribal strife within nations; not from grand strategies hatched in capitals but from conflicts in back alleys and hinterlands that spread across borders, destabilize neighboring countries, and turn civil wars into regional ones; not from strong states but weak ones.

The converse is equally apparent: more than ever before, strong states—what have often been called the major powers—have the capacity and the incentive to buttress international peace and order. But to do so, they must act in concert with one another. Collective security is the only real security. Powerful states must also define strength and security in a way that protects and advances their citizens' political, legal, and civil liberties, as well as guarantees of social justice and economic opportunity. Otherwise, they will discover, to their peril, that they are not as strong as they thought.

Atlanticism has always included a commitment to these precepts. It is implicit in the idea of a compact based on shared values as well as shared interests. But the fulfillment of that commitment depends on the efficacy with which the governments involved adhere to those values in practice through representative democracy, separation of powers, checks and balances, rule of law, and accountability of public officials to their constituents. It also depends on the extent to which the community as a whole enforces those principles and abides by them in its own institutions. In short, Atlanticism today is as much about how the participating nations govern themselves individually and collectively as it is about how they defend themselves against external enemies.

Finally, Atlanticism requires a shared perception of threats and a reasonable sharing of burdens. By and large, the United States and Europe have managed to accomplish this, despite challenges emanating from the end of the Cold War and 9/11. But new challenges loom, including fiscal pressures on both sides of the Atlantic and weariness over the toll of wars in Iraq and Afghanistan.

The Crisis

Every system of governance has an ideological dimension—a set of ideas that guides the formulation and enforcement of rights and rules, ends and means. The Cold War was an ideological contest as well as a geopolitical one. Competing "isms" were the object of passionate intellectual and political debate when *Wehrkunde* was founded in 1963 and for decades afterward. Atlanticism took on the connotation of both a synonym for a community of values *and* an antonym of communism.[1]

But that globe-spanning contest has passed into history. For many, the very word "ideology" has a somewhat anachronistic ring to it now that the world is no longer a Manichean battlefield.[2] Communist totalitarianism is dead in what used to be the Soviet empire; and in China, Maoism has morphed into state capitalism.

As for the winning ideology in the Cold War—democratic capitalism— it is very much alive. However, it is not healthy. Nor, for that matter, is any method of national administration. In most of the 196 countries on earth, the powers that be—whether democratic or authoritarian, capitalist or socialist, republican or monarchial, long-established or recently installed, civilian or military, secularist or theocratic, Confucian or Western—have discovered, often rudely, that they have less power at their disposal and more trouble with their citizens than they had realized. There is, in short, a worldwide decline of confidence in governance—in the ability of governments to get things done to the satisfaction of their own citizens and to the advancement of global goods.

This nearly universal contagion of underperforming national authority and rising public expectations is replete with ironies, starting with its precipitating event: a financial debacle in the world's most successful capitalist economy, combined with a prolonged seizure of political dysfunction in the birthplace of modern democracy and a decline in the influence of the mightiest country on earth—not to mention the country that, through economic rescue and military protection, made Atlanticism possible.

The disaster of 2008 first shook the American economy, damaging if not destroying banks, investment houses, and insurance companies that were thought to be too big to fail. But it quickly generated political tremors. The crash gave rise to two populist movements that were similar in their anti-establishment thrust but at opposite ends of the political spectrum. The Tea Party is ultra-libertarian, while the loosely defined agenda of the Occupy Movement—which is actually more of a primal scream than an articulated program—gestures in the direction of more regulation of capitalism.

Another difference is that the Tea Party was conceived and has remained, like its eighteenth-century namesake, a uniquely American phenomenon. It is also a party-within-a-party. Its members who won seats as Republicans in the US Congress have polarized the legislative branch of government to the point of near-paralysis.

The Occupy Movement, by contrast, has had little effect in the United States other than amplifying rhetorical complaints against income inequality. But largely because of its emotive, all-purpose character, it went viral, spawning similar movements in more than ninety cities on nearly every continent within a month of its birth in New York in September 2011.

In July 2013, massive anti-austerity protests took place in a number of major European cities. In China, there have been an estimated 100,000 protests annually, often targeted against flagrant—and in the case of shoddy school construction, sometimes fatal—cases of official ineptitude and corruption. India has experienced a wave of backlashes against endemic bribery and law-enforcement agencies' indifference (or worse) toward violence against women. In Israel, more than half a million people—10 percent of the adult population—joined rallies and tent cities for over six weeks of demonstrations against the soaring cost of living and lack of affordable housing. In Russia, tens of thousands defied the bitter cold and the threat of a crackdown by the authorities to challenge Kremlin-orchestrated election fraud and Vladimir Putin's consolidation of one-man rule. Last year, Turkey was convulsed by public rage that was, at first, directed at the unpopular plan to pave over an oasis of greenery in central Istanbul. Brazil's summer of discontent was triggered by urban dwellers' frustration with inadequate city services.

The two biggest national upheavals in the world last year, in Syria and Egypt, were not just political and sectarian in origin—they were fueled by citizens seething against their government's failure to govern competently. The Syrian civil war had roots in the Assad regime's feckless response to a severe drought, and the meltdown of Egypt's first democratically elected government was initially caused not just by the animosity between secularists and Islamists but also by power outages, gasoline shortages, and a collapse of basic services.

For all their differences, these and other cases had something in common. Throughout modern history, there has often been a correlation between downturns in the economy and spikes—if not sustained outbreaks—of civic disapproval of governments. While economic distress can sometimes rouse citizens to demand more accountability from their governments, it all too often feeds the politics of fear, anger, and irrationality, sometimes leading to the adoption of official policies that reflect those qualities.

There have been signs of precisely that cause-and-effect worldwide over the last few years. During decades of global growth, many countries gave the impression of being effectively managed or at least firmly controlled. The 2008 financial and economic earthquake, with its epicenter on Wall Street, exposed weaknesses below the surface of these societies and polities. As a result, whole systems of governance were strained and in some instances shattered.

While the shockwave radiated in all directions, it swept like a tsunami across the Atlantic and hit Europe triply hard, shaking national economies, pan-European institutions, and international confidence in Europe's effort to reinvent how nations govern themselves in the era of globalization.

Therein lies another irony: during the past five years, Europe has paid a heavy price for its success over the previous six decades in pioneering not just an innovation but a transformation in governance that can still, if it survives its current crisis, benefit the whole world.

The Project

The story of Europe—and of the Atlantic community—over the past hundred years is both a cautionary tale and an inspirational one. It is germane in both respects to the complexities confronting the world today.

In the first half of the twentieth century, Europe was the bloodiest region of all time and a source of woe for the entire planet. Its politicians and generals ignited two global conflagrations; its ideologues bred two predatory totalitarian regimes, one of which perpetrated the Great Terror and the other a massive genocide. As Margaret MacMillan has put it, "Europe laid waste to itself."[3]

Then it redeemed itself. It did so thanks to the three generations of European leaders since the end of World War II who have, step by careful step, pooled authority, concerted policies, and institutionalized consensus-based decision-making on issues that can best be managed collectively. They called their undertaking the European Project, a phrase that compared what they were doing to designing and building permanent structures alongside those that governed individual states. To this end, they adopted some key aspects of federalism, a concept originally and still primarily applied to a single state. The result was, up until a few years ago, almost universally regarded as a bold, skillful, and promising experiment in multiple states governing themselves simultaneously on the national and supranational levels, an achievement in its own right and a precedent and example for other regions.

The European Union not only serves as a bulwark against any repetition of the horrors perpetrated between 1914 and 1945—it has distilled and updated the best in European history and culture. Europe, while scarred by countless depredations over the millennia, was also home to Periclean Greece, Roman law, the Renaissance, the theory of federalism as conceived by Dante and elaborated by Hume, the Hanseatic "confraternity of trade," the Age of Reason, and the Kantian vision of a democratic peace. In the late eighteenth century, European civilization had bred a new polity in the New World—not just a nation-state but an idea-state, animated by Classical and Enlightenment values.

Europe has also seized the best of modernity and made a virtue of globalization—a term that was invented by Europeans to describe an economic condition with profound political consequences.

The interaction of nations is an ever-thickening skein of transactions, some of them virtually instantaneous and many unobstructed by physical distance or national boundaries. The challenge for governments is to facilitate, and at the same time regulate, the movement of goods, services, money, information, ideas, and people across borders. While sovereignty remains a sacred principle in international law, the reality of international life honors it more in the breach than in the observance; the de facto interdependence of nation-states coexists with, and sometimes trumps, their de jure independence. For the leaders of countries whose national rivalries had triggered two world wars, interdependence is not just a fact to get used to—it is a godsend, to be exploited as the basis for the iterative process that has led to the formation of the European Union.

That process was, from the beginning, economic in its means and political in its purpose. But the economic means had to work in their own right in order to achieve the political purpose: economic integration would encourage political integration, not the other way around.

This strategy was largely conceived and successfully advocated by two Frenchmen, Jean Monnet and Robert Schuman. Their method was to create economic facts on the ground that would incentivize politicians of the nation-state to think, act, and govern on the level of pan-European structures.

In 1951, the Treaty of Paris lowered duties and restrictions between France and Germany on the coal that fired factories and the steel they manufactured, spurring economic cooperation between the two long-time political antagonists, who were soon joined by Italy, Belgium, Luxembourg, and the Netherlands.

As the fifties unfolded, customs unions among the Nordic and Benelux countries vindicated the Monnet-Schuman method, leading to the Treaty of Rome's formation of the European Economic Community and the empowerment of its trade commissioner to negotiate tariffs on behalf of all members.

The EEC was a common market designed, over time, to become a common political space. That finally happened nearly four decades later, in 1992, with the Treaty of Maastricht, which strengthened existing institutions, such as the European Parliament and Court of Justice, and established a Common Foreign and Security Policy.

From the beginning, the European Project was an Atlanticist one as well. It had been, even before either of those terms had been coined. Woodrow Wilson sent doughboys "Over There" to end World War I, and he went to Versailles to take charge of the peace conference, redraw the map of Europe, and, he hoped, usher in an era of permanent peace.

Three decades later, after World War II, Monnet and Schuman were the fathers of a renewed attempt to turn Europe into a zone of prosperity and peace, but Harry Truman and his two secretaries of state, George Marshall and Dean Acheson, were the godfathers. The European Recovery Plan that Marshall proposed in 1947 underscored the crucial importance of economic buoyancy for political stability in general and the bolstering of democracy in particular.

In addition to a massive infusion of American dollars, helping Europe rebuild after a decade of devastation required US protection from the new bloc of nations conquered by a hostile and predatory Soviet Union. The self-congratulatory cliché about NATO being the most successful alliance in history has the virtue of being true. During the Cold War, it achieved its goal of deterring Soviet aggression, and—while there were some close shaves, notably during crises over Berlin—it did so without firing a shot.

By keeping the enemy in check at a price that its European members could afford, NATO fostered an environment in which Europe could thrive economically and politically. In addition to open markets, the project was based on a commitment to open societies. From the outset, only genuine democracies were eligible for membership in the treaty-based community as it expanded. In 1979, that criterion was made explicit through a declaration that "the principles of pluralist democracy and respect for human rights form part of the common heritage of the peoples of the States brought together in the European Communities and are therefore essential elements of membership of the said Communities."[4]

NATO was less choosy. Turkey, a member since 1952, experienced several episodes of military government. The alliance operated on a variant of the principle that the enemies of its enemies could be members, even if they were right-wing dictatorships like those of Antonio Salazar's Portugal and Greece after the 1967 colonels' coup. Still, there was relief and approval on both sides of the Atlantic when those nations dismantled their military regimes in the seventies and, in the following decade, joined the European Economic Community.[5]

NATO was already an alliance of democracies when the Berlin Wall, the Iron Curtain, the Soviet Union, and the Warsaw Pact came tumbling down in the heady period between 1989 and 1991. The compatibility of their membership criteria allowed NATO and the EU to undertake the joint venture of expanding eastward.

NATO enlargement, while undertaken during the Clinton administration, owed its basic logic to George H. W. Bush. His vision of "a Europe whole and free" could not be fulfilled unless Europe was also safe. That condition could not be met if the nations liberated from Soviet domination were left in geopolitical limbo.

It was the first President Bush who took the initial step in expanding NATO by supporting the absorption of East Germany into a Federal Republic that remained in the alliance. The German chancellor at the time, Helmut Kohl, became convinced that NATO must move further east, in particular to Poland, so that Germany would no longer be the easternmost nation of the political West, a position that he felt had contributed to his country's fraught history.

NATO began the formal process of opening its door to what had been Soviet bloc countries in 1997, thereby literally securing the ground for the EU's own accession process the following year. It is highly unlikely that the

EU would have been able to expand were it not for the extension eastward of the transatlantic defense umbrella. NATO gave former Soviet bloc countries confidence that their security would be protected as members of the European Union.

NATO and the EU became the twin foundations for a network of some seventeen organizations that brought together more than fifty countries that had been adversaries or nonaligned during the Cold War.[6] The area they occupied stretched west-to-east all the way across North America, the Atlantic, and Eurasia—as was often said, from Vancouver to Vladivostok.

Some endeavors, like the Partnership for Peace, were dedicated to political security cooperation, others to cross-border commerce. The cultivation of these interlocking ventures was dubbed "the Hanseatic strategy." It was the brainchild of the late Ronald Asmus, who had been recruited by the State Department to work on European integration and NATO enlargement. The evocation of a commercial arrangement five hundred years in the past had particular resonance for him as an historian as well as a strategist, since the Hanseatic League had included Immanuel Kant's hometown of Königsberg (now the Russian city of Kaliningrad) and Novgorod.

Kant had been thinking globally, and so was Asmus. The web of institutions with different functions but overlapping memberships (sometimes known as "variable geometry") was intended to serve as a model for other regions—and so it has, particularly the Organization for Security and Cooperation in Europe. Statesmen on the Pacific Rim have, for decades, been talking about an "Asian OSCE." The Association of Southeast Asian Nations and its Regional Forum are a step in that direction. Leaders elsewhere have had the European precedent in mind in their efforts to increase the efficacy of the African Union, the Southern African Development Cooperation Conference, the South Asian Association for Regional Cooperation, the Organization of American States, and subregional bodies like Mercosur and the Andean Pact. "Our mirror will be the European Union, with all its institutions," remarked Eduardo Duhalde, a former president of Argentina and the head representative of Mercosur.[7]

A distinguishing feature of Atlanticism has always been a conscious effort to make the most of the synergy between hard and soft power—that is, the power to coerce and the power to persuade and lead by example.

There is, however, a paradox in the way that NATO has used its hard power. During the forty-year standoff with the Warsaw Pact, the Western alliance was prepared to wage World War III. Yet because that threat deterred and contained the Soviet Union, NATO never had to fire a shot in anger. Since the end of the Cold War, the alliance has turned much of its energy to a soft version of hard power by fostering partnership and collaboration in the realm of security and peacekeeping with former enemies. Yet during that same period, NATO has gone into combat four times. Its interventions in Bosnia and Kosovo in the nineties brought an end to genocide and ethnic cleansing. Both conflicts were ended with the active diplomatic assistance of Russia under the presidency of Boris Yeltsin.

Having already expanded its membership, post-Cold War NATO extended its military reach "out of area," notably in Afghanistan and Libya. In the latter case, it enlisted support from the armed forces of four Arab countries (the United Arab Emirates, Qatar, Jordan, and Morocco). NATO has initiated coordination and cooperation with four US Pacific allies: Japan, the Republic of Korea, Australia and New Zealand.

In 2008, Victoria Nuland, then US permanent representative to the North Atlantic Council (NAC), publicly advocated further steps to make the alliance "the core of a global security community of democracies that work together in common purpose."[8] (Last year, she was nominated by President Obama and confirmed by the Senate as assistant secretary of state for Europe.)

While NATO has always relied on the overwhelming military predominance and political authority of the United States, the end of the Cold War created the conditions for Europeans to demonstrate leadership of their own. Through much of the nineties and the first decade of the twenty-first century, Javier Solana personified the ethos of the post-Cold War collaboration among NATO, the EU, and the successor states of the former Soviet Union. In 1995, during the Balkan crises, Solana replaced Willy Claes as secretary general of NATO when the alliance was, for the first time, at war. Yet while chairing the NAC throughout the seventy-eight-day bombing of Serbia, he simultaneously worked with the Russians and Martti Ahtisaari, the president of Finland, which held the presidency of the EU, to make peace on NATO's terms. Solana was also instrumental in expanding NATO and, in his subsequent capacity as Europe's high representative for common foreign and security policy, negotiated vigorously with the Iranian government over its nuclear program and with all the parties to the Middle East conflict.

While the danger of a major war can never be written off, it has been supplanted by climate change as the single greatest threat to the planet. Here too, Europe has distinguished itself. In 2005, the EU adopted a cap-and-trade scheme designed to limit, and over time reduce, the carbon footprint of a grouping of nations whose economy was then, and remains, approximately the same size as that of the United States—a country that has so far failed abysmally in passing national legislation to control carbon emissions.

More generally, the very existence, not to mention the efficacy, of the EU's supranational structures and rules has had a salutary influence on manufacturing and commercial practices in other regions. Since the EU's internal market is the largest in the world, companies everywhere have tended to adopt European regulatory standards for their own goods, even for those intended for markets with lower standards. Anu Bradford, a professor of law at Columbia University, has termed this phenomenon "the Brussels effect."[9]

Even while the EU was on a roll, "deepening and broadening" integration, it suffered setbacks and deficiencies, notably including persistent complaints about a "democracy deficit," inefficiencies and inequities in carbon trading, and impatience among European publics with the expensive bureaucracy in Brussels and the labyrinthine regulations that emanated from it. The EU also made a colossal mistake over and over—pretending to encourage Turkey's accession to the Union while actually, and all too effectively, erecting barriers to that prospect.

Still, up until the last months of 2008, the European Project seemed, as a general proposition and with every passing year, to solidify its progress and promise as the greatest experiment in transnational governance ever undertaken.

The Misstep

Then came the pterodactyl-sized black swan of that fall. The Lehman Brothers crash and all that ensued cast a shadow over the Maastricht Treaty, which had been signed with much fanfare sixteen years before.

Maastricht set the criteria for EU member states to enter the European Economic and Monetary Union, thereby introducing a single currency in three stages that would culminate, seven years later, when the euro fully replaced local currencies. But not all EU member states accepted the new currency; the United Kingdom and Denmark negotiated formal opt-outs of the eurozone, and Sweden, through a series of parliamentary maneuvers, has so far avoided joining.

A common currency had long been regarded as the linchpin in consolidating the European Project. Monetary union, it was believed, would serve as a predicate and incentive for a more complete political union. In theory, the pan-Europeanists, led by Jacques Delors, the president of the European Commission until 1995, were following the Monnet-Schuman strategy. They hoped that the creation of the euro would set off a benevolent chain reaction:

making a common currency work would require a more coordinated fiscal policy, a greater role for the European Central Bank and the European Commission, and more coordination in the banking and financial sectors. It was hoped that these needs would lead to "more Europe" in the political space and a greater role for the European Parliament, which would bolster the democratic legitimacy of integration.

However, in practice—and certainly in consequence—for the first time in the evolution of the EU, the political cart was too heavy for the economic horse to pull. Many economists said as much at the time. Europe, they argued, should have waited until it had a single fiscal policy and a single treasury before it established a single currency.[10]

Since neither of those preconditions had been established at Maastricht, the creation of the euro was, at best, an act of faith and a risky gamble and, at worst, a serious misstep on the path to integration.

On New Year's Day 1999, the euro replaced the franc, lira, peso, deutschmark, and other currencies of the seventeen EU member states. For nine years, the bet seemed to be paying off. There was even speculation, including by Delors, that the euro would replace the dollar as the world's preferred reserve currency.

But the eurozone could maintain the appearance of structural viability only as long as its southern tier—despite large public deficits in countries such as Greece and real estate bubbles in others such as Spain—was buoyed by the rising tide of global growth. Then came a rude reminder, in 2008 and its aftermath, that interdependence globalizes damage and danger as well as growth and prosperity.

Much as the Great Depression had exacerbated the unintended economic consequences of the Peace of Versailles, the Great Recession of 2008—which technically ended in the United States a year later but continued for five years in the eurozone—exposed a fault in the European Monetary Union, perhaps hastening and worsening a crisis that many experts believe was inevitable. Negative growth and rampant unemployment devastated the nations of the south, leading Greece and Portugal to negotiate formal bailouts and Spain and Italy to implement strong austerity-oriented policies. Portuguese, Spaniards, Italians, and Greeks chafed at the demands by Germany and other northern European countries whose own people and governments reciprocated by reproaching the south for its profligacy.

At a time when the cohesion of the EU was in jeopardy, the federal ties within individual states were strained. Faltering national economies activated a resurgence of ethnically, religiously, and linguistically driven centrifugal forces. Parliamentary elections in Catalonia in late 2012 produced a majority for parties seeking independence from Spain. In the United Kingdom, Prime Minister David Cameron agreed to a referendum on Scottish independence that would take place in 2014.

Separatism in outlying regions was accompanied by the manifestations of nativism and nationalism in capitals. In an interview with *Der Spiegel* in March 2013, Jean-Claude Juncker, the prime minister of Luxembourg and a former president of the Eurogroup (a conclave of eurozone finance ministers), saw in some of the anti-European and anti-immigrant populism a reminder of thirties fascism—perhaps the single most vivid and vicious example of the connection between a bad economy and bad politics. "The demons haven't been banished," said Juncker. "They are merely sleeping." Worse, he implied, they were stirring.[11]

In the course of a few years, the integrative process that had been the best news of the twentieth century seemed in danger of going into reverse. A specter was haunting the EU—the specter of disintegration. Speaking for many friends of the European Project around the world, Kevin Rudd, then Australian foreign minister, said at the Munich Security Conference in 2012: "The danger that I see is Europe progressively becoming so introspective and so preoccupied with its internal problems on the economy and on the eurozone in particular that Europe runs the risk of talking itself into an early economic and therefore globally political grave."

The Revival

As 2013 drew to a close, many feared for the EU's survival, while some longtime eurosceptics openly hoped for its demise—an outcome that would be profound and protracted bad news not just for Europe but for the entire international community.

There is nothing preordained about that outcome. In fact, there were signs of resilience to counterbalance the pessimism and the naysaying. On the all-important economic front, several newcomers have weathered the storm better than longtime members of the transatlantic community. In 2012, the Polish economy grew by 1.9 percent while the Slovakian economy grew by 2 percent, and the three Baltic economies grew by over 3 percent— that is, at rates ahead of the United States, not to mention the eleven EU member states that had negative or nearly flat growth.

Moreover, EU manufacturing standards continue to exert a gravitational pull toward a worldwide acceptance of commercial and regulatory best practices. According to Mark Leonard, the director of the European Council on

Foreign Relations, this is evidence that the region still has a form of hard power in its economic might.[12]

So the "Brussels effect" has, so far, survived the recession, and not just in the economic realm. In the eyes of former East Bloc countries still outside NATO and the EU, prospective membership remains an incentive to develop democratic institutions, nurture open societies, respect national minorities, and reconcile disputes with their neighbors. For example, Kosovo's and Serbia's aspirations to join the EU helped Catherine Ashton, Solana's successor as EU foreign policy chief, forge an agreement between the two nations. She was able to succeed largely because she had something valuable to offer: three days after the agreement was signed, the European Commission recommended to EU national governments that Serbia be given a date to begin membership talks. The magnetism of prospective membership was still a force for good governance inside countries and accommodation among them.

If the EU can build on these areas of resilience, remediate its structural weaknesses, and shake off its doldrums, it will be able to reclaim its leadership role in reinforcing the positive dynamics of globalization. The restoration of Europe as a robust market for imports from other regions and a vigorous exporter of its own products would revitalize global trade; and rebuilding public support for the premise and goals of the EU would enable its leaders—who have been on the political defensive within their own countries—to turn outward again, concerting their diplomatic influence on the world stage.

The prerequisite for that to happen is to get the economics of integration right, first and foremost by repairing the defects in the euro. That means channeling Monnet and Schuman's guiding principle that pan-European political structures must be aligned to the realities—and differences—of national economies. The challenge will be to reconcile the diverging nature of what various members are willing to accept, with some ready to move forward with greater pooling of sovereignty and political integration, while others remain strongly opposed.

A proposal that has found support among both political leaders and influential economists who think about Europe's future would strengthen attempts to give existing institutions, particularly the European Commission, the power to require national governments to cut their deficits and then to monitor and enforce progress in that direction. That plan has the potential to mitigate North/South divisiveness within Europe, while maintaining a common currency and advancing the goal of an all-inclusive monetary union.

It is also important that Europe regain the high ground that it had attained in 2005 in meeting the challenge of climate change. Since then, the EU has slipped backward. That was largely because the recession contributed to a decline in the value of carbon permits, distorting the price signal and leading businesses to lock in investment decisions that failed to ensure meaningful greenhouse gas reductions over time. As the EU recoups its self-confidence and its economic health, it should recommit itself to emissions reductions more stringent than those it adopted in 2005. That would help raise the price of carbon and create expectations of a stronger forward carbon price on which to make investment decisions. It would also set an example—a variation of the Brussels effect—not least because the failure of the EU's cap-and-trade scheme would be a boon for those seeking to block or unwind similar efforts in other countries.

The revival of the EU is more assured if, like its creation, it is part of a transatlantic effort. And once again, wise geoeconomic policies are the key to ensuring geopolitical peace and stability.

The single most important task confronting the twenty-nine nations on both sides of the ocean is the successful negotiation of the Transatlantic Trade and Investment Partnership (TTIP)—an idea that former Secretary Hillary Clinton first floated publicly on behalf of the Obama administration in a speech at Brookings in November 2012. TTIP would be the biggest "bi-regional" trade deal of all time. It would create the largest internal market in the world, with 830 million consumers, and it would liberalize one-third of global trade. A study by the Centre for Economic Policy Research in London estimates that its passage would be worth 119 billion euros per year to the EU and 1.26 trillion dollars per year to the United States.[13] TTIP can go a long way to "reversing the reversal" that resulted from the Great Recession.

Prime Minister David Cameron of the United Kingdom hailed the prospective deal as a "once-in-a-generation prize" that could create two million jobs on both sides of the Atlantic, and the UK's ambassador in Washington, Sir Peter Westmacott, described TTIP as the "Holy Grail" for resuscitating transatlantic economies.[14]

As welcome as official British optimism is on this score, it would be more so if the UK's continuing membership in the EU were a certainty. Instead, Cameron has promised a referendum on the UK's continued membership of the EU before 2017, if the Conservative Party wins the next general election. In 2013, polling showed that 43 percent of Britons wanted to leave the EU, compared to 35 percent who wished to remain members.[15] Fortunately, polls also show that the younger generation in Britain is more European than the older ones.[16]

The US government has signaled, publicly and otherwise, that it is counting on Cameron—and his successor in No. 10 Downing Street—to keep anti-EU forces in the UK Parliament from prevailing. Otherwise, the relationship between the United States and the United Kingdom would be somewhat less special. In May 2013, in a joint press conference with Cameron in Washington, President Obama made that point, stressing that "our capacity to partner with a United Kingdom that is active, robust, outward-looking, and engaged with the world is hugely important to our own interests as well as the world. And I think the UK's participation in the EU is an expression of its influence and its role in the world."[17]

At the same time, however, Obama and, perhaps, his own successor will have their work cut out for them in getting the TTIP approved, given the partisan polarization of Congress. In its remaining years in office, the Obama administration should modify the way it explains and applies the priority it is giving to Asia. In her speech at Brookings, Secretary Clinton stressed, that "our pivot to Asia is not a pivot away from Europe. On the contrary, we want Europe to engage more in Asia along with us, to see the region not only as a market but as a focus of common strategic engagement."[18] That caveat has faded somewhat and needs not just to be emphasized from Washington, but also translated into concrete initiatives.

Linking TTIP to the Trans-Pacific Partnership will be key to Washington's "rebalance" toward the East. That linkage—which might well include a Latin American and Caribbean dimension—would bring with it a level of coordination and collaboration that could blunt the danger of competitive regional free trade areas and preserve the spirit of the World Trade Organization until it can be reenergized. An organic connection between the two communities—one on the littoral zone of the second largest body of water on the planet, the other on the rim of the largest—would solidify the constructive role that Atlanticism will play in a globalized world.

Strobe Talbott is president of the Brookings Institution. He served as US deputy secretary of state from 1994 to 2001.

Notes

1 The concept of Atlanticism, if not the term, predated the Cold War. For example, the values of Atlanticism inspired Clarence K. Streit's 1938 book *Union Now: A Proposal for a Federal Union of the Democracies of the North Atlantic* (New York: Harper & Brothers, 1938).

2 For some, however, ideology is staging a comeback. See, for example, Robert Kagan, *The Return of History and the End of Dreams* (New York: Random House, 2008).

3 Margaret MacMillan, *The War That Ended Peace: The Road to 1914* (New York: Random House, forthcoming 2013).

4 11979H/AVI/COM. Documents Concerning the Accession of the Hellenic Republic to the European Communities, Commission Opinion of 23 May 1979 on the Application for Accession to the European Communities by the Hellenic Republic. Official Journal L 291, 19/11/1979, 3–4.

5 For an explanation of how NATO served the goal of creating a "community of values" even before the end of the Cold War, see Alexandra Gheciu, *NATO in the New Europe* (Stanford: Stanford University Press, 2002), 23: "[The inclusion of countries with undemocratic governments] was a compromise that, as many NATO members pointed out at the time, threatened to undermine the Euro-Atlantic community of liberal democratic values embodied in NATO. As a way to compensate for the increasing importance of the geostrategic dimension of the organization, its decision makers initiated a series of activities meant to contribute to the consolidation of a liberal democratic community throughout the Euro-Atlantic area."

6 They included the Council of the Baltic Sea States, the Central European Free Trade Association, the Treaty on Conventional Armed Forces in Europe, the Council of Europe, the Euro-Atlantic Partnership Council, the Economic and Monetary Union, the Nordic Council, the NATO-Ukraine Commission, the Organization for Security and Cooperation in Europe, Partnership for Peace, the NATO-Russia Council, the Southeastern European Cooperative Initiative, the Barents Euro-Arctic Council, the Stability Pact Agreement, the Southern Europe Defense Ministerial.

7 See "South American Summitry: Fraternity at 3,300 metres," *The Economist*, December 9, 2004, www.economist.com/node/3485922.

8 "Ambassador Nuland Advocates Strengthening NATO's Role," excerpts: iipdigital. usembassy.gov/st/english/article/2007/10/20071024173754dknosille0.493313.html#ix zz2bMqKRzXG. Similar proposals include McCain's League of Democracies, the Princeton Project on National Security's Concert of Democracies, and Ivo Daalder and James Goldgeier's notion of a "Global NATO." For an overview, see Tobias Bunde and Timo Noetzel, "Unavoidable Tensions: The Liberal Path to Global NATO," *Contemporary Security Policy* 31:2 (2010), 295–318.

9 Anu Bradford, "The Brussels Effect," *Northwestern University Law Review* 107:1 (2012): 1–67.

10 While some prominent European economists registered their opposition to the EMU at the time, the most adamant skeptics were Americans, in particular Martin Feldstein, the president of the National Bureau of Economic Research; Barry Eichengreen, Professor of Economics at the University of California, Berkeley; and Lawrence Summers, who occupied the three top jobs in the US Department of Treasury.

11 Interview with Jean-Claude Juncker, *Der Spiegel*, March 11, 2013, English version: www. spiegel.de/international/europe/spiegel-interview-with-luxembourg-prime-minister-juncker-a-888021.html.

12 Europe's Foreign Policy: Emerging from the Crisis, public event at the Brookings Insti-

tution, February 12, 2013, transcript: www.brookings.edu/events/2013/02/12-europe-foreign-policy.

13 Joseph Francois, et al.,"Reducing Transatlantic Barriers to Trade and Investment: An Economic Assessment," *Centre for Economic Policy Research*, March 2013.

14 Irwin M. Seltzer, "USTR Hopes TTIP+TPP = Faster Growth," *The Weekly Standard*, July 13, 2013. www.weeklystandard.com/blogs/ustr-hopes-ttiptpp-faster-growth_7393 22.html.

15 Steven Kellner, "The EU Referendum Paradox," *YouGov*, May 7, 2013, yougov.co.uk/news/2013/05/07/eu-referendum-paradox/

16 Henning Meyer, "New Poll: Young Brits Want To Stay In The EU," *Social Europe Journal*, January 18, 2013. www.social-europe.eu/2013/01/new-poll-young-brits-want-to-stay-in-the-eu/.

17 Remarks by President Obama and Prime Minister Cameron (Speech, Washington, DC, May 13, 2013), White House, www.whitehouse.gov/the-press-office/2013/05/13/remarks-president-obama-and-prime-minister-cameron-united-kingdom-joint-

18 U.S. and Europe: A Revitalized Global Partnership, public event at the Brookings Institution, November 29, 2012, transcript: www.brookings.edu/events/2012/11/29-trans atlantic-clinton

The Future Isn't What It Used to Be

François Heisbourg

Long-standing participants at the Munich Security Conference can be recognized not only by their graying hair (assuming there is any left); they are also prone to referring to the gathering as *Wehrkunde,* an abbreviation of its original name, which translates literally as "military science." During the Cold War, the correlation of forces between the blocs, the specter of World War III, deterrence theory, and NATO's performance as a collective defense pact were the bread and butter of the meetings held under Ewald von Kleist's aegis. Although the end of the Cold War led many to assume that the currency of power was being replaced by the power of currency, the wars of Yugoslav succession, not to mention the First Gulf War and the genocide in Rwanda, reminded us that the use of force was not going to take its leave as easily as all that. Nor were power politics going to be replaced by universal amity.

From Western Dominance to the Diffusion of Power

The Munich conference's second age was going to be no less busy than the *Wehrkunde* phase, minus the Soviet empire and a divided Europe, plus a

▲
Omid Nouripour (right) and François Heisbourg (second from right)
at the MSC's 2013 Future of European Defence Summit in Berlin

world in which the United States enjoyed its unipolar moment, with Western values shaping the global agenda intellectually (à la Fukuyama) and strategically (à la Krauthammer). If conflict and disorder still prevailed (à la Huntington), such violence was an anomaly that Western-inspired *devoir d'ingérence* and subsequently Responsibility to Protect would bring under control. The success of humanitarian intervention in Kosovo, East Timor, and Sierra Leone showed the way. Conversely, the West's failure in Somalia, its absence in Rwanda, and slowness to intervene in Bosnia were counter-examples of the refusal to use force in a timely and decisive manner. Despite occasional differences between the Western allies, there was a basic dominance of the West built around the US pivot. A shattered post-Soviet space and a China that was still exporting less than twenty million Taiwanese offered no counterweight; and although Islamist terrorism was a threat, it was more remote to the Europeans than the waves of Red, Black, or Palestinian terrorism of the Cold War decades.

From 1992 onwards, the West as a whole enjoyed close to a decade of robust economic growth, with Germany stuck in *Reformstau* (reform gridlock) appearing as an exception which some called the "sick man of Europe." This sense of progress was compounded by the West's mastery of the revolution in information technology, springing forth from its Silicon Valley incubators, spinning out its World Wide Web invented near Geneva, exponentially facilitating the access of all to information and knowledge hitherto the preserve of only the mightiest bureaucracies. Despite the post-Cold War shrinkage of NATO's defense spending, this technological leap forward generated a revolution in military affairs in which the West would exercise total battle space dominance through the conduct of network-centric warfare: the great military buzzword factories in the Pentagon were working overtime. More broadly, globalization became a household word, a process denounced by its detractors as yet another manifestation of American hyper-power. In Europe itself, the European Union and NATO borders moved steadily eastward, while the creation of a common currency would give Europe growth and stability: the "eurosclerosis" of the Reagan years was definitely behind us.

The West's Golden Nineties came to a sudden end, first with the hyper-terrorist attacks of 9/11, which heralded an age in which power, including the use of force, is no longer the monopoly of the state, including the most powerful. In some ways, and not solely because of terrorism of mass destruction but also as the state divests the use of force to private actors, and as the larger powers seek to shift front-line duty to lesser players, this is a world that harkens back to the pre-Westphalian age. The other closing episode to the years of the West's post-Cold War ascendancy played itself out in the harsh split occasioned by America's decision to invade Iraq, come what may. The Munich Conference of 2003 was at the epicenter of this drama. None of those who were present then will ever forget the *dialogue de sourds* between a Donald Rumsfeld determined, along with his team, to make what he subsequently called "old Europe" knuckle under his unstoppable will, and a Joschka Fischer pushed to tears at this postmodern version of "Und bist du nicht willig, so brauch ich Gewalt." Nor was the spectacle behind the stage any less dramatic. For my part, I had until then been divided in my own mind on the prospective war in Iraq: it was hardly less legal than our recent and justified intervention in Kosovo; Saddam Hussein was a mass murderer who had used chemical weapons against his own people; and there was the unresolved question of Iraq's chemical and biological capabilities. These considerations were about equally balanced by my concerns about the "day after" in a post-Saddam Iraq. However, the brutality with which my friends (no irony meant here) in the American delegation treated my own hesitations made up my mind to counter the war: when allies are considered as *quantité négligeable* and as it was clear that these people did not have a clue about what to do after the invasion, it was time to leave them and the US to their own misguided devices, putting in effect an end to the American Century.

Less Hegemony, More Disruption

We know what has unfolded during the following ten years. Globalization became truly global, with more Internet users in China and more cell phone owners in Africa than in the US. China became a great power after a two-century eclipse. The BRICS (Brazil, Russia, India, China, and South Africa) became more than a Goldman Sachs acronym, while Russia pulled herself up from the carpet. The West's contribution to the annual growth of gross domestic product currently stands at less than one-quarter of the world's total. Europe as a whole has not yet recovered its pre-2008 GDP, and its defense spending is now less than that of East Asia.

So what will the Munich Security Conference be talking about during the next twenty years?

First, this is a world in which the exercise of Westphalian great power contests for hegemony will become more difficult. Although the state will remain the only permanent full-spectrum actor, its stage is limited by borders that information-technology-enabled players can cross more or less at will. Furthermore, the growing scale of cross-border challenges linked to the disorders of globalization, from epidemics to financial crises, from climate change to cyber security, makes the Westphalian state operating on a stand-alone basis a weakening actor when it comes to responding to such developments. Working with others (state and nonstate actors) and delegation of sovereignty will be increasingly required: yet these developments are emphatically resisted by the neo-Westphalian majority of countries who have been victims of colonial or imperial interference in the past.

If old-style hegemony and stand-alone sovereignty will be less easy to achieve, this is also a world in which the ability to disrupt increases along with the diffusion of power to all and sundry, whether the disruption is active (cyber attacks, for instance) or passive (for example, not accepting international constraints on the emission of greenhouse gasses). This is a world that will be friendly to free riders, obstructionists, and activists.

Nor should these two basic traits—less hegemony, more disruption—be considered as entailing a relaxation of the quest for power. In a post-Westphalian world, new alliances between state and nonstate will emerge, along with the corresponding potential for violence. Indeed, the ease and scale of disruption will lead to a renewed quest for stability from the people at large as well as from the elites. Only powerful entities are well positioned to provide stability through means good or foul. The use of torture, administrative detention, and massive surveillance as publicly accepted responses to the violent disruption caused by the terrorist attacks of 9/11 give us a taste of what this new world may look like.

Demographic change and the accession of China to great power status will be singled out here as key shaping factors of the world during the coming decades, interacting with developments in other regions and combining with growing cross-border challenges.

Demography Is Destiny?

Auguste Comte's aphorism about demography being destiny has to be taken with a grain of salt. Low birth rates or small families do not mechanically lead to a lower propensity to run military risks, as was demonstrated by France's willingness and ability to counter a demographically dynamic German empire on the battlefields of World War I. In the present age, China's or India's massive gender imbalances in favor of male births have not, or not yet, led to military postures markedly more bellicose than those of, for instance, the United States. Japan, with the world's oldest population, is undergoing a patriotic revival, not a retreat.

However, several current demographic trends have demonstrable strategic consequences. First is what demographers and sociologists call the "youth bulge," that is, the massive arrival on the job market of the cohorts born during the population explosion of the previous decades. When the youth bulge emerges at a time of rising economic growth—as it did in postwar Europe or Japan, or in post-Mao China—it sustains and boosts the economy, in what is referred to as the "demographic sweet-spot": well-trained cheap and energetic labor on the one hand, very low dependency ratios and therefore low social welfare costs on the other. Even so, the massive injection of youthful energy will challenge the ruling elites: the 1968 generation in the industrialized countries and the student uprising of 1989 in Tiananmen Square provide examples of this. If the youth bulge surges in the face of an underperforming economy and an unprepared society, the disruption becomes unmanageable. The rapid urbanization of the planet is both a consequence and a cause of the youth bulge's transformational nature. The Arab revolutions bear witness to such a process in which the urbanized, college-trained masses hit a political, social, and economic scene utterly unable to cope with their arrival. Furthermore, the problem has yet to reach its fullest extent, notably in the oil-rich Gulf monarchies. Saudi Arabia, the world's number one oil exporter, is a ticking time bomb in this regard, with its yet-to-be resolved succession problem, its massive youth unemployment, and close to total social and political disenfranchisement of its subjects. In the Gulf states, the youth bulge will interact with another unique factor: the massive (and in the case of the United Arab Emirates, Kuwait, and Qatar, majority) presence of foreign-born populations, whose sheer numbers and place in the local economies make them a permanent fixture. There is no historical precedent of such a combination. Since an energy-independent United States is a priori less likely than before to intervene in the countries of the region, the knock-on effects for oil-dependent Europe and Asia could be severe.

One of the great unknowns is the manner in which demography and economy will combine in sub-Saharan Africa, where the "mother of youth bulges" is building up as the continent's population exceeds that of India. Nigeria's population alone will soon surpass Brazil's, and Ethiopia is already more populated than Germany. In parallel, the economy is growing at more than 5 percent a year overall: although dependency on the export of raw materials remains high in many countries, on average, resource extraction is no longer the prime mover. With information technology, and notably cell phones (including a rapidly rising share of smartphones), reaching a majority of urban and rural households with knock-on effects in terms of literacy enhancement and inclusion in the formal economy, a number of important countries, such as Kenya, Ghana, or Senegal, are now poised on a development path like that of similar Asian countries two or three decades ago. However, rampant insecurity and deprivation in the Sahel, the Horn, and the Great Lakes area weigh heavily on the negative side of the ledger, as does crippling corruption in Nigeria, Africa's demographic pivot. The EU's basic interest will be to focus much more than it has done hitherto on Africa in helping to tilt the balance toward an Asian rather than a Middle Eastern scenario in terms of the youth bulge's consequences.

The ageing of society is the other trend. Over time, this is in most instances the inevitable companion of the youth bulge: European, Japanese, and South Korean baby boomers are now swelling the ranks of the retired, with erstwhile producers and savers becoming a net economic burden. The same process will progressively affect countries which have only recently moved below the replacement threshold of 2 to 2.1 children per woman: most of Latin America, South East Asia, part of the Middle East (Iran, Tunisia), Bangladesh. India, with a fertility rate of 2.4, will probably enter into demographic transition quite soon. China, which no longer experiences natural demographic growth, will enter before 2030 an ageing process of unprecedented scale and brutality, as the large pre-"one-child policy" cohorts retire, while the depleted ranks of the one-child working-age generation will have to bear the corresponding burden.

The effects of what is becoming a global trend are clear enough. Economic growth suffers as the proportion of productive-age people diminishes. A growing share of production will have to be set aside to cater for the needs of the aged (whose numbers also increase as a result of growing life expectancy, which remains even in mature societies at close to three months a year every year since the end of World War II). Ageing countries will be under growing economic pressure to import foreign labor. Within a generation or so, "old" emerging powers (China, Turkey, Brazil, Mexico, Thailand) will see their economic growth rate flatten along lines similar to those of the industrialized world: by then they will have clearly surpassed the latter in terms of economic power, and China's military spending will equal or overtake that of the US. Having "grown old before growing rich" in per capita terms, there will be room for frustration in China and other 'first generation' emerging economies *vis-à-vis* the relatively affluent Westerners. At the same time, a successor generation of emerging powers will rise to prominence, undercutting the labor-cost advantages of the likes of China. Another source of tension will result from the combined "emigration push" of youth-bulge countries and "immigration pull" of ageing countries. When these are in relative synch, this can be managed: Canada and Australia served by the combination of maritime isolation and their historically liberal approach to immigration come to mind. But as is clear in Europe, the US, but also in an affluent Asian country such as Singapore that the process can become highly corrosive domestically and internationally. Close to total locking-in as practiced by Japan avoids the friction, but it does not solve the wider problem: there are probably economic, and possibly social and psychological, limits to what robotization can accomplish for healthcare and household tasks. In the meantime, the "push" of climate-change refugees and of the unemployed youth from underperforming youth-bulge countries will place the ageing countries of the West and of the recently emerged powers under increasing pressure: the EU's *limes* at Ceuta and Melilla, and the American-Mexican borders are harbingers of things to come.

A Place in the Sun: China, the West, and the Rest

Historians of the future will marvel at the simplicity, wisdom, and effectiveness of Deng Xiao Ping's decision to act on the classical Chinese precept "conceal brilliance, cultivate obscurity" after China's last war—its bloody and inconclusive attempt to "teach a lesson" to Vietnam in 1979. During the following thirty years, China acted as a status quo power with a low-profile, essentially reactive, foreign policy, focusing relentlessly on its economic development. Foreign investment flowed into a rapidly reforming country seen as basically unthreatening: only when the status of Taiwan came into play did China show her claws. When massive repression was used to quell the student demonstrations in Tiananmen Square, the outside world protested and took limited economic countermeasures (for example, the EU arms embargo, the US annual renewal of trade relations), but in the absence of a Chinese strategic threat the West refrained from shutting China out from the process of globalization. Not only was Deng's policy effective in its stated goal of "aiming to do something big," but it also provided a conveniently clear lodestone to the numerous central and provincial agencies involved in the production of foreign, security, and defense policy.

The problem is that this very success in transforming China into a superpower also makes Deng's policy inapplicable: concealing brilliance and cultivating obscurity are no longer tenable options.

This became evident during the closing years of Hu Jintao's leadership. China's posture *vis-à-vis* the opposing territorial and maritime claims in the South China Sea, the world's busiest maritime space, appeared less as a product of a given policy than the result of the competing actions of the "nine dragons"—the various state and provincial agencies militarily and administratively present in the area. Interagency incoherence was also apparent in the handling of the situation in the Korean Peninsula. With the leadership change under Xi Jin Ping, Beijing has the opportunity as well as the motive to formulate a post-Deng foreign and security policy. Although there are obvious differences between modern China's position in a globalized world and the post-unification rise of Wilhelminian Germany, there are elements of analogy. In both cases, a "new" great power emerges (or reemerges) on a world stage in which rules and practices had already been set by others. In both cases, the economy is export-driven in the framework of a financially and commercially interdependent world economy. And in each case, there was an objective as well as a subjective need to define the country's foreign and security positioning—hence "the place in the sun" allusion.

For Wilhelm II, the choice, as it appears in retrospect, was basically between a European-centric positioning, exemplified by Chancellor Bismarck, and a global approach. For China, the options appear to be more numerous, at least seen from close-up. Elements of each option are practiced in the real world—what remains to be decided is where the center of gravity will lie:

- A regionally focused remake of the Middle Kingdom, as practiced in the management of the South China Sea claims or the military emphasis on the ability to project force to the first and second "chain of Pacific islands."
- A "Rest" versus the West posture, with strong South-South solidarity toward the satisfied countries of the West and its allies. China's handling of climate change issues is an example of this.
- A UN Security Council /G-20 "responsible shareholder" policy. China was heavily involved via the G-20 in the handling in 2009 of the global financial crisis.
- A G-2 China-US duopoly: although disowned both in Washington and Beijing as a policy, the US pivot to Asia and China's reaction thereto make this a real option, whether cooperative or adversarial (or both).
- A global influence-and-power projection option, with strategic positions being built up in the Indian Ocean space, including the "collar of pearls" concept (not a Chinese expression, though) in a multipolar world.

The manner in which Beijing will articulate its basic choices, or absence thereof (unpredictable opportunism flowing from a weak political power center is not entirely excluded), will in turn depend primarily on domestic factors and secondarily on external considerations. One thing that has not changed with China's restoration to power is the extreme concern of

Chinese leaders toward domestic factors. This has been true since the beginning of China's history as a self-perceived nation: the overriding imperative is to hold together a continent-sized polity of 1.4 billion inhabitants. No foreign policy doctrine will leave that consideration to the side: hence the importance given by Beijing to the question of who sees and does not see the Dalai Lama, although he is a leader without control of a territory, which itself consists of only a few million people readily subjugated by Han China. The fear of "splittism" is deep and takes precedence over the rest. This traditional concern is amplified by the fear of social and political instability. A rapidly rising plugged-in urban middle class can no longer be governed by an old-style communist dictatorship that is mired in the boundless opportunities for corruption opened by the combination of political opacity and economic growth. As a consequence, the Chinese leadership will tend to promote foreign policy decisions that it sees as uniting people and party above and beyond their intrinsic merit. Nationalism and anti-Japanese sentiment are widely espoused by the newly affluent urban middle class. It can be tempting to play to that gallery rather than preach and practice moderation. The manner in which Chinese mainstream media, and particularly the prime time television news, hypes growing Chinese military prowess is a sign of the times, particularly when the Senkaku/Diaoyu Islands issue flares up. This is not a Chinese specificity, historically or geographically, but there is a high risk that a communist party seeking legitimacy will pander dangerously to such sentiment, not unlike what happened in late Wilhelminian Germany.

These remarks imply that the Chinese Communist Party will continue to exercise unfettered political power. Such an assumption may be entirely wrong: but it is the only one we can work with, given the unknowable nature of possible regime change in China. What is clear, though, is that the regime deeply fears massive political change—after all, in the space of a century, China has lived under an emperor, a republic of sorts, asserted warlords, Japanese invasion, and various permutations of communist rule—and that this fear drives foreign and security choices to an exceptional degree.

However, China's actions will also be influenced by the policies of the United States, not only by virtue of America's unique global power status but more directly as a consequence of its strategic role in the Asia-Pacific region at the center of a hub-and-spokes alliance system extending from Japan and Korea to Australia and New Zealand. The US, like China, has to adapt a system devised in the early years of the Cold War to the realities of the Chinese restoration. Two basic models are usually put forward in this respect. The first is an updated form of containment sometimes called "constrainment" to emphasize the differences with the US-Soviet confrontation, with the hubs-and-spokes system morphing into a more integrated NATO-like multilateral security space. This is what the US signaled in 2011 with President Barack Obama's announcement of the pivot to Asia. Although Washington was at pains to emphasize the nonmilitary dimension of the rebalancing, and while the pivot was more symbolic than material, China perceived it as a challenge: not only was the rebalancing often explained to the region through speeches by Secretary of Defense Leon Panetta in a "the medium is the message" situation, but Secretary of State Hillary Clinton herself struck a deliberately assertive stance on the South China Sea claims. At the same time, the countries of the region—South Korea and Japan, but also the Philippines and Vietnam—seized the opportunity to draw the US into a tighter security embrace in the face of China's policies. Thus, the pivot led to China seeking to balance the rebalance. The US is now pivoting away from the pivot, with Secretary of State John Kerry toning down his predecessor's South China Sea rhetoric and Secretary of Defense Chuck Hagel watering down his predecessor's moves toward establishing a strategic relationship with Vietnam, China's southernmost neighbor. In a softer mode, the US is also using its soft power to maintain its regional position while operating as the global strategic pivot in the face of China's rise. The parallel transpacific (TPP) and transatlantic (TTIP) trade and investment negotiations are seen in that light in Beijing.

The other model, formalized by the Australian analyst Rory Metcalf, would be an attempt to create a concert of nations system in East Asia, akin to that of nineteenth-century Europe. The difficulty here lies both in the concept itself, which does not appear to figure in China's intellectual repertoire nor in the US's vision of its alliance relations, and in the practicalities: in Europe, large powers with small or nonexistent colonial empires (Russia, German, Austria-Hungary) coexisted with large (Britain, France, Italy) and small (Belgium, the Netherlands, Spain, Portugal) with substantial overseas territories or histories; even Sweden and Denmark could make themselves heard in the concert. In East Asia, the strategic reach and alliance relations of the US on the one hand and the massive weight of ascendant China on the other overshadow the strategic scene. A new model remains to be defined.

The same remark applies more broadly to the West as a whole: the countries of the "Rest" are no longer content with responding to norms proposed by the old industrialized world, whether the issues are about forceful intervention notably in the form of Responsibility to Protect or cross-border challenges such as climate change. Since Europe is often in the lead here (*droit d'ingérence,* but also the Kyoto protocol or the creation of the International Criminal Court), and since Europe is both declining economically and incapable of acting as a coherent whole, the Europeans will be even harder pressed than the American superpower to cope with the growing assertiveness of the world's new middle class of nations. The process will be all the more laden with risk as the West responds in a divided way (with the Copenhagen environmental summit of 2009, the Libyan war of 2011, and the Syrian crisis of 2013 as examples), while the emerging states are more effective at blocking Western-originated norms and policies than at promoting their own. Yet emerging powers need agreed norms no less, and arguably more, than the *vieux riches* of the West. Stating the primacy of Westphalian sovereignty is a powerful glue for the BRICS, but it hardly suffices to answer the question of what needs to be done.

The Nuclear Wild Card

This essay began with a reminder of how the Cold War order functioned under the shadow of a potential nuclear holocaust. As complete accounts of the Cuban missile crisis and other nuclear near misses emerge along with new knowledge on accidental atomic close shaves, we realize today that the world danced on the brink of catastrophe even more dangerously than we thought at the time. With the end of the Cold War, the threat of a deliberate or inadvertent World War III has dissipated as a result of the breakup of the USSR and, along with it, the disappearance of the all-consuming contest between East and West. Not only has no similar global confrontation emerged, but overall the leaders of the key powers are neither risk-takers of the Wilhelm II "school" nor ideological bearers of permanent revolution. Even if this is a reversible situation, one should be grateful for small mercies: 2013 actually looks better in that regard than 2003. On the nuclear side, the situation also looks better than we could have expected. The number of operational nuclear warheads has been divided by at least two since the end of the Cold War. Notwithstanding North Korea's ability to detonate nuclear devices and justified concerns about Iran's nuclear program, the number of countries with nuclear arsenals has remained surprisingly stable over the decades. South Africa's nuclear weapons have been destroyed, while the non-Russian successor states of the former USSR have all relinquished the nuclear weapons deployed on their territory. Furthermore, until now, "loose nukes" have been prevented from leaking out of the post-Soviet space as a result of the admirable preventive diplomacy initiated by the US and Russia in the aftermath of the USSR's collapse. Countries as different as Sweden, South Korea, Brazil, and Taiwan have abandoned (or in the case of Iraq and Libya been compelled to abandon) their nuclear weapons programs. The nuclear crises between India and Pakistan have been successfully defused, and none appears to have taken place in recent years.

Yet this is a fragile situation. Runaway nuclear proliferation in the Middle East is entirely possible if the Iranian nuclear issue is not convincingly resolved. North Korea's ability to feed international proliferation networks of the sort run for many years by Pakistan's Dr. A. Q. Khan is substantial and growing, while its nuclear program creates uncertainty about South Korea's (or a united Korea's) and Japan's future nuclear status. The potential for conflict in South Asia remains high.

It would take only one nuclear weapon, used in earnest, to upset the entire international system. Breaking the taboo that has prevailed since the bombing of Hiroshima and Nagasaki in August 1945 would remove a key underpinning of the global order, breaking one of the few elements of positive continuity in global affairs since humanity emerged from the ruins of world war. The fact that since the late forties nuclear weapons have been folded by the UN into a single category of weapons of mass destruction along with chemical and biological weapons creates an additional layer of complexity—and connected obligations. Nuclear nonproliferation, the reaffirmation of the use of any weapon of mass destruction, and nuclear disarmament are essential requirements, not only as abstract goals but as practical aims. North Korea's nuclear adventurism, Iran's nuclear ambitions, the fate of Syria's chemical arsenal unleashed by the government against the inhabitants of its own capital, the 2015 Nuclear Non-Proliferation Treaty review conference are real and present tasks, and there will be others.

However, one threat will definitely not materialize: the Munich Security Conference will not run out of business any time soon.

François Heisbourg is chairman of the council of the Geneva Centre for Security Policy and of the London-based International Institute for Strategic Studies. He is special advisor of the Paris-based Fondation pour la Recherche Stratégique. His career has included positions in government, industry, and academia.

Munich Security Conference 1963–2063: The European Union as a Superpower?

Radosław Sikorski

I have a special affection for 1963—it was the year I made my first public appearance. And that year saw the launch of the distinguished *Wehrkunde* conference series, whose fiftieth anniversary we celebrate.

As 1963 began, the world was tense. Only months earlier, the Cuban missile crisis had seen the United States and the Union of Soviet Socialist Republics close to full-scale conflict. Perhaps this was inevitable: in a frenzied arms race, both countries were testing their nuclear arsenals *every week,* often high in the atmosphere, spreading radioactive debris far and wide. The blast of the USSR's Tsar Bomba over Novaya Zemlya in 1961 far exceeded the combined force of all explosions in World War II.

Elsewhere, Vietnam was slipping into crisis. Nigeria and Kenya gained their independence, and the Organisation of African Unity was founded. In Europe, Cyprus had become independent in 1960 but was not yet a divided island. The core principles of future European integration were still forming. In early 1963, President Charles de Gaulle vetoed the United Kingdom's membership in the European Economic Community, but a few weeks later France and West Germany signed the famous Élysée Treaty and moved to a new level of cooperation and friendship.

In 1963, Washington and Moscow started to change course. In June they inaugurated the famous "hotline" to help manage their disagreements. Then in August, the US, the USSR, and the UK signed the Partial Test Ban Treaty that banned nuclear weapons tests in the atmosphere, outer space, and at sea. China and France continued atmospheric nuclear tests for more than a decade.

When the most optimistic people at the first *Wehrkunde* conference looked to the future, what progress on European and global security issues might they have hoped to see by 2014?

First and foremost, they would have wanted a hugely reduced nuclear threat. That has happened. Under successive international treaties, the number of nuclear weapons has dropped sharply (although thousands of warheads—mainly American and Russian—remain). Nuclear tests have almost come to a halt. Most countries on earth have forsworn nuclear weapons completely.

Second, they would have wanted major steps forward in other arms control areas. That has happened. The 1972 Biological Weapons Convention was the first major disarmament treaty banning the production of an entire category of weapons. The 1993 Chemical Weapons Convention has led to significant progress toward eliminating chemical weapons stocks around the world. The international response to the sickening chemical weapons atrocity in Syria in August 2013 exemplified global opposition to these weapons. The Organization for the Prohibition of Chemical Weapons was a worthy recipient of the Nobel Peace Prize 2013.

Third, the first *Wehrkunde* would have wanted Europe's divisions to end. And that has happened. The snaking barbed wire fences and watchtowers that marked the brutal border between freedom and authoritarianism have been demolished, and the European Union has removed most administrative obstacles to travel, work, and business. Back in 1963, a Polish couple might have dreamed of escaping communism to reach America and start a new life. That couple's children or grandchildren can now present an ID card and hop on a bus from booming, modern Warsaw to another European Union capital to visit friends, work, or start a new business.

In short, the fifty years since the founding of the Munich Security Conference series in the fall of 1963 have seen a transformation in the global security picture, helped by the historically unprecedented improvement in Europe's fortunes delivered by the European Union. This has helped drive reform and surging prosperity around the planet: billions of people are linking up through new, cheap technologies, finding a democratic voice and a chance to take part in the global economy. Politicians and officials across the planet are in constant contact, usually searching for common ground on myriad technical issues, while strategic differences or rivalries among them do not lead to devastating military conflicts.

Do we feel more secure? In that old Cold War-era sense, we do. The threats of nuclear annihilation, massive conventional wars, and aggressive conquest of the sort the world justifiably still feared in 1963 have receded.

Political-military disasters still occur in many parts of the world, typically when states are weak or badly governed and unable to manage change. North Korea, Belarus, and Cuba linger in a communist twilight zone. The Arab Spring was a reaction to decades of Cold War-style bad government across the Middle East. Helping different Middle East countries find their way to a modernizing political stability will probably be the main security challenge for Europe in the coming decades: Syria demonstrates how the international community struggles to deal with greedy regimes that cling to power by inflicting horrendous costs on their own people.

What will participants at the centenary Munich Security Conference in 2063 think when they look back on how the world has changed since 1963?[1]

They will be living in a world in which the focus of human energy represented by the planet's young people is shifting from Asia to Africa. In 2063, India will be the largest country in the world in terms of population, several hundred million more than China. But the driver of global population growth will be Africa. In 2063, the combined populations of Nigeria, Tanzania, Uganda, and Kenya will well exceed the number of EU citizens. These demographic changes have obvious implications for economic and political power, and for cultural and human values.

The very idea of military security will have changed in ways we cannot predict today. I suspect that in the decades to come, a major theme for Munich Security Conference events will be adapting the classic laws of war to meet new global security challenges. We will move from weapons of mass destruction to weapons of micro-destruction. Why waste money and energy working out how to blow up possible enemies when you can use computer viruses to disable their critical infrastructure, or target individual enemies with tiny biodrones? What is the line between war and assassination—and who decides where and how to draw it? What will "national self-defense" mean in a world like that?

These debates will take place against a background of ever more acute environmental issues. A 2063 world population of around ten billion will be accumulating environmental and climate effects that far exceed those we currently see. Finding ways to alleviate these issues will become steadily more difficult.

Finally, in the decades to come the gap between fast, flexible communities and slow, stagnant communities will grow in leaps and bounds. Failing societies that do not deliver efficient participation in modern life to their people—and above all to women—will spread instability well beyond their borders.

So where will the European Union fit into a world where security issues are becoming harder to classify, let alone to tackle? Should we be aiming at being a global force, or should we be seeking an unobtrusive role in world affairs, humbly "cultivating our own garden," as Voltaire put it in *Candide*?

I am an optimist.

First and foremost, Europe's economic and intellectual weight is a formidable strategic asset. The European Union is the world's largest economy and free trade area. It is the world's biggest exporter and the second-biggest importer. Six of the top ten competitive economies in the world are from the EU. European universities and research institutes compete strongly with the best and attract millions of young people from around the world. The EU and its member states provide more than half of global development assistance and together have two thousand overseas missions of different shapes and sizes, an unrivalled network for influence and communication.

This explains why a Transatlantic Trade and Investment Partnership that combines the demographic and economic potentials of the US and Europe will be so powerful. Transatlantic trade and investment generate half of the global gross domestic product and a third of global trade. With a new framework for making these mighty relationships even closer—and perhaps, in due course, bringing in Ukraine and Turkey too—Europe will have no problem maintaining a major role in global economic governance for the foreseeable future. Furthermore, the redefinition of the rules of the game in favor of the transatlantic community will give it an edge in becoming a regular rising normative power.

Second, the European Union is leading the way for the world in addressing the question of modern government around the world: How shall shared national sovereignty be made compatible with growing international integration? The European Union has become a mighty "civilization machine," bringing its member states together to work to make their legislative and regulatory systems more sensible, market-driven, integrated, and transparent. Our way of doing things helps drive peaceful change and modernization in Europe's neighboring countries, and far beyond. Slowly but steadily, the

EU External Action Service will come to serve as the focus of our collective foreign policy work.

This is not to say that what we do is ideal, let alone a model for what Africa or Asia should do. But the modern European method with its unwavering emphasis on peaceful persuasion and shared interests is unsurpassed anywhere else on earth. And as power migrates from places, structures, and organizational hardware to networks, relationships, and organizational software, the EU model will become ever more important.

Second, when we recall the way the world looked in 1963, the US and the USSR were seen as "superpowers" primarily because they alone had vast arsenals of nuclear and other weapons of mass destruction. Superpower meant military power. Fifty years later, the United States is by far the most powerful country in terms of military might. Its spending and military technology are in a quite different class.

In contrast, our share of global military expenditure is some 20 percent— half of that of the United States. But let us be true to facts: this is by far more than China's 5, Russia's 3, and India's 2 percent. The EU conducts four military and twelve civilian missions and operations with a staff of over 6,200. We are present in Europe, Asia, and Africa, and in places ranging from Niger, Mali, and Kosovo to Georgia and Afghanistan. The problem we have, however, is familiar and stubborn. Today, most European states are trimming defense spending. At the same time, we spend far too much money on defense for far too little operational return. Out of 1.8 million European soldiers, only some 6 percent may be immediately deployed, a dismal consequence of the fact that Europe's administrative and logistic military expenditures are far too high.

We need a serious debate on the future of the Common Security and Defense Policy that takes full account of our responsibility within the NATO Alliance. European military power must remain credible. Joint command structures, a permanent military planning unit, enhancement and better use of the battle groups, coordinated initiatives within smart defense: all these and more need to be looked at in the years to come.

While we are doing that, we need to keep an eye on what the *purpose* of military force really is. We do not want to end up in a situation where we have invested expensively and well in military capabilities that do not help us tackle the enemies we in fact face: small and shadowy terrorist groups, the decay of national border arrangements, or intractable security dramas caused by collapsing states not far from our borders in which the problems are not susceptible to classic military interventions, even with the smartest weapons imaginable.

In late 2011 I held a talk at the German Council on Foreign Relations in Berlin. I said that we in the European Union represented "the world's largest area of peace, democracy, and human rights ... if we get our act together, we can become a proper superpower."

So what does this mean in practical terms? In our case this means more Europe. More Europe in banking supervision and overall economic coordination to underpin the Eurozone. More Europe that makes the EU's top leadership democratically accountable. More Europe through continuing EU enlargement when candidate countries are ready. More Europe in the form of a firm, united foreign policy voice led by the External Action Service, and a firm ambitious voice in EU trade that does the hard negotiation job with Washington to set up a new, shared transatlantic economic space.

In his famous speech delivered at Harvard University in 1943, Winston Churchill said: "Let us go forward in malice to none and good will to all. Such plans offer far better prizes than taking away other people's provinces or lands or grinding them down in exploitation. The empires of the future are the empires of the mind."

This is the point. In the world that our children inherit, what defines a superpower will not be its weapons of mass destruction that can never be used or its ability to conquer and destroy. It will be its ability to combine and build, its power of mass innovation and mass teamwork based on flexibility, tolerance, and inclusion.

When we look back at how European integration looked to the participants of that first *Wehrkunde* we realize just how far we have come. I hope that in fifty years' time, the participants at the centenary Munich Security Conference will be no less impressed at what Europe has achieved—and is still achieving.

Radosław Sikorski has been foreign minister of the Republic of Poland since 2007. He also served in numerous other roles in government, including as deputy minister of national defense, deputy minister of foreign affairs, and as minister of national defense (2005–2007). In 2007, he was elected to the Lower House of the Polish parliament from the Civic Platform list.

Notes

1 Technically, the 100th conference would take place in February of 2064. But since, in 2063, it would be precisely a hundred years since the conference's beginnings, 2063 was chosen here as point of reference.

Appendix*

* You can find additional material to this book on our website:
www.v-r.de/Munich-Security-Conference

This is the agenda and the list of participants of the second *Internationale Wehrkunde-Begegnung* in 1964. The four main topics discussed were: "The future of the Atlantic Alliance"; "An analysis and evaluation of the changes in the East and between East and West"; "Necessities of Western security policy in Europe"; and "The reform of the Atlantic Alliance." Presentations were given by, among others, Helmut Schmidt and Zbigniew Brzezinski. Until the mid-seventies, the meeting would take place at the Hotel Regina, before moving to the Hotel Bayerischer Hof. (Source: Archiv für Christlich-Soziale Politik, Nachlass Jaeger Richard: D 242)

"II. INTERNATIONALE WEHRKUNDE-BEGEGNUNG"
in München, Hotel Regina, am 5. und 6. Dezember 1964

P R O G R A M M

Freitag, 4. Dezember

Ankunft und Unterbringung von Teilnehmern
Abendessen für Teilnehmer im Hotel Regina
Ab 21 Uhr Kontaktgespräche im Palais-Preysing-
Club, München 2, Residenzstraße 27/V.

Samstag, 5. Dezember

Frühstück für Teilnehmer im Hotel Regina
Ankunft und Unterbringung von Teilnehmern

10.30 Uhr   Erste Arbeitssitzung

Generalthema der Tagung:

DIE ZUKUNFT DER ATLANTISCHEN ALLIANZ

Referat: D. Dr. Eugen G e r s t e n m a i e r , Präsident
des Deutschen Bundestags

Diskussion

13.00 Uhr   Essen des Oberbürgermeisters der Stadt München,
Dr. Hans-Jochen Vogel, im Rathaus

Abfahrt mit Autobus um 12.45 Uhr vor dem Hotel

15.30 Uhr   Zweite Arbeitssitzung

Diskussionsthema:

Analyse und Beurteilung der Veränderungen im Osten,
sowie zwischen West und Ost

Referate: Zbigniew B r z e z i n s k i , Columbia University,
New York

Robert S t r a u s z - H u p é , Pennsylvania-Uni-
versity, Philadelphia

20.00 Uhr   Abendessen für Teilnehmer im Hotel Regina, nach dem
Abendessen Kontaktgespräche im Palais-Preysing-Club.

./.

Sonntag, 6. Dezember

Frühstück für Teilnehmer im Hotel Regina

10.00 Uhr Dritte Arbeitssitzung

Diskussionsthema:

Notwendigkeiten der westlichen Sicherheitspolitik in Europa

Referate: Robert E. O s g o o d , Washington Center for
Foreign Policy Research

Senator Helmut S c h m i d t , Hamburg

Diskussion

13.00 Uhr Mittagessen für Teilnehmer im Hotel Regina

14.30 Uhr Vierte Arbeitssitzung

Diskussionsthema:

Die Reform der atlantischen Allianz

Referate: Jacques B a u m e l , Generalsekretär der
U.N.R./U.D.T., Paris

Dr. h.c. Franz Josef S t r a u ß , Vorsitzender der CSU.

20.30 Uhr Essen der WEHRKUNDE im Hotel Regina
Abschluß der offiziellen Tagung
Kontaktgespräche im Palais-Preysing-Club
Abreise der ersten Teilnehmer

Montag, 7. Dezember

Abreise der Teilnehmer und Auflassung des
Sekretariats im Hotel Regina bis 16.00 Uhr.

II. INTERNATIONALE WEHRKUNDE-BEGEGNUNG
in München, Hotel Regina, am 5. und 6. Dezember 1964

TEILNEHMERLISTE

PARTICIPANTS

LES PARTICIPANTS

DR. CARLOS KRUS ABECASSES
Staatssekretär a.D., Lisboa/Portugal

EDUARD ADORNO, MdB
Mitglied des Verteidigungspolitischen Ausschusses
Bonn/Tettnang (Südwürttemberg)

DR. JOHANN CHRISTOPH BARON VON ALLMAYER-BECK
Leiter der Militär-wissenschaftlichen Abteilung im
Bundesministerium für Landesverteidigung,
Wien/Österreich

DR. HANS ARNOLD
Auswärtiges Amt, Bonn

DR. GÜNTHER BACHMANN, Ministerialdirigent
Bundeskanzleramt, Bonn

JACQUES BAUMEL, Sénateur
Sécrétaire Général de l'U.N.R./U.D.T., Paris

KURT BECKER, Redakteur
"Die Welt", Ressortleiter für Politik, Hamburg

OBERST i.G HANS GEORG BIEDERMANN
Bundesverteidigungsministerium, Bonn

ROBERT R. BOWIE
Cambridge, Massachusetts/USA
Harvard University
Director, Center for International Affairs

JEREMY BRAY, M.P.
House of Commons, London

HELMUT BRENNECKE
Stellvertretender Leiter der
Presse- und Informationsabteilung im
Bundesverteidigungsministerium
Bonn

ZBIGNIEW BRZEZINSKI
Columbia University, Director Research
Institute on Communist Affairs, New York

ALFONS DALMA, Chefredakteur der "Wehrkunde", München
Leitender Redakteur "Die Presse" (Wien)
Lehrbeauftragter der Hochschule für Politik und
Strategie, München

DR. ERNST DÖLKER, Stadtrat
der Landeshauptstadt München

KLAUS DOHRN, Schriftsteller
Zürich/München

WALTER C. DOWLING
US-Embassador
The Atlantic Institute
Director Boulogne sur Seine/France

BURGHART FREUDENFELD
Chefredakteur des Bayerischen Rundfunks
München

OBERST i.G. K.H. FRIEDRICH
Führungsakademie der Bundeswehr
Hamburg

GENERAL PIERRE M. GALLOIS, Paris

GEORG VON GAUPP-BERGHAUSEN
Major der Reserve
des österreichischen Bundesheeres
Hohenweiler, Vorarlberg

JOHN GELLNER, writer
Toronto, Canada

GENERALMAJOR C.U.- V.GERSDORFF
Chefredakteur der "Wehrkunde"
München

PROFESSOR DR. WILHELM GREWE
Botschafter der Bundesrepublik Deutschland
bei der NATO
Paris/Bonn

KARL THEODOR FREIHERR VON UND ZU GUTTENBERG, MdB
Schloß Guttenberg

JOHN HAY, M.P.
House of Commons, London

DR. FRANZ HEUBL, MdL
Bayerischer Staatsminister für
Bundesangelegenheiten
München/Bonn

DR. RICHARD JAEGER, MdB
Vizepräsident des Deutschen Bundestags
Bonn/Dießen

J. VINCENZ JOYCE
Public Affairs Counselor, USIS
US Mission to the North Atlantic and
European Regional Organizations
Paris/France

GEORG KAHN-ACKERMANN, MdB
Mitglied des Verteidigungsausschusses
des Bundestags

DR. ELMAR J. KAMMERLOHER
Bonn/Lengsdorf

LORD KENNET
House of Lords, London

HENRI DE KERGORLAY
Correspondant du "Figaro"
Bonn

EWALD HEINRICH v. KLEIST
Herausgeber der "Wehrkunde"
München

DR. HERMANN KOPF, MdB
Vorsitzender des Außenpolitischen Ausschusses
des Bundestags

HANNS KÜFFNER
Abteilungsleiter im Presse- und
Informationsamt, Bonn

DR. HANS LEHMANN, Schriftsteller
"Nürnberger Nachrichten",
München/Nürnberg

FRED LUCHSINGER, Redakteur
"Neue Zürcher Zeitung", Zürich

OTTO MERK, leitender Redakteur
"Münchner Merkur" München

FRITZ MEURER, Chef vom Dienst
"Münchner Merkur", München

HANS J. MORGENTHAU jun.
University of Chicago, Director
Center for the Study of American
Foreign and Military Policy
University of Chicago

MULY MURGER   Editor
"Washington Post", Washington

ROBERT E. OSGOOD, Assistant Director
Washington Center for Foreign Policy Research
Washington

WOLF POSSELT
Zweites Deutsches Fernsehen
Leiter des Studios Bayern
München

OBERSTLEUTNANT a.D. VON RAVEN
Militärpolitischer Schriftsteller
Bonn

JOSEF RIEDMILLER, Redakteur
"Süddeutsche Zeitung", München

PROFESSOR DR. OTTO ROEGELE
Professor für Zeitungswissenschaft
auf der Ludwig-Maximilians-Universität
Herausgeber des "Rheinischen Merkur"
München/Köln

LOUIS SANGUINETTI, député
Rapporteur de la Commission de Défense Nationale
Paris

HELMUT SCHMIDT, Senator der Hansestadt Hamburg
Vorstandsmitglied der SPD
Hamburg

OBERST SCHMIDT
Bundesverteidigungsministerium, Bonn

BRIGADEGENERAL GERD SCHMÜCKLE
Vertretung der Bundesrepublik Deutschland
bei der NATO, Paris

DR. OTTO SCHULMEISTER, Chefredakteur
"Die Presse", Wien

FRITZ RUDOLF SCHULZ, MdB
Vorstandsmitglied der FDP
Mitglied des Verteidigungsausschusses
im Bundestag, Bonn

DR. MAX SCHULZE-VORBERG
Bonner Korrespondent des Bayerischen Rundfunks

- 5 -

DR. URS SCHWARZ, stellvertretender Chefredakteur
"Neue Zürcher Zeitung", Zürich

DR. KLAUS SEEMANN, Ministerialrat
Bundeskanzleramt, Bonn

DR. THEO SOMMER, Redakteur für Außenpolitik
"Die Zeit", Hamburg

HANS SPEIER
"Rand Corporation, Director
Political Department
Santa Monica, California

OBERSTLEUTNANT GERD STAMP
Bundeskanzleramt, Bonn

MAJOR i.G. HEINRICH STÄRKE
Bundesverteidigungsministerium, Bonn

DR. h.c. FRANZ JOSEF STRAUSS, MdB
Vorsitzender der CSU, München

ROBERT STRAUSZ-HUPE
Pennsylvania University
Director Foreign Policy Research Institute
Philadelphia

REGIERUNGSRAT MAX STREIBL, MdL
Vorsitzender der Jungen Union in Bayern

OBERST i.G HASSO VIEBIG
Leiter der Presse- und Informationsabteilung
im Bundesverteidigungsministerium
in Bonn

DR. GISELHER WIRSING, Chefredakteur
"Christ und Welt", Stuttgart

ARNOLD WOLFERS, Director
Washington Center for Policy Research
Washington

DR. FRIEDRICH ZIMMERMANN, MdB
Vorstandsmitglied der CSU
München/Bonn

OBERST a.D. HORST VON ZITZEWITZ
Militärschriftsteller
Oberursel/Hessen

CHRYSOSTOMUS ZODEL, Chefredakteur
"Schwäbische Zeitung", Leutkirch

ANTHONY ROYLE, M.P.
House of Commons, London

In the fall of 1996, after Ewald von Kleist had indicated his intention to retire as chairman, it became obvious that there would be no meeting in 1997, and that the conference's future as a whole was uncertain. Here, we document two of the letters that were sent during this period—one by then-NATO Secretary General Javier Solana to Ewald von Kleist, the other by Richard Burt, the former US ambassador to Germany, to Chancellor Kohl. "When I … received … the answer that there would be no Wehrkundetagung next year or indeed any time, I could hardly believe it," Solana wrote to von Kleist. Burt, urging Chancellor Kohl that the conference should continue, wrote: "[I]n creating and sustaining the Wehrkunde meetings, Ewald von Kleist made a significant contribution to stability and peace in Europe. It would be a terrible shame to lose this legacy." Also included is a note by the German embassy in the United States concerning Burt's letter. The embassy asked the German Federal Foreign Office to make sure that a copy of the letter to the chancellor would also be handed to both Foreign Minister Klaus Kinkel and Defense Minister Volker Rühe. Comments by diplomats at the margin include "Good letter!" (Source: Politisches Archiv des Auswärtigen Amts, Bd. ZA 254334)

**ORGANISATION DU TRAITÉ
DE L'ATLANTIQUE NORD**

**NORTH ATLANTIC
TREATY ORGANIZATION**

LE SECRÉTAIRE GÉNÉRAL
SECRETARY GENERAL

Javier Solana Madariaga

SG/96/1180

18 November 1996

Dear Mr von Kleist,

When I inquired about the date for next year's
Wehrkundetagung in Munich and received instead of a date the
answer that there would be no Wehrkundetagung next year or indeed
any time, I could hardly believe it. The legendary gathering of
cognoscenti and decision makers in the field of security and
defence that you invented and then chaired for 33 years had
become an institution. It is a tribute to the unique role that
your initiative and your personality played in shaping this
yearly gathering that the institution comes to an end with your
decision to relinquish the chair. As one paper put it, the
Wehrkundetagung was your salon. As so many of your admirers I am
sad to see it closed.

All I can do now is to wish you well and to assure you that
through your extraordinary achievements you have earned the
gratitude of many people.

Yours sincerely,

Javier Solana

Mr Ewald von Kleist
██████████████████
████ München
Federal Republic of Germany

Boulevard Léopold III - B-1110 Bruxelles
TEL. : (32-2) 707.49.17/707.41.11 - FAX : (32-2) 707.46.66

Botschaft
der Bundesrepublik
Deutschland

Embassy
of the Federal Republic of Germany

AZ: Prot- 704.03

000273

Auswärtiges Amt

2 0. JAN 97 15 :56

Ministerbüro I

221-

2 7. JAN. 1997

AZ. 371.00 (USA)

Büronotiz

Betr.: Weiterleitung der Kopie eines Schreibens des ehemaligen Botschafters in Deutschland, Richard R. Burt, an Herrn Bundeskanzler Dr. Helmut Kohl

Anlg.: -1- (Umschlag)

Auswärtiges Amt 3 0. JAN. 1997

Vorab: *[handschriftlich]*

Referat 221 wird gebeten, beiliegende Fernkopie eines Schreibens des ehemaligen Botschafters in Deutschland, Richard R. Burt, das im Original an Herrn Bundeskanzler Dr. Helmut Kohl ging, auch an Herrn Minister Kinkel sowie Herrn Verteidigungsminister Volker Rühe weiterzuleiten.

An das
Auswärtige Amt
Bonn
Referat: 221

Washington, 17. Januar 1997
Schö/rt

Adresse:
4645 Reservoir Rd., N.W.
Washington, D.C. 20007 - 1998
USA

Post:
Postfach 40680
Washington, D.C. 20016 - 0680
USA

Telefon:
(202)298-4000

Telefax:
(202)298-4249

Telex:
197685
Kennung:
AAWN UT

RICHARD R. BURT

January 13, 1997

His Excellency Helmut Kohl
Chancellor of the Federal Republic
of Germany
Bundeskanzleramt
Bonn
Germany

Dear Mr. Chancellor:

I have not seen you recently, but have been able to follow your successes from news reports and from old friends in Germany. I wish you and your government all the best in the new year, particularly your efforts to strengthen NATO, to create a common European currency, and to stabilize and improve Germany's ties to the east.

I am writing concerning the cancellation of this year's conference on European defense and security (Wehrkunde) in Munich. I wanted you to know that in recent discussions with many members of Washington's defense and foreign policy community, a number of people have expressed their deep concern that the Wehrkunde meetings may have come to an end. In fact, several have suggested that I should report this concern to you and this is the purpose of my writing.

As a frequent participant in the Munich conference, you know the special role it occupied during and after the Cold War. By attracting senior politicians and security specialists from both sides of the Atlantic, Wehrkunde over the years became an important vehicle for building an international consensus on pressing security and arms control problems. It was particularly effective, in my view, in exposing international participants in the conference to "the German point of view" on these problems.

The conference also served another important function. Because of the strong support it enjoyed from serious members of both the U.S. Senate and House of Representatives, such as Sam Nunn, John Tower and William Cohen, the conference always attracted a large group of members of the U.S. Congress. At a time when the current climate in Washington makes members of Congress reluctant to travel abroad, Wehrkunde was thus able to serve as an indispensable seminar on German and European security. As you know, one of the "graduates" of this seminar is William Cohen, who led the U.S. congressional delegation to Wehrkunde and is now preparing to serve as Secretary of Defense.

I recently spoke to Senator Cohen, and told him of my intention to contact you concerning the Wehrkunde conference. He urged me to do this, and pledged his strong support for reviving the Munich meetings. He also suggested that I speak with Senator John McCain, who was asked by Senator Cohen to take over the leadership of the Wehrkunde congressional delegation. I have done that, and Senator McCain has asked me to assure you that if Wehrkunde can be restarted, he will work enthusiastically to assure strong U.S. congressional participation.

Needless to say, this will be an important year for the Alliance and security in Europe. While it is of course not possible to convene the Wehrkunde conference at its traditional time - early February - I would hope that a meeting could be scheduled later in the year. If this is not possible, then I hope that Wehrkunde could be revived by early 1998 at the latest.

I hope you do not mind my intervention in this matter. But in creating and sustaining the Wehrkunde meetings, Ewald von Kleist made a significant contribution to stability and peace in Europe. It would be a terrible shame to lose this legacy.

With great respect,

Richard Burt

The issue of the conference's continuation also preoccupied the German government during the fall of 1996. The third document, a note prepared at the Federal Foreign Office, allows a glimpse into the internal deliberations concerning the future of the conference. Dated November 21, it points out the "very urgent" need to find a successor to von Kleist, and sketches out options. In a handwritten comment, Wolfgang Ischinger, then political director at the Federal Foreign Office, expresses his view that the only viable option would be "Horst Teltschik with the Quandt Foundation." (Source: Politisches Archiv des Auswärtigen Amts, Bd. ZA 254334)

Planungsstab
VLR Dr. Freytag von Loringhoven

Bonn, 21. November 1996
HR: 3235

Herrn Staatssekretär Hartmann

Betr.: Zukunft der "Tagung für europäische Sicherheitspolitik" ("Wehrkunde"-Tagung)
Bezug: 1) Aufzeichnung des Planungsstabs vom 18. 09. (vergl. Anlg.)
2) BM-Weisung auf Vermerk 013 vom 14. 11.
3) Weisung StS Hartmann vom 20. 09.

Anlg.: 2
Zweck der Vorlage: Zur Billigung des Vorgehens zu 2.

Sie hatten um nähere Informationen und konkrete Vorschläge zur Fortsetzung der Wehrkunde-Tagung gebeten.

1. Zur Finanzierung konnten wir - ohne Direktinformationen einzuholen - bislang lediglich folgendes in Erfahrung bringen: BMVg hat sich mit einem Zuschuß von DM 500.000,- p.a. beteiligt. Die bayerische Staatsregierung hat ein Festbankett finanziert.

2. Die Sache eilt sehr, da inzwischen sehr fraglich ist, ob die Frühjahrstagung noch durchgeführt werden kann. Es wird deshalb folgendes Vorgehen vorgeschlagen:

a) Möglichst bald Hausbesprechung unter Leitung der Staatssekretäre (BM-Weisung auf Vermerk von 013 vom 14. 11., vergl. Bezug zu 2).

b) Bitte an Herrn von Kleist, die Tagung im kommenden Frühjahr ein letztes Mal durchzuführen. Dies dürfte nur dann Erfolgsaussichten haben, wenn der BK persönlich Bitte ausspricht und wenn dies sehr rasch geschieht. Bei dieser Gelegenheit stellt Herr von Kleist seinen Nachfolger vor.

d) Als Nachfolger kämen h.E.in Frage:

Verteiler:
mit Anlage
MB   1x
BStSe   3x
BStM Sch   1x
D2, Dg 20
Ref. 201

- <u>Politiker</u>. z.B. BM a.D. Prof. Scholz, Stoltenberg,
  Mitglieder des Deutschen Bundestags, z.B. Carsten Voigt.
- <u>Wissenschaftler</u>: Prof. Karl Kaiser (DGAP), Prof. Werner Weidenfeld haben
  einschlägige Erfahrung in transatlantischen und in Sicherheitsfragen.

Herr von Kleist hat trotz jahrelanger Suche keinen geeigneten Nachfolger gefunden.
Einzelheiten konnten wir nicht in Erfahrung bringen, da Herr von Kleist gegenwärtig
nicht erreichbar ist. Wir wissen lediglich (vertraulich), daß er BMW-Vorstandsmitglied
Teltschik vorgeschlagen, dieser jedoch abgelehnt hat.

gez. Klaiber

Awards given by the Munich Security Conference

The "Peace through Dialogue" Medal

2005   Kofi Annan
2006   John McCain
2007   Javier Solana
2008   North Atlantic Treaty Organization
        (medal presented to a Canadian soldier)

The Ewald von Kleist Award

2009   Henry Kissinger
2010   Javier Solana
2012   Joseph I. Lieberman
2013   Brent Scowcroft

The Ewald von Kleist Award medal given to Henry Kissinger in 2009. The silver medal, as well as a diamond pin, are designed and donated annually by the Munich jeweler Maximilian Heiden.

Image Credits

Darchinger / Körber-Stiftung: 399
Dettenborn / MSC: 143, 203, 243, 277, 287, 329
Getty Images: 29
Heider-Sawall: 45
Hughes: 49
Kan / MSC: 119, 335, 417
Kuhlmann / MSC: 19, 23, 193, 215, 229, 269, 303, 319, 341, 363, 389
Mörk / MSC: 15, 37, 133, 177, 207, 235, 259, 295, 351, 371, 383, 447
US Department of Defense photo: 161, 223, 367, 377
picture alliance / dpa: 93, 103, 113, 129, 167
Plitt / MSC: 359, 411
Svet / MSC: 151, 309, 403
SZ Photo: 171, 185
Trenkel / MSC: 435
Wegmann / Bundesregierung: 81
Wuest / MSC: 253
Zwez / MSC: 393

Illustration Section

List of Abbreviations

AICGS	American Institute for Contemporary German Studies
AOR	area of responsibility
AR5	Fifth Assessment Report of the United Nations Intergovernmental Panel on Climate Change
ASEAN	Association of Southeast Asian Nations
AU	African Union
AWACS	Airborne Early Warning and Control System
AZ	Arizona
BBC	British Broadcasting Corporation
BR	Bayerischer Rundfunk (Bavarian broadcasting service)
BRICS	Brazil, Russia, India, China and South Africa
CCS	carbon capture and storage
CDU	Christlich Demokratische Union Deutschlands (Christian Democratic Union of Germany)
CESS	Centre for European Security Strategies
CFE	Treaty on Conventional Armed Forces in Europe
CFSP	Common Foreign and Security Policy
CIA	Central Intelligence Agency
CNN	Cable News Network
CoDel	congressional delegation
COP	Conference of the Parties
CSDP	Common Security and Defence Policy
D	Democrat

DNA	Deoxyribonucleic acid
EAPC	Euro-Atlantic Partnership Council
EASI	Euro-Atlantic Security Initiative
ECFR	European Council on Foreign Relations
EDA	European Defence Agency
EEAS	European External Action Service
EEC	European Economic Community
EIA	Energy Information Administration
EMU	European Monetary Union
ERW	enhanced radiation weapon
ESDI	European Security and Defence Identity
ESDP	European Security and Defence Policy
EST	Eastern Standard Time
EU	European Union
FDP	Freie Demokratische Partei (Free Democratic Party)
FRG	Federal Republic of Germany
GA	Georgia
GATT	General Agreement on Tariffs and Trade
GDP	gross domestic product
GDR	German Democratic Republic
IAEA	International Atomic Energy Agency
ICBM	intercontinental ballistic missile
ICT	information and communication technologies
IEA	International Energy Agency
Ifo institute	Leibniz-Institut für Wirtschaftsforschung an der Universität München e. V. (Leibniz Institute for Economic Research at the University of Munich)
IISS/ISS	International Institute for Strategic Studies/Institute for Strategic Studies
IMF	International Monetary Fund
IN	Indiana
INF	Intermediate(-Range) Nuclear Forces
IPCC	Intergovernmental Panel on Climate Change
ISAF	International Security Assistance Force
KFOR	Kosovo Force
LNG	liquefied natural gas
LRTNF	long-range theater nuclear forces
MBFR	Mutual and Balanced Force Reductions talks
ME	Maine
MIRV	multiple independently targetable reentry vehicle
MSC	Munich Security Conference
MT	Montana
MYL	Munich Young Leaders
NAC	North Atlantic Council

NACC	North Atlantic Cooperation Council
NATO	North Atlantic Treaty Organization
NGO	Nongovernmental Organization
NPT	Treaty on the Non-Proliferation of Nuclear Weapons (Non-Proliferation Treaty)
NSA	National Security Agency
NSC	National Security Council
NTI	Nuclear Threat Initiative
OEF	Operation Enduring Freedom
OECD	Organisation for Economic Co-operation and Development
OH	Ohio
OPCW	Organisation for the Prohibition of Chemical Weapons
OSCE	Organization for Security and Co-operation in Europe
PfP	Partnership for Peace
R	Republican
R2P	Responsibility to Protect
RAND	Research and Development Corporation
SALT II	Strategic Arms Limitation Talks II
SCADA	supervisory control and data acquisition
SDI	Strategic Defense Initiative
SPD	Sozialdemokratische Partei Deutschlands (Social Democratic Party of Germany)
START	Strategic Arms Reduction Treaty
SWP	Stiftung Wissenschaft und Politik (German Institute for International and Security Affairs)
TPP	Trans-Pacific Partnership
TTIP/T-TIP	Transatlantic Trade and Investment Partnership
UÇK	Ushtria Çlirimtare e Kosovës
UK	United Kingdom of Great Britain and Northern Ireland
UN	United Nations
UNFCCC	United Nations Framework Convention on Climate Change
UNSCR	United Nations Security Council resolution
US/USA	United States of America
USSR	Union of Soviet Socialist Republics
WEU	Western European Union
WMD	weapons of mass destruction
WTO	World Trade Organization